Ozu

Ozu

A Closer Look

Kathe Geist

Hong Kong University Press
The University of Hong Kong
Pokfulam Road
Hong Kong
https://hkupress.hku.hk

© 2022 Hong Kong University Press

ISBN 978-988-8754-17-5 (*Hardback*)

All rights reserved. No portion of this publication may be reproduced or transmitted in any form or by any means, electronic or mechanical, including photocopying, recording, or any information storage or retrieval system, without prior permission in writing from the publisher.

British Library Cataloguing-in-Publication Data
A catalogue record for this book is available from the British Library.

10 9 8 7 6 5 4 3 2 1

Printed and bound by Sunshine (Caimei) Printing Co., Ltd. in Hong Kong, China

For Robert, Margaret, and Gretel, with whom I first encountered Japan

Contents

List of Illustrations	viii
Introduction	1
Part I. The Silent Films	7
Chapter 1: The Gangster Films	9
Chapter 2: Signs, Symbols, and Motifs	28
Chapter 3: The Sound of Silence	54
Chapter 4: Narrative Strategies, Texts, and Subtexts	65
Afterword Part I: ". . . when the studio was in Kamata"	86
Part II. War and Peace: The Sound Films, 1936–1952	87
Chapter 5: The Calm	89
Chapter 6: The Storm	101
Chapter 7: The Reckoning	121
Afterword Part II: "Then it's good we lost."	158
Part III. Religion, Sex, and Other Matters	161
Chapter 8: Narratives Strategies in the Late Films	163
Chapter 9: Religion	180
Chapter 10: Gender Issues	195
Chapter 11: A Two-Dimensional Art Form	209
Chapter 12: The Ozu Touch: Influencing Others	229
Afterword Part III: But is it modern?	250
Plot Synopses	253
Selected Bibliography	271
Index	277

Illustrations

Figure 1.1:	Jyoji's moment of truth comes at the conclusion of *Dragnet Girl*.	13
Figure 1.2:	Tokiko's quick conversion, from hate to love for Kazuko, takes place in front of a Christian church in *Dragnet Girl*.	16
Figure 1.3:	The policemen who arrest Kenji wear a variety of hats in *Walk Cheerfully*.	25
Figure 2.1:	At the boxing club, Jyoji sits next to a poster with actor George Bancroft on it in *Dragnet Girl*.	36
Figure 2.2:	*Tagasode-byobu*, c. 1600–1650	45
Figure 2.3:	Notomo steps on his shredded credentials in *I Graduated, But . . .*	48
Figure 2.4:	Omura uses his fan to calculate his costs during the reunion in *Tokyo Chorus*.	50
Figure 3.1:	Tokiko reacts angrily to the sound of Misako's intrusion in *Dragnet Girl*.	60
Figure 4.1:	Cigarette smoke blows over a goldfish bowl in *I Flunked, But . . .*	67
Figure 4.2:	Takahashi is blowing the smoke.	67
Figure 4.3:	As Jyoji and Tokiko embrace in *Dragnet Girl*, there is no yarn on her shoes.	73
Figure 4.4:	In the following close-up, Tokiko's shoes are tangled in black yarn.	74
Figure 4.5:	Chikako's customer waits for her in a car in *Woman of Tokyo*.	78
Figure 4.6:	Okajima holds his baby's pacifier in his mouth as he dresses for work in *Tokyo Chorus*.	79
Figure 5.1:	Marlene Dietrich's face appears prominently in shots of Setsuko reading her magazine in *What Did the Lady Forget?*	98
Figure 6.1:	Praying at his mother's altar, Ryohei, a new recruit, takes on the appearance of a priest in *There Was a Father*.	112
Figure 7.1:	A conflicted Tokiko gazes into her mirror as she decides prostitution is her only option in *A Hen in the Wind*.	129

Figure 7.2: *Record of a Tenement Gentleman* ends with Saigo's back turned to the audience. 131

Figure 7.3: In *Late Spring*, exterior shots of the train Somiya and Noriko take into Tokyo show the white stripe on the car designated exclusively for American Occupation personnel. 133

Figure 7.4: The American flag on the Pan Am Stratocruiser's tail moves slowly out of the frame as onlookers wave in *The Flavor of Green Tea Over Rice*. 152

Figure 9.1: St. Luke's International Hospital in *Equinox Flower* 181

Figure 9.2: Okajima's talisman hangs prominently from his waist in *The Lady and the Beard*. A poster for *The Rogue Song* appears behind him. 184

Figure 9.3: A large wheel stands between Kihachi and Otaka as they argue in *A Story of Floating Weeds*. A larger wheel appears out of focus to the right. 187

Figure 10.1: Tomio, with a patch on his eye, stands in front of the carp banner that hangs in the doorway of Otome's restaurant in *Passing Fancy*. 205

Figure 11.1: Akiko and Noriko walk next to the Katsura River in *The End of Summer* 213

Figure 11.2: Utagawa Hiroshige, *Kinryusan Temple, Asakusa*, from the series *One Hundred Famous Views of Edo*, 1856 213

Figure 11.3: Torii Kiyonobu I, *Courtesan Painting a Screen*, c. 1711 217

Figure 11.4: Komiya and niece Setsuko walk together in *What Did the Lady Forget?*, demonstrating the "twinning" prevalent in Ozu's films and in *nihonga*. 221

Figure 12.1: Chishu Ryu and Kuniko Miyake play innkeepers in Wim Wenders's *Until the End of the World*. 237

Colorplate 1A: Disappointed in love, Michiko winds a dressmaker's measuring tape around her fingers in *An Autumn Afternoon*. (after p. 6)

Colorplate 1B: A large, ghostly stupa appears in the inn's interior garden during the reunion sequence in *Equinox Flower*. Ureo Egawa appears here in a cameo role. (after p. 6)

Colorplate 2A: Shallow space becomes deep space in a series of successive matched shots from *The End of Summer*, beginning with the front door of a restaurant in Osaka. (after p. 6)

Colorplate 2B: Back door of the same restaurant (after p. 6)

Colorplate 3A: An alley near Sasaki's house in Kyoto (after p. 6)

Colorplate 3B: Manbei comes into the same alley, confirming it as a deep space. (after p. 6)

Colorplate 4: Saeki Shunko, *Tearoom*, 1936 (after p. 6)

Introduction

Two black-and-white photographs hang, one above the other, on one wall in my study. On top is the sculpted figure of St. John the Baptist from the north portal of Chartres Cathedral. The figure is rendered so spare and angular as to appear almost modern; from his stooped shoulders and sad eyes we understand that he foresees his own fate and that of the man he came to proclaim; but this portrait of weary sorrow also speaks to the inherent pathos of human life itself.

Below St. John, Yasujiro Ozu stares out from a movie set designed to look like a Japanese house. The photograph, cropped from a still for *What Did the Lady Forget?*, has been incorporated into a poster for the New York Japan Society's 1982 retrospective of his work. Ozu's eyes are crinkled in a benign half-smile, one we might associate with the portrait of a Chinese sage, one that laughed at human folly while it mourned life's limitations and was no stranger to the resigned sorrow we see on the face of St. John.

These photographs bookend my academic career. I first saw Chartres Cathedral at the age of twenty-one and decided then and there to study medieval art history. Sometime later I switched to cinema studies. The medieval cathedral was, after all, an early exercise in creating narratives for the masses out of successive images. My dissertation completed, I obtained a press pass to the 1982 Ozu retrospective in New York, with the promise that I would write an article on it for *Film Quarterly*. I have been writing about Ozu ever since.

While still a medievalist, I saw my first Ozu film, *The End of Summer*, in the early 1970s, soon after Dan Talbot of New Yorker Films brought Ozu's films to the United States. Prior to immersing myself in Europe and European art, I had spent a good deal of my childhood in Okinawa. Seeing *The End of Summer* felt like coming home.

Once I began a more serious study of Ozu, I realized I had come into contact with the director many years before. While in Okinawa, my father's secretary offered to accompany him to a celebrated comedy called *Ohayo*. The next morning at breakfast he entertained us with his description of this very funny film in which little boys played farting games. (No one in a Hollywood film at the time ever went to the bathroom, much less farted; the closest thing to it were Andy Griffith's saluting toilets in *No Time for Sergeants*.)

Initially, Dan Talbot distributed *Ohayo* under the translated title *Good Morning,* which is the title Donald Richie used in *Ozu,* his seminal book on the director. The more I read about *Good Morning,* the more I wondered if this was the hilarious film my father had seen over twenty years earlier. Eventually, I realized it was the same film, and, with some excitement because this was now my favorite director, I asked my father if he remembered the Japanese film with the little boys who played farting games. He had no recollection of it whatsoever! What had lodged itself so firmly in my eleven-year-old mind had long since vanished from his. (He would not live into the DVD era when he might have revisited *Ohayo.*)

The book that follows is based on avenues of research I have pursued over the past thirty years, the last of which have been particularly intense. It is intended to both complement previous works on Ozu and to challenge aspects of them with which I disagree. Readers may perceive it as something of a gloss on David Bordwell's *Ozu and the Poetics of Cinema,* and they would not be completely wrong. Bordwell's *Ozu* remains, to my mind, the most important work on the director in English and is a rock on which I stand.

In the 1980s and 1990s I gained a reputation as the anti-Bordwell when, in fact, as an art historian, I had immediately gravitated to his and Kristin Thompson's formalist approach as a foundational way to understand cinema. I was not willing to be limited to this approach, however, and this is where disputes have arisen.

Works of art that describe people and things have meaning, but not all interpretations are equal. Medieval works have iconographic programs based on the theology of the time. The iconography of twentieth-century art is more elusive, but close reading combined with a knowledge of history and culture can unlock it. Bordwell believes, essentially, that Ozu was too preoccupied with his intricate parametric designs to give much thought to his narratives or their meaning, but I contend that the iconographic programs discernible in Ozu's films rival the complexity of his formal structures. The question arises as to whether anyone watching his films as theatrical entertainment would have been aware of these networks of signs and symbols, to which I would answer: probably not. But neither would they have comprehended his formal complexities in their entirety; yet both contribute to the aura the films project.

This book concerns only Ozu's extant films and fragments from films that have otherwise been lost, and it is divided into three parts. Part I is devoted solely to the silent films and begins with his so-called gangster films, which were a full-throttle foray into the modernism that accompanied Ozu's coming of age. Focused on only three films, Chapter 1 nevertheless introduces both the concerns and methodologies that run throughout the book: iconography and meaning discerned through motifs and symbols, Ozu's narrative strategies, and influences on Ozu's art that have not previously been discussed at length, in the case of the gangster films, those of Germany's Weimar cinema.

Chapter 2 isolates Ozu's recurring motifs, discusses their relevance to his stories, and the extent to which they reveal the story he intends to tell. Drawing on the work

Introduction

of Michel Chion, Chapter 3 investigates the ways in which Ozu visualized sound in his silent films to heighten drama, further his narration, create humor, and/or to suppress or delay narrative information.

Chapter 4 analyzes the narrative strategies that dominate Ozu's silent period, such as his use of synecdoche, reverse of cause and effect, or substitution of one character's emotions for another's. This chapter refutes the widely held notion that Ozu's stories are open-ended and ambiguous by illustrating the narrative logic that informs them. Although Ozu's style and content would evolve somewhat over time, the methodologies for analyzing his films demonstrated in Part I, the interpretation of signs and symbols and the investigation of how he narrates, will undergird successive chapters as they pursue additional lines of inquiry.

Part II examines chronologically Ozu's sound films from his first, made in 1936, to the one he made in the last year of the American Occupation of Japan, 1952. These were years in which history was accelerated. As militarists came to dominate the government, Japan moved into Germany's fascist sphere, into all-out war with China, and eventually into war with the United States and its allies. The seven-year-long American Occupation would follow.

From 1937 to 1939, Ozu served in a combat unit in China. Chapters 5 to 7 chronicle, respectively, the sound films he made in three distinct periods: before he went to China, after he returned until the end of the war, and during the American Occupation. My analysis of these films pays particular attention to the ways in which they were influenced by political and historical events. In this respect Ozu's films are indeed ambiguous, darting and dodging between an outright approbation of government policies and a veiled critique.

Part III takes up particular topics that tilt toward the late films but incorporate evidence from the entire body of extant films. Chapter 8 looks at narrative strategies in what can be thought of as Ozu's life-cycle films (those most familiar to Western viewers). While some critics view these films as repetitive and tired, this chapter reveals instead elegant and seamless narratives that never deviate from Ozu's essential story even while seeming, at times, to mislead the viewer.

Chapter 9 takes on the much-debated topic of religion in Ozu's films and demonstrates that while they may not be religious objects in themselves, as some have portrayed them, they are nevertheless informed and influenced by a wide array of religious iconography, sentiment, and impulse. Chapter 10 examines Ozu's attitude toward a variety of gender issues, particularly those concerning women, and finds him generally sympathetic to the reforms advocated by Japanese feminists and Occupation authorities in their efforts to liberate Japanese women.

Ozu's work has been compared to Noh drama and other Japanese art forms. Chapter 11 looks specifically at the ways in which his work compares to Japanese painting and printmaking, both classical and contemporary to his time. Ozu was aware of traditional art, dabbled in watercolors, and was friends with renown painters. Accordingly, his work reflects spatial strategies and other interests similar to both traditional and contemporary Japanese painting.

Ozu's influence on other directors has drawn considerable interest over the years and is the particular focus of Jinhee Choi's anthology *Reorienting Ozu: A Master and His Influence*. My final chapter adds to this discourse, discussing Ozu's influence on six directors, Japanese, German, and American, whose admiration for or dependence on him is either well documented or obvious. Each director has a different relationship to Ozu and a different understanding of his work, and each borrows distinct aspects of Ozu's content, style, and ethos.

Each of the book's three parts concludes with an "Afterword." That for Part I discusses Ozu's demonstrated nostalgia for his early films while Part II ends with a discussion of the persistence of war memory in the post-Occupation films. Part III's "Afterword" engages the debate over whether or not Ozu can be considered a modernist.

Because I have not always included a plot synopsis each time I discuss a particular film, a chronological list of plot synopses is available for quick reference at the end of the book. The actors involved in each film are noted, as is information about current DVD copies of the films. Because thorough and detailed filmographies exist in English in Donald Richie's, David Bordwell's and Kiju Yoshida's books on Ozu, I have not included one here. Kyoko Hirano's filmography in Yoshida's *Ozu's Anti-Cinema* has corrected earlier mistakes and omissions.

Although it has become customary in recent writing on Japan to give Japanese names in the Japanese order, i.e., family name first, I have written them in the Western/ English order because that is less confusing for English-language readers, not all of whom will be academics or Japanologists. Exceptions to this will occur in Chapter 11, in which the names of Japanese painters are given in the Japanese order because many of these individuals have international reputations based on the Japanese version of their names. I have also followed the custom of referring to these artists by their given names. All Japanese words and names have been romanized using the Hepburn system without macrons.

Footnotes containing the usual references, as well as additional observations, useful information, and interesting trivia, have been placed immediately following each chapter for the reader's convenience. Enjoy them!

Besides Donald Richie and David Bordwell, many individual scholars have contributed to our understanding of Ozu over the last thirty-plus years. I have not always agreed with everything they have written, but, as with Bordwell, I am profoundly grateful for their contributions to this field. Without their insights and, particularly, the background their research has provided, this book would not have been possible.

In addition, I would like to thank the following individuals for their personal assistance: Patricia Murray, Tamotsu Nagano, and Penelope Herbert for their invaluable help with translations; Kiyoshi Kabira, Akiko Miyamoto, Rowland Abiodun, and Jennifer Rutledge for finding and forwarding materials to me from Japan or from American libraries I could not access; David Desser, Woojeong Joo, and Chris Berry for

Introduction

critiquing the manuscript and offering advice; and Linda Ehrlich, Gina Marchetti, and Markus Nornes for their advice and encouragement. Special thanks go to my husband, Steven Sternbach, who not only assisted me with both image preparation and a listening ear, but who, at a time when authoring a book like this seemed out of reach, kept buying Ozu DVDs as they came on the market to encourage what he knew was my abiding interest in this amazing director.

Colorplate 1A: Disappointed in love, Michiko winds a dressmakers' measuring tape around her fingers in *An Autumn Afternoon*.

Colorplate 1B: A large, ghostly stupa appears in the inn's interior garden during the reunion sequence in *Equinox Flower*. Ureo Egawa appears here in a cameo role.

Colorplate 2A: Shallow space becomes deep space in a series of successive matched shots from *The End of Summer*, beginning with the front door of a restaurant in Osaka.

Colorplate 2B: Back door of the same restaurant

Colorplate 3A: An alley near Sasaki's house in Kyoto

Colorplate 3B: Manbei comes into the same alley, confirming it as a deep space.

Colorplate 4: Saeki Shunko, *Tearoom*, 1936. Panel; ink, color, and silver on paper. Photograph © 2011, Museum of Fine Arts, Boston.

Part I

The Silent Films

Ozu went to work for the Shochiku studios, located at that time in the Kamata district of Tokyo, in 1923. Beginning as an assistant cameraman, he worked his way up to assistant director and, in 1927, was elevated to director. Beginning in Shochiku's period film (*jidai-geki*) unit, he switched to the modern film (*gendai-geki*) unit when the former moved to Kyoto in 1928. From 1928 to 1936, he made thirty-three narrative films, of which only thirteen complete films and three fragments still exist.[1] For all that he admired American films, Ozu was slow to adopt their technical advances and thus made silent films until 1936.

Beginning with the so-called gangster films, the following chapters examine the foundations of his storytelling: his early narrative techniques and story structures, his use of symbolism, and the ways in which he pictured sound. Because the chapters are arranged by topic and draw on examples from all of Ozu's extant silent films, readers less familiar with these films are encouraged to make use as needed of the Plot Synopses, located on pages 253–269.

Note

1. Ozu also made a short documentary about Kabuki, *Kagamijishi*, in 1935. The title refers to the Kabuki lion dance by the same name. This film, made with sound, still exists.

1
The Gangster Films

The *ankokugai eiga* (underworld film) . . . offered contested spaces in which reality and imagination, ordinary life and crime, domestic space and "foreign" space directly interacted.

—Mitsuyo Wada-Marciano[1]

Ozu's so-called gangster films exemplify many of the themes that will be elaborated throughout this book: the intricacy of his narrative structures, his elaborate use of motifs, as well as symbolism and political commentary. In keeping with the modernist aesthetic afforded by the gangster genre, Ozu's enchantment with German Expressionist cinema is most evident in these films.

Foreign crime films as well as Japanese crime fiction inspired the Japanese *ankokugai* films, which featured the netherworld of gangs, prostitutes, detectives, and "seedy dockside spaces."[2] These films offered writers and directors the opportunity to explore foreignness and modernization in a quasi-fantasy world not completely tied to the reality of Japanese life, in what has been called a "*mukokuseki* (stateless) aesthetic."[3] At least one Japanese film scholar saw Ozu's underworld films, *Walk Cheerfully* (1930), *That Night's Wife* (1930), and *Dragnet Girl* (1933), as the most successful of this genre though they have little in common with the Hollywood crime films on which they are supposedly modeled.[4]

Tadao Ikeda, Ozu's scriptwriter on two of the gangster films, has described the romantic mixture of old Japan and modern America that inspired Ozu and himself. "In the end, we imagined both Edo and San Francisco . . . as if a playwright of Edo attempted to imitate the dandy style of American films."[5] Such was the sense of romance that generated the *mukokuseki* aesthetic.[6]

Iconography

Ozu's so-called gangster films use the iconography of American crime films, including fist fights, boxing, jazz clubs, beer barrels, the flapper, and, of course, the gun. Ozu shows guns in close-up multiple times in *That Night's Wife* and *Dragnet Girl* because they were (and are) rare in Japan. By 1930, guns were taken for granted in a variety of American film genres, but for Ozu's audience, they remained exotic.

The beer barrels in the back room of the jazz club in *Dragnet Girl* betray an iconography borrowed from American films that made little sense in a Japanese context. They correspond to that phenomenon, identified by art historians, in which a design element with a function in one object has been appropriated by another purely as design without the corresponding function. American gangster films were largely about trafficking illegal booze during Prohibition and frequently featured beer barrels in illicit factories and delivery trucks. Since there was no Prohibition in Japan, references to free-flowing alcohol and beer barrels are irrelevant; nevertheless, they make an appearance in *Dragnet Girl*.

Moral Tales and Love Stories

In contrast to most Western crime films, Ozu's gangster films are mainly moral tales and love stories. In this respect, Ozu's gangster films are similar to Joe May's *Asphalt* (Germany, 1929) in which the crimes depicted serve as backdrop to a story about love and redemption. According to Michael Raine, "*Asphalt* was a major touchstone for Ozu and his friends."[7]

Walk Cheerfully traces the developing affection between a kimono-clad "nice girl" and a hoodlum, whom she inspires to go straight. The tense crime scene at the beginning of *That Night's Wife* is an excuse for the long night waiting for a child's recovery, which reveals the father's intense affection for her, the intimate feelings he shares with his wife, and the longsuffering policeman's humanity. *Dragnet Girl's* story of love and commitment between a gangster and his moll is the most complex exploration of modern love in this group and, perhaps, in all of Ozu's extant films.

When *Dragnet Girl* begins, gang leader Jyoji proclaims, with pride, that he is "living off a woman" in response to his trainer's suggestion that he get back in shape and start boxing again. (See Figure 2.1, p. 36.) He means to say he is enjoying too much sex to perform well in the ring, but his phraseology suggests that his relationship is both casual and exploitative. Later he will modify his excuse to "I have a woman who loves me," when asked again about a comeback, but it is still the woman who loves *him*, not vice versa.

His live-in girlfriend, Tokiko, treats their relationship equally casually, accepting a ring from her boss's son, Okazaki, in exchange for unspecified sexual favors. At the jazz club, Jyoji flirts with Tokiko's friend Misako, who has a crush on him, while her date makes overtures to Tokiko. When Jyoji emerges from a back-room brawl at the club, Ozu frames him between the two women, backs to the camera, anxiously waiting, Misako on the left and Tokiko on the right. Although Jyoji and Tokiko are clearly infatuated with one another and acknowledged by gang members as a couple, the gang ethic does not recognize real commitment. This sets up a conflict between the couple's real feelings and the ethics they live by. When Jyoji notices the ring Tokiko has acquired from Okazaki, he says, "Don't make me worry." She responds, "A guy like you worried about a girl like me? You touched Misako's cheek three times tonight."

Here she broaches a theme that will be repeated later in the film. As a gang leader, Jyoji enjoys great respect and status. (Unlike an actual *yakuza*, he appears to be autonomous, answering to no one but himself.) Apart from being Jyoji's girlfriend, Tokiko enjoys no status at all. Merely a typist in an office typing pool, she, as a Japanese woman living outside the norms of middle-class life, is not entitled to anyone's respect.

The audience, of course, knows that Tokiko is much more than a conventional movie flapper or *moga* (modern girl). Played by a young Kinuyo Tanaka, pert and adorable, she is distinguished by her costumes, which, though all Western, are tasteful and beautiful. At the jazz club, Tokiko wears all white, Misako all black. This color distinction, symbolizing, with little subtlety, good and bad, will resurface later in the film. Although she is part of the gang milieu, smoking and playing pool, Tokiko's sweet nature and concern for others differentiate her from a *moga* like Misako, a fast-living gossip, or the criminal *moga* characters played by Satoko Date in two other Ozu films, *Walk Cheerfully* and *The Lady and the Beard*. Although Tokiko deems herself "selfish" at one point, her instinctive sympathy for others drives the plot at several junctures.

Infidelities aside, Jyoji and Tokiko are enjoying a normal, youthful boy-girl relationship when Jyoji develops a serious crush on a kimono-clad "nice girl." She is the sister of Hiroshi, a student whom Tokiko, out of consideration for his sponsor, gang member Senko, has encouraged Jyoji to take into the gang. The sister, Kazuko, suggests to Jyoji that he could be more than just a gangster, but when Tokiko, similarly inspired by Kazuko, demands as much, Jyoji rebels, suggesting that Tokiko, a "delinquent," is not worthy of his reformation. Hurt and frustrated, Tokiko storms out and toys with the idea of becoming Okazaki's mistress. Significantly, the first thing she says to Okazaki when he proposes an arrangement is, "Do you think I'm worthy?" She then proceeds to enumerate all of her bad qualities, but a validation of her worth is clearly important to her.

Still considering Okazaki's proposition, Tokiko looks out the window of the apartment he has taken her to and into another apartment with a coffee pot similar to Jyoji's. A two-pronged heating vent sits just outside the window, pouring out steam or smoke. Like the steaming tea canister in Sonya's room when she meets Agent 326 in Fritz Lang's *Spione* (1928), the vapor here reflects the passion Tokiko feels for Jyoji and does not feel for Okazaki. Understanding in this moment that "going straight" means giving up Okazaki and his gifts and being true to her man, she surrenders the expensive ring and bracelet he has given her. A box of cigarettes on the table where she deposits the jewelry prominently displays the words "Lucky Strike," suggesting she's on the right track and that Okazaki has struck out.[8]

Jyoji, who has expressed his lovesickness by systematically breaking glasses in a bar, is by turns joyful at her return, stoic as she begs him to forget Kazuko and love her more, and sullen when she repeats her demand that they reform. When Kazuko appears at their door looking for Hiroshi, Jyoji is again framed between two women, Tokiko at one end of the room and Kazuko near the door. Jyoji stands facing the table. This is more or less where Jyoji, Tokiko, and Hiroshi were standing the first time Hiroshi appeared in the apartment, and in both scenes Jyoji fiddles with an alarm clock as though it were a ball, a forewarning of trouble ahead. In contrast to the earlier scene in which the couple had welcomed Hiroshi, Jyoji is unsympathetic and rude to Kazuko, explaining to Tokiko afterward that he had to act that way "to get over her" and proclaiming that as twin "thugs" she and he belong together. Tokiko is crushed, first by his admission that his feelings for Kazuko had run deep and second by his continued unwillingness to see her as a potentially "decent woman." She continues urging him to reform, and finally he agrees.

The couple has started to embrace when a shamed-faced Hiroshi shows up, desperate because he has lifted money from his sister's place of business, a record store, to pay gambling debts. Despite Tokiko's reluctance, Jyoji insists they must help Hiroshi. No longer in possession of Okazaki's jewelry, she offers the necklace Jyoji has given her, but he reveals that it's fake. By this point he must have noticed that her other jewelry is missing and is delighted when she whispers something to him, presumably the plan to rob Okazaki himself, which will constitute a complete repudiation of her relationship with him. As they begin to imagine their reformed life together, Jyoji lights their gas heater—something he did earlier in the film prior to their lovemaking—and sets a teapot, not his coffee pot, on it, a nod to Japanese domesticity.

The heist is successful, and Jyoji leaves the money with Hiroshi and Kazuko, telling them to be good to one another and literally walking away from his attraction to Kazuko. The police, however, are hot on the couple's trail. They escape out their window, despite Tokiko's plea that they simply give themselves up. When, in an alley, she refuses to go any further, Jyoji hits her and insists on continuing his escape alone. In response, the ever-impulsive Tokiko shoots him in the leg. When she runs after him weeping and apologizing, he tries to throw her off but finally surrenders to his pain and her pleas, swallowing hard as she insists they will have a chance for a better life after prison. The police appear, and when she starts to run toward them, he calls her back and embraces her, tears spilling from his eyes. With everything else stripped away, he finally acknowledges the full depth of his love for her (Figure 1.1).

Ozu has prepared us for this climactic moment in several ways. First, he has twice denied our desire to see Jyoji and Tokiko reconcile in a full embrace. Once near the beginning of the film and once near the end, they argue about their relationship then make up just as Hiroshi arrives and interrupts their intimacy. Free of the distraction, disruption, and errant life choices Hiroshi represents, their embrace is finally consummated at the end of the film, satisfying our delayed gratification.

In addition, Jyoji's tears bring full circle a comment initially made by Hiroshi, who boastfully asks gang member Senko, "Have you ever made a woman cry?" These words appear on the screen before we actually see Hiroshi speak them, emphasizing their importance as thematic material. Hiroshi admits that the woman he made cry is only his sister, who is chagrinned by his delinquent behavior; but Jyoji makes Tokiko cry as she begs him to forget his infatuation with Kazuko, accept her as a "decent woman," and go straight. At the end he, too, is crying.

The Gangster Films 13

Figure 1.1: Jyoji's moment of truth comes at the conclusion of *Dragnet Girl*.

Western viewers may question Tokiko's need to shoot her lover to save their relationship, but extreme reactions by Japanese women thwarted in love are not unusual in Japanese cinema. We see the abandoned moll Chieko rolling on the floor and beating up her lover's friend Senko in *Walk Cheerfully*, for example. However, Ozu embedded a more subtle justification for Tokiko's act in *Dragnet Girl*. Tokiko shoots Jyoji right after he has hit her for refusing to continue their flight. Men striking women may well have been common in 1930s Japan; yet, in keeping with the generally feminist agenda of *Dragnet Girl*, Tokiko responding to violence with violence is understandable.

Beyond that, there is a structural parallel in the story that helps us understand how Ozu viewed Tokiko's action. Hiroshi is making a joke when he brags that he made a woman cry, but, in fact, he, like Jyoji, has a woman who loves him—his sister. In addition to the film's love triangle, then, there are two parallel love stories, Tokiko/Jyoji and Kazuko/Hiroshi, and Kazuko proves her love by going to great lengths to reform Hiroshi. Consequently, once Tokiko decides to reform Jyoji, not only her undignified begging but her decision to shoot him are all part of the same effort to save him that Kazuko has already modeled. Ozu insisted he was more interested in familial love than in romantic love,[9] so despite his touching evocation of romantic love and the subordination of the familial couple to the romantic couple in *Dragnet Girl*, we should understand that he took the film's familial bond and what it had to say about real love very seriously.

After the police take the couple away, one policeman remains behind and picks up a small knitted sock still attached to some yarn and hangs it on the nearby fence. The little sock points to the knitting and yarn motif that weaves its way throughout the film. Knitting is associated with Kazuko, domesticity, and decency. In the first shot of Kazuko at home, we see only her hands knitting. In this scene, she scolds Hiroshi for his delinquency, which he denies, but on the floor we see two balls of yarn, one light, one dark, indicative of the good sibling and the bad sibling. When Tokiko goes to the RCA shop to find Kazuko, she is knitting. Persuaded by Kazuko's goodness to go straight, Tokiko herself buys light yarn and dark yarn with which she promises to knit Jyoji some socks. Asking him to hold the dark yarn in an effort to domesticate him, she tries to wind a ball, but he throws the skein away angrily so that it becomes tangled throughout the apartment. At the end of this scene Tokiko storms out, but later, when she and Jyoji make up and it appears they may live happily ever after, a shot of her from the waist down shows her feet tangled in the black wool, an indication that they won't escape their gangster world so easily. (See Figure 4.4, p. 74.)

The sock the policeman finds after the couple's arrest is knitted with the same light and dark yarn, and, as the policemen give the all clear to one another, Ozu takes us back to the cop investigating Jyoji's apartment. He picks up a ball of light yarn, then tosses it away; it rolls next to a ball of dark yarn. Although the two balls lie close together, the light ball is in the center of the shot, bathed in light. The film cuts to another part of the floor, where the dark yarn still lays tangled, and from there to the window, where a plant stands against the night's darkness. Suddenly light fills the window. It's morning, and the light—true love, purity, redemption, symbolized by the light yarn—has won out.

Dragnet Girl was based on Ozu's 1930 gangster film, *Walk Cheerfully*, and although the plot is inverted—the good girl gets the gangster hero in the earlier film—it recycles many of the same elements: the gang leader caught between a good girl and a bad girl; sexual harassment from one girl's boss; a sidekick named Senko; a connection between gangsters, boxing, and jazz clubs; and the eventual reformation of the gangster heroes, who sustain gunshot wounds shortly before being arrested.

However, *Walk Cheerfully*'s love story remains on the level of a fairy tale; the bond between Kenji, the gang leader, and his friend Senko is at least as strong as that between Kenji and Yasue, the heroine. The bad girl, Chieko, is rejected by Kenji even before we meet her. Certain connections between the two films, however, work to inform and reinforce our understanding of *Dragnet Girl*. For example, the good girl, Yasue, in *Walk Cheerfully* is once shown knitting, although the motif goes no further. In lieu of a boxing club, Kenji's apartment in *Walk Cheerfully* is filled with boxing equipment and memorabilia. When he decides to go straight, he takes down the boxing posters and pictures in his apartment, thus rejecting this gang-related activity. Consequently, when *Dragnet Girl*'s Jyoji declines to continue his boxing career because of his woman, he is, without knowing it, already halfway reformed. (Kazuko picks up on this when she suggests Jyoji is only pretending to be a tough guy.)

In *Walk Cheerfully*, a bed sits in the middle of Kenji's apartment on which he and Chieko sit in her first scene with him, which suggests that sex is the main reason they are together. Although *Dragnet Girl* implies a robust sex life between Jyoji and Tokiko, Ozu is not so indelicate as to introduce a bed into the middle of their apartment, inviting the audience instead to observe the genuine chemistry between the two.

The first time the audience meets Chieko in *Walk Cheerfully*, Kenji has already lost interest in her, but he, nevertheless, reassures her with the same words that Jyoji uses to reassure Tokiko toward the end of *Dragnet Girl*: that a hoodlum [delinquent] like her suits him best. This helps us to understand why Tokiko is not at all assuaged when these words come from Jyoji. Not only are they denigrating, they are simply a "line," one that reiterates and thus traps her in the gangster ethic of non-commitment that she is trying to escape. When, in the same scene, Jyoji suddenly promises to go straight, he is not simply offering to get an honest job but to commit to a serious love relationship.

Finally, when, in *Walk Cheerfully*, Kenji and Senko are arrested—Senko having insisted on accompanying Kenji to jail—they are handcuffed together. The camera lingers on a medium two-shot of them with their cuffed hands in the bottom center. Senko grasps Kenji's hand and speaks cheerfully about the benefits of going to jail. At the end of *Dragnet Girl*, a policeman pries Tokiko and Jyoji's hands away from their embrace and, in close-up, locks them together. As with Kenji and Senko, the couple's strong emotional bond is now signaled by their locked wrists.

In Jyoji, Ozu created a complex hero, a mixture of Japanese and American types and virtues. Critic Tadao Sato has identified archetypal Japanese heroes as either *tateyaku* or *nimaime*. *Tateyaku* were samurai or samurai-type heroes who were victorious, sagacious men, "never permitted to place love for his wife or sweetheart above loyalty toward his lord."[10] Conversely, *nimaime* were handsome, romantic heroes, often weak, careless, or imprudent and, while sufficiently loyal to their sweethearts to commit suicide with them, were often the cause of their need to commit suicide. Ozu's hapless fathers and salarymen defied these stereotypes, but, rather than creating a new type in *Dragnet Girl*, Ozu mixed the two traditional male types in Jyoji. For cinematic and literary purposes, Japanese gangsters, or *yakuza*, were, to some extent, extensions of the samurai-type, i.e., *tateyaku*; and Jyoji, a former boxing champion who enjoys great respect from his gangland subordinates and inspires Hiroshi's hero worship, proves his mettle in one scene by single-handedly defeating three members of a competing gang in a fist fight. Afterwards he demonstrates a degree of nobility in ordering that glasses of water be taken to the defeated trio. Nevertheless, in his very first scene, Jyoji tells us that he no longer intends to box because he is "living off a woman," which sounds more characteristic of the weak *nimaime* than the proud *tateyaku*. However, his pretended indifference to Tokiko as well as his strength of character in both quelling his infatuation with Kazuko while still protecting her from Hiroshi's imprudence and setting the boy on a better path characterize him as *tateyaku*. This characterization breaks down at the end, however, when, in tears, he comes to terms with his love for Tokiko and the cost of their misdeeds. While Jyoji seems to be a combination of *tateyaku* and *nimaime*, Ozu channels Western humanism to soften the former and elevate the latter. Projecting such humanism was, in fact, one of the goals set by Ozu's boss, Shiro Kido, for Shochiku's Kamata studio.[11]

Although Ozu maintained that he was not interested in romantic love, the director made two films, *Dragnet Girl* and the lost *Until the Day We Meet Again* (*Mata au hi made*, 1932), both with Joji Oka as the male lead, which were celebrated for their poignant portrayal of romantic love.[12] Oka's tough-guy machismo combined with his dimpled smile and large expressive eyes made his portrayals of men conflicted over love particularly compelling, but Ozu never used him again or created such nuanced love stories. For unspecified reasons, the director found his work on *Dragnet Girl* difficult and draining.[13]

Beyond humanism, Ozu's films at times make very specific references to Christianity, and *Dragnet Girl* is the first of these. The redemption of the fallen woman looms large in the Gospel narratives, and, with its quick conversions, themes of repentance, reformation, and sacrifice, as well as its light/dark (good/evil) motif, *Dragnet Girl* leans heavily on Christian tradition. It is no accident that Tokiko's own quick conversion takes place in front of a Christian church (Figure 1.2). The film is set in Yokohama, an international port city suffused with foreign influence; thus its invocation of Christianity suits its location.

Figure 1.2: Tokiko's quick conversion, from hate to love for Kazuko, takes place in front of a Christian church in *Dragnet Girl*.

Bohemia vs. the Police State

Underground almost since its inception, Japan's Communist Party nevertheless continued to exert enough political influence that on March 15, 1928, more than 1,600 Communists and fellow travellers were arrested in a crackdown on the left that would only intensify in the coming decade. Ozu's oddly staged *That Night's Wife*, with its gratuitous robbery, surreal police chase, and unconventional apartment setting, where most of the story unfolds, should be viewed through the lens of this political reality.

The film begins with a shot of a street at night, lit by two street lamps, outside a large, imposing colonnaded building, which reminds one of the opening title from Josef von Sternberg's *Underworld* (1927): "A great city in the dead of night . . . streets lonely, moon-flooded . . . buildings empty as the cliff dwellings of a forgotten age." But whereas Western gangster films of the time include large imposing buildings—the bank in the beginning of *Underworld* and the colonnaded police station in Fritz Lang's *Spione* (1928)—and while these sets may imply the power of commerce and the state, their screen time is limited to their purely narrative function, usually captured in a single shot. Moreover, the institutions they represent are subsequently undermined by the respective gangsters and spies referenced in the films' titles. The bank at the beginning of *Underworld*, for example, is immediately blown up.

In *That Night's Wife*, shots containing the over-large stone buildings comprise approximately one-quarter of the first twenty minutes of the film. The opening scene, in which a policeman, dwarfed by the enormous colonnaded building next to him, chases away a bum trying to sleep next to one of the columns and then goes off duty, is composed of ten shots (compared to three or four, one of which contains an explosion, in the opening sequence of *Underworld*). In an extreme long shot of the policeman lighting a cigarette, he appears miniscule next to the colonnaded building. The police in this film will appear more bureaucratic and inept than malign, but the huge buildings, the faceless state that the police serve, come across as an intractable, menacing presence.

The scene shifts to the police station and eventually to the robbery, the motivation for the story. However, the huge buildings, among which the policemen run trying to catch the thief Hashizume, return after these interior scenes: first, after a lengthy scene in the Hashizume apartment, in which his wife consults with a doctor about her sick child, and again after a scene in a telephone booth, in which Hashizume contacts the same doctor, who tells him he must return home. These opening sequences conclude with the same large colonnaded building with which the film began: Hashizume, still trying to elude capture, runs in front of the building, then spots and hails what he thinks is a taxicab.

The inspiration for using the stone buildings as a symbol of oppression may have come from *Lady Windermere's Fan* (Ernst Lubitsch, 1925), with which Ozu was familiar. Oversized interior sets, particularly doorways, were common in Hollywood films because they facilitated camera movement, allowed for lighting, and did not crowd the actors.[14] However, in *Lady Windermere* Lubitsch frames his characters within huge sets, holding on extreme long establishing shots, and having characters move to the back of these shots away from the camera to suggest that the Windermeres and their class move through life like little dolls trapped in a social system over which they have no control.[15] Lubitsch's use of oversized sets to make a point about society was, apparently, not lost on Ozu, for whom Lubitsch was a model. He would use the stone buildings in *That Night's Wife* to evoke the faceless oppression of an oligarchic state.

These massive stone buildings are always associated with those servants of the state, the police, who are wonderfully characterized by the film's second sequence, which cuts from a close-up of the first policeman's hands, in which he, ready to go off duty, holds his white gloves behind his back, to a close-up of his hands dumping the gloves into his hat in the police station. A small sign next to the hat identifies him as a "Sanitation Officer," consequently his need to clean up the human garbage next to the elegant building in the film's opening sequence. He picks up his hat and gloves, salutes, and we cut to the "General Affairs Officer" at his desk, after which the camera travels back to reveal the two-volume "Daily Digest of Government Records" on another desk and finally stops behind an officer who is manning the telephone. This survey of one section of the police station establishes the orderliness and bureaucratic zeal of the police before the plot moves forward as the cop on the phone gets a call from the victim of an ongoing robbery. We watch the robbery conclude and then cut back to the police, who swarm out among the stone buildings on motorcycles and on foot.

For the most part, *That Night's Wife* is not particularly light-hearted or funny, but in one hilarious sequence we see a police captain addressing his "troops," a line of about fifteen policemen, with orders that seem to have more to do with straightening up their appearance than with catching the crook, for the next two shots show them straightening their hats, ties, and gloves. Subsequently, the captain takes out his false front teeth, top and bottom, and, looking for all the world like Dracula, charges off to lead his men into battle. Author Gregory Barrett asserts that the "police were above parody in [Japan's] predominantly authoritarian society,"[16] but not in Ozu's hands.

Later we see the cops gathering to plan strategy. There is a close-up of a policeman's hand drawing, on the street, a map of several city blocks to which many other hands point. This map, with its arrow drawn along one block, ties into Ozu's obsession with direction, discussed in detail in Chapter 4. Suffice it to say here that it proves as useless as all the other police actions. Despite their large numbers, high morale, and efficient organization, the uniformed policemen prove completely ineffective. Even when they spot the thief and give chase, he manages to elude them. Instead, a single wise detective, inefficient in his humanity, tricks the robber.

The contrast between Detective Kagawa and the police force generally elevates humanism over bureaucracy, but the visual contrast between the massive cold stone buildings and the chaotic display of objects in the Hashizume apartment signals an escape from a cold, faceless, and oppressive bureaucratic society into an alternative bohemian universe.

Not a professional gangster, the thief Hashizume is a sign painter, and his one-room apartment is filled with the tools of his trade, paint buckets and brushes, signs and posters he has presumably worked on. These include a sign for "Siegfried" (a reference either to Wagner's opera or, more likely, Part I of Fritz Lang's *Die Niebelungen*, 1924) and another that says "Dance Hall." In addition there is a photograph of a pretty woman and a dog, a poster for a film starring Walter Huston, another for a revue called "Broadway Scandals," and a large map of the "Empire of India." Besides signs in English and a wall covered with graffiti in mangled English, there is one sign in Russian. We also see a large assortment of art objects and collectors' items, which include: a straw boater, an Indonesian puppet, a Chinese doll, a large oval painting of a woman with an elaborate headdress, a painted plate, an intricately decorated fabric, and a vase painted with bats. There is a swing with a long-limbed cloth doll, a laundry line, and a Mission-style chair. Although outfitted with Japanese bedding, a Western-style iron-framed bed, on which the sick child Michiko sleeps, dominates the apartment, which has no tatami mats on which to lay out a Japanese bed.[17]

The room's décor celebrates the foreign, the modern, and, given the Russian poster, the political left. The large map of India that dominates the décor indicates a cause célèbre across the political spectrum in Japan, the Indian independence movement. The Indian National Congress had declared January 26, 1930, a day of complete self-rule.[18] Ozu would have had plenty of time to incorporate a commemoration of that event into *That Night's Wife*, his fourth film of 1930, released in July.

Dragnet Girl likewise embraces internationalism in its movie poster for *All Quiet on the Western Front* (Lewis Milestone, 1930) in Kazuko and Hiroshi's apartment. While the glowering soldier's head at the top of the poster may reflect the degree to which Kazuko feels under siege because of Hiroshi's bad behavior—it appears behind her while she's arguing with him—it is particularly interesting because it is in French. Thus we have a French poster for an American movie based on a German novel about German soldiers; as such, it evokes the international, cosmopolitan culture still popular in Japan, despite the growth of an inward-looking nationalism.

Ozu's lost *Until the Day We Meet Again* (1932) was, at the time of its release, considered an antiwar film.[19] The inclusion of the poster for *All Quiet on the Western Front* in *Dragnet Girl* suggests a continuing antiwar sentiment.

All three of Ozu's gangster films posit a prison term as a cleansing, redeeming punishment that permits love and restores the hoodlums to normal society. By all accounts Japanese prisons are not a place anyone would want to be, but these endings acknowledge Japanese aspirations for a cohesive, harmonious society. *That Night's Wife* speaks most compellingly to this notion. Having spent the night watching over his captive, Hashizume, watching over his child, the detective Kagawa gets ready to leave with him, donning a coat and hat and getting out his handcuffs. In doing so he comes upon the child's coloring book, her medical record, and an empty medicine bottle. Forsaking his "duty" out of sympathy, he deliberately allows his prisoner to escape. Hashizume leaves but returns on his own, convinced that he cannot be a good father until he sets himself right with society by going to prison for his crime. The two men leave together, share a cigarette, and then link arms, no handcuffs necessary. Like the endings of *Dragnet Girl* and *Walk Cheerfully*, which show the two friends/lovers cuffed together as emblematic of their strong feelings for one another, this one depicts not only the moral growth of the characters—Kagawa having found compassion more compelling than "duty" and Hashizume having seen the necessity of maintaining the social compact—but celebrates both the personal bond between the policeman and his prisoner and, by extension, social healing. The police morph in this film from being bureaucratic fools in the service of an oppressive state to human beings capable of eliciting reform.

Although the police are not humanized in either *Walk Cheerfully* or *Dragnet Girl*, they nevertheless serve as agents of reform. Ozu was often criticized for not following through on the bleak leftist vision many of his films begin with. Whether from personal belief, a wish to avoid censorship, or from a desire to create a Hollywood-like happy ending, his films generally end with a moral rather than a political vision.

The German Connection

According to Tadao Sato, Japanese filmmakers were influenced by German films from the 1920s.[20] The influence of German Expressionist cinema as well as that of Austrian émigré Josef von Sternberg is evident in Ozu's films, particularly the gangster films. A series of von Sternberg films starring George Bancroft appear to have been particularly influential. *Underworld* has already been mentioned. *The Dragnet* (1928), which involves a female gangster, undoubtedly inspired the title of *Dragnet Girl* and possibly the character of Tokiko, while *Thunderbolt*'s plot (1929) is propelled by a moll who wants to go straight. The influence of von Sternberg's *Docks of New York* (1928) will be discussed in Chapter 3.

All three gangster films borrowed at times from the city symphony formula, popularized by Walther Ruttmann's groundbreaking *Berlin, Symphony of a City* (*Berlin: Sinfonie der Grossstadt*, 1927), which was released in Japan in 1927.[21] Ozu would borrow directly from it for his office sequence in *Walk Cheerfully*.

Ruttmann's first two "acts" show the city waking up, and *Akt II* includes a sequence of shutters and curtains being raised and opened in homes and stores. Later there is a long sequence of an office opening up, mostly picturing legs and feet walking or hands and arms working rather than entire human bodies. It runs like this:

1) MS of people, photographed from behind and from the waist down, going up steps and into an office building.
2) CU of people's feet going up the steps.
3) FS of people going up steps.
4) A service elevator going up the side of a building.
5) Two successive shots of freight elevators going up.
6) Two successive shots of a passenger elevator going up.

The Gangster Films 21

7) Two dumbwaiter-type elevators, one going up, the other going down.
8) A cabinet being unlocked and a roll-up cover falling away.
9) A roll-top on a desk being pushed back.
10) A roll-up shutter on a cabinet being lifted.
11) Two smaller cabinets being unlocked and roll-up shutters falling away.
12) The arms of a typist putting on sleeve protectors.
13) The back of a man seated at a desk as he gets his pens out.
14) A hand opening a leger.
15) A woman's hands taking typing paper out of a drawer.
16) A woman's hands lifting the cover off a typewriter.
17) The hands and arms of two women typing.

This sequence continues alternating close-ups of the typewriter keys with close-ups of the women typing, ending in a surreal swirl of lettered keys, followed by a telephone sequence.

The office sequence in *Walk Cheerfully* is introduced well into the film, after Kenji has vowed to go straight. In it we see:

1) From the outside: a metal window shutter going up on a lower window with a bar across it.
2) From the outside: a metal window shutter going up on an upper three-part window.
3) From the inside: another shutter going up.
4) People walking along a sidewalk, framed from the waist down.
5) People going into a building, framed from the waist down.
6) Hats being hung up inside the building.
7) People's feet going up the office steps.
8) More hats being hung up until the row is filled.
9) Typewriters being uncovered by women's hands.
10) A woman powdering her nose.
11) CU of her compact on the windowsill.

At this point the narrative resumes. Heroine Yasue's feet are among those shown walking along the sidewalk. She sees the reflection from the compact and looks up to see Kenji washing windows high above her, but he disappears, and she sees no more of him until later in the day when the office closes, much as it opened.

The first three shots in the office-closing sequence show the shutters coming down on the same three windows as shots #1, 2, and 3 above but in reverse. The typewriters are covered by the same hands that uncovered them, and hats are taken from the rack. Men, framed from the waist down, go down the office steps, feet walk past a corner of the building, and more hats are taken from their hooks. Feet go down the office steps again, including some female feet. Seen from outside, the shutter over the main entrance goes down, then more feet walk away from the building. There is a closer shot of feet walking on the sidewalk, then Yasue comes into the frame.

In *Berlin's Akt IV*, very few shots are devoted to the office closing. Rather, we see factory workers washing up and only two shots related to the white-collar portion of the factory: a woman's arm closing the roll-up cabinet shutter and the service elevator going down.

Undoubtedly influenced by *Berlin*, Ozu borrowed his shutter shots from the scenes of shutters going up on stores and domestic buildings and attached them to *Berlin's* shots of people going into the office building and of typewriters being uncovered and used. In contrast to *Berlin*, Ozu repeated his opening sequence more or less in reverse as Yasue leaves her office. What Ozu added to the sequence are the hats, which, as we will see, play a significant role in all three gangster films.

Ozu, who saw *Dragnet Girl* as a variation on *Walk Cheerfully*, repeated his office opening and closing sequences in that film, with some changes:

1) Very high shot of three tiny men, casting long shadows, walking across pavement in two directions.
2) A window blind, situated on the left, is closed partway over part of an office window, seen from inside.
3) Two pendulum time clocks side by side.
4) A row of hats next to the time cards.
5) A third wall clock.
6) The row of hats; one falls off onto the floor.
7) CU of the fallen hat.
8) Traveling shot showing the backs and hands of women typing.
9) Traveling shot across the row of hats with one missing to another row of hats with none missing.
10) Traveling shot of women typing, seen from the opposite side of the table; camera pauses on a typewriter without a typist.

The director used what had been the office-opening sequence in *Walk Cheerfully* as the film's opening sequence in *Dragnet Girl* for more overtly narrative purposes. Unlike that in *Berlin* and *Walk Cheerfully*, the office in *Dragnet Girl* is not actually opening. The clocks tell us that it is already 3:35. One hat falls from the hat rack, creating an empty spot, and when we see the typists, all in dark colors, one is missing. Tokiko comes into that spot wearing a bright striped sweater in contrast to the other typists. She is the fallen hat, and we will soon learn why.

As in *Walk Cheerfully*, the office in *Dragnet Girl* closes with almost the same series of shots that introduced it:

1) Typewriters being covered by women's hands.
2) Twin trash cans overflowing with crumpled pages that the typists have spoiled.
3) A very high shot of the street outside the office building with men leaving work and casting long shadows as in the earlier shots introducing the office.

The Gangster Films

4) A shot through a decorative window grating; we see Tokiko on the street through this window.

5) Tokiko using a shop window as a mirror to straighten her hat and scarf, an echo of the office worker powdering her nose in *Walk Cheerfully*.

Ozu calls on these twin sequences again when Tokiko and Jyoji rob Okazaki in his office, flipping shot #2 from the opening sequence so that the blind half-covering the window is on the right, then showing the twin clocks from which the camera travels in a continuous shot over all the hats before cutting to Jyoji and Tokiko coming down the hallway.

In *That Night's Wife*, the city symphony is evoked in a morning sequence in which a shot of a dark window is replaced by the same window filled with light, followed by a light on the outside of the apartment building going out, then a boy delivering milk with a horse-drawn wagon. None of this appears to be drawn directly from *Berlin*, but the light filling the dark window would be repeated in the very last shots of *Dragnet Girl* in a highly symbolic statement. Ozu thus borrowed, added to, manipulated, and sometimes gave symbolic meaning to shots and sequences inspired by the city symphony; Ruttmann's *Berlin* appears to have been the catalyst.

Ozu would borrow bits and pieces from other German films. If von Sternberg's *Underworld* informed his image of "the street" as it appears in *That Night's Wife*, German films like *The Street* (*Die Strasse*, 1923), *The Joyless Street* (*Die Freudlose Gasse*, 1925), and *Asphalt* (1928) also contributed. Gangster hero Kenji's moniker "Ken the Knife" in *Walk Cheerfully* derives from *The Three Penny Opera* (*Die Dreigroschenoper*).[22] The sequence in *Dragnet Girl* in which Tokiko shuts Jyoji's front door on gang member Senko's arm in her eagerness to begin severing ties with gang life is similar to an early sequence in *Pandora's Box* (*Die Büchse der Pandora*, 1929), in which Lulu shuts a door on her stage manager's arm as she tries to win back her lover.

The office sequences in *Dragnet Girl* that borrow from *Berlin* begin and end with extreme high shots of men walking to and away from the office building, a camera setup favored by Fritz Lang, and the shot in *Walk Cheerfully* of Kenji and Senko being taken down a stairwell and away to jail uses exaggerated, menacing shadows in the vein of *Nosferatu* (1922) and other German Expressionist films. These particular shots stand out because they don't really fit with Ozu's dominant style in his gangster films, as do his other borrowings, but they attest to the creative latitude he seems to have felt this genre afforded him.

Several of Ozu's recurring symbols, which are not confined to the gangster films, also appear to have been influenced by German Expressionist cinema. These will be explored in Chapter 2.

Hat Tricks

Chapter 2 will detail a wide variety of Ozu's motifs and symbols as they appear in the silent films, but one in particular, his play with hats, is confined mainly to the gangster films. In both *Walk Cheerfully* and *Dragnet Girl*, Ozu added hats to a sequence of shots otherwise copied quite faithfully from Ruttmann's *Berlin*, and, as we have seen, Tokiko is compared to a hat in *Dragnet Girl*. Hats drive the narrative at several points in that film. When Hiroshi is accepted into the gang, he makes a point of changing his student cap for the street punk's "poor boy" hat, then changes back again while looking at himself in a shop window. Ozu frames this action through the window of the store next door, a shot which he "vignettes" by smearing the window with soap, leaving enough of it clear so that we can see Hiroshi. Meanwhile, looming very large in the right foreground of the shop window is a fedora. Thus while Hiroshi plays with his hats, we look at a huge hat in the foreground.

Hats are used synecdochically to indicate a person's presence before we actually see that person. For example, another Hiroshi sequence begins with a close-up of his student hat, his books, and another gang member's hat hanging on hooks, the first scene in which we see him gambling with the gang.

The scene in which Tokiko retreats to a private apartment with boss Okazaki begins with a close-up of her hat and suitcase along with Okazaki's hat. This same hat and suitcase combo is the first thing Jyoji notices when he comes back to his apartment and realizes Tokiko has returned to him. It also introduces a scene after the robbery in which she waits for him to return. Initially this last close-up of her hat, purse, and suitcase suggests she is "ready to run" as Jyoji has instructed, but the camera moves around the table to another on which a different suitcase and a similar hat sit amid a certain amount of disarray, indicating that perhaps she is not really ready.

In *That Night's Wife*, Hashizume and his wife, Mayumi, are shown mainly as worried parents desperate enough to commit crimes, but both are linked to their more light-hearted bohemian universe through Hashizume's fedora. When Mayumi lies to detective Kagawa, insisting Hashizume is not at home, the policeman spots the fedora and pops it on Mayumi's head, invoking an alternative image of the *moga*, a kimono-clad beauty sporting a fedora. At the end of the film, a disheveled Hashizume returns to the apartment after his escape, wearing the fedora pulled down over his forehead, creating a roguish *mobo* (modern boy) look.

Of all three gangster films, the earliest, *Walk Cheerfully*, makes the greatest and most varied use of hats. Early in the film when bad girl Chieko demands money from a male victim she has wooed, she first takes off his hat. Realizing his predicament, the victim runs off. When she throws his hat after him, he runs back hesitantly to retrieve it. Similarly, toward the end of the film, hero Kenji punches gang member Gunpei for taunting him (for reforming), then throws Gunpei's hat out the door after him. There is a close-up of the hat on the floor as Gunpei picks it up and dusts it off. When, in the previous scene, Kenji breaks up the gang, sending a tearful Senko off on his own, he takes off Senko's white bowler hat, smoothes his sidekick's hair like a mother, and places the hat back on his head.

Senko's white bowler becomes an object of amusement, presumably for Chieko, when it is twice thrown out of their vehicle and Senko jumps out of the car to retrieve it. Subsequently, Senko's white bowler becomes a foil for the black bowler hat of the President, who lures Yasue to a hotel, intending to rape her, before Kenji comes to the rescue. As the President recovers from Kenji's knock-out punch, he picks up his black bowler and dusts it off. The last shot in the Luna Hotel scene is a close-up of the black hat. With obvious irony, Ozu contrasts the open-hearted, ever-faithful Senko with the black-hearted President (already characterized by the filthy towel on which he has wiped his hands earlier in the scene) via their hats. Senko will wear a different-style hat in his new, honest job, but it will remain white.

When the unsmiling police detectives come for Kenji at the end of the film, each wears a different hat, one an Ascot cap, one a bowler, the third a policeman's patrol cap (Figure 1.3). The policemen never vary their stern expressions, but their assortment of hats is funny and part of Ozu's subtle mockery, which will expand so prominently in *That Night's Wife*.

With synecdochic economy, Ozu established place, character, action, pathos, and humor in these films via hats. They figure only slightly in later films. Kihachi and Jiro,

Figure 1.3: The policemen who arrest Kenji wear a variety of hats in *Walk Cheerfully*.

protagonists in *Passing Fancy*, are distinguished by their very different hats, a beret for Kihachi and a military cap for Jiro, and the kimono-clad woman with a bowler is revived in *A Mother Should Be Loved*. Nowhere, however, are hats used as extensively as in the gangster films.

Ozu made only three gangster films, and we are lucky that all three have survived. More even than his nonsense comedies, the *mukokuseki* world of the gangster films afforded him great creative and imaginative latitude because it had little to do with actual Japanese society. In these films Ozu could exhibit the modern: fashionable Western dress, jazz clubs, and Nipper dogs; explore the utopian: equality in relationships; and mock the unjust: sexual harassment and an oppressive police state. Quite possibly he developed similar themes in some of his lost films, but less so in those other silents that have come down to us. They, however whimsical, are tied much more closely to the realities of Japanese life in the 1930s.

Notes

1. Mitsuyo Wada-Marciano, *Nippon Modern: Japanese Cinema of the 1920s and 1930s* (Honolulu, HI: University of Hawai'i Press, 2008), 32.
2. Wada-Marciano, *Nippon Modern*, 34.
3. Wada-Marciano, *Nippon Modern*, 37.
4. The critic is Kikuo Yamamoto. See Wada-Marciano, *Nippon Modern*, 37n54.
5. Woojeong Joo, *The Cinema of Yasujiro Ozu: Histories of the Everyday* (Edinburgh: Edinburgh University Press, 2017), 76.
6. For more on the origins of the silent crime film in Japan, see David Bordwell, *Ozu and the Poetics of Cinema* (Princeton, NJ: Princeton University Press, 1988), 197.
7. Michael Raine, "A New Form of Silent Cinema: Intertitles and Interlocution in Ozu Yasujiro's Late Silent Films," in *Reorienting Ozu: A Master and His Influence*, ed. Jinhee Choi (New York: Oxford University Press, 2018), 106.
8. Baseball was introduced into Japan in 1872 and to this day retains its American terminology.
9. Donald Richie, *Ozu: His Life and Films* (Berkeley, CA: University of California Press, 1974), 216.
10. Tadao Sato, *Currents in Japanese Cinema*, trans. Gregory Barrett (Tokyo: Kodansha, 1982), 16.
11. Bordwell, *Poetics*, 21.
12. Richie, *Ozu*, 216; Bordwell, *Poetics*, 244.
13. Richie *Ozu*, 217. In an interview entitled "Talking of My Own Work," originally published in 1964, Ozu says almost nothing about either *Walk Cheerfully* or *Dragnet Girl*. "Ozu on Ozu: The Silents," *Cinema* (USA) 7, no. 3 (Winter 1972–1973): 24.
14. Norman Gambill, "Harry Horner's Design Program for '*The Heiress*'," *Art Journal* 43, no. 3 (Fall 1983): 224.
15. This aspect of the film is made particularly clear in the garden scene in which Lady Windermere dallies with Lord Darlington; they are photographed in long shots from in front of a medium-height hedge so that, as they stand up from a bench behind the hedge

The Gangster Films 27

and then sit down again, they pop in and out of the picture like puppets manipulated from behind a puppet stage.

16. Gregory Barrett, "Comic Targets and Comic Styles: An Introduction to Japanese Film Comedy," in *Reframing Japanese Cinema: Authorship, Genre, History*, ed. Arthur Nolletti, Jr. and David Desser (Bloomington, IN: Indiana University Press, 1992), 216.

17. Jun'ichiro Tanizaki's description of furnishing a Western-style house in *Naomi* gives some insight into Ozu's choice of objects in *That Night's Wife*: "We bought some inexpensive India prints . . . At a Shibaguchi shop that specialized in Western furniture, we found an old rattan chair, a sofa, an easy chair, and a table . . . On the walls we hung photographs of Mary Pickford and several other American movie actresses." *Naomi*, trans. Anthony H. Chambers (New York: Vintage International, 2001), 19.

18. *Purna Swaraj* Day.

19. Yuki Takinami, "Modernity, *Shoshimin* Films, and the Proletarian-Film Movement," in Choi, *Reorienting Ozu*, 144.

20. Sato, *Currents in Japanese Cinema*, 32.

21. Abe Mark Nornes, *Japanese Documentary Film: The Meiji Era through Hiroshima* (Minneapolis, MN: University of Minnesota Press, 2003), 15. Dziga Vertov's *Man with a Movie Camera* (*Chelovek s kinoapparatom*, 1929) was not released in Japan until March of 1932. Yuki Takinami has detailed parallels between it and the home movie shown in *I Was Born, But . . .* See Takinami, "Modernity, *Shoshimin* Films, and the Proletarian-Film Movement," 145ff.

22. Though not filmed until 1931 (G. W. Pabst), *Three-Penny Opera*'s most famous song, "Mack the Knife," had been a hit since the play's debut in 1928.

2
Signs, Symbols, and Motifs

Ozu's refusal to adopt the codes of Hollywood illusionism results in an excess of film language, of signs and signifiers.

—Catherine Russell[1]

David Bordwell, leading film scholar and Ozu expert, has inveighed at length against the idea of interpreting films or assigning meaning to the objects in them.[2] The rigorous formalist was, perhaps understandably, uncomfortable with the imprecision of critical interpretation, which is, at best, subjective and intuitive. To make matters worse, artists also work intuitively and may not always be conscious of the meaning with which they have endowed their art. Nevertheless, interpreting signs and symbols and discerning how they fit into patterns of meaning in a film require a rigor similar to detecting formal patterns as well as a knowledge of both the culture and history of the country and the period in which the film was made. A compelling interpretation involves evidence and logic and is not simply invented out of thin air. If art history confined itself to formal analysis alone, it would be a dull subject indeed. Art historians regularly interpret the intent of pictures which don't move or talk or sing or dance as to the story they wish to tell, the moral, religious, philosophical, political, and social themes they express, and the attitudes they convey. Doing the same for moving pictures is not novel, frivolous, or specious.

To this we can add that Japanese write in pictures, and these pictographs (*kanji*) have multiple meanings, which Japanese writers play off one another. Many objects in traditional Japanese culture have meanings, much as they did in medieval European culture. Consequently, endowing objects with meaning would hardly have been an alien exercise for Ozu.

In his attempt to denigrate and discredit interpretative readings of Ozu's films, Bordwell piles on arguments and examples that reach well into the realm of absurdity. In *Ozu and the Poetics of Cinema*, he creates a fictional "interpretative critic" who advances silly interpretations so that Bordwell can shoot them down and prove that interpretation is useless.[3] He and frequent co-author Kristin Thompson have also formulated a list of axioms related to the interpretation of signs and symbols within films

Signs, Symbols, and Motifs 29

that are both arbitrary and nonsensical. One of these holds that using obvious symbols is ipso facto heavy-handed and thus more or less unthinkable of Ozu.[4]

Obvious Symbols

Such reasoning is, of course, tautological, but, for the record, Ozu was not above availing himself of symbols that might be considered clichéd. The black-and-white symbolism in *Dragnet Girl* is hardly subtle or original. Other obvious symbols have to do with death and dying—small animals battling for life, for example. In *Tokyo Chorus* the father stops by to collect his son, who is playing in a creek with friends. The boy catches a fish in his father's straw hat and then announces that his sister is ill. He dumps his fish on the ground as the two hurry off. The final shot in the sequence is of the beached fish, gasping for life, clearly a reference to the sister's plight. In a subsequent hospital sequence, father and son are reading a picture book when they look up to watch to a moth batting its life out against a hanging light. This motif would be reprised in several of Ozu's sound films. In *An Inn in Tokyo*, a similar hospital scene includes two shots of an insect struggling in a pan of water.

Mikio Naruse's short film from 1931, *Flunky, Work Hard!* (*Koshiben ganbare*), characterizes the health crisis of the protagonist's son with a montage composed of a close-up of a clock's pendulum, then a dripping faucet (life dripping away) that tilts down to reveal an insect struggling in a pan of water. A later shot of the faucet and the pan of water shows the insect nearly dead. In contrast, *That Night's Wife*, from 1930, does not use any of these symbols; the clocks in the film are included primarily to inform us of the long night in which the parents watch the child and the detective watches the parents. Ozu would not use the particular image of the bug struggling in water until 1935. From this we understand both that these images suggesting impending death and/or a struggle for life were not unique to Ozu and that he was not too sophisticated to avail himself of them.

Nooses and rope constitute another category of signs or symbols associated with death. We first encounter the noose as a joke in *I Flunked, But . . .* We are shown a premonitory noose but soon discover it is really part of an overhead lamp cord. Eventually we are shown a student agonizing in front of his dean. We know from the story that he is not very bright, and we suppose he has flunked; but two sequences later we learn he is pleading not for himself but for the protagonist, Takahashi, who tutored him. (Takahashi was busy working out an elaborate cheating scheme instead of studying the night before the exam.) Of the three sequences involving the dim-witted student and the dean, two are preceded by the "noose" shot. In a typical Ozu reversal, the doom implied by the noose is real, but it applies to Takahashi and his friends, not to the anguished underachiever.

In *That Night's Wife*, from the same year, ominous loops of heavy rope are draped over the beams in the stairwell outside the protagonists' apartment. The rope may signal the husband's eventual downfall, but, since he goes off companionably with his captor at film's end and is not facing a death sentence, the rope, like the police chase and robbery at the beginning of the film, acts as another token of the scary crime film that never materializes.

In *Woman of Tokyo*, however, bits of rope combine with other symbols, including two pairs of *hanging* gloves, to portend and communicate the brother Ryoichi's suicide. Having learned that his sister, Chikako, moonlights as a prostitute, Ryoichi confronts her, then runs out of their apartment. In a subsequent sequence, a tracking shot follows him through an unkempt alley. In the alley we see bits of rope, shards from broken pots, and overturned barrels and tubs. Ryoichi sits, pulls a button off his coat and throws it away. At his feet are a little flame from a lantern, an upright tub, and more rope.

A cut to his girlfriend Harue's home begins with a close-up of her brother, Kinoshita's, white policeman's gloves *hanging* on the wall with his saber, casting a shadow on the wall. A similar shot began the sequence between Harue and her brother the day before when she returned from the movies. In that shot, however, the gloves did not cast the prominent shadow that they do in the shot that begins this second Harue-Kinoshita sequence. In this second sequence, another shot begins with the saber and gloves in the foreground left, out of focus, *hanging* from Kinoshita's side. Two other gloves hang, separately, from a clothesline on the balcony and are silhouetted behind the frosted glass of the sliding door. They appear ominously in the background every time the camera points in that direction during this extensive sequence, which consists: first, of Kinoshita trying to reassure Harue, distraught from the fight she has had with Ryoichi the previous night; second, of his departure for work; and, finally, of Chikako's arrival and her conversation with Harue. This last, the interview with Chikako, includes a call from Kinoshita with the news that Ryoichi has committed suicide. When Harue goes to answer the call at a neighbor's clock shop, we see boots *hanging* in the hallway, to which Ozu deliberately calls our attention when he has the boy who has come for her bat at them while he waits. Subsequently in Chikako's home, we see the shadow of a loop of rope on the wall next to Ryoichi's kimono. Not once are we told that Ryoichi has committed suicide by hanging, but can there be any doubt?

In addition to the rope and hanging objects in *Woman of Tokyo*, Ozu adds clocks as a symbol of mortality. While Chikako waits in Harue's house for her to return, she looks up at a clock on the wall. Cut to a wall of clocks in the shop with the phone. Harue comes into the shot, and there are cuts back and forth between Harue and Kinoshita on the telephone. Each shot of Harue has the clocks in the background. Finally, there is a close-up of the wall of clocks, Harue hanging up the phone, the same close-up of the wall of clocks, then a cut back to the clock on the wall of her home. The scene continues with Harue telling Chikako of Ryoichi's suicide and ends with her collapsing in tears.

Vessels of various kinds create a less obvious but persistent motif that runs through the story, from our first glimpse of Chikako as a prostitute to Harue and Chikako mourning over Ryoichi's body. It begins with a sink full of dirty water at the disreputable cabaret where Chikako picks up her johns, an obvious comment on what she does there. The motif continues in the form of the overturned tubs and shards seen on

Ryoichi's walk through the back alleys. These connect to the tub of wash water Chikako sees in the alley behind Harue's home while she waits for Harue, who returns with the news of Ryoichi's death. Subsequently we see basins in Chikako's home, presumably used to wash Ryoichi's body, which is laid out for mourning. Thus we go from the dirty business of the club, which, when known to Ryoichi, upends his life and shatters his faith (the overturned tub and pottery shards) to the washtub under the hanging laundry (to which other motifs pointing to hanging and death have been added) to the washbasin that has been used to wash his body. This is a journey from the profane to the sacred through the agonies of the heart. These motifs, combined and interwoven with one another, elevate Ryoichi's death above the merely melodramatic to something more elegiac. Despite Chikako's castigating him as a weakling, these various symbols give Harue's sentiment, "I feel terribly sorry for Ryoichi," equal weight.

Critics typically view *Woman of Tokyo* as a Mizoguchi-esque, *shinpa*-inspired story of an impoverished, misunderstood woman, for whom prostitution is the only way to earn enough money to support her brother; but Ozu's story is more Shakespearean than Mizoguchian, and Ozu's symbols guide us to this conclusion. This film is about the bad choices every single major character makes. Chikako's desire to indulge Ryoichi, not simply pay for his schooling—indicated in the conversation between her supervisor and a policeman ("She's very generous to her brother")—has caused her to take up "dirty" work instead of the honest translating she claims to be doing on the side. The shot of the sink full of dirty water, reminiscent of the dirty towel Hiroko's boss wipes his hands on in *Walk Cheerfully*, justifies this reading. Smaller missteps lead to tragedy: Harue's brother wants to warn Chikako that the police are investigating her, but he allows Harue to take on the task instead. When Harue finds Ryoichi instead of Chikako at home, she lets him pressure her into telling what she knows, and his extreme reaction leads him to commit suicide.

These are all bad choices, but critics tend to side with Chikako, who sees herself as a victim—"You never understood me, Ryoichi," she says to his dead body—and dismiss Ryoichi's very legitimate question to her: "Don't you care that your actions may ruin our lives?" Through his piling on of signs and symbols, Ozu helps us to understand Ryoichi's heartbreak and the tragic irony of the bad choice each character makes.

From Motif to Symbol

Another of the Bordwell/Thompson axioms is that an object endowed with symbolic meaning must have the same meaning from film to film, both within a director's oeuvre and even within that of any other director. In fact, Ozu's use of particular objects in his films often moves from a simple motif or even a singular image to a more complex sign or symbol. One wants to say such usage "evolved," but an image could as easily move back again to being a simple motif. Certainly Ozu had an affection for certain objects and how they photographed and introduced them into his films for no other reason than that, but at times he invested them with meaning when the story suggested it.

Victrolas are a good example of this change from motif to symbol. Ozu used close-ups of record players in a number of his early films. One begins the pawnshop sequence in *Days of Youth*, in which protagonist Watanabe trades in his friend Yamamoto's books for ski equipment. In *I Flunked, But . . .* a record player is used as a gag, a means for the roommates to determine who will pay for their snacks. One scene in *Walk Cheerfully* begins with a close-up of a 78 record playing. Subsequent shots reveal gang member Senko singing "I'm a Gay Cabalero" along with the record, the words having been written in English on the wall behind him.

In *Dragnet Girl*, however, the Victrola is given a more active role in the plot and more meaning. We see a close-up of one playing three times, twice in the RCA store where Kazuko works and once in Jyoji's apartment, where he is listening to the classical music record he has bought at Kazuko's store. The cut directly from Tokiko's boss, Okazaki, fingering the bracelet he will give her, to the Victrola summarizes the twin attractions— Jyoji's infatuation with Kazuko and Okazaki's attentions to Tokiko—which threaten the couple's relationship. We see Jyoji's Victrola again after he and Tokiko have made peace and decided to go straight. Associated with Kazuko and legitimate culture (as opposed to jazz-age decadence), it stands for the decent life she represents, which both Jyoji and Tokiko now aspire to. Tokiko, who earlier resented the Victrola's implications, winds it up and plays it while Jyoji lights their gas heater and puts a kettle on it.

Clocks also function in a variety of ways in Ozu's films. Often they simply let us know what time it is or how much time has passed as in *I Graduated, But . . .* , *That Night's Wife*, *Where Now Are the Dreams of Youth?*, *Dragnet Girl*, and *A Story of Floating Weeds*. We see the clock as a metaphor for passing, passed, or past time in *Passing Fancy* when main character, Kihachi, picks up a pocket watch from a pile of belongings he hopes to sell and moans about how he has no education and no savings to pay the hospital for the treatment of his son Tomio. Time to do these things has run out. He has wasted his time.

In *Woman of Tokyo*, however, clocks not only tell time but indicate that time has literally run out for one individual. The wall of clocks behind Harue as she learns of Ryoichi's death from her brother's phone call insists on this interpretation, and the symbol is repeated in *A Mother Should Be Loved*, where the sons return home from school to be told their father has died. We see two successive shots of a grandfather clock, the exterior of the family's house, a cut to the boys having breakfast, the dead father's picture in the background, and a medium shot of the picture, draped with a black ribbon. A dialogue sequence with the boys' uncle follows, then a final shot of the grandfather clock. When, later in the film, the mother, unpacking after the family has moved to the suburbs, holds her husband's pocket watch to her ear, there is a cut to a picture of her dead husband.

Most intriguing of all Ozu's clocks, however, are the old-fashioned alarm clocks with twin bells on top. All of the students and salarymen in Ozu's silent films have them.

Signs, Symbols, and Motifs

The odd sequence in *Passing Fancy* in which the boy Tomio is shown drawing his alarm clock suggests that Ozu found their bulbous shape fascinating. Most of the time, the alarm clocks serve as background, but in two instances they enter more directly into the story. In *Days of Youth* Ozu created an alarm clock gag in which Watanabe takes an alarm clock off the sleeping Yamamoto's desk and sets it so it will wake him up. It goes off, and Yamamoto, without waking up, puts it inside his *haori* (short robe) to silence it. When Watanabe finally joggles Yamamoto awake, he doesn't know why the clock is inside his *haori* and takes it out sheepishly. Thus begins Watanabe's shameless manipulation of the pliant Yamamoto.

More subtle is Ozu's use of an alarm clock in *Dragnet Girl*. In the scene in which the student Hiroshi first comes to Jyoji's apartment asking to join the gang, Jyoji sits on his table, tossing an alarm clock up and down in his hands as one might a ball. He senses that Hiroshi is trouble, but Tokiko persuades him to let the boy into the gang. When, later, we see Hiroshi pretending to study, there is an alarm clock on his desk, typical of Ozu's students. Yet here the clock and the person it belongs to connect to the clock Jyoji was juggling earlier. That gesture is reprised when, toward the end of the film, Kazuko appears at Jyoji's door urgently looking for Hiroshi. He speaks to her tersely and dares her to "call the police." In accord with this dangerous suggestion, he picks up the alarm clock and starts juggling it again.

Visual Puns

In *Making Meaning*, a book devoted to discouraging critics from interpreting films, David Bordwell denigrates the idea of metaphor or symbolic film language by referring to metaphors as "puns," which, he says, "are . . . attractive because they are highly *available* . . . and call on no specialized knowledge."[5] Every high school English teacher knows that a metaphor is not a pun. A metaphor is an image that stands for something else, and Ozu used them frequently. One of the most obvious is the lingering shot of an empty room, seen most frequently in his later films but sometimes in the early films, which indicates a person's absence, usually because of death or marriage.

A pun, in contrast, is a play on a word that has two meanings, Shakespeare's "grave man" (Romeo and Juliet III:1), for example, by which Mercutio indicates that his imminent death is a serious matter. Ozu, in fact, loved visual puns, which he created either from two images that were alike but different or from juxtaposing written words and images. In *Days of Youth*, lanky Yamamoto wears a jacket embroidered with a giraffe. In *A Story of Floating Weeds* we see troupe leader Kihachi on stage being followed by the boy Tomibo dressed as a dog. A kerfuffle ensues when Tomibo steps out of character and starts to bawl because Kihachi has hit the "dog" a little too hard. Later in the film an actual dog follows Kihachi back to the theater—the acted dog replaced by a real dog. In the same film we're told it's hard to play "the horse," as two men practice prancing inside a horse costume. Subsequently, we see a cartoon-like horse painted on the dressing room wall, visible behind actress Otaka when she sits at her dressing table.

Smoking chimneys perform a variety of functions in Ozu's films, but in *Tokyo Chorus* he used them to create a visual pun. While the protagonist Okajima visits an employment office, Ozu's camera occupies itself with two unemployed laborers, who are salvaging cigarette butts and are quick to grab the one Okajima throws away. A cutaway to smoking chimneys has preceded the shots of these laborers. As in *An Inn in Tokyo*, the smoking chimneys represent the factory jobs the men don't have, but they also correspond to the "smoke" they will have once they collect enough cigarette butts.

Near the end of *Passing Fancy*, Kihachi punches his friend Jiro to keep him from joining a work crew on its way to Hokkaido. Jiro lies on the ground with his fiancée, Harue, kneeling over him in front of a poster for a samurai film, which shows the head of the samurai hero facing outward and a woman behind him. Harue, with her traditional *shimada* hairdo, looks almost identical to the woman on the poster, but Jiro—a military vet who exhibits many samurai traits: self-sacrifice, loyalty, a feigned indifference to women—is crumpled on the ground beside her. He is, in effect, missing from what would otherwise be a real-life duplication of the poster.

Laundry, ubiquitous in Ozu's films, becomes the subject of another pun in *Passing Fancy*, where a sign in Japanese across from Kihachi's house advertises "Western Laundry" (which may refer to laundry done in a machine). The sign is analogous to the "non-Western" laundry ever-present in the little alley by Kihachi's home.[6]

In *That Night's Wife*, a poster for the 1928 Hollywood movie *Broadway Daddies* appears on the wall of the main characters' one-room apartment toward the end of the film, as the detective Kagawa and Hashizume's wife, Mayumi, look out from the apartment into the hall. Kagawa has purposely let Hashizume escape, so both he and Mayumi are shocked to find the culprit in the hall, hat cocked roguishly forward, insisting he can only be a good father to daughter Michiko if he turns himself in and cleanses his crime. His *mobo* mien makes him in one sense a "Broadway daddy," but he is, in fact, a real daddy, not the "sugar daddy" the film's title implies. That Ozu's intent here was to correlate the different "daddies" is clear from the fact that only at this time do we see the *Broadway Daddies* poster. Every other shot into the apartment from the hallway shows only the poster below *Broadway Daddies*, one for the 1929 film *Broadway Scandals* (presumably a reference to the scandalous, criminal actually, behavior of Hashizume and his wife).

Movie Posters and Related Art

Ozu used movie posters and other advertising art not simply to convey his enthusiasm for foreign, usually American, films and products, but to create a variety of gags and/or commentary. In *Walk Cheerfully*, a poster for *Our Dancing Daughters* (Harry Beaumont, 1928) appears, somewhat incongruously, in the office heroine Yasue shares with Chieko, Kenji's moll. The "dancing daughters" of the title are two women, one pure, one not, in love with the same man, who thus echo Ozu's two women in love with Kenji.[7]

Signs, Symbols, and Motifs

In *I Flunked, But . . .* the roommates have a poster for *Charming Sinners* (Robert Milton, 1929), an early sound film, which frequently appears directly behind Takahashi, the one who spends the evening before their big exam preparing an elaborate cheating scheme rather than studying. Later the shirt on which Takahashi has written all his answers hangs in front of the poster. The "sin" in the American movie is adultery while that in *I Flunked, But . . .* is cheating on exams, but the attitude toward both is indulgent, and the cheaters, in both cases, are charming.

The poster for *Seventh Heaven* (Frank Borzage, 1927) in *Days of Youth* echoes the boys' hopes for romance in their garret, and at one point Watanabe, inspired by the poster, imitates *Seventh Heaven*'s Chico when he tells Yamamoto: "I'm such a wonderful fellow! Look up!"

Days of Youth contains several other jokes based on advertising. To ready the prospective groom Hatamoto's hair for his *omiai* (introduction to a potential marriage partner), the boys consult a magazine picture of a Caucasian male. They work back and forth carefully from the picture to Hatamoto, but in the end Hatamoto's hairdo looks nothing like the magazine picture, a jab at Japanese imitating Westerners. Later, in the ski hut where Watanabe broods over losing the girl Chieko to Hatamoto, two boys from the club chat amiably about Hatamoto's impending marriage. "He won't be doing any sudden ski jumps anymore!" comments one, while directly behind them Ozu has placed a poster of a ski jumper.

In *I Graduated, But . . .* a poster for Harold Lloyd's *Speedy* (1928) in protagonist Nomoto's apartment plays on the fact that Nomoto, taking his time to find a job, is anything but speedy. Bordwell suggests that the movie posters, pennants, and so on in *I Graduated But . . .* are meant to contrast American prosperity with Japanese poverty, but these objects occur in all Ozu's student comedies even after the United States was deep into its own Depression.[8] Such artifacts were part of Japanese students' culture of the time and corroborate Nomoto's confession that he is "too carefree." He retains a student mentality, which is not only carefree but too entitled to accept a lowly job. Recognizing his need to change, he accepts the disappointing job offered to him early in the film, only to be offered a professional position instead. Sharing the good news with his wife, he throws his hat onto a trunk surrounded by books that sits under his student-era pennant wheel, as if bidding good-bye to all that.

In protagonist Okajima's room in *The Lady and the Beard*, there is a big poster for *The Rogue Song* (Lionel Barrymore, 1930), MGM's first all-talking, Technicolor film. While we cannot actually see the title of the film in any of the shots that have the poster in the background, what we see very clearly at times is "All Talking" and "Technicolor," written on the poster. (See Figure 9.2, p. 184.) This is the comparison Ozu wishes to make with America—innovations in cinema that were far ahead of what was current in Japan at the time. These were, of course, precisely the innovations that Ozu resisted until long after they had become standard in the Japanese industry, but *The Lady and the Beard* is still too early for us to read any intentional irony here.

The sequences from *If I Had a Million* (Ernst Lubitsch, 1932) included in *Woman of Tokyo* are famous and the only funny part of that tragic story. There is a cut from sister Chikako typing at her day job to the film's credits, so that it looks like she is typing the credits. A segment of the film follows, stopping short of the final gag. The film plays a more somber role the next day, however, when girlfriend Harue, who had been attending the film with Chikako's brother, Ryoichi, the previous day but is now estranged from him, picks up the program, looks at it briefly and closes it abruptly in a succinct acknowledgement of the difference one day can make.

In the anteroom of the boxing club in *Dragnet Girl* there is a poster for King Vidor's *The Champ* (1931), the story of a washed-up boxer and his son, which would provide the inspiration for Ozu's next film, *Passing Fancy*. We see the poster most often when Jyoji is in the anteroom. A retired boxer whom everyone looks up to, he is truly "the champ." Inside the training room, Jyoji sits next to a huge poster with actor George Bancroft's face (Figure 2.1). Bancroft had starred in Josef von Sternberg's *Docks of New York*, a popular, critically acclaimed film in Japan. Joji Oka, who plays Jyoji in *Dragnet Girl*, had played the Bancroft role in a Japanese adaptation titled *First Steps Ashore* (*Joriku no dai-ippo*) the previous year. The Bancroft poster is thus an extra-diegetic tribute to the actor rather than to the character he plays.

Figure 2.1: At the boxing club, Jyoji sits next to a poster with actor George Bancroft on it in *Dragnet Girl*.

Signs, Symbols, and Motifs

Four movie posters appear in the brothel that the older son, Sadao, frequents in *A Mother Should be Loved*. Bordwell suggests Ozu's movie-poster syndrome was by now a "tic," but in fact all four films are relevant thematically.[9] One, *Rain* (Lewis Milestone, 1932), is about a prostitute (Joan Crawford) and appears as Sadao is trying to get his friend Hattori away from one of the women in the brothel. Two others, *Poil de carotte* (*The Red Head*, Julien DuVivier, 1932) and *Die Tochter des Regiments* (*Daughter of the Regiment*, Carl Lamac, 1933), are about adopted children who are much loved by those who adopt them, a parallel to the eponymous mother who loves her older son very much, despite not being his birth mother and despite his apparent rejection of her when he becomes an adult. *Die Tochter* appears in the prostitute's room in which Sadao seeks refuge when he tries to flee his family, *Poil de carotte* in the bar below. In one sequence there is a close-up of the little boy in the *Poil de carotte* poster with a shadow cutting him in half. Later, when Sadao's mother shows up at the brothel and begs him to come home, shots of Sadao have the poster in the background, thus identifying him with the adopted child.[10]

The fourth poster, which also appears in the prostitute's room, is for *Don Quixote* (1933), a Hollywood film by the German director G. W. Pabst, which was based on the famous Spanish novel and shot in three versions, French, English, and German. Including it may have been a nod to internationalism, like the *All Quiet on the Western Front* poster in *Dragnet Girl*. The other three films referenced in *Mother*, representing the American, French, Austrian, and German industries, reinforce this notion. *Die Tochter des Regiments*, about a Scottish regiment that rescues and adopts a foundling during World War I and later helps to apprehend smugglers in Bavaria, would seem to be advocating world peace and cooperation.[11] Prior to making *Mother*, Ozu had been called up to serve for two weeks with his army reserve unit and had been trained in poison gas warfare.[12] World peace, which by 1934 must have seemed as elusive as Don Quixote's quest for chivalry, might well have been on his mind as he started work on the film.[13]

Something Borrowed

We have seen in Chapter 1 that Ozu borrowed from German films, and several of his recurring symbols also appear to have been influenced by German Expressionist cinema. The use of characters' reflections in mirrors or other reflective surfaces was used in German Expressionist films to evoke a doppelgänger motif, indicative of a split personality, as in the famous shot from Fritz Lang's *M* in which the murderer sees his face reflected in the window of a cutlery shop, surrounded by knives.[14]

According to Ruth Benedict, Japanese see the mirror as a symbol of purity, one of three sacred symbols of Shinto.[15] Ozu, however, used mirrors in the German film tradition, which became fairly standard throughout Western cinema, as an image of duality. In *That Night's Wife*, for example, Hashizume, devoted father, husband, and thief, examines his reflection in a mirror, as does the hypocritical boss in *Walk Cheerfully* just before he attempts to rape heroine Yasue.

In *Dragnet Girl*, Tokiko examines her reflection in a window after she's allowed her boss to make overtures to her. Her duality is twofold. Most immediately she is in the process of two-timing her lover. In a larger context, she is a gang member, comfortable with wielding a gun, but she is also a sweetheart who will, eventually, long to go straight. In the same film Hiroshi, student-turned-punk, also examines his reflection in a shop window as he changes back from his punk "poor-boy" hat to his student cap.

In *A Story of Floating Weeds*, the actress Otaka sits at a mirror to do her make-up while hatching a plot to have the younger actress, Otoki, seduce her boss/lover Kihachi's son, Shinkichi. She lies, saying she is no longer upset by her fight with Kihachi, but all the while she is plotting her revenge. Likewise, Otoki is using her make-up mirror when she accepts Otaka's bribe. Later Shinkichi checks his face in a small mirror before going to see Otoki. He even hides the mirror under his *zabutan* (cushion) before he goes downstairs, where he tells his mother he's "going for a walk." (His duplicity is reinforced by the large *kanji* for "snake" [*hebi*], one of the Chinese zodiac signs, on the wall above his desk; among the snake's characteristics are intelligence, cunning, and unscrupulousness.[16]) Although we the audience don't actually see the reflected image in these examples from *A Story of Floating Weeds*, the characters' use of a mirror, nevertheless, suggests their duplicity.

Woman of Tokyo has the most extensive and complex play with mirrors. As she gets ready to go to work, we see Chikako go to her mirror in the back of a shot; her action is and remains out of focus. There is a cut to a focused shot of her face in the mirror, but when she gets up, the camera stays focused on the mirror surface while the distant objects it reflects are out of focus. Ozu cuts immediately to a policeman making inquiries about her, introducing the possibility that she may not simply be the loving, homemaking sister we saw in the earlier scene.

At the cabaret, the prostitutes look at themselves in their compact mirrors. Chikako does the same, then looks in the mirror over the sink. We don't see her reflected face in these mirror shots, only her actual face, made up to look vampish. When she returns home from her assignation, having changed back into a modest kimono, she looks in a mirror in the hallway, removing a last vestige of her cabaret make-up. Again, we don't see her reflection. Her brother, Ryoichi, comes out into the hall, and she goes into the apartment, oblivious of his dark mood.

After their confrontation, Ryoichi leaves, and she rushes after him, then comes back inside and sits down at her mirror. This time we see her reflection: she looks crushed and defeated; the marks on her face from where he has slapped her are visible. The contrast with the first time we saw her in this mirror couldn't be starker. All of these mirror shots walk us through the stages, not only of Chikako's duality but of her deception, her obliviousness to Ryoichi's feelings, which imply a continuing disregard for how he *would* feel if he found out the truth about her evening employment, and finally the wreck of all she had hoped for their happiness.[17]

Although we the audience don't actually see the reflected image in many of these examples, the characters' use of a mirror implies their duplicity. That Ozu intended his mirror shots to convey duality seems clear from the scene in *Walk Cheerfully* in which pure-as-the-driven-snow Yasue sits at her make-up table and begins to lift the cover off her mirror when she is interrupted by her little sister. She lets the cloth drop, and the scene ends without her ever uncovering the mirror.

Fritz Lang's *Spione* (1928) suggests a possible German source for Ozu's steam motif in his silent films. The scene of the initial tryst between Agent 326 and Sonya, his lover-to-be, contains a steaming samovar—she has invited him to have "real Russian tea." When Agent 326 arrives, it is clear that the two are attracted to one another. He kisses her hand, and there is a cut back to the steaming samovar, then back to the two captivated lovers. Clearly Lang meant to correlate the steam coming from the samovar with the passion of the lovers. As we have seen in Chapter 1, *Dragnet Girl* correlates the steam coming from the vent pipe Tokiko sees outside the room she has gone to with her boss, Okazaki, and the passion she feels for her lover, Jyoji, as she weighs it against the easy life of a concubine that Okazaki has offered her. This is the only extant film in which Ozu depicts, if subtly, strong physical passion, but in many of his silent films, the presence of smoke or steam tracks with strong emotion.

Transience in the Silent Films?

Steam and smoke

In my very first article on Ozu, I suggested that the steam and smoke, ubiquitous in his films, were meant to evoke the idea of transience—water turns to steam and blows away.[18] Bordwell, despite his aversion to interpretation, restates this in his *Ozu and the Poetics of Cinema*.[19] Steam or smoke as transience, however, holds for Ozu's later films, many of which are preoccupied with the life cycle, nostalgia, and ephemerality, but in his silent films, from the earliest to the latest, the presence of steam from kettles and other devices generally tracks with heightened emotions rather than the quietist notion of "transience," although at times it suggests both. The silent films are, after all, those of a young man. Ozu made them while he was between the ages of twenty-six and thirty-three, and in most of these films, steam and smoke accompany strong emotions. When *Dragnet Girl*'s Tokiko looks out the window past the steaming vent pipe, "transience" is not what's on her mind.

When, in *Walk Cheerfully*, for example, Kenji confronts Yasue's boss in the hotel room where the latter has trapped her, he knocks over the stovepipe, which adds smoke to that already created by the boss's cigar. Along with the symbolism of the stove itself, the smoke suggests the heat, anger, and passion in the room. Contemplating the supine boss at the end of the scene, Kenji lights up a cigarette, which adds more smoke. In *Dragnet Girl*, Jyoji sits alone, angry and confused over his relationship with Tokiko, in a bar filled with smoke. Some of the smoke comes from his cigarette, but a long shot of him at the bar reveals extra smoke being blown up from an unseen source. No one else but the bartender is in the bar to produce this smoke, but clearly Ozu wanted the bar to be extra smoky, the better to convey Jyoji's emotional state.

In *Walk Cheerfully*, steam pours out of a teakettle both times Yasue discusses her job with her mother. The first time she voices her desire to quit because of her boss's advances, and later, after he has fired her for evading him, she expresses anger. Yasue's mother sits near the steaming pot, which reflects the high emotion in the room: complementing Yasue's anger is her mother's fear of what a loss of income will mean. In a third, almost identical, scene, Yasue sits with her mother and reports that she has found a new job. This time the teakettle is not steaming. However, during Yasue's reunion with Kenji at the end of the film, a steaming coffee pot suggests an abundance of happy, conjugal feelings.

A short sequence in *I Flunked, But...* shows protagonist Takahashi blowing smoke at a goldfish in a bowl on a table in the bakery the boys frequent. (See Figure 4.2, p. 67.) He is, of course, brooding about his failure to graduate, something he comes to see in a positive light only toward the end of the film. In his room he continues brooding while a teakettle boils just off-camera, its steam floating into the room, visible against Takahashi's back. As the sequence continues, the steam is not always obvious, but when Takahashi agrees to join the rest of the boys for dinner, it becomes prominent again. The final shot in the sequence is the kettle steaming away beneath the *Charming Sinners* poster.

In *A Story of Floating Weeds*, large puffs of smoke come from a little pipe actress Otaka smokes as she waits for companion, Otoki, to come home after being sent to seduce the boss's son, Shinkichi. Savoring her victory, she is still smoking the next day as the group does its laundry in a mountain brook. Troupe leader Kihachi, brooding over their lack of revenue and his fight with Otaka, is also smoking.

In *An Inn in Tokyo*, in which Ozu recycles the same names, protagonist Kihachi begs his friend Otsune for a loan, but she refuses, piqued by his attentions to the younger woman,Otaka, in preference to herself. Throughout this tense exchange, smoke issues from a hibachi in every shot of Otsune.

A crossover between strong emotion and the idea of transience occurs when the strong feeling is one of loss. Something that is lost has "gone up in smoke," thus the convergence of loss with transience. Ozu would merge these two ideas in his earliest extant film, *Days of Youth*. The title itself—in which "youth" refers very specifically to college days, something on which the Japanese, at least in Ozu's day, heaped nostalgia—pays homage to that which passes very quickly, never to return. The film contains an extraordinary amount of smoke and steam, most of it associated with high emotions, often having to do with loss, but some—all of the college boys smoke cigarettes—is less particularized and can be seen as referencing the boys' college days, which will soon be gone.

On the students' ski trip, sad sack Yamamoto smokes while nursing his resentment at how Watanabe stole Chieko, their mutual love interest, away from him while

Signs, Symbols, and Motifs 41

Watanabe creates clouds of steam with a hot iron he uses to wax his skis. The next day, Watanabe, having realized that Chieko is engaged to the captain of the ski club, broods in a ski hut filled with smoke and steam. The sequence begins outside the Hutte Arlberg, where smoke pours out one side of a two-pronged chimney. The camera travels down the smoke stack and then cuts to the stovepipe inside the Hutte, travels down that and comes to rest on a steaming teapot atop a woodstove. Watanabe and two disinterested boys drink coffee, eat raisins, and smoke pipes. A medium shot of Watanabe shows him surrounded by smoke and steam, reflecting his disappointed, brooding mood, but those cuts that include all three boys have much less smoke. When the other boys leave, Watanabe stokes the fire, and the steam increases. There is a final close-up of the steaming kettle as the camera travels back up the stovepipe, cuts back outside, and travels up the smokestack, where smoke now pours from both sides of the chimney.

Back in the inn, Watanabe and Yamamoto both sit smoking and nursing their disappointment apart from the others, who are celebrating the engagement in high spirits. Chieko, the object of their desire, enters and throws them some of the persimmons she is passing around.

Persimmons are a symbol of triumph; hence Chieko passes them out in celebration of her successful *omiai*, but they can also be astringent and make one wince. On the train going home, in fact, Yamamoto manages to squirt some persimmon juice in his eye. The boys continue to smoke on the train, during which time Watanabe puts all the persimmons in the hand-knitted sock he had earlier begged off Chieko and throws it out the window.

At home in their room, Yamamoto stares out the window, smoking and looking wistful. Chimneys, reprised from an earlier sequence, echo his smoke. As in the earlier sequence, vent tops whirl and a windmill turns. What had earlier meant merely "snow in the mountains" now stokes nostalgia and indeed suggests transience—dreams and illusions that blow away. But when Watanabe puts the "for rent" sign—their ploy for meeting girls—back in the window, both boys go to bed happy, and there is no more smoke or steam.

The prototype for this closing sequence occurs earlier in the film when Ozu cuts from the smoking chimney outside the apartment to Yamamoto studying intensely, accompanied by smoke from a cigarette and a hibachi. Study gives way to horseplay with Watanabe, and there is no more smoke.

A late sequence in *A Story of Floating Weeds* begins with a little steam issuing from a hanging kettle in Kihachi's former mistress Otsune's restaurant. Kihachi comes looking for his son, Shinkichi, who, at the time, is out on a date with the young actress Otoki. By this time Kihachi has learned how his current mistress, Otaka, set Shinkichi up to be seduced by Otoki. "I let Shinkichi ruin his future," he ruminates. The next time he comes, a coil of insect-repelling incense is burning. The troupe has disbanded, and Kihachi and Otsune discuss his moving in, but, after a confrontation with Shinkichi, Kihachi concludes that such an arrangement would not work. Otsune is crestfallen. As Kihachi collects his bundle to leave, the incense coil is smoking mightily. By the end of the scene, Shinkichi, Otoki, and Otsune are all weeping. The last shot in the sequence is the empty room with the smoking incense coil, strong emotion combined with loss.

When the boys in *I Was Born, But . . .* return from the home movie screening that embarrassed them so much, they start throwing a tantrum, much to their mother's surprise. A teakettle is sitting on the hibachi and steaming slightly. When their father arrives home and the boys persist in confronting him, the kettle is steaming more. After the boys are in bed, the father lights a cigarette, adding smoke to the steam. When they are finally asleep, the parents go into their room, and the father admonishes them not to "become miserable apple-polishers like me." The scene ends with a long shot of the parents in the boys' room, kneeling beside them, while the teakettle steams away in the foreground. The emotion has moved from anger to sadness and resignation, and the steaming kettle follows this transition from high emotion to a sense of depletion and loss.

In *Woman of Tokyo*, steaming teakettles accompany the strong emotions expressed in multiple scenes from the time her brother, Kinoshita, tells Harue about Chikako's dubious moonlighting to the penultimate scene in which Ryoichi's body is laid out at home. In the initial scene, Harue, upon hearing her brother's suspicions, turns, and a teakettle in the background is obviously steaming. She sits near it and suggests that she talk to Chikako herself as Kinoshita smokes.

When Harue subsequently arrives at Chikako's, Ryoichi lights a gas heater and offers to give his sister Harue's message as he puts a teakettle on the heater. Harue hesitates, Ryoichi is peeved, and she finally breaks down. "What if your sister isn't who you think she is?" she asks. The teapot is steaming as she tells him the rest. Ryoichi demands she leave, and she runs out crying while the teakettle steams away. He throws her wrap after her, then sits crying with the kettle steaming in the background. The final shot in the sequence is a close-up of the kettle, steaming so furiously that its top is bouncing up and down.

Sometime later, with Ryoichi still at home, there is a cut to the same kettle in the same close-up, but it is completely still, no steam, no fire under it. This is not a continuity failure. The time is late, the kettle is "dead," and we can read this either as a portent of Ryoichi's death or understand that something inside him has already died or both. In contrast to most of Ozu's other highly emotional scenes, the subsequent fight between Ryoichi and Chikako has not a single wisp of smoke or steam. The relationship between brother and sister is over.

At Harue's the next day, we see, along with the hanging gloves, a steaming kettle. After Harue takes the phone call from her brother announcing Ryoichi's suicide, we cut from her hanging up the phone to the wall of clocks in the clock shop where she takes the call to the wall clock in her house to the hibachi with its steaming kettle. Here, in this sequence with the clocks, the steaming kettle stands not only for strong emotion but also for transience, in this case death, and it will continue this double duty to the end of the film, for in the following scene the steam from a teakettle is linked to the smoke from a chimney.

Signs, Symbols, and Motifs

Back at Chikako's on the following day, Ryoichi's body is laid out, and a kettle steams as Chikako berates the body, calling him a weakling. Harue weeps; there is a close-up of the kettle. Outside the window a whirling vent fan appears behind the kettle. Then there is a cut to two chimneys, one pouring out black smoke. In an early scene Chikako looked at both the vent pipe with its onion-dome fan and the chimneys as she fetched Ryoichi's socks off their balcony, but now one of the chimneys is smoking copiously. Back inside, Chikako is weeping while the kettle steams behind her.

The chimneys we see at the end of *Woman of Tokyo* point to another image that recurs throughout Ozu's oeuvre, which can change in meaning from film to film. We see industrial chimneys in Ozu's films from the earliest extant one, *Days of Youth*, to his very last, *An Autumn Afternoon* (1962). He was obviously drawn to these tall, dominating icons of an urban, industrialized landscape. In *Walk Cheerfully* he used a close-up of a vent chimney and a man working on it to link a sequence in which friends Senko and Kenji chat on one section of their office-building roof with a subsequent scene of Yasue taking a break with other office workers on another section of the roof. In *An Inn in Tokyo* smoking chimneys indicate the jobs protagonist Kihachi is not able to get.

At the extreme end of the chimney-as-symbol spectrum is their ultimate referent: the crematorium chimney, certainly a symbol of transience and a sacred one, given that this is part of the Buddhist funeral rite. Such a chimney appears literally in the final sequence of *The End of Summer* (1961). Thus the chimneys Chikako sees at the end of *Woman of Tokyo* comport with the steam from her teakettle and ultimately reference the crematorium. When Chikako first looks at them from her balcony at the beginning of the film, they seem innocent enough and little smoke comes from them, but, even as they create a formal closure to the film—much as they do towards the beginning and end of *Days of Youth*—their appearance at the end of *Woman of Tokyo* is much more freighted than it was at the beginning.

A Mother Should Be Loved connects smoke very directly to the idea of death and transience. The family moves to the suburbs and starts unpacking. The boys, now young men, find their deceased father's pipes and smoke them throughout the rest of the scene. They discover their father's top hat and playfully put it on the mother's head, noticing thereupon that she has a gray hair. She remarks that the father wore the hat to a flower exhibition exactly one year before he died. Their aunt arrives with a paddle that had belonged to her husband, their uncle, Okazaki, who had rowed in college along with their father. Okazaki himself has died close to one year before, and the mother comments, "One's life is so fragile." The aunt replies, "Everyone returns to the earth in the end."[20] While the boys help their aunt to some lunch and the mother makes tea, she notices the picture of her dead husband standing upside down on the floor in an adjacent room. She rights it and dusts the glass. If this scene comes across as particularly heavy-handed, it might be because Ozu's own father died while he was making the film, but the idea of transience and the many signs and symbols that accrue to it—in this case, smoke, flowers, gray hair, and references to death—would become increasingly dominant in the director's sound films.

Hanging laundry

The ubiquitous hanging laundry in Ozu's films also has the potential to suggest transience—water evaporates from it—and it comes closest to that meaning in *Tokyo Chorus*. When the father, Okajima, returns home after his wife and children have seen him doing manual labor, carrying banners to advertise his former teacher's restaurant, his mortified wife reproaches him. He tries to explain his situation to her and then looks outside. We see the following sequence:

1) Okajima from behind, standing and looking outside while undressing.
2) A smoking chimney or vent pipe.
3) A continuation of shot #1 with Okajima.
4) 180° cut to Okajima and his wife, from the front, sitting/kneeling; he is still undressing and looking outside.
5) Laundry hanging on a line to dry.
6) 90° cut to Okajima from the side, still sitting and looking outside.
7) The laundry.
8) Continuation of shot #6; Okajima, undressing, looking out, then speaking:
9) Title: "I feel like I'm getting old. I've lost my spirit."
10) Mrs. Okajima, still kneeling, looks up.
11) Okajima from behind (Mrs. O's point of view), still sitting.
12) Mrs. Okajima, follows his gaze and looks outside.
13) The laundry.
14) Okajima and Mrs. Okajima, still sitting, from behind; they bow their heads; she turns to him and speaks:
15) Title: "I'll go with you to help tomorrow."

The sequence is a good example of Ozu's use of a 360° shooting space (see Chapter 4), but the point of describing it here is to show hanging laundry being used in the context of sadness, discouragement, and transience. In the sequence, Mrs. Okajima comes to understand her husband's sense of desperation and agrees to help him at the restaurant. Okajima's reference to getting old, his wife's change of heart, and the fact that, by its end, the film is completely steeped in sadness and nostalgia support the notion that the laundry here implies transience, as does the smoking vent pipe.

Like the smoking chimney in *Woman of Tokyo*, we see this smoking vent pipe in the beginning of the film, where it has less resonance, but when it recurs near the end of the film, it comports with the transience and sorrow expressed in the sequence. Not only does the meaning of certain Ozu motifs vary from film to film, it can also vary within a single film, as in these examples. Showing an object at the beginning and again at the end of a film achieves a formal balance, but it also tracks with our understanding of what has happened in the course of the film. A motif that had little meaning early on takes on meaning at the end because it has gained a context.

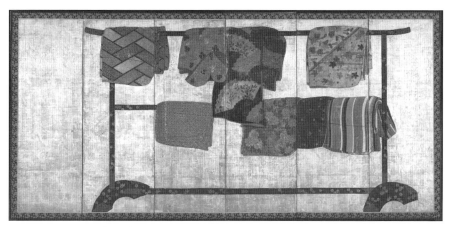

Figure 2.2: *Tagasode-byobu,* c. 1600–1650. Six-panel folding screen, ink, color, gold on gilt paper. Courtesy of the Metropolitan Museum of Art, H. O. Havemeyer Collection.

In *Walk Cheerfully* laundry transitions us from the trauma of Kenji being shot by fellow gang members and arrested to the joy of his reunion with Yasue at the end of the film. The first hanging laundry we see in *Walk Cheerfully* is the wet towels used to clean Kenji's wound after he has been shot. After he returns from prison to celebrate with Yasue and her family, the film ends with a shot of an empty laundry line, followed by a shot of multiple lines full of laundry, strung between apartments, flapping cheerfully, as per the film's title, in the wind. (This is the only time Ozu shows an empty laundry line close-up, and whether this sequence is meant to suggest a movement from emptiness to fulfillment or barrenness to fecundity or simply shows two variations on laundry lines I leave to the viewer's imagination.)

Ozu's hanging laundry has a precedent in a type of Japanese gold screen art from the Momoyama/Edo periods called *tagasode-byobu*, which depict kimono and other accessories hanging from lacquered racks (Figure 2.2). The kimono have lovely patterns, but they are folded over the racks and draped with the various ties that held them together, not hung in full-length displays as they are in museums (or in Kon Ichikawa's *Makioka Sisters* [*Sasameyuki,* 1983]). Thus they register primarily as hanging clothing, and, although more elegant than Ozu's laundry, are definitely related. The Japanese are perhaps the only culture to appreciate the aesthetics of hanging clothes; certainly there is no counterpart in the West.

Drying laundry is Ozu's most enigmatic, shape-shifting motif. As per above, it can be appreciated on purely aesthetic grounds. It also helps to create the ambiance of middle- and lower-middle class life. In *That Night's Wife*, laundry, principally a smock or apron, hangs on a line inside the apartment and serves to orient us as the camera moves around the couple's cluttered living space.

Laundry fluttering in the morning breeze denotes a bright new day, fresh with possibilities. We see it used this way in *I Was Born, But . . . , An Inn in Tokyo, A Story of Floating Weeds*, and once, among many other shots of laundry hanging in Kihachi's alley, in *Passing Fancy*.

In *Woman of Tokyo*, however, Chikako looks out at laundry hanging in the yard outside Harue's home, and it comports with all the other "hanging" objects we have seen and thus looks gloomy and ominous. In two later films, *Record of a Tenement Gentleman* (1947) and *Ohayo* (1959), laundry would become a principle story element, disclosing the indiscretions of young boys, and, possibly, disguising a subversive caricature of an American flag.[21]

Trains

Trains are another of Ozu's ubiquitous motifs that may or may not imply transience. He liked trains, Ozu told Donald Richie, adding puckishly, "I also like whales."[22] In fact, many people born in the era of the steam engine, as well as many born after, like trains.

Lynne Kirby has written about the historical conjunction with and the similarities between trains and silent cinema: "the cinema finds an apt metaphor in the train, in its framed, moving image, its construction of a journey as an optical experience, the radical juxtaposition of different places, the 'annihilation of space and time.'"[23] Classic cinema, silent and sound, from *The General* to *North by Northwest*, has memorable train sequences.

Ozu's trains would join a complex of images signifying "passage," going from one place to another, emblematic of the life cycle, with which so many of his later films were preoccupied. Like many of his signs and symbols, however, trains didn't start out with that meaning, and in his earliest films they are, as he says, simply a record of his predilection. His earliest extant film, *Days of Youth*, stages three scenes on a train or a streetcar. In the streetcar sequence, Ozu shows us not only the drama that transpires there, but the outside of the whole streetcar, the mudguard on the front, the springs, the tracks, the wires above that fuel it, the interior, the conductor and the cord he pulls to signal a stop, Yamamoto standing between two cars while looking for his wallet, and finally the driver, along with a close-up of the mechanism he uses to stop the streetcar. In the subsequent train sequences, we see the tracks, the interior with its hard seats, the station-purchased bento boxes (a ubiquitous feature of Japanese trains), the sign indicating the station's name, the station exit and the ticket collector, and, later, the shadow of the train against a snow-covered slope. Some of these shots play into the drama, but most do not.

A train appears in *Walk Cheerfully* when Kenji and Yasue are out for a drive. After it disappears, shots of the car that is following them include the empty tracks. In *That Night's Wife*, an elevated train appears near the phone booth when the thief/father Hashizume calls the doctor, making their already fraught conversation even more difficult. In *Tokyo Chorus*, the streetcar sequence, during which Okajima's wife and children see him engaged in manual labor, corresponds to Kirby's understanding of the train as a

Signs, Symbols, and Motifs   47

"movie": as it moves through space, the streetcar affords the Okajima children a movie-like view of their father carrying the restaurant banners.

The fact that the family house in *I Was Born, But...* faces the commuter rail tracks tells us that, although father Yoshii has moved to his boss's suburb, he doesn't live in the same neighborhood. It is also the earliest extant film in which trains take on a symbolic meaning, one that is the opposite of "passage." The commuter trains that go back and forth in front of the house, at the crossing, and next to the fields where the children play signify the same thing as the wheel stuck in a rut at the beginning of the film: Yoshii is stuck in his job, subservient to his boss, and that will never change. By extension, these commuter trains take an army of salarymen like Yoshii into the city and back every day.

A Story of Floating Weeds begins and ends in the village train station, and, similar to *Days of Youth*, examines the station and the arriving train in detail. It is the first extant film in which the idea of trains as passage, passing time, and separation arises. The young lovers, Otoki and Shinkichi, meet near a railroad track. Otoki stands by the tracks, wondering where she and Shinkichi will be "next year," and warning him to forget about her. As it turns out, the lovers are not parted, but, whether out of a distorted sense of responsibility—not wanting Shinkichi to have to live with a "no good" father—or simply because he cannot give up his wandering ways, Kihachi takes the train away from the village, away from Shinkichi and his mother, Otsune. He reconciles with his estranged lover, Otaka, on the way, and they agree to start a new acting troupe. This is not, as in Ozu's later films, "passage" in the sense of going on to a new phase of life but rather a return to a life Kihachi cannot give up and an escape from the dullness of village life. For all that this film strikes critics as part of a "nostalgia-for-the-countryside" trend, Ozu, who spent a year teaching in a mountain village, makes it clear that there isn't much to do there, and the train is, in actress Jean Seberg's words, "a way out."[24] Nevertheless, it signifies separation and sadness as it takes Kihachi away from his son. In the film's last shot the train disappears into the distance, with smoke, which in this instance indeed signifies transience, pouring from its stack.

Torn paper

In *Walk Cheerfully*, the heroine, Yasue, feeling abandoned by her beau, Kenji, tears up some paper she is holding and throws it off the roof of her office building where colleagues are socializing. The pieces of paper float down, and a shot from the front of the building records them falling to the ground. For some reason Bordwell, generally opposed to interpretation, believes they represent "evanescence,"[25] another word for transience, but the bits of paper we see at this moment in *Walk Cheerfully* instead represent, in a very literal way, the heroine's shredded hopes and dreams. If this were to become her permanent state, we might well speak of transience, but on this same day, Yasue discoverers that Kenji has remained true to her, and the film ends happily.

Prior to shredding paper on the roof of her office building, Yasue has torn up the notice of her dismissal from her previous job, in which her boss harassed her, and let the

Figure 2.3: Notomo steps on his shredded credentials in *I Graduated, But...*

shreds fall to her lap in a similar gesture of anger, frustration, and disappointment. This sequence ends with a close-up of the shredded paper.

In one of the preserved fragments of *I Graduated, But...* the protagonist, Nomoto, tears up his résumé and lets the pieces fall to the ground after he has been offered the lowly job of receptionist. We see him leaving the office with his credentials in hand, then a cut to his feet coming down the office steps and the shredded credentials falling onto the mat at his feet, again signifying anger, frustration, and shredded dreams. Nomoto steps on the shreds, and the shot ends (Figure 2.3).

After confronting Otoki, who has seduced his son, *A Story of Floating Weeds*' Kihachi sits in the empty theater, and little bits of paper, part of an earlier show perhaps, start to float down from the rafters like early snow. He has lost everything. His show has been spoiled by bad weather; his mistress has betrayed him; his son's future has been compromised. His hopes and dreams, too, are in shreds. Unlike Yasue's dreams in *Walk Cheerfully* and Nomoto's in *I Graduated, But...*, Kihachi's dreams are not fulfilled by the end of the film, which concludes in disappointment and regret. Nevertheless, he gets his mistress back, they aspire to start a new acting troupe, and, when he leaves his son, who will marry the actress Otoki, he admonishes her to help him become "a great man." Thus his dreams are restored, but whether they will be realized remains in question.

Signs, Symbols, and Motifs   49

While the origin of the shredded paper in *A Story of Floating Weeds* and the outcome of Kihachi's hopes for the future are vague, compared with those in the earlier films, one can still be more precise in interpreting the torn paper than simply calling it a symbol of "evanescence."

Uniquely Japanese

Arguments have swirled as to whether Ozu was traditional or modern, steeped in his own culture or thoroughly Westernized, too urban to have understood the countryside, and so on. These arguments say more about our own limitations than they do about Ozu. He was an artistic genius with an intellect most of us can barely fathom. He was Westernized and modern, Japanese and traditional, an urbanite who had spent his youth in the countryside. He drew on what he knew about Japan and the world for his materials. As with the origins of his hanging laundry, some of his images and symbols are deeply embedded in traditional Japanese culture.

Fans

Bordwell has noted the fan motif in *Where Now Are the Dreams of Youth?*, which includes electric floor fans, ceiling fans, and a folding fan that sad sack Saiki, fearful of losing his fiancée, picks apart; but fans are even more prominent and creatively employed in *Tokyo Chorus*.[26] In that film, we see three kinds of fan: the electric table fan, the *sensu* (folding fan), and the *uchiwa* (flat fan). The protagonist Okajima's insurance office has many electric fans, humorously employed in various ways. The first we see is drying the polish on one character's shoes. At his own desk, Okajima, ever the prankster, sharpens his pencil in an electric fan, while another worker uses the fan at his desk to dry out the bonus money he's dropped in the urinal. These provide a link to the boss's office, where an electric fan stands at one end of the boss's desk.

In his office, the boss unwraps an elegant *sensu*, which he raps on his desk with authority when Okajima confronts him. In the heat of their argument, Okajima takes it from him and starts banging it on the boss's desk. The boss then takes out another *sensu*, and both men open their fans so that they look like fighting cocks. The fans they use are the same kind that dancers use, which, in the course of a Japanese dance, can become anything—waves, butterflies, swords, and so on. That they turn into fighting roosters in this scene is hilarious; it also connects the scene to Japanese dance and theater.

Flat fans or *uchiwa* appear in the hospital scene, where they are used to fan the sick child and the baby. Later we see one in Okajima's home being used once again to fan the baby. In the scene in which Mrs. Okajima scolds her husband for stooping to manual labor, the *uchiwa*, like the *sensu* earlier, becomes a vehicle for expressing emotion: agitated, Okajima, who has been fanning the baby, twists the *uchiwa* around in his hand, then drops it abruptly and leaves the room.

Figure 2.4: Omura uses his fan to calculate his costs during the reunion in *Tokyo Chorus*. His head is framed by the American and Japanese flags.

Both *uchiwa* and *sensu* appear in the reunion scene, which ends the film. Most of the men at the party are vigorously fanning themselves with one or the other, indicating that the old teacher is too cheap or too poor to provide electric fans. (In an earlier scene in the restaurant, *uchiwa* are hanging on the wall for use by customers.) Aesthetically, these fans dominate many of the shots of the men around the table. The old teacher appears in formal dress, holding his *sensu*, which he unfolds and folds ceremoniously and uses to punctuate his short speech to the former students. Ozu then undercuts his dignity by having him use the end of the *sensu* to "write" on the table, figuring out how much the party is costing him (Figure 2.4). The many fans in *Tokyo Chorus* constitute a motif derived from traditional culture and used with amazing creativity to express emotion and evoke humor.

Fireworks

In Japan, small towns, villages, and districts within cities celebrate ancient summer festivals on different days all summer long, and each festival sends up fireworks, which can be seen from miles around. The fireworks, which occur seemingly out of nowhere in three of Ozu's films, can be attributed to the Sumida River festival or to any of dozens of similar festivals taking place in or near Tokyo. Among Ozu's extant films, fireworks first appear in *Tokyo Chorus*, then in *Passing Fancy*, then *An Inn in Tokyo*. In the last two, they occur as the protagonist, Kihachi, develops and acts on a very desperate idea, and they seem to correspond to the energy of his desperation. In *Passing Fancy*, Kihachi decides to take Jiro's place in a work gang headed to Hokkaido—Jiro has borrowed money to pay hospital bills for Kihachi's son—and he knocks his friend unconscious in the process (whereupon Jiro undoubtedly sees a different kind of fireworks). In *An Inn in Tokyo*, the Kihachi character commits a robbery to save his friend Otaka from prostitution by paying for her child's hospital stay with the stolen money.

In *Tokyo Chorus*, fireworks explode as Okajima and his son leave the hospital after his child, Miyoko, finally starts to recover. Prior to this his wife has said, "Can we pay the bill?" He nods "yes" but is clearly worried. The camera remains with Mrs. Okajima, who continues to look worried. She goes to the window, raises it, and waves to her husband and son, now outside. We see a firework explode. The next shot is of Mrs. Okajima's hands fidgeting with the string on the window shade. Off-screen Okajima will make the draconian decision to sell his wife's kimonos to pay for Miyoko's hospital bills. In contrast to the two later films, in *Tokyo Chorus* we don't know exactly when Okajima makes his decision because we only learn of it after his wife comes home and finds her kimonos missing. However, the film initiates a pattern connecting fireworks with a drastic decision, which becomes more explicit in the later films. In each case, the fireworks, which can be associated with childish delight, accompany an extreme idea for obtaining the money necessary to pay for a child's hospital bills.

Fireworks take on a different connotation in *Where Now Are the Dreams of Youth?* and in another part of *Passing Fancy*. After the confrontation between hero Horino and his former girlfriend Oshige toward the end of *Where Now Are the Dreams of Youth?* Oshige looks out her window and sees a single firework exploding. Obviously, it has nothing to do with inspiration or sick children but punctuates the heated exchange that has transpired and the emotional exhaustion she feels.

In *Passing Fancy*, the initial fireworks relate to Kihachi's determination to replace Jiro on the boat to Hokkaido, but he subsequently shocks the barber, who has lent Jiro the money, restaurant owner Otome, and son Tomio with his decision. Stunned, they look after him as he runs off, and two more fireworks explode over them, highlighting their shock and dismay. Far from maintaining fixed meanings from film to film, Ozu's signs could, as here, shift in significance even within a single episode in a single film.

Ozu's signs and symbols range from the obvious to the highly nuanced, culturally embedded and multilayered, from gratuitous "puns" to intertwined, complex metaphors, from the silly to the elegiac. A motif, bare of meaning in one film or in one scene in one film, can take on significance in another film or sequence. Signs like smoke could do double or triple duty, signifying loss, death, high emotion, or transience all within one film, sometimes within one shot. More importantly, Ozu's signs and symbols allow us to better understand his meaning in a given film. How does he understand and want

52   *Ozu*

us to understand prostitution or attempted rape, for example? Are they similar? A dirty towel in one case and a sink full of dirty water in another make it clear that Ozu thought they were. The fact that these signs and symbols can be something of a moving target is no excuse for not trying to follow their significance or, worse, for denying their existence altogether.

Notes

1. Catherine Russell, "Insides and Outsides: Cross-cultural Criticism in Japanese Film Melodrama," in *Melodrama and Asian Cinema*, ed. Wimal Disanayake (Cambridge: Cambridge University Press, 1993), 150.
2. See David Bordwell, *Making Meaning: Inference and Rhetoric in the Interpretation of Cinema* (Cambridge, MA: Harvard University Press, 1989).
3. See Bordwell, *Poetics*, 258, for an example.
4. Bordwell, *Poetics*, 104; Kristin Thompson, *Breaking the Glass Armor* (Princeton, NJ: Princeton University Press, 1988), 328n13.
5. Bordwell, *Making Meaning*, 141.
6. Ozu's films abound with diegetic words embedded in the mise-en-scène. Michel Chion's *Words on Screen*, trans. Claudia Gorman (New York: Columbia University Press, 2017) is a detailed, theoretical analysis of all the words we see on a movie screen. See page 59ff for his analysis of words embedded in the mise-en-scène.
7. *Our Dancing Daughters* ends with bad girl Ann falling down the length of a flight of stairs, which may have suggested Tokiko's tumble down a flight of stairs in *A Hen in the Wind* twenty years later. (Other sources proposed as possible inspiration for the *Hen in the Wind* scene are *Gone With the Wind* [1939] and Naoya Shiga's novel, *A Dark Night's Passing*. See Shinnosuke Kometani, *Chasing Ozu*, trans. Kimiko Takeda [Tokyo: The Publishing Arts Institute, 2021], 169.)
8. Bordwell, *Poetics*, 193.
9. Bordwell, *Poetics*, 254.
10. Robert Lynen, the red-headed star of *Poil de carotte*, was among the many casualties of World War II. Lynen, who had fan clubs throughout the world, including in Japan, joined the French Resistance as a teenager, calling it his "finest role." Captured by the Nazis in 1943, he was executed in 1944. Lynne Olson, *Madame Fourcade's Secret War* (New York: Random House, 2019), 126ff.
11. *Die Tochter des Regiments* was distributed by the Nazis but had been shot prior to Hitler's taking power in Germany and well before the *Anschluss*. It was based on a popular nineteenth-century French opera, *La fille du regiment*.
12. Richie, *Ozu*, 218.
13. Mikio Naruse, often considered closest to Ozu in style, would follow him in embedding movie posters to comment on his film's storyline. In his 1934 *Street Without End*, the heroine, Sugiko, accompanies her upper-class boyfriend, Hiroshi, to see Ernst Lubitsch's *The Smiling Lieutenant* (1931), a film about a love triangle. A poster in the theater lobby advertises *White Woman*, a 1933 potboiler starring Carole Lombard and Charles Laughton. The poster appears behind Hiroshi as he confronts the very Westernized, upper-class

Signs, Symbols, and Motifs

woman his family wants him to marry. Played by Yukiko Inoue, the woman is not only dressed in beautiful Western-style clothing but, with her small round face and shoulder-length, crimped brown hair, looks semi-Caucasian, i.e., like a "white woman," in contrast to Sugiko, who looks and acts the part of the ideal Japanese woman.

14. The doppelgänger motif was introduced to Japan from Germany in the early twentieth century and was employed by serious literary figures like Ryunosuke Akutagawa and Jun'ichiro Tanizaki. Ozu adopted a softened version of the doppelgänger, one which does not convey the tortured psychology or murderous intent of characters in German literature and Expressionist cinema. See Baryon Tensor Posadas, *Double Visions, Double Fictions: The Doppelgänger in Japanese Film and Literature* (Minneapolis, MN: University of Minnesota Press, 2017), Ch. 1.

15. Ruth Benedict, *The Chrysanthemum and the Sword* (New York: Houghton Mifflin, 2005 [originally pub. 1946]), 288.

16. The snake *kanji* does not denote the year of Shinkichi's birth unless we assume the story takes place in 1925, not 1934.

17. Woojeong Joo offers an interesting if different explanation of how the mirrors operate in *Woman of Tokyo*, but he doesn't take into account all the times characters gaze at themselves in mirrors in Ozu's early films, some of which belie his notion that "Ozu's male characters hardly look into themselves through a mirror." He notes that the film's Harue never looks at herself in a mirror, which is in keeping with the fact that none of Ozu's "good" women do so. Joo, *Ozu*, 94–95.

18. Kathe Geist, "Yasujiro Ozu: Notes on a Retrospective," *Film Quarterly* 37, no. 1 (Fall 1983): 6.

19. Bordwell, *Poetics*, 192.

20. The mention of "one year" before or after these deaths is significant because Japanese, following Buddhist tradition, hold memorial services for their dead at set intervals, the first being after one year.

21. See Edward Fowler, "Piss and Run: Or How Ozu does a Number on SCAP," in *Word and Image in Japanese Cinema*, ed. Dennis Washburn and Carole Cavanaugh (Cambridge: Cambridge University Press, 2001), 283ff. Naruse's silent films also feature a great deal of hanging laundry, but it serves to characterize the working-/lower- middle-class milieu of his films more than being either an aesthetic or symbolic presence.

22. Richie, *Ozu*, 14; 254n17.

23. Lynne Kirby, *Parallel Tracks: The Railroad and Silent Cinema* (Durham, NC: Duke University Press, 1997), 2.

24. David Richards, *Played Out: The Jean Seberg Story* (New York: Random House, 1981), 27.

25. Bordwell, *Poetics*, 202.

26. Bordwell, *Poetics*, 234.

3

The Sound of Silence

> Silent cinema . . . sometimes expressed sounds better than sound could itself.
>
> —Michel Chion[1]

A salient feature of Ozu's films is the extent to which he represents sound through images. This ranges from fairly lengthy performances, cheers and dances, to a hearer's sudden reaction indicating an off-camera sound, to more subtle images of people hearing the sound of someone's approach. Sometimes titles, indicating speech belonging to a character we do not see, appear before the interlocutor, who only listens. Sometimes titles indicating speech appear at the beginning of a new scene. Our understanding of these instances of silent "sound" is complicated by the fact that Japanese theaters employed *benshi* or narrators to accompany silent films despite, by the 1920s, widespread frustration on the part of the production end of the industry with the *benshi* presence.

How Silent Were Ozu's Films?

Among major film-producing countries in the silent era, Japan was more or less unique in having narrators accompany silent films.[2] The *benshi* were analogous to the reciters in Kabuki and Bunraku and most closely resembled the narrators for lanternslide shows in the nineteenth century. They stood on stage as the film was projected, explained the film's background and action, and read (or improvised) the dialogue. Beginning in 1923, *benshi* scripts were introduced to keep the *benshi* from going too far off track in creating their own stories.[3] In addition to the *benshi*, Japanese theaters had large or small orchestras, which were also equipped with native instruments used to accompany period films (*jidai-geki*).

For decades, the *benshi* were a movie theater's main attraction, which, in the course of the 1920s, became problematic for studios. As films became more coherent and self-contained, and studios, directors, and stars became famous in their own right, studios attempted to mitigate domination by the *benshi*, the only group in the industry to be unionized.

Just as sound, pioneered in the United States, allowed theaters to dispense with orchestras and other live musical accompaniment, it allowed the Japanese industry to dispense with the *benshi* as well, although this proved to be a difficult and nasty divorce. By 1932, the major Japanese studios had become serious about adopting sound, but even then most films were still silent, and talkies did not dominate the industry until 1935. Ozu's studio, Shochiku, made thirty of the forty-five talkies produced in 1932, but the industry's entire output was 400 films, most, obviously, silent.[4] Consequently, *benshi* continued to accompany films well into the mid-1930s.

When Shochiku was founded in 1920, film critics as well as the industry itself had become concerned about the effect of the *benshi* because each film could be changed in the theater by the varying interpretations *benshi* gave to it. Specifically intending to emulate Hollywood production methods, Shochiku was particularly hostile to the *benshi* as an institution; in retaliation, thugs hired by the *benshi* union in 1932 attacked Shiro Kido, Shochiku's head.[5]

Given Shochiku's goal of making American-style, self-sufficient films and Ozu's own inclination in that direction, we should assume that the "sound" Ozu portrays visually was to his mind sufficient, whether or not a *benshi* added narration or an orchestra sound effects. (One has to wonder if one motivation for Ozu's penchant for showing a close-up before its context [cart-before-the-horse cutting] was to confuse the *benshi*, who could only view a film once or twice prior to performing with it.)

One technique for encouraging the departure of the *benshi*, while studios worked out the technicalities of full-sound film production, was adding tracks known as *saundoban* with background music and sound effects only. Ozu's first *saundoban* film was the lost *Until the Day We Meet Again* (1932) and his last *An Inn in Tokyo* (1935).[6] The only soundtrack from his *saundoban* films to survive is from *An Inn in Tokyo*. No *benshi* script for any Ozu film survives.

Of *An Inn in Tokyo*, Ozu commented that Shochiku made him "make it just as though it were sound," by which he meant not simply with a *saundoban* track but with an increased use of intertitles, implied off-screen "sound," and so on.[7] Michael Raine has analyzed Ozu's increased use of intertitles in his late silent films and concluded that with these Ozu hoped to make a form of silent film hitherto unknown in Japan, one without *benshi* narration and without spoken dialogue.[8] We can conclude, however, that between the *benshi* and the *saundoban*, Ozu's films were not particularly silent but that he wished them to be.[9]

Ozu did not make his first talkie until 1936. One of his stated objections to making sound films was that he felt his films were already complete, and he "did not much like music and [sound] effects being added to silent films he considered finished."[10] He was not alone in this. Michel Chion, author of numerous books on film sound, writes, "ce cinéma s'était déjà constitué et structuré autour de son manqué de telle façon que le son réel n'a pas pu s'y adjoindre autrement que comme un *intrus*." ([Silent] cinema was already constituted and structured around the lack of sound in such a way that adding real sound could only seem like an intrusion.)[11] A good illustration of this perceived intrusion is one critic's assessment of the sound effect of a train pulling into the station on the *saundoban* track at the beginning of *A Story of Floating Weeds*. He called it a "cheap gimmick."[12]

Ozu has not left us his own thoughts on the *benshi*, but the *naniwabushi* storyteller at the beginning of *Passing Fancy* invokes the origin of the *benshi* narrators. Joseph Anderson points out that "the *katsuben* [*benshi*] and the movies that accompanied them were the principal competitors of these traditional storytellers."[13] In towns without movies, the storyteller and the *taishu engeki*, Kihachi's art form in *A Story of Floating Weeds*, still flourished. Possibly Ozu was signaling his wish to situate live narrators back where they belonged—in a world without movies.

Visible Sound

Michel Chion notes that "the silent cinema was swarming with implied noises."[14] Indeed, we are able to imagine the sound of most things we can see in silent films, things that would be accompanied by sound effects today. Ozu's ubiquitous trains, for example, can all be imagined with accompanying sounds. In my observation, however, few of these imagined train sounds affect Ozu's stories. In this chapter I will discuss mainly those implied or visual "sounds" that have narrative import.

Like most silent films, Ozu's have instances where the close-up of an object making noise or an actor screaming forces us to imagine the racket being portrayed, for example, the screaming, sometimes stomping, children in *Tokyo Chorus*, *I Was Born, But . . .* or *Passing Fancy*. The child Tomibo not only bursts dramatically into tears several times in *A Story of Floating Weeds*, but a close-up of him "barking" through his dog costume contrasts with his human tears that come later in the scene. In *Passing Fancy*, a drunken Kihachi claps his hands insistently, demanding more sake. A telephone rings in *An Inn in Tokyo*, alerting a policeman to Kihachi's robbery. In *Days of Youth* and *I Flunked, But . . .* a monitor walks through the college courtyard ringing a bell, signaling the end of a class period, as the boys pour out of buildings. There are close-ups of instruments in the jazz club sequence in *Dragnet Girl* and classical music playing on records in Kazuko's RCA store in the same film. We're asked to imagine the scratchy sound of a needle going off the 78 record Jyoji is playing, which interrupts his conversation with Kazuko in the store. (It isn't clear how Jyoji and Kazuko can converse through the window of what is supposed to be a soundproof booth, but Bordwell sees this as a gag based on the fact that, since the film is silent, their, like our, ability to "hear" is hypothetical.[15] In other words, silent "sound" here moves from the imagined to the magical.)

Additional silent "sounds" in *Dragnet Girl* include Tokiko slamming her purse down on the table when she finds Jyoji at home listening to a record from Kazuko's store, after which she abruptly pulls the needle off the record. Later we imagine the sound of tinkling glass as Jyoji breaks one aperitif glass after the other in the bar sequence. During the couple's attempted escape at the end, a wine bottle slides off the roof and smashes on the ground, potentially alerting the police. And, of course, there

The Sound of Silence

is the sound of the gun, signified by the huge cloud of smoke it produces, when Tokiko shoots at Jyoji.

Very often, Ozu's visible sound took the form of performances, games, and cheers. Jazz musicians play in nightclubs in *Walk Cheerfully* and *Dragnet Girl*, and *Walk Cheerfully* also features Senko singing "Gay Cabalero," its words written in English on the wall behind him. Most of Ozu's extant silents have at least one performance, beginning with the earliest, *Days of Youth*, in which the students, during their ski trip, perform the *okesa*, a folk song and dance, which, appropriately, recounts a lovers' dialogue. Richie notes that Ozu liked to film complete performances.[16] Even if they are not truly complete, they certainly seem so, requiring substantial screen time. *Days of Youth's okesa* lasts close to three minutes and includes shots of the boys dancing while two others sing, clap, and drum.

Ozu utilized such performances not simply to engage the audience, who would have known the words and music portrayed on the screen, but also to carry his story along. The *okesa* performance in *Days of Youth* comes the evening after Watanabe has made a fool of Yamamoto on the ski slopes, ruining his chances, or so he believes, with Chieko. Yamamoto joins the dance reluctantly—still unaware of its actual meaning, i.e., the upcoming *omiai* between Chieko and ski club president Hatamoto—and looks sad throughout. Meanwhile, Watanabe joins the dance looking smug, still gloating over his imagined success with Chieko and his prior acquisition of the socks she knitted, which provides a sharp contrast with Yamamoto's sad mien. Two lines from the song appear in a title card and seem to be directed at Yamamoto: "Stop your crying and wailing. Though we part, we'll meet again."

Ozu would use performances to show one or more characters trying to cheer up amid sorrow in two other films, *Tokyo Chorus* and a *Story of Floating Weeds*. In *Tokyo Chorus*, protagonist Okajima initiates a clapping game to celebrate his daughter, Miyoko's, recovery at the same time his wife discovers he has sold all her good kimonos to pay for Miyoko's hospital stay. Throughout the game, we watch her struggle to absorb this shock while he struggles with the guilt and shame of having had to do it. During the reunion at the end of the film, the former students and teacher sing a sentimental song commemorating their school days. Ozu accompanies the song with many visual "sound effects," the men beating time with their fans, the women and children, who are sitting on the sidelines, clapping in rhythm. Again he uses this performance, which lasts ninety seconds, to let his characters silently express emotion. Okajima struggles to remain cheerful against not only the nostalgia invoked by the reunion and the song but against the knowledge that he must leave Tokyo to take his new job. The teacher, too, looks sad and exchanges glances with Okajima. Both understand that the teacher, once the victim of Okajima's naughtiness, has reached the last phase of his life.

In *A Story of Floating Weeds*, Otaka leads the actors in a valedictory song prior to the troupe's dispersal. They clap and sing, but Kihachi looks distressed throughout, as does the oldest member, Tomibo's father, who leaves the group and weeps, bringing the ninety-second performance to an end amid his sobs and the "sound" of Tomibo bawling (as only child actor Tokkankozo could).

In *An Inn in Tokyo*, the Kihachi character drowns his sorrow over lost love in sake and, accompanied by a waitress, claps and sings. Drunk, he claps insistently for more sake, as does the Kihachi character in *Passing Fancy*, who is drinking for the same reason.

Other performances include the students' college cheers in *I Flunked, But . . .* and *Where Now Are the Dreams of Youth?* At the end of *I Flunked, But . . .* the boys who failed to graduate lead their classmates in a cheer at the beginning of the new term. It lasts two-and-a half minutes and becomes "sound over," i.e., off-screen sound, when the film cuts to the roommates who passed their exams. The cheer awakens them, and they first whistle along with it, then lie back down and beat the rhythm with their feet as the film cuts back to the clapping students and the cheerleaders yelling and gesturing.

In *Where Now Are the Dreams of Youth?* a student-led cheer begins the film. We see an audience of students clapping, then the cheerleaders leading them. Two separate conversations follow, and when we get to the second, between the bakery girl Oshige and student Saiki, we realize that the cheer has continued over these conversations because Oshige and Saiki both beat out the rhythm as they talk. Cuts back to the cheerleaders and the clapping boys confirm this. In *Passing Fancy*, we credit the *naniwabushi* performance at the beginning of the film with continuing throughout the introductory scene, which includes the purse gag, the flea outbreak, and an introduction to our main characters.[17]

Another instance of "sound over" occurs in *An Inn in Tokyo*. The fireworks, in that film, *Tokyo Chorus*, and *Passing Fancy*, must all make a noise. In *Inn*, however, we can assume that that "noise" continues over the shots of Kihachi steeling himself for the robbery by drinking an overflowing glass of sake inside a bar because a shot of the ongoing fireworks is cut between shots of the bar and Kihachi drinking. To the extent that the fireworks have an inspiring/instigating effect on the desperate measures the men in all three films undertake to secure money, the continuing presence of the booming fireworks while Kihachi drinks is significant.

Gags Based on Sound

If, in *Dragnet Girl*, Ozu created extra-diegetic gags based on sound that cannot be heard, either by plaster Nipper dogs or men in glass booths, he set up straightforward, diegetic gags based on sound in earlier films. The alarm clock gag in *Days of Youth* works only if we imagine the sound of the alarm going off underneath Yamamoto's robe.

In *Where Now Are the Dreams of Youth?* a sequence with the college bell ringer begins with a close-up of the ringing bell, emphasizing its noise, which carries in "sound over" into the bake shop, summoning the boys to their classes. Later the bell ringer finds a change purse on the ground and shakes it to see if there is money in it, inadvertently ringing his bell. "Sound over" resumes as Ozu cuts to the classroom where the boys listen, assume their class has ended, and begin to leave. Outside, the bell ringer

The Sound of Silence

hides while students pour out of the building, only to be herded back by their teachers once the error is discovered.

The Docks of New York

Close-ups of a sound source were a sure way to cue an audience to "silent sound," but sometimes films sought to make sound visible by showing the reaction to a sound without actually showing the cause of the sound. Such an instance occurs in Josef von Sternberg's 1928 *Docks of New York* in a sequence in which an aggrieved wife, Lou, shoots her husband, Andy, while he is trying to seduce the heroine, Mae. We see Lou enter Mae's room where we know she is fighting off Andy, but instead of seeing the inside of the room again, the film cuts to pigeons outside the window suddenly fluttering around. The hero, Bill, drinking coffee in the restaurant below, looks up. There is a cut to others in the restaurant getting up and rushing out. Five more shots of Bill and others rushing to and staring at the door to Mae's room follow before we find out what actually happened. (Lou has murdered Andy.) Von Sternberg combines visible sound with a suspenseful withholding of narrative information by showing the reaction to the sound instead of the sound source.

The Docks of New York was well known in Japan. It won best foreign film in *Kinema Junpo*'s poll of film critics in 1929, and in 1932 Yasujiro Shimazu made a sound film for Shochiku based on *The Docks of New York* called *First Steps Ashore* (*Joriku no dai-ippo*) starring Joji Oka, who would subsequently star in *Dragnet Girl*.

Not surprisingly, Ozu adapted von Sternberg's technique in *Dragnet Girl*. The sequence in which Jyoji engages competing gangsters in a fistfight at the jazz club unfolds as follows:

1) In a back storeroom the gangsters take off their coats.
2) Senko takes Jyoji's coat and returns to the dance floor.
3) FS of gang members, including Senko, Tokiko, and Misako, on the dance floor suddenly looking toward the storeroom.
4) Other women in the club look toward the storeroom and stand up.
5) Repeat of shot #3 as gang members look toward the people in shot #4, then back toward the storeroom, then (presumably) toward what we see in shot #6.
6) Older people seated in another part of the room stand up.
7) Repeat of shots #3 and #5 as the gang members look again toward the storeroom, then consult together.
8) Senko walks over to the bandstand and instructs the musicians to keep playing.

The sequence continues with people dancing while Tokiko and Misako wait for Jyoji to emerge from the back. This dramatic and lengthy example of silent "off-screen sound" was clearly derived from von Sternberg, but Ozu included shorter examples in other films.

More Off-screen Sound

A preview of *Dragnet Girl*'s "fight" sequence occurs at the beginning of *I Flunked, But...* We see two boys arguing, and one pushes the other. Three reaction shots—students observing the fight, their heads moving back and forth—follow. Then the students gather around the two pugilists and try to broker a peace.

After Tokiko, Jyoji, and their friends return from the jazz club to Jyoji's apartment, Tokiko, eager to engage Jyoji in lovemaking, quickly suggests it is time for the friends to leave. Misako, who has a crush on Jyoji, leaves under protest. Tokiko begins to sit on Jyoji's lap, then turns and jumps up angrily (Figure 3.1). Cut to Misako's head peeking in the door. She comes in, then suddenly turns and rushes back out as Tokiko comes into the frame. These abrupt dramatic actions are motivated by sounds we must imagine: Misako opening the door, Tokiko's outburst, and so on.

The same startled reaction to an off-screen sound occurs in *An Inn in Tokyo* during a scene in which Kihachi tries to rouse his sleeping boys for school. One complains that Kihachi is being "noisy," and a brush comes flying into the shot. The boys jump up and then settle back down. Suddenly, with no brush or flying object to prompt them, they sit bolt upright. The next shot reveals Kihachi standing by the doorway, glowering at them. We have to presume he has just yelled at them.

Figure 3.1: Tokiko reacts angrily to the sound of Misako's intrusion in *Dragnet Girl*.

The Sound of Silence   61

Typically, Ozu shows a character reacting to a sound before we see its source. When the lovers, Shinkichi and Otoki, in *A Story of Floating Weeds* sit near a train track, they look down the track, and Otoki stands up before we see the passing train. Later Kihachi confronts Otoki, whom he has seen with Shinkichi. She starts to walk away, but then stops and looks at him. He has obviously yelled at her. In *An Inn in Tokyo*, a policeman picks up a telephone, which presumably alerts him to Kihachi's robbery. Ozu first shows us the policeman reacting, then the phone.

In a pivotal scene from *A Mother Should Be Loved*, the disaffected son Sadao befriends a cleaning woman, offering her a cigarette. To get her attention, he makes a sound, probably something like "Oi!" but we only know this because we see her turn toward him. In the shot of Sadao that follows, his lips are still, and Ozu does not dignify this short call with a title card. They share a cigarette, and she starts to leave when he calls her back. Ozu repeats the sequence: she turns, then we cut to Sadao, lips still.

Other than dialogue, which I will discuss shortly, the off-screen sound Ozu's characters react to most often is that of someone at the door. Typically, a person arriving at a Japanese-style house slides back the door, which may cause a little bell to ring, and calls out a greeting—"I'm home," (*tadaima*) if it's a family member, or "Excuse me," (*onegaishimasu* or *gomennasai*) if not. A non-family member arriving at a Western-style door opening to an apartment might knock but would also be likely to call out the appropriate greeting. This is what Ozu's characters are hearing when they look up suddenly because someone has come in or is at the door.

Misako's reentry in *Dragnet Girl*, to which Tokiko reacts so angrily, is only the first in a series of interruptions by people at Jyoji's door whenever the lovers start to become intimate. Each time, they detach from one another upon hearing someone at the door. The most dramatic of these instances occurs when, near the end of the film, Jyoji breaks away from a weeping Tokiko because he has heard Kazuko's voice. Without looking at the door, he invites her in. As she enters, he stands facing his table: this is the moment he must decide between the woman he truly loves and the gentle girl who has caught his fancy and touched his heart. This internal struggle has been initiated by the off-screen "sound" of Kazuko's voice. Later in the story he and Tokiko stop arguing when they hear the police at their door, represented by the door handle twisting back and forth in the locked door.

Sometimes the character who looks up upon hearing someone at the door knows, like Jyoji, who it is even when the audience does not. In *Dragnet Girl* Kazuko looks up suddenly, and we cut to Hiroshi in the hallway of their building getting rid of his cigarette. But often characters are surprised. In *A Story of Floating Weeds*, Otsune is fetching sake for herself and Kihachi when she hears someone at her door, and some seconds pass before she reaches it and is surprised to discover that her son, Shinkichi, has come home. In *Woman of Tokyo*, Ryoichi looks up, expecting Chikako to come home, when Harue arrives instead; and the next day Harue, wishing Ryoichi would stop by, hears someone at her door who turns out to be Chikako. Later, both women register surprise upon hearing someone at the door before they see the neighbor boy summoning Harue

62   *Ozu*

to the phone. In *I Flunked, But . . .* different characters react to hearing people on the stairs to the boys' rented room. At one point the landlord's child, who is visiting protagonist Takahashi, hears someone coming but doesn't understand the visitor's significance: it's the bakery girl, and Takahashi quickly shoos the little boy back downstairs.

Title Cards and Sound Bridges

The "sound" which precedes the picture of what or who made the sound is part of Ozu's cart-before-the-horse cutting style, which forces the audience at many junctures to read the film backwards. (See Chapter 4.) Ozu sometimes uses dialogue title cards in the same way, in which case an audience may "hear" words without knowing who has spoken them. At other times, we know who is involved in a conversation, but shots of those conversing don't always match up with who is speaking the words on the title cards. Sometimes we experience "sound over" conversation, i.e., we see someone listening, a title card, then back to the person listening before cutting to the actual speaker. At a critical moment in *Dragnet Girl*, Tokiko accompanies Hiroshi to the door, brushing off his coat sympathetically (because Jyoji has punched him). We see a close-up of her, the title "We'll do one last job," and a shot of Tokiko reacting to the words, then a shot of Jyoji, who has spoken them. In *Woman of Tokyo*, we cut from Chikako hanging up a payphone outside her club to the title "I wonder who you were calling" to the speaker, that evening's john, whom we've never seen previously. (See Figure 4.5, p. 78.) *Passing Fancy* is famous for repeatedly putting a speaker's words ahead of his or her face. The very first shot is a title card, "A geisha tells a client she loves him," which is followed by another card, "He lies and says he'll come again." Cut to a traveling shot over an audience, and nine shots later we see the *naniwabushi* narrator who spoke the opening lines.

Using a title card at the beginning of a scene, Ozu could effectively create a "sound bridge." After *Passing Fancy*'s Otome formally petitions Kihachi to persuade his friend Jiro to marry her ward Harue, Ozu transitions to the next scene as follows:

1) CU of Kihachi's hand reaching for a piece of sushi and Otome's hands pouring him sake.
2) Title: "I'm choosy about women. If I don't want her, that's that."
3) MS of Kihachi, brow furrowed, standing outdoors.
4) Title: "How dare you say that! She's too good for you."
5) FS of Jiro seated on a log and looking up.

Not only do we not see the speaker of the line that begins this sequence until the fourth cut, but by beginning with the title card, Ozu uses "sound" to transition into the new sequence.

After Jyoji admits Hiroshi into the gang in *Dragnet Girl*, we see Hiroshi, still in Jyoji's apartment, change from his student hat to his poor-boy punk's hat, then the title "Hiroshi is a full-fledged punk now," then two of the gang members standing on the street, waving to Hiroshi. Again, a silent "sound bridge."

The Sound of Silence 63

Bordwell writes that eliminating shots of the speaker in Japanese silent films of the 1930s was not uncommon, and Joseph Anderson notes that, "Japanese literature . . . also has this tendency to elide the speaker."[18] That said, Bordwell concludes that "while other filmmakers use this tactic sporadically to create a momentary flourish, Ozu organizes it to create playfully suppressive patterns."[19] In other words, Ozu played with inserting titles without direct reference to the speaker more frequently and systematically than did his contemporaries to create the synecdochic or "cart-before-the-horse" narration that will be discussed in Chapter 4. He also used them to suppress transitions, or, viewed another way, to create "sound bridges" from one scene to the next.

As a Japanese filmmaker, Ozu could have availed himself of several possibilities for adding sound to his otherwise silent films, but, whatever the studio or the theaters did to add either *benshi* narration or *saundoban*, he remained committed to creating silent films that were complete in themselves. As a filmmaker who continued making silent films well into the sound era, he was obviously aware of what sound added to a film, including its dramatic and humorous possibilities, and sought to exploit these in silence. His use of "silent sound" is as imaginative, quirky, and contrary as every other aspect of his filmmaking.

Notes

1. Michel Chion, *Audio-Vision: Sound on Screen*, trans. Claudia Gorbman (New York: Columbia University Press, 1994), 137.
2. Some very early narrative films in the West were accompanied by live storytellers, but by 1910 these were replaced by intertitles. See Michel Chion, *Film, A Sound Art*, trans. Claudia Gorman (New York: Columbia University Press, 2009), 10.
3. Raine, "A New Form of Silent Cinema," 103.
4. Joseph L. Anderson and Donald Richie, *The Japanese Film: Art and Industry* (Princeton, NJ: Princeton University Press, 1982), 77.
5. Anderson and Richie, *The Japanese Film*, 78.
6. Woojeong Joo, *Ozu*, 61–63.
7. Richie, *Ozu*, 221.
8. Raine, "A New Form of Silent Cinema," 113.
9. Raine writes, "Whether or not the benshi was actually present, I argue that Ozu made his late silent films *as if* they were not." "A New Form of Silent Cinema," 110.
10. Richie, *Ozu*, 221.
11. Michel Chion, *Le son au cinema* (Paris: Cahiers du cinéma [Editions d l'Etoile], 1985), 28.
12. Raine, "A New Form of Silent Cinema," 110.
13. Joseph Anderson, "Spoken Silents in the Japanese Cinema; or, Talking to Pictures: Essaying the Katsuben, Contextualizing the Texts," in Nolletti and Desser, *Reframing Japanese Cinema*, 282.
14. Chion *Film, A Sound Art*, 7.
15. Bordwell, *Poetics*, 67.
16. Richie, *Ozu*, 118ff.

17. The flea outbreak in *Passing Fancy* may have been inspired by Harold Lloyd's *Hot Water* (1924), in which a crab gets away from boys who have been fishing and is passed from passenger to passenger on a streetcar.
18. Bordwell, *Poetics*, 66; Anderson, "Spoken Silents," 285.
19. Bordwell, *Poetics*, 67; see also Raine, "A New Form of Silent Cinema," 107.

4
Narrative Strategies, Texts, and Subtexts

Cinema is drama, not accident.

—Yasujiro Ozu[1]

Master at discerning and describing Ozu's "parametric" style, David Bordwell was less discerning when it came to Ozu's stories. Early on he insisted that Ozu's plots were subordinate to his style, stating "the constraints of stylistic patterning [impose] their will on the [plot], or at least . . . the narration limits itself to presenting events that display the style to its best advantage."[2] Of Ozu's themes, he wrote, "parametric film-makers have tended to employ strikingly obvious themes. Not much acumen is needed to identify . . . *Tokyo Story* as examining the decline of the 'inherently' Japanese family . . . It is as if stylistic organization becomes prominent only if the themes are so banal as to leave criticism little to interpret."[3] But just as Ozu's signs and motifs carry meaning beyond mere patterning, his methods of narration, arbitrary though they appear, also lead us to subtexts and a deeper understanding of his stories.

An Obsession with Direction

Ozu invoked direction, in the sense of something heading one way or the other, as a means of both structuring and commenting on the world he created in his films. In his 1930 *Walk Cheerfully*, the gangsters Kenji and Senko pull off a robbery/scam, and, when they meet up afterwards and move on to other locations, a series of mysterious arrows, always pointing to screen left, appears along their route. The arrows have been drawn on various buildings and a post box and are accompanied by carefully placed cigarette butts and ashes. All this intrigue, however, amounts to nothing. At the end of this sequence, Kenji's infatuation with Yasue begins, the arrows cease to appear, and no mention is ever made of them by anyone.

In *That Night's Wife* from the same year, the policemen pursuing Hashizume draw, on the sidewalk, an elaborate sketch of the neighborhood's city blocks with arrows pointing this way and that. This deliberate, calculated approach to catching the thief likewise comes to nothing. (More than a generation later Arlo Guthrie would mock

66 *Ozu*

Officer Obie in "Alice's Restaurant" for his "circles and arrows" on glossy photographs of garbage. Ozu had anticipated him by thirty-seven years.)

Toward the beginning of *Dragnet Girl*, two gang members walk down the street with Tokiko. Seeing a policeman, they run off to the left, leaving Tokiko to continue straight ahead. The policeman stands looking, deciding whom to follow. He chooses to follow Tokiko, but, like other direction-determined strategies, this one comes to nothing.

During Okajima's fight with his boss in *Tokyo Chorus*, the heel of the boss's secretary's shoe comes unglued. After Okajima tosses it to him, the secretary turns it back and forth, trying to find the right direction to fit it back on.

Much later in 1949's *Late Spring*, one sequence involves the father's friend guessing the direction to the sea, the shrine, Tokyo, and so on. He points one way and the father invariably contradicts him, pointing in the opposite direction. Kristin Thompson sees this sequence as Ozu's self-reflexive commentary on his 360° cutting style.[4] Meanwhile, David Bordwell has identified the geometry lesson in *The Only Son* (1936), in which a teacher uses an illustration of a triangle inscribed on a circle, as also illustrating Ozu's cutting pattern.[5]

Indeed, Ozu's fascination with direction is most evident in his refusal to respect continuity editing's 180° rule, which helps an audience watching a film's two-dimensional surface to stay oriented to the 360° space that has been filmed. One result is that the images of Ozu's characters often flip back and forth from screen left to screen right or vice versa, even though the characters have not actually moved or changed their orientation in the story (diegetic) space. Ozu is said to have compared examples of sequences that maintained the 180° line with those that crossed it and declared, "It's all the same, isn't it?" by which he probably meant that the story was still understandable.[6] That notwithstanding, his flaunting the 180° rule makes the spaces his characters inhabit more difficult for an audience to comprehend. Nevertheless, his insistence that an abrupt change in screen direction made no difference is consonant with the uselessness of the arrows in *Walk Cheerfully* and *That Night's Wife* and the policeman's decision to follow Tokiko in *Dragnet Girl*.

Reversing screen direction in Ozu's films is also related to reversing cause and effect. As we saw in Chapter 3, he often showed dialogue title cards before an image of the person speaking, forcing the viewer to think back from speaker to title. He frequently began sequences with a close-up of an object, the goldfish bowl surrounded by smoke in *I Flunked, But . . .* , and then cut to a medium shot of someone manipulating that object: Takahashi blowing smoke on the bowl (Figures 4.1 and 4.2). One scene in *The Lady and the Beard* begins with a coat flying onto a sofa; hands pick it up, followed by a match-on-action to a medium shot of a servant holding the coat. Disembodied hands and feet often manipulate objects, as in the party preparations toward the end of *Tokyo Chorus*. These sequences create a visual reversal of cause and effect. We see the smoke before the smoker, hands, legs, or feet before their owners. Significantly, the two jokes the boy Tomi tells in *Passing Fancy* are both based on a reversal of cause and

Narrative Strategies, Texts, and Subtexts 67

Figure 4.1: Cigarette smoke blows over a goldfish bowl in *I Flunked, But...*

Figure 4.2: Takahashi is blowing the smoke.

effect. Why does a hand have five fingers? So it will fit in a glove. Why is seawater salty? Because salted salmon swim there.

Just as Ozu challenged his audience to reconstruct his spaces when he crossed the 180° line, he challenged viewers to mentally straighten out cause and effect. In *Tokyo Chorus*, he illustrated the method for following his narration that he expected his viewers to use. Okajima comes home to find that his wife won't speak to him. He takes off his coat and looks around the room. He sees the following:

1) his wife's good kimono hanging out
2) some packages laid beneath the kimono
3) two white *tabi* (socks) sitting on the windowsill to air

Cut back to Okajima taking this in, then the title: "Did you go out today?" Of course, clues in any detective movie are presented in more or less this way, but in Ozu's films, the audience is constantly required to read such clues in order to figure out what is going on.

Often Ozu's audience is required to assemble clues across the film as they become available. *A Story of Floating Weeds* opens with Kihachi's troupe arriving at the station. The sequence ends with a long shot of the last member leaving the station, followed by:

1) two vertical banners
2) a poster advertising the show
3) Title: "Are you going to see the show tonight?"
4) a man having his hair cut

The speaker, the man in the barber chair, is an actor from Kihachi's troupe. The scene in the barbershop continues, and we are left wondering about the banners that began the sequence. Later they are established as being outside the theater and precede a number of scenes that take place in the theater, so that we come to understand that their initial appearance indicated that, upon arrival, the troupe had established itself in the theater.

In this example, the single shot of banners stands not simply for a place but for an entire activity. However, confirming the nature of that activity requires the audience to read backwards. Like the reversal of cause and effect, the necessity for reading backwards results in a time-bound puzzle which denies viewers immediate access to narrative information but instead requires them to put the pieces together as they become available.[7]

More Ways to Confuse the Viewer

Similar to requiring the viewer to read backwards is Ozu's practice of deliberately miscuing the viewer when scene changes occur. In *Walk Cheerfully*, Kenji meets Senko, who has found a job as a chauffeur. Senko invites Kenji to get in his car, and the scene ends with Senko and Kenji driving away. A title reading "The Job Kenji Found" appears,

Narrative Strategies, Texts, and Subtexts   69

followed by a traveling shot taken from the hood of a moving car. We assume that Kenji is still riding with Senko and that we will watch him find his job. Instead, when the car stops, Senko and his boss get out of it and look up to where Kenji is washing windows on the company's building. Instead of indicating the continuation of the previous scene, the traveling shot from the car occurs at a much later time after a major story event—Kenji finding his job—has taken place.

Three times *Dragnet Girl* repeats a close shot of a Victrola that then tracks out away from the record player: first in the RCA store where Kazuko works, then in Jyoji's apartment, and again in the record store. Each time we expect the record player plus tracking shot to be in the place we last saw the Victrola, but each time we are fooled, as Ozu shifts from the record store to the apartment and back to the record store.

Miscuing the viewer to scene changes by showing similar objects or activities at the beginning and end of scenes or through graphic matches or by repeating similar shots in different locations occurs in many of Ozu's films and deliberately confuses viewers, who are forced to rethink their reading of the action. Ozu's mise-en-scène also works at times to retard a viewer's comprehension. His camera frequently refuses to reframe shots to keep characters' faces and upper bodies in the frame. Early in *Tokyo Chorus*, for example, there is a shot of protagonist Okajima in the foreground, framed from his elbows down, speaking to his wife, who is in the background, kneeling next to their baby's mosquito tent. She stands up and comes to him so that we now see both of them from the elbows down as they say good-bye and leave the frame. Meanwhile the camera holds on the baby's tent, out of focus, in the background. We know who and what are in this shot, but it is disorienting nonetheless and brings us to another aspect of Ozu's early style, his frequent disregard for keeping people and objects in focus.

A scene in *I Was Born, But . . .* begins with a close-up of the family's belongings piled near a doorway in the new house. The truck encountered at the beginning of the film drives into the frame and can be seen through the doorway as the little boys get out and the older one calls to his mother. However, the view through the doorway is out of focus and remains so. Only a cut to a full shot of the boys satisfies our desire to see them clearly. Ozu continues to play with focus in this scene: a long shot of the mother, boys, and the truck has everything in focus, but subsequent shots of two helpers unloading the truck has the one near the camera in focus and the one near the truck out of focus, and so on throughout the sequence.

A scene in *An Inn in Tokyo* begins with an out-of-focus long shot of Kihachi's boys eating in Otsune's restaurant. Kihachi walks into the still out-of-focus shot with his new friend, Otaka, and her child. Cut to medium shots of Kihachi, Otsune, and Otaka, all in shallow focus with the background, including the eating boys, still out of focus. In these shots, Kihachi asks Otsune to feed his guests. After she agrees, Ozu cuts back to his long shot, now in focus.

(Yet Ozu was not indifferent to the possibility of deep focus. During the sale of the troupe's props and costumes in *A Story of Floating Weeds*, a deep-focus shot worthy of Renoir allows us to see clearly from the men buying the theatrical paraphernalia to the back of the scene where actress Otaka sits smoking, separated and alone because of her feud with boss Kihachi.)

We're forced to conclude, therefore, that by all of these different methods—crossing the 180° line, cart-before-the-horse editing, forcing the viewer to read backwards across many shots and scene changes, making scene changes hard to anticipate, and playing with focus—Ozu deliberately sabotaged the viewer's ability to immediately comprehend his story, and the question is why? To some extent his film style imitates the ambiguities of Japanese spoken discourse, where obfuscation is an art form. Japanese literature also prizes indirectness and ambiguity. Joseph Anderson writes, "Japanese written literature, including modern novels . . . has this tendency to elide the speaker as well as not indicate what is direct or indirect speech."[8] But if Japanese literature gave Ozu a model, simply imitating some of these tendencies does not constitute a rationale. He did, after all, belong to a studio dedicated to being "modern" and making American-style films, and most of his colleagues complied with the requirements of the continuity style.[9]

For Bordwell, Ozu is just having fun, and this is certainly a valid observation.[10] His reputation as a jokester was well known, and his tendency to insert humor into his films in various ways is prolific, but a more profound impulse may also be at work, and *Tokyo Chorus*, which teaches us how to read singular objects from effect back to cause, suggests one. The hero Okajima has met Yamada, the older gentleman whose firing has led to Okajima's own job loss, at the zoo. Suddenly, everyone starts running in the same direction. Yamada inquires and discovers that a bear has escaped, so he starts to run after the crowd, but Okajima stops him, saying, "The bear won't affect our lives in any way." Following the crowd, following a comparatively simple story line, *following a defined direction*, will not enrich our lives in any way, but following Ozu's artful twists and dodges and taking time to look more deeply into his texts and subtexts will.

Puzzles and Mazes

In his seminal work on Japanese film, Noël Burch insisted that many of Ozu's still life (unpeopled or "empty") shots were inserts that had nothing to do with the diegesis, and in their early work on Ozu, Bordwell and Thompson claimed Ozu was indifferent "to the temporal and causal chain of the narrative."[11] Indifference, however, is not the same as deliberately deceptive. Bordwell would later back off the claim of indifference but still emphasize narrative gaps, ambiguities, and open-endedness in Ozu's stories.[12] For the most part, however, the gaps are eventually filled, and there is far less ambiguity and open-endedness than he imagines. There is, for example, an obvious cause-and-effect sequence in *Walk Cheerfully* in which, as an office building opens up, a young woman stands by a window powdering her nose. She leaves her open compact on the windowsill. There is a cut to a circle of light on the sidewalk, which causes the heroine Yasue to look up to see where the light is coming from. She spots what appears to be her boyfriend, Kenji, washing windows high above.

Bordwell, however, insists on reading this sequence as not only "roundabout," an established part of Ozu's narrative style, but as "fundamentally ambiguous," because "what [Yasue] is looking at is not the window with the compact but Kenji . . . washing another window . . . So perhaps the reflection is not that of the compact but of Kenji's window."[13] It's true that, when Yasue looks up, there is no window corresponding to the window where the compact was left; however, Kenji's window could not create a circular disk of light. The secretary with her compact plays no role in the film *other than* to direct Yasue's gaze upward so that she becomes aware that Kenji may be working at the same place she is working.

Bordwell further questions whether Yasue actually works in this building at all when that is not only suggested by this scene, in which everything converges on this particular office building, but is made clear by the subsequent sequence of chimney shots, which link Yasue's roof to Kenji and Senko's. In the scene in which Kenji chats with Senko on the roof, Kenji's back is to a vent chimney with its onion-domed fan. After the men look at a biplane, there is a cut to a close shot of a man working on what may be the same chimney, then a cut to the office workers on their section of roof, apparently at a lower level than the one Senko and Kenji are on. Coming up from that roof is a chimneystack with the same cast iron rungs the chimney worker was standing on in the previous shot. These are not three different chimneys but Ozu's way of linking the shots and the spaces, not simply formally but narratively.

Furthermore, when Yasue leaves work that day, she discovers Kenji behind her building arguing with his former gang members, who subsequently shoot him. The fact that Kenji, Senko, and Yasue all work in the same building allows Kenji's friends to rescue him when he is shot. Ergo, the fact that Kenji, Senko and Yasue all work in the same building is crucial to the narrative and not at all up for debate.

In another example, the prologue for *Tokyo Chorus* ends with the hero, Okajima, sitting alone, leaning against a large wooden rack after the rest of his class has marched off with their teacher, Omura. Bordwell wonders whether he moved to this spot before or after the rest of the boys marched off when logic insists he would not have moved from the spot where the teacher had left him standing as punishment as long as the teacher was present.[14] The point of this last, short sequence of Okajima sitting alone and looking out at his surroundings, is, in any case, the breeze he watches blowing through the trees. It pairs with the smoke he sees blowing from a chimney near his home in the scene that follows. Although, as argued in Chapter 2, the notion of transience does not dominate the early films as it does the later ones, Ozu establishes the idea of transience in these two shots right at the beginning of this film about growing up, growing old, meeting old friends, and leaving home.

Ozu's narratives are puzzles and mazes we are asked to figure out in terms of space, time, cause and effect, and meaning, but they are not ambiguous. Everything we need to understand the plot as Ozu intended it is there, but it is not always obvious. As noted above, Ozu's filmic discourse is, at times, similar to Japanese spoken discourse. If I ask a Japanese to do something for me, and he replies that it would be "difficult" (*muzukashii*),

I might interpret this as ambiguous: maybe he will or maybe he won't. But there is no ambiguity in my interlocutor's mind; he knows exactly what he means: he won't. In the same way, Ozu's narration is frequently indirect, but it is never ambiguous. He knows exactly what his story is, and he leaves enough clues that we can eventually figure it out.

The baby bootie at the end of *Dragnet Girl* is another case in which Bordwell sees "open-ended" narration. Did it actually belong to Tokiko? he asks. Did she knit it? Is she pregnant?[15] He suggests several times that, based on the baby bootie, Tokiko might be pregnant, but we have only to consider the extent to which such a plot point would completely deform Ozu's story to realize that this suggestion is absurd. First of all, if fast women like Tokiko or Misako were to get pregnant by their gangster boyfriends, they would have an abortion. If Tokiko were pregnant, and, unbeknownst to anyone else in the film, decided to keep her baby, she would hardly need Kazuko to convince her to go straight. Upon considering her boss's suggestion that she become his mistress, she tells him she is selfish, extravagant, and can't keep house. He praises her frankness, which does not include her saying "and by the way, I'm pregnant." Finally, she puts great pressure on Jyoji to go straight, even shooting him in the leg at the end of the film. Surely, pregnancy would have been yet another pressure point she would have applied if that indeed were the case. These characters reform because they love one another and awaken to a better sense of themselves, not because an unseen, unacknowledged, and disruptive force—a pregnancy—forces them to reform. The motivation, logic, and outcome of this story is clearly laid out. It is neither open-ended nor ambiguous.

The primary purpose of the baby bootie is to indicate that Tokiko has joined the ranks of "decent" women, most of whom sew or knit in Ozu's films. (See Chapter 10.) Tokiko had promised to knit Jyoji some socks, but those who remember the hand-knit socks in *Days of Youth*, which got pitched out the train window, will probably agree that a man's sock hanging on the fence would be far less poignant than the small baby's sock. The baby sock also suggests the new life Jyoji and Tokiko will undertake once they are out of prison and the new life they may yet engender. The suggestion of *future* fecundity is, after all, conceivably present at the end of *Walk Cheerfully*, from which *Dragnet Girl* takes its basic story, in the shot of an empty clothesline that gives way to a full clothesline. The baby bootie likewise suggests what may lie ahead, not a current condition.

While the baby bootie doesn't indicate an open-ended narrative, it does tell us that Ozu privileged his subtexts and symbolism over complete narrative coherence or credibility. Most storytelling requires the viewer or listener to suspend disbelief to a certain degree, and Ozu's stories are no different. The problem with the little sock at the end of *Dragnet Girl* is not that it is ambiguous but that it requires us to believe that between the time Tokiko makes up with Jyoji and they execute their robbery and getaway, there has been time for her to roll up the yarn and knit the little sock. (Remember: all on the same day Tokiko comes home from work, meets and threatens rival Kazuko, shops for yarn, fights with Jyoji, goes out with her boss in the evening, makes up with Jyoji, hears Hiroshi's predicament, and formulates a plan for their robbery. Did she also stay up for the rest of the night knitting?) Yet the subtext, the black-and-white symbolism, is rendered perfectly: the sock is knit from the light and dark yarn we've seen Tokiko bring home, the two balls of yarn lie near one another on the floor of Jyoji's apartment, and some tangled black yarn—the couple's heretofore tangled life—remains elsewhere on the floor.

The black yarn/white yarn symbolism also contains a continuity failure, which similarly indicates that Ozu's interest lay as much with his subtext as with his text. After Jyoji agrees to go straight, there is a long shot of him and Tokiko embracing (Figure 4.3), then a cut to her feet tangled in the yarn that had been thrown around during their fight (Figure 4.4). In the long shot of the embrace, however, no yarn touches her shoes. Intent on his symbolism, Ozu ignored continuity, guessing rightly that, in most cases, audience members would not notice. The narrow window in *Walk Cheerfully* where the unknown secretary has placed her compact, which is missing from Yasue's POV shot of Kenji washing windows, is simply another example of Ozu ignoring continuity, not an example of ambiguity.

There are, in fact, quite a number of continuity failures in Ozu's early films. Bordwell might be inclined to attribute them to Ozu's "play," particularly when they involve time-pieces, but some are obviously oversights.[16] In *Woman of Tokyo*, for example, Ryoichi slaps Chikako very hard, but, although she faces toward the camera while she chastises him, there are no marks on her face until, some minutes later, we see her reflection in her mirror, by which point the make-up crew has painted the imprint of Ryoichi's hand

Figure 4.3: As Jyoji and Tokiko embrace in *Dragnet Girl*, there is no yarn on her shoes.

Figure 4.4: In the following close-up, Tokiko's shoes are tangled in black yarn.

on her face very prominently. When Tokiko in *Dragnet Girl* turns around angrily to face Misako, who has come back into Jyoji's apartment, the medium shot of her staring at Misako reveals that the strap on her dress has fallen off her shoulder. (See Figure 3.1, p. 60.) The fallen strap emphasizes the intimacy of the moment that Misako has interrupted, but Jyoji has not pulled the strap down, and, even though we see Tokiko turn, we never actually see the strap fall off her shoulder. Ozu was more concerned about the impact and import of his shots than about perfect continuity.

Numerous witnesses have testified to Ozu's relative indifference to continuity. In general, their comments reflect on the director's desire to frame shots perfectly, thus moving props around to create the desired composition. Clearly, Ozu also ignored continuity when he wanted his shot to make a dramatic or symbolic point.[17]

Substitution

Another example of Ozu's indirectness is his occasional substitution of a minor character for a major one as a way of tamping down the emotional temperature in his films. The most obvious example is the student we see in *I Flunked, But* . . . who is agonizing in front of the dean because the protagonist, Takahashi, who tutored him, has failed the final exam. Later he comes into the coffee shop where Takahashi is blowing smoke

Narrative Strategies, Texts, and Subtexts

at the goldfish bowl and again expresses his anguish over the unfairness of it all. The smoke (see Chapter 2) and this student cue us to Takahashi's own low feelings while he himself never expresses them overtly.

In *Tokyo Chorus*, the hero, Okajima, passes unemployed laborers on his way to the employment office. Instead of following Okajima on his fruitless visit, the camera stays with the laborers, two of whom are scrounging cigarette butts, including one Okajima throws away. The men are not meant to contrast with Okajima but to represent his desperation. The smoking chimneys, shown early in the sequence, link to the chimney Okajima sees from his house at several points in the film. By staying with the laborers, Ozu avoids showing us Okajima's emotional state, giving it to us through the workers by inference. Later, when Okajima must perform manual labor and afterward confront his mortified wife, he describes himself as "a drowning man." This confrontation between Okajima and his wife, the film's emotional climax, comes across as especially strong because we have not seen him describe his desperation before. Yet by identifying him with the laborers in the earlier scene, Ozu has prepared us for it.

In *A Story of Floating Weeds*, well before we learn about Kihachi's son and former mistress, the barber's wife, a pretty if plump middle-aged woman, expresses her infatuation with Kihachi, much to her husband's discomfiture. Later we see her in the theater, clapping enthusiastically for Kihachi, even after Tomibo as the "dog" has ruined his performance. Through her we understand the process by which Otsune, Kihachi's former mistress, fell in love with him twenty years earlier while Otsune herself, although still in love, remains much more subdued.

Misreading *Woman of Tokyo*

Bordwell is not alone in occasionally misreading Ozu's stories. In Chapter 2, based on my analysis of Ozu's signs and symbols, I presented an alternative to the usual view of *Woman of Tokyo*, which is generally seen as the *shinpa*-inspired story of a woman sacrificing herself for her brother. Bordwell, Tony Rayns, Anthony Nield, Mitsuyo Wada-Marciano, and Woojeong Joo all discuss the film in these terms.[18] Rayns admits that Ozu did not generally use *shinpa*-inspired stories but believes *Woman of Tokyo* is an exception.

On the surface the film appears to be a *shinpa*-esque melodrama, but Ozu had other mentors. The name of the film is taken from Chaplin's *Woman of Paris*, in which the eponymous woman, separated from her fiancé, becomes a Parisian courtesan whose inability to leave the riches of that life drives the fiancé, who has managed to find her again, to suicide. Chastened, she departs for the countryside to spend her life caring for young orphans. Bordwell notes that "Ozu was immensely impressed by *Woman of Paris* and throughout his career cited it as a model of the well-constructed film."[19] Given the Japanese setting and the myriad stories of victimized women in Japanese literature, it is natural for critics to read *Woman of Tokyo* in that light.[20] As we have seen in Chapter 2, however, Ozu's story is closer to Chaplin's moral tale.

Isolde Standish, who sees Chikako's prostitution as somehow "modern" as defined by 1930s Japan, interprets *Woman of Tokyo* as "patriarchal masculinity . . . being criticized for its inability to come to terms with the modern world."[21] On the contrary, Ozu is far from equating prostitution with the demands of the modern world. (It is after all the "oldest profession.") Chikako's brother, Ryoichi, who will eventually commit suicide, is shocked, disillusioned, and afraid for their reputations and their already fragile status as middle-class citizens. It is Chikako's insistence on sacrificing herself for him that is more in keeping with feudal patriarchy than is his desire to preserve their middle-class respectability.[22]

(Chikako is the film's central character and, unlike Chaplin's heroine, does not repent but remains defiant at the end of the film. She has, after all, sacrificed everything for her brother, and he has, indeed, not understood her sacrifice in that light. She is a tragic character, and we sympathize with her, but Ozu makes it clear that the tragedy is of her own making. She is not a victim, as *shinpa* drama tends to cast its female characters.)

Wada-Marciano goes further in misreading this film by assuming that an original subplot involving Chikako's allegiance to the Communist Party remains intact.[23] In the original script, money from Chikako's moonlighting as a cabaret hostess went to the Party as well as to her brother. Wada-Marciano believes this element remains in the film and that, given the leftist purges in Japan at the time, a contemporary audience would have understood this from all the whispering and the announcement at the end of the film that a "criminal gang" had been apprehended.[24]

In keeping with what Darrell Davis describes as "an overwhelming fashion for Marxism in the late 1920s," Ozu made several nods to communism in his early films.[25] Marx's picture hangs, rather improbably, in the young baron's home in *The Lady and the Beard* and appears behind the hero in a number of shots. (The portrait may reference his rebelliousness if not his politics.) In *I Flunked, But . . .* the roommates raise clenched fists while forming the word "Bread" with their arms and legs —a riff on the communist slogan "Peace, Land, Bread!"— as a signal to the baker's daughter that they want her to bring them some bread to snack on. In addition, the theme of workers' solidarity runs throughout *Tokyo Chorus*, beginning with Okajima's protest against Yamada's firing, then the interchange between Okajima and the boss's secretary when the latter loses the heel of his shoe, the laborers who are identified with Okajima when he visits the employment office, and the manual labor he is forced to undertake soon after. A painted sign in the Hashizume apartment in *That Night's Wife* is in Russian, and certainly images of the oppressive state and the comical policemen at the beginning of that film serve as an oblique commentary on the government's communist purges.

That said, the idea that *Woman of Tokyo*'s Chikako would have been understood as a Communist Party member, even though it had been written out of the script, seems fanciful. Like an architectural work that has been repurposed, in which traces of its original form and uses are still evident, the present form of *Woman of Tokyo* contains elements that don't quite fit. The policeman at the film's beginning who comes to Chikako's office to inquire about her seems like a heavy-handed plot device if the complaint against Chikako is that she is an unlicensed prostitute. Such women must have been a dime a dozen in the 1930s, yet that is the ostensible reason for the interest the police take in Chikako in the finished version of the film. Two rumors about Chikako are revealed to Harue by her brother, Kinoshita, and then by Harue to her boyfriend, Ryoichi, Chikako's brother. Kinoshita tells Harue first that Chikako is working as a cabaret hostess and then whispers something to her, presumably that the police suspect she is also working as a prostitute. But when Harue tells Ryoichi, she whispers something first and then says aloud that Chikako is working as a cabaret hostess. What did she say when she whispered? The worst first, that the police suspect Chikako is a prostitute? Possibly Harue started with the suspicion and ended with the confirmed fact that Chikako is moonlighting as a cabaret hostess, but it would all make more sense if one of the suspicions was that she was involved with the Party. Finally, the intrusion of the reporters at the end of the film disrupts what is otherwise a highly structured, unified diegesis with intense moral and religious overtones. The indifference of the self-seeking, secular, callous reporters is the point, but that doesn't make the ending fit with the rest of the film. If, however, Chikako were a communist, the interest on the part of the press would make more sense.

These are the elements that lead Wada-Marciano to conclude that the communist storyline is still present but disguised. I read these rather as remnants and inconsistencies left over from a script that was changed very quickly since Ozu made the film in only one week. That he left in the grossly caricatured journalists is understandable, given how short the film is, presumably because the subplot was eliminated. In backing her Communist Party reading, Wada-Marciano doubts that Chikako really is a prostitute: "This information [what Harue whispers] effectively undercuts the possibility that Chikako's . . . disgrace involves prostitution."[26] But Ozu makes it very clear that Chikako is a prostitute when he shows her getting into a taxi with a leering customer (Figure 4.5) after calling her brother to tell him that she will be home late. This man is clearly a john, not a comrade.[27]

Finally, allowing the audience to assume Chikako is a Party member without ever saying so leaves no room for the filmmaker or the audience to contest the meaning of such in the same way that Chikako's prostitution is contested by Ryoichi, Harue, the police, and Chikako herself, all of whom perceive it somewhat differently. Ozu himself characterizes it with a shot of a sink full of dirty water as well as the striped shadows that fall on her and the other bargirls, such shadows being a Hollywood cliché for compromised characters. (They will be echoed in the striped bruise on her cheek in a subsequent sequence.) No opinion is or can be offered regarding a supposed affiliation with the communists because it is never mentioned.

Ozu's films pursued many lines of inquiry, some obvious, some subtle, but they were not intentionally ambiguous and did not contain hidden, unmentioned storylines. His camera placements, mise-en-scène, and cutting style make us work to reconstruct his stories, and his use of substitution, as well as a hefty dose of symbolism, guides us to

Figure 4.5: Chikako's customer waits for her in a car in *Woman of Tokyo*.

meanings that may not be apparent on the surface but which can be demonstrated by each film's own internal evidence.

Of Men and Children

In the prologue to *Tokyo Chorus*, the hero, Okajima, is presented as an irreverent, playful, rebellious schoolboy, who carries a yo-yo, a child's toy. At scene's end he tries to light a cigarette, a grown-up activity, but can't manage it. Transitioning to the adult Okajima, a title tells us that "Several Years Later" he works for an insurance company. However, the shots that follow this title are not of an insurance agent or an office and only belatedly include a person at home, among his children, getting ready for work. This would appear to be Ozu's usual obfuscation of plot, but it reveals an important subtext. The sequence runs as follows:

1) A desk with books, an alarm clock, a child's hat and a doll; hands reach in and pull several things out of this mélange.
2) A man in his underwear—the camera showing only his hips and waist—holds two objects, a mirror and a baby's pacifier.
3) His hands place the mirror on a bookshelf.

Narrative Strategies, Texts, and Subtexts   79

4) MS of the man, Okajima, tying his tie in the mirror with the pacifier in his mouth; he looks up.
5) Cutaway to a smoking chimney; wind is blowing the smoke to screen left.
6) Repeat of shot #4; Okajima looks back down at his mirror, and a child's paper balloon comes flying at him.
7) Match-on-action as the balloon falls to his feet; we see Okajima from the knees down only; his hand reaches down to pick up the balloon.
8) Match-on-action to a FS as Okajima tosses the balloon.
9) Match-on-action with a 180° cut to a FS of his daughter catching the balloon.
10) 180° cut to FS of Okajima reframed so that there is enough room for his daughter to come into the shot; he finally takes the pacifier out of his mouth and finishes tying his tie.

While we wait for the sequence to show us an insurance agent and get on with the story, Ozu instead shows us the story he wants to tell, namely that, like the student we saw in the prologue, Okajima is still a child. If that seems like an unfair assessment—he is, after all, surrounded by his three children and their toys—consider that throughout this sequence Okajima has the pacifier—which he has picked up from the desk, not taken from his baby—in his mouth (Figure 4.6). This is another example of Ozu

Figure 4.6: Okajima holds his baby's pacifier in his mouth as he dresses for work in *Tokyo Chorus*.

privileging a symbol over narrative logic, for there is no logical explanation for Okajima picking up the pacifier, much less putting it in his mouth.

These introductory shots are also an example of not following the bear. Although they seem to be merely Ozu's roundabout way of introducing a scene with parts rather than a whole establishing shot, they prepare us for the real story: Okajima growing up.

When we finally see the insurance agent we have been told to expect, we find that most of the agents in his office are also childish as they sneak off to the urinals to inspect their bonuses. Okajima, however, outdoes them all by, on a dare, going to the boss to defend Yamada, an older worker who has been fired, and not simply registering a complaint but becoming so worked up over his cause that he starts assaulting the boss physically.

Okajima is, understandably, fired, and, hoping to cut back on expenses, gets his son a scooter instead of a promised bicycle. His son rebels and provokes Okajima to the point that he spanks the boy soundly, a parallel to his own childish behavior with the boss and the extreme consequences.

Ozu continues his adult-as-child motif when Okajima meets Yamada, the laid-off former co-worker, outside the zoo. They see a child throwing a tantrum, and Yamada remarks on the freedom children have to "just bawl their heads off." Okajima agrees; it is the first time he admits to understanding the difference between adults and children. Subsequently, he meets his teacher, Omura, first seen in the prologue, in the street, and he reverts back into his student-self, consciously standing up straight the way Omura taught him. Later Omura will admonish him to stand up straight while carrying banners that advertise the retired teacher's restaurant. Although Okajima remains cooperative, he makes it clear, both before and during, that this task is as annoying as his drills in school. The scene ends with little children pestering him as he carries the banners, much as his own children pester him at home.

His moment of epiphany comes when he faces down his wife, Sugako's, criticism after she has seen him carrying the banners like a common laborer. He looks in one direction at the smokestack visible from his house, then in another direction at laundry flapping in the wind and says, "I feel like I'm getting old." Ozu doesn't leave much daylight between the irresponsibilities of childhood and the disappointments of adulthood, but Okajima has finally come to recognize the inevitability of the latter. At this point he and Sugako reach a moment of mutual understanding—both are growing up. Later she agrees that he should accept the less-than-perfect job he is offered at the end of the story.

The shot in which Okajima and Sugako mull over the job offer, which will require them to leave Tokyo, is framed with their baby in the foreground. In a subsequent two-shot of the couple, Sugako looks back at the baby, then says, "I'm sure we can return to Tokyo someday." Their responsibility for the next generation overwhelms her disappointment, and both parents accept the need to set aside their own desires for the sake of their children.

The interplay and occasional role reversal between men and children is one of the recurrent subtexts in the silent films. Bordwell often mentions the humiliation Ozu's men endure, a reversal of their society's patriarchal ideals.[28] Frequently that humiliation involves identifying them with children.

In the films that followed *Tokyo Chorus*, *I Was Born, But . . .* and *Passing Fancy*, Ozu continued to explore variations on the need to grow up. In *I Was Born, But . . .* the little boys have to accept some of the realities of adult life, namely, the economic necessity of submitting to a hierarchical society even at the cost of one's dignity. The adults' indulgence in child or college-boy play in this film appears to be safely confined to the home movie, which shows zoo animals, the father's boss, Iwasaki, flirting with geishas, and the father, Yoshii, clowning—except that neither Yoshii's boys nor Iwasaki's wife are willing to grant this behavior a safe space, and both men have some explaining to do. We don't see the probable exchange between Iwasaki and his wife, but Yoshii, of course, is forced to explain some of what is involved in putting food on the table. The boys' brief hunger strike helps them to accept this aspect of the adult world.

As soon as the boys give their father permission to greet his boss in an appropriately subordinate manner, harmony is restored. Questioning the boss's son, Taro, as to who has the best father, each boy concedes that the other's father is best. Taro submits to the children's "killing" ritual, but then jumps up, and the three walk off with arms around each other's shoulders. They meet Kamekichi, the bully, who is stumped by the ring puzzle he stole from the brothers some days earlier. Older brother Ryoichi solves the puzzle, then reassembles it, and returns it to the still mystified Kamekichi. The boys bow to their passing teacher, and Kamekichi, having been preoccupied with the puzzle, runs after him to register his bow. Then he walks amiably to school with his pals. Other boys run into the street until a fairly large mass of happy children is making its way to school, and the film ends. The harmony we see here has been based on cooperation, compromise, and knowing one's place.[29]

Citing American films as Ozu's inspiration, Gregory Barrett calls the fathers in *Tokyo Chorus* and *I Was Born, But . . .* "democratic fathers" because they seem to be on the same level as their children.[30] However, Ozu's portrayal of these fathers is a good deal more complex than their seemingly egalitarian relationship to their children: they wrestle with life's compromises vis-à-vis their offspring. The adults are less sanguine than the children regarding the concessions their lives require, but in one way or another most of them grow up. Ozu's Kihachi series provides the exception to this rule.

In *Passing Fancy*, the little boy Tomio has been forced to become the adult in the family because of his father's refusal to grow up, which does not change throughout the film. In the beginning we see Tomio acting as a parent, waking up both his father and their neighbor Jiro in the morning and helping his father to dress. There is obvious irony when father Kihachi says: "Obey your parents while they're alive," because it is Tomio who acts like the parent in this scene. This irony is reinforced by Tomio's calligraphy exercise, which hangs next to his desk and reiterates the importance of filial piety.

In addition to caring for his father, Tomio takes it upon himself to excel at school despite their poverty. Throughout this early portion of the film, Tomio wears an eye patch. (See Figure 10.1, p. 205.) We don't know what happened to his eye, but the patch reminds us that, despite the adult role he has taken on, he is still a vulnerable child.

Halfway through the film, Tomio's "adultness" literally breaks down. When some children bully him, citing his father's illiteracy and irresponsibility, he starts to cry and doesn't stop until he has destroyed his father's bonsai gingko tree, beaten his father's head, and, eventually, thrown himself sobbing into his father's arms. By this time, Tomio has ceased wearing the eye patch, and from this point on he acts much more like a child: he lets Kihachi dress him, eats too much candy and gets sick, and bursts out crying again when Kihachi leaves for Hokkaido.

For his part, Kihachi tries for a time to be a responsible parent but ultimately fails. He nurses Tomio through his illness, but three times offers Tomio up for dead, speculating once on what to wear to his funeral, telling ingénue Harue that Tomio would have gladly died to hear of her generosity, and expressing exasperation by telling Tomio that he should have died. To his neighbors' horror, he abandons his son in order to join a work crew going to Hokkaido (ostensibly to pay Tomio's hospital bills) and insists that "kids can grow up without parents." Although the film leaves him swimming back to Tomio, we understand that, despite his obvious affection, he will never grow up or care for Tomio properly.

The American film *The Champ* (1931) is said to have inspired *Passing Fancy*, and both celebrate the bond between an irresponsible father and a son who seeks to care for him. However, the American film ends with the father's death and the boy passing into the responsible care of his divorced mother and her new husband. In *Passing Fancy*, nothing changes for Tomio.

Ozu made two more "Kihachi" films, *An Inn in Tokyo* and *A Story of Floating Weeds*, both about fathers with sons. Although not as obviously irresponsible as the Kihachi of *Passing Fancy*, both men abandon their sons.

In *The Chrysanthemum and the Sword*, Ruth Benedict described, in 1946, the differences between childrearing practices in Japan and the West. Japanese children, she reported, were greatly indulged until the age of nine, at which point their freedoms were increasingly restricted, reaching a nadir just before and after marriage. Having known the freedoms of childhood, however, men in particular did not always make the transition from childhood to adulthood completely.[31]

Ozu frequently portrayed men who either had difficulty transitioning to adulthood or found ways around it, and he knew these men well: he had himself turned his youthful passion into a career, thereby prolonging his childhood; he failed to marry, living most of his life with his devoted mother; and he drank too much. In addition, he channeled an irrepressible sense of both rebellion and humor into his art.[32]

Ozu briefly revisited his men-as-children theme in *The Only Son*, his first talkie. Discouraged with his lack of advancement, despite a good education, the protagonist, Ryosuke, tells his mother he wishes he had stayed with her in their mountain village

Narrative Strategies, Texts, and Subtexts

and later sticks the nipple end of his son's baby bottle in his mouth. The many shots of his sleeping baby echo those at the end of *Tokyo Chorus* and stress the need to sacrifice for the baby's future. But the drawing of a child, hung upside down in Ryosuke's home, alludes more to an upside down, i.e., failed, process by which education no longer helps a man advance in life than to Ryosuke's failure to grow up.

The drawing of the upside down child pinned to a *fusuma* (sliding screen) in Ryosuke's home is yet another example of Ozu's fascination with the meaninglessness of direction, whether in society, politics, police work, film editing, or story construction. Although many of his films end by reaffirming the necessity of conforming to society's norms, a tension always exists between that affirmation and an equally strong belief that "following the bear won't affect our lives in any way," a rejection of prescribed or popular directions. He observed morals in important things, he would say, but "I stick to my own path when it comes to art."[33]

Notes

1. Quoted in Kiju Yoshida, *Ozu's Anti-Cinema*, trans. Daisuke Miyao and Kyoko Hirano (Ann Arbor, MI: Center for Japanese Studies, 2003), 2.
2. David Bordwell, *Narration in the Fiction Film* (Madison, WI: University of Wisconsin Press, 1985), 288.
3. Bordwell, *Narration in the Fiction Film*, 282.
4. Thompson, *Breaking the Glass Armor*, 347. Thompson also relates Tadao Sato's anecdote of Ozu setting up shots and making his assistants move furniture several inches one way or another. "When all the assistants grew tired, Ozu used to . . . joke . . . 'Toward Tokyo!' or 'Toward Atami!' instead of to the left or right."
5. Bordwell, *Poetics*, 272.
6. Richie, *Ozu*, 152–53.
7. David Desser refers to this phenomenon as "retrospectivity." See "Introduction: A Filmmaker for All Seasons," in *Ozu's Tokyo Story*, ed. David Desser (Cambridge: Cambridge University Press, 1997), 6.
8. Anderson, "Spoken Silents," 285.
9. David Bordwell has described the difference between Ozu's "parametric" style and the less consistent "flourishes" common in his contemporaries' work in both his *Poetics*, 24–25, and in a subsequent article: "A Cinema of Flourishes: Japanese Decorative Classicism of the Prewar Era," in Nolletti and Desser, *Reframing Japanese Cinema*, 328–37. Mitsuyo Wada-Marciano seems unaware of both these works when she writes in *Nippon Modern* that "Bordwell's exhaustive work on Ozu ascribes the technical and narrational refinements of Ozu's filmmaking style to his singular creative talents without acknowledging that many of the same stylistic elements are shown in equal measure in the works of other Kamata filmmakers such as Shimazu Yasujiro," and concludes that "the overwhelming sense is that Japanese cinema itself has not been extensively researched and that many films have simply not been seen" (Wada-Marciano, *Nippon Modern*, 113). The latter assertion is to a large extent true, but both Bordwell and Donald Richie had seen a great many Japanese films when they wrote about Ozu's singularity, and Bordwell points clearly to the fact that

"Ozu and the norms of his early period cannot, of course, be starkly separated, since he also shaped them. Many Shochiku directors of the 1930s . . . were his pupils" (Bordwell, *Poetics*, 25). Shochiku's head, Shiro Kido, told Mikio Naruse, "We don't need two Ozus," when Naruse was inclined to imitate Ozu, and Bordwell notes, moreover, that Shimazu borrowed from *I Was Born, But . . .* in *My Neighbor, Miss Yae*, one of the films Wada-Marciano analyzes in detail. See Wada-Marciano, *Nippon Modern*, 114ff.

10. Bordwell, *Poetics*, 64ff.
11. Noël Burch, *To the Distant Observer: Form and Meaning in the Japanese Cinema* (Berkeley, CA: University of California Press, 1979), 160ff; Kristin Thompson and David Bordwell, "Space and Narrative in the Films of Ozu," *Screen* 17, no. 2 (Summer 1976): 70.
12. Bordwell, *Poetics*, 65ff.
13. Bordwell, *Poetics*, 201.
14. Bordwell, *Poetics*, 219.
15. Bordwell, *Poetics*, 65, 247.
16. Bordwell, *Poetics*, 131.
17. Keisuke Kinoshita and Shohei Imamura, both of whom worked for Ozu as assistant directors, as well as art director Tatsuo Hamada, have testified to Ozu's indifference to strict continuity. See Tadao Sato, *The Art of Yasujiro Ozu 4*, trans. Goro Iiri (1974), 94; Kazuo Inoue, *I Lived, But . . . [Ikite wa mita keredo]* (Tokyo: Shochiku, 1983).
18. Bordwell, *Poetics*, 237; Tony Rayns, "The Melodrama Option," *Three Melodramas* (London: British Film Institute, n.d.), 2; Anthony Nield, "Woman of Tokyo," *Three Melodramas* (London: British Film Institute, n.d.), 6–7; Wada-Marciano, *Nippon Modern*, 91; Joo, *Ozu*, 97.
19. Bordwell, *Poetics*, 152.
20. Scott Nygren, *Time Frames: Japanese Cinema and the Unfolding of History* (Minneapolis, MN: University of Minnesota Press, 2007), 35. See also Russell, "Insides and Outsides," 146. The sacrificial woman is also a trope in Chinese literature, a kind of collective Christ figure for Confucianism.
21. Isolde Standish, *A New History of Japanese Cinema: A Century of Narrative Film* (New York: Continuum International, 2005), 61–62.
22. Standish insists on interpreting the title of this film as "*Women of Tokyo*," thus undercutting its obvious relationship with Chaplin's *Woman of Paris*. She also misreads the story's time-frame and the location of the final scenes. See Standish, *A New History of Japanese Cinema*, 72.
23. Wada-Marciano, *Nippon Modern*, 92.
24. Wada-Marciano, *Nippon Modern*, 93–94.
25. Darrell William Davis, *Picturing Japaneseness: Monumental Style, National Identity, Japanese Film* (New York: Columbia University Press, 1996), 60.
26. Wada-Marciano, *Nippon Modern*, 92.
27. Woojeong Joo follows Wada-Marciano in supposing the script's communist element remains in the film and in being uncertain that Chikako is a prostitute despite no evidence for the former and clear evidence for the latter. See Joo, *Ozu*, 90, 93, 101.
28. Bordwell, *Poetics*, 43 (and frequently thereafter).
29. Tadao Sato sees Ozu's films aiming for "harmony rather than confrontations." See Sato, *Art of Yasujiro Ozu 4* (1974), 90. Ozu is quoted in a 1955 interview saying, "I do cherish the harmony among people above all else." See Kometani, *Chasing Ozu*, 44.

30. Gregory Barrett, *Archetypes in Japanese Film: The Sociopolitical and Religious Significance of the Principal Heroes and Heroines* (Selinsgrove, PA: Susquehanna University Press, 1989), 169–70.

31. Benedict, *The Chrysanthemum and the Sword*, 254, 286ff.

32. Ozu's identifying adults as children and vice versa is captured in the subtitle he gave to *I Was Born, But . . .*—"A Picture Book for Grown-Ups"—and to a poem he wrote many years later in honor of his deceased mother, which he described as "a nursery song for the aged." Inoue, *I Lived, But . . .*

33. Yoshida, *Ozu's Anti-Cinema*, 14.

Afterword Part I: "... when the studio was in Kamata"

Ozu's silent films had been made at Shochiku's Kamata studio in Tokyo, but as sound came in, filming in Kamata became increasingly difficult because the city, with all its industrial noises, was growing up around it, and in 1936 Shochiku relocated to the Ofuna district in Kamakura. Typically, Ozu was the last one out the door of the Kamata studio, making his last silent film, *College Is a Nice Place* (*Daigaku yoitoko*, 1936), as well as his first talkie, *The Only Son*, there.

From time to time Ozu cited his earlier films in later ones, although it can be difficult to distinguish a deliberate citation from all the bits and pieces he recycled from one film to the next. However, in his first color film, *Equinox Flower*, he made obvious references to four of his silent films. "Ever with us are the dreams of youth," says one character in the film's reunion sequence. *Dreams of Youth* is the title of Ozu's second film (*Wakodo no yume*, 1928). No longer extant, it concerned college-boy high jinks, but the title was recycled into *Where Now Are the Dreams of Youth?* which combined comedy with a serious look at the strains on friendship post-college life can bring. Star of that film, Ureo Egawa, appears, gray-haired and middle-aged, in a cameo in *Equinox Flower*'s reunion scene. (See colorplate 1B.) Kinuyo Tanaka, who plays the mother in *Equinox Flower*, starred in both *Where Now Are the Dreams of Youth?* and *Dragnet Girl. Equinox Flower* makes specific reference to *Dragnet Girl* with a shot of an all-neon Nipper dog beaming from the top of Tokyo's RCA building. Meanwhile, window washers, seen from both inside and outside the protagonist's office building in *Equinox Flower*, are an obvious reference to *Walk Cheerfully*.

The Japanese New Wave was beginning to emerge at the time Ozu made *Equinox Flower*. Takashi Kawamata, who worked for a decade on Ozu films as an assistant cameraman, went on to become the chief cinematographer for many New Wave films. Not long before his death, Ozu congratulated Kawamata on his success in the new genre, then added wistfully, "I used to be one [avant-garde filmmaker] myself when the studio was in Kamata."[1]

Note

1. Makoto Igarashi, *Ozu's Films from Behind the Scenes* [Ozugumi no seisaku genba kara] (Tokyo: Shochiku, 2003). This short film is available on Criterion's *Early Summer* DVD, 2004.

Part II

War and Peace: The Sound Films, 1936–1952

Ozu's first ten sound films were made against the backdrop of Japan's war in China, the Pacific War, and the American Occupation of Japan. Chapters 5 through 7 examine the content and context of each film in light of this history.

5
The Calm

As the [1930s] advanced, the graphic record of these brittle years conveys stress and contradiction in every direction.

—John Dower[1]

Nationalism and Internationalism

The first time *All Quiet on the Western Front* (Lewis Milestone, 1930) was shown in Berlin, December 5, 1930, Hitler's minions staged a preplanned, well-orchestrated demonstration against it: Nazis planted in the audience rose up to shout it down. The projectionist was forced to turn off the film, whereupon Joseph Goebbels gave a speech from the balcony, after which his comrades threw stink bombs and released white mice into the audience. With Nazi help, protests against the film spread throughout Germany. Six days after its Berlin premier, the film was banned in Germany.[2]

Nothing similar happened in Japan. The already prestigious pacifist film opened in the fall of 1930, won the *Kinema Junpo* first prize for a foreign film, and evoked tears from a Japanese audience, torn between the ideals of war and peace. Peter B. High writes that, since Japan, unlike Europe, had never known the devastation of total war, "there was [in 1930] neither the ideological nor the essential basis for widespread, deeply rooted pacifism." The film could never have evoked the extreme partisanship in Japan that it did in Germany, in which both the film and the novel it was based on were set; nevertheless, it caught the eye of Japanese censors. It was cut in 280 places, losing 20 percent of its length. The deleted scenes included those depicting death in battle, the screams of the wounded, and the hero's ambivalence toward killing. Even before the Manchurian Incident on September 18, 1931, the Japanese government had no intention of dampening the public's perception of war as worthy and valorous.[3]

Ozu included a poster for *All Quiet on the Western Front* in *Dragnet Girl* (1933). The multinational contributions to both the film and the poster—Ozu managed to come up with a French version of the poster—reflect the internationalism continually present—via advertisements, movie posters, and other props—in his early films. One wonders, though, if his choice of a French poster in this instance was motivated by his desire to avoid the censors' notice, for by 1933 Japan was at war in Manchuria.

Filmmakers in this period were forever dodging or throwing bones to the censors.[4] The latter often took the form of inserting pro-military content into scripts and films. Ozu did this with his boys' stories: not only do the little boys in *I Was Born, But . . .* want to be generals, but a reference to a 1932 suicide mission by soldiers in Manchuria, whipped up in the press and recounted in popular movies, is prominently displayed on a sign in the classroom scene.[5] High reports that the scripted ending to the movie had the older boy meeting up with some soldiers before returning home.[6] Obviously, that scene never made it into the final film, and it is hard to believe Ozu ever intended that it should. Other reminders of militarism, possibly censor-driven, in his early films include the many references to Jiro's military service in *Passing Fancy* as well as movie posters referring to Manchuria in that film. In addition, the company test in *Where Now Are the Dreams of Youth?* contains a question about the Manchurian Incident.

While Ozu threw sops to the censors, he also included sly references that either undercut or questioned his government's positions. In *Passing Fancy* Tomio practices his calligraphy with a paean to filial piety, a moral precept the Japanese government wished to see reinforced, but his father, of course, is nothing like the patriarch imagined in Confucian orthodoxy. In *A Story of Floating Weeds*, Kihachi's play is an 1870 Kabuki drama called *Murubashi Chūya* or *Keian Taiheiki*, based on an abortive 1651 uprising against the shogun, which, nevertheless, sparked uprisings throughout the country in succeeding years. In 1931 and 1932 militarists had assassinated two prime ministers. A third had already been assassinated in 1921. Ozu's choice of drama for Kihachi's performance suggests the fragility of Japan's government in the face of determined opposition.

Along with the compliance and subversion observable in the early films are the many props that suggest Ozu's enthusiastic embrace of foreign influences in keeping with Japan's internationalism in the 1920s and early 1930s. These include the plethora of foreign or Western-inspired objects in *That Night's Wife*; almost the entire milieu of the gangster films, including jazz, boxing, Victrolas, English graffiti, and movie posters; the posters, pennants, and advertisements, mainly in English, in the student films, and the array of foreign movie posters in *A Mother Should Be Loved*. Of particular note in this regard are the international flag decorations used in the party sequences of *Walk Cheerfully* and *Tokyo Chorus*.[7] These are on-screen longest in *Tokyo Chorus*, where they arch above the teacher, Omura, as he sits at the head of the table. Five medium shots of Omura show his head framed by the American flag to the left and the Japanese flag to the right. (See Figure 2.4, p. 50.) For Japanese at this time, the United States stood for everything that was modern and progressive. (It was also heralded as a fellow colonizer).[8]

Countering such unabashed enthusiasm for things foreign were Japan's growing militarism, nativism, and isolationism. In 1933 both Japan and Germany withdrew from the League of Nations. Meanwhile, Japan's slide into economic depression worsened.

The Calm 91

Depression (*The Only Son*, 1936)

As the Depression deepened, Ozu's films, already laden with irony regarding education (or the lack of it) and work in 1930s Japan, became darker with *An Inn in Tokyo, College is a Nice Place,* and *The Only Son.* For Ozu's characters, any work is difficult to find, good jobs impossible, and the value of education questionable. Despite his characters' vows to keep on trying, prostitution, robbery, despair, and death come to seem like reasonable responses to hopeless poverty.

The Only Son specifically critiques the value of education as a guarantee of upward mobility. Early in the film, the son, Ryosuke, sits at the top of a stairway in his mother's home, listening as she speaks with his teacher, Okubo. Ryosuke has lied to the teacher, telling him that his mother will send him to high school, which is news to Otsune, his mother. She struggles to maintain face while listening to Okubo describe the necessity of higher education and his own ambition to leave their village and continue his studies in Tokyo. When Okubo leaves, Otsune calls Ryosuke, who comes down the stairs, emblematic of the upward mobility he seeks, and tells him she cannot afford to send him to high school. Throughout the scene, we hear the sound of the spinning machines from the silk factory in which Otsune works. This sound effectively announces the path Ryosuke will follow if he doesn't get more education.

Later, Otsune relents and spends all she has sending Ryosuke to high school and college in Tokyo, but a visit to him thirteen years later reveals that her sacrifices did not bring the promised status or security. Neither Ryosuke nor Okubo has done well in Tokyo. Ryosuke's only job is teaching night school, and Okubo, now burdened with four children, runs a small cutlet (*tonkatsu*) restaurant. Ryosuke lives in a poor neighborhood where textiles are manufactured, and, ironically, the sound from this small cottage industry permeates his home just as the sound of the spinning wheels was constantly present in his mother's home.

Of the many shots in Ryosuke's house, some include a bookshelf crammed with books, but his education has not brought him a decent living. In a hospital sequence, Ryosuke stands near a medical manikin, half of whose "skin" is intact but whose other side is exposed to reveal the inner anatomy. Ryosuke's juxtaposition to the half-flayed manikin suggests his vulnerable state.

Competing narratives, however, suggest varying reasons behind Ryosuke's failure. Are the times so bad that even the highly educated cannot get ahead, or is Ryosuke simply not ambitious enough as his mother insists? He has, for example, married the daughter of the owner of the restaurant near where he boarded during college—a character familiar to us from *I Flunked, But . . .* and *Where Now Are the Dreams of Youth?*—which implies he may not have studied very hard in college or, at the very least, wasn't willing to wait for a more advantageous match. (If the latter, education is, indeed, not all that is needed to get ahead.) He has also lied to his mother, like Notomo in *I Graduated, But . . .*, telling her he had a good job in his ward office. (He later tells her he quit that job, and Bordwell wonders why he left, but I think we are to assume he never held this position.)[9]

A second narrative involves the Buddhist concept of fate. Okubo has resigned himself to his failure to make good in Tokyo, saying, "things go as they're destined." We might suppose this to be a mere rationalization except that Ozu includes many shots of wheels in the film. The wheel is a Buddhist symbol of the endless cycle of birth and death and the fate we cannot change until and unless we reach enlightenment (*satori*). (See Chapter 9.) The film's second shot, an exterior in Otsune's village of Shinshu, and almost every shot inside Otsune's house, include a wheel of some sort. The Tokyo sequences include fewer wheels, but there are large wheels on a cart associated with the noodle vendor near Ryosuke's home. Do concepts like fate still apply in modern, progressive Tokyo? Or are people kidding themselves to think they do not?

Finally, there is the narrative of three "only sons:" Ryosuke, his own baby, and Tomi-chan, neighbor Otaka's son, all trapped in a cycle of downward mobility. Toward the middle of the film, Otsune walks outside with the baby, asking "What will you become?" Ozu employs his morning-laundry iconography to begin this sequence, but the "bright-new-day-full-of-promise" meaning attached to it in the silent films is muted here. As she does throughout most of the Tokyo sequences, Otsune looks worried while she queries the baby about his future.

At least five close-ups of the sleeping baby, one in which the baby is in the foreground with the family out of focus in the background, tell us that he is not only a liability to Ryosuke but, with two poor parents, unlikely to have much of a future. At the end, Ryosuke vows to work harder to give his son a better future, but little in the film encourages us to believe that this will happen.

Meanwhile, the third "only son" Tomi appears as Otsune walks with the baby. An eager student, he begins reciting Japan's prefectural capitals for her. Earlier Ozu has made a point of showing him studying, and at one point he sharpens his pencil like a boy we have seen in Ryosuke's night class. If teaching night school is a dead-end job, what of the students who attend it? Tomi, too, is the son of a poor single mother. Will night school be all he can afford? Subsequently, Tomi is kicked by the horse around which he was playing in order to show off for his friends because one of them refused to lend him a baseball mitt. Tomi had no mitt because his mother is too poor to buy him one. The entire episode emphasizes the spiraling vulnerability of the poor.

Okubo has given Ryosuke a charm, a picture of a child with writing around it, which, when hung upside down, is supposed to stop babies crying at night. This upside-down child, hung on a sliding door in the room with the hibachi, is, like the baby, the subject of three long holds and is seen directly over Ryosuke's shoulder at several points and behind wife Sugiko at others. It is present in many of the shots in or of the hibachi room. The nighttime sequence in which Otsune, unable to sleep, broods in the hibachi room begins with a focused shot of the upside-down child, while Otsune, still in the adjoining room, remains out of focus. This sequence ends with a cut from the sleeping baby to the upside-down child, with Sugiko's crying on the soundtrack. This final shot

The Calm 93

lasts for an entire minute while the sun comes up and Sugiko's crying is replaced by the sound of the textile machines. In contrast to the stairway in Otsune's home that suggested Ryosuke could rise in life, this picture suggests that, for these only sons, the opposite is true. The times are upside-down, and these sons won't rise.

The film ends with Otsune back at the silk factory, where she now lives in a dormitory, resting in a courtyard surrounded by a wall topped with barbed wire. This enclosure represents the world without promise that Ryosuke and Okubo face ever more starkly. Otsune is deeply sad: she forfeited her house to pay for her son's education and has little to show for it. The film's last three shots, however, are not of her but of the wall's large wooden gate. Thus the emphasis is less on the enclosure than on the way out, but the way out, of course, is death. "Old Black Joe" plays on the soundtrack. It may be, as Bordwell points out, a "lilting vibraphone" rendition,[10] but the song, popular in Japan since the Meiji era, is about an old Black man, presumably a slave, whose friends have all died and are calling him to follow: "I'm coming, I'm coming / Though my head is bending low. / I hear those gentle voices calling Old Black Joe." The Japanese translation of the song is faithful to the English lyrics.

Given all that Otsune has been through, her impending death seems like an appropriate ending to the film, but, in fact, death has also been invoked at both the beginning and in the middle of the film. "Old Black Joe" plays over the film's opening credits before we ever meet Otsune, Ryosuke, or Okubo and hear of their aspirations. Midway through the film, Otsune and Ryosuke walk out in the industrial wasteland near his house and sit down in view of a garbage incinerator plant. The plant's four chimneys are all smoking strongly, which, as in *Woman of Tokyo*, suggests the crematorium. The fact of *four* chimneys also signifies death, because the Japanese word for "four" (*shi*) is the first syllable in *shinu* (to die). The Japanese avoid the number four much as Westerners avoid the number thirteen. One can, for example, never buy a set of four dishes in Japan (unless specifically manufactured for Western tourists). Thus a film about dead dreams and dead ends repeatedly invokes the ultimate dead end.

While the film's story, predicated on Depression-era poverty, invokes both the sociological and the cosmic, two other topics relevant to Japan's prewar history are gratuitously introduced: environmental degradation and the growing influence of Germany. During their visit with Okubo in Tokyo, Otsune mentions that the riverbanks in Shinshu where Okubo played with Ryosuke are now all concrete. As Ryosuke and Otsune observe the garbage incinerator near his house, he remarks on the large amount of garbage it processes each day. Ozu would not have viewed these harbingers of environmental degradation as we do today, something out of control and liable to destroy the world as we know it, but rather as casualties of progress, much like the speed-up evident in Otsune's silk factory from 1923 to 1935 and the industrial wastelands where Ryosuke and Okubo live.

There had been a worldwide backlash against modernization after the massive slaughter of World War I revealed what machines were capable of doing. Chaplin's *Modern Times*, released in February of 1936, epitomized that backlash, and in Japan it dovetailed with the right-wing reaction against Westernization. *The Only Son* suggests modernization has not only failed to bring continued prosperity but has left a certain level of devastation in its wake; and the film was prescient. Today most of Japan's streams and rivers are concrete channels,[11] and in Ozu's own lifetime air pollution in Tokyo reached intolerable levels, much like Beijing today.

Evoking a long tradition in East Asian arts, birds as a motif crop up in this film to slightly mitigate its uglier themes. As with the introduction of fate into the discussion of failure, Japanese tradition again squares off against sociological reality. A still life shot outside Otsune's home near the beginning of the film features two adorable chicks. Okubo has a caged bird in his home, and each time the subject of environmental degradation comes up, Ryosuke mentions birds: they can hear mountain birds in Tokyo and skylarks near the garbage incinerator (but apart from some vague chirping on the soundtrack neither the mountain birds nor the skylarks make an actual appearance in the film).

The film treats the growing influence of Germany in prewar Japan negatively, but subtly so. For the same reason that some of Ozu's other characters keep unlikely posters in their homes and offices, Ryosuke's home has a large poster promoting travel to Germany. It features an imposing statue of a man on horseback, and the word "Germany" written below in English. In one of Ozu's visual puns, the horse in the poster recurs as the real horse that kicks Tomi in the latter part of the film. Whatever Ozu intended with this parallel, it is certainly less than positive and suggests that Germany or fascism could give Japan a nasty kick.

After World War I, in which Japan sided with the Allies, Japan's relations with Germany cooled but warmed again throughout the 1920s and 1930s. In the 1920s, partly because of America's anti-Asian policies, 80 percent of Japanese students who studied abroad studied in Germany, and by the 1930s many of those running the government had attended German universities.[12]

As Japanese militarism increased in the 1930s, an alignment with Hitler's Germany became increasingly attractive. *The Only Son* was released in September of 1936. In October, the Anti-Comintern Pact, which pledged that Japan and Germany would support one another in resisting Russian Communism, was initiated. In November it was signed.

It seems logical that Ozu, as a highly individualistic director, welcomed neither Japanese militarism nor an alliance with fascist, racist Germany, but he reserved special opprobrium for what German cinema had become. Inspired by Walther Ruttmann, Fritz Lang, G. W. Pabst, émigré director Ernst Lubitsch, and Austrian-born Josef von Sternberg to the point of imitation, Ozu was obviously appalled by what had become of the industry once the Nazis were in charge. In a sequence reminiscent of the *If I Had a Million* sequence in *Woman of Tokyo*, Ozu cuts directly from a still life shot in Ryosuke's home, which includes pictures of both Joan Crawford and, obliquely, the upside-down child, to a startling close-up of Martha Eggerth singing loudly in Willi Forst's *Leise fliehen meine Lieder*, a 1933 biopic based on the life of Franz Schubert. Distributed in

The Calm   95

England as *The Unfinished Symphony*, the Austrian-German co-production was not a Nazi film per se. But with the very blond Eggerth cast as a countess, flouncing about in a dirndl while playing at being a peasant girl, it captured Nazi aesthetics and sentiments perfectly and was light years away from the Weimar films that Ozu admired. In 1934, leftist critic Akira Iwasaki had accused the German film industry of plummeting "into an abyss from which it may never again rise . . . After the enforced flight of Jews and liberals from the industry, those who remain are little more than hacks."[13] Like the Japanese economy, the German film industry had turned upside down.

After the initial shot of Eggerth singing, Ozu cuts to the theater where Ryosuke has taken his mother to see her first "talkie," but since the "talk" is in German, she promptly falls asleep. In the next cut from the film, Eggerth concludes her song, and Hans Jaray as Schubert kisses her hands. Subsequently he chases Eggerth's Countess Esterhazy through a field of grain on the pretense of returning her shawl. The scene ends with a coy cut to the shawl being tossed into the stalks of grain. When seen in toto the entire sequence does not come across as quite so bald and ridiculous as the cuts Ozu chooses to show us, which leaves no doubt that he intended to lampoon the film, whose artlessness was not only at odds with his own work but with that of the Weimar directors he had learned from. If the specter of death hangs over *The Only Son*, mourning the loss of upward mobility in mid-1930s Japan, the specter of fascism is also present, and in this sequence Ozu points to one of its casualties.

The cut from Joan Crawford's face staring out at us defiantly from a poster in Ryosuke's home to the Austro-German film suggests a comparison between the American films Ozu loved and Nazi-era films. Crawford had starred in two of the films whose advertising posters appeared in Ozu's silents, *Our Dancing Daughters* and *Rain*, and he seems to have admired the strength she projected along with her beauty. The poster with her face appears numerous times in the interior shots in Ryosuke's home and signals a quiet resistance.

Good-bye to All That (*What Did the Lady Forget?* 1937)

Although Ozu could not have anticipated the apocalyptic reckoning toward which Japan was heading, *What Did the Lady Forget?* functions in retrospect as a kind of valedictory for the prewar genres, characters, values, and to some extent stylistics that had characterized his films up to that time. It would be his last in which we see the innocent affectation of Western culture, endemic to both the upper classes and to youth, as evidenced in *A Mother Should Be Loved*, *The Lady and the Beard*, the gangster films, and the student comedies. We see it in Dr. Komiya's Western-style study, with its drink caddy, fencing foil, deer-head trophy, and, incongruously, samurai armor; in the formal Western dining room, bedecked with Impressionist-style paintings, where Okada tutors Fujio; in the women's fox stoles; in the Western-style coffee shops in the department store and haberdashery; and in the "Cervantes Bar," with its quote in English from "Don Quichotte." All are emblematic of a privileged class embracing and absorbing

Westernization happily and, except insofar as it denotes their status, unselfconsciously. It would not happen again in Ozu's lifetime.

A reaction against Westernization had been underway in Japan throughout the 1930s, but with the outbreak of war in China, Japan's military government would stigmatize Western affectation as unpatriotic and dissolute. After the war it would be associated with the Occupation and the paternalistic relationship between America and Japan. When Lars-Martin Sorensen sees the gangsters' love of jazz and Western dress in Akira Kurosawa's *Drunken Angel* as obliquely critical of the Occupation, one has to ask if this is not just a continuation of the gangsters' love of Western culture as seen in prewar films.[14] It may well be; it may also be a form of "embracing defeat," as John Dower describes the mindset of occupied Japan,[15] but, for postwar Japanese, Westernization might be seen as inevitable but never again as neutral or completely innocent, nor would it be portrayed as such in Ozu's films.

The *moga*, too, would disappear. *Moga* were featured in a number of Ozu's early films, but most of these have been lost, leaving mainly the gangster *moga* for today's audiences to contemplate. In *What Did the Lady Forget?*, however, *moga* Setsuko is an upper-class brat (whose male counterpart is Horino in *Where Now Are the Dreams of Youth?*), and she is Ozu's last.[16] Although his later films would be populated by pert young women, none would evoke the elegant independence of the *moga*.

Self-reflexively, the film also reminds us of two Ozu genres that flourished in happier times, the gangster film and the student comedy. When Komiya and Setsuko sneak away from his house, their hats are pulled low over their foreheads and remain so when they finally return home. (See Figure 11.4, p. 221.) They sneak back into the Komiya house (hoping to avoid wife Tokiko) and are photographed in low light from behind, silhouetted against the light-colored *fusuma*. Co-conspirators, they look like Ozu's vaguely comic gangsters.

The student comedies are invoked early in the film when Dr. Komiya lectures to a theater full of medical students. He teases one who has fallen asleep, played by the same heavy-set actor who was frequently the butt of jokes in *I Flunked, But . . .* and *Where Now Are the Dreams of Youth?*.

When Osaka-bound Setsuko lunches with Okada, Komiya's student to whom she has become engaged, she promises to return to Tokyo for the Waseda baseball game. (The Waseda-Keio baseball game was celebrated as a national event.) Okada remarks that he, too, is a Waseda fan. Waseda is, of course, the prestigious university where Ozu's hapless students have all (improbably) matriculated and where many of them serve as cheerleaders for the famous baseball team.[17]

Among the stylistic features that would disappear after this film is the camera traveling on the running board behind the front wheel hub of a car, which begins the film. The shot had appeared in *Walk Cheerfully* and *The Only Son*.

Ozu uses selective focus in the first Cervantes Bar sequence. After tracking along the quote from Don Quixote at the top of the wall, the camera cuts to a long shot of Chiyoko's husband, Sugimoto, and the bar hostess at the bar, but they remain out of focus until Ozu cuts to a medium shot of them. He would drop his play with focus after this film.

The film maintains Ozu's roundabout approach to narrative, which combines with symbolic content to create meaning. In the second of four interactions between Komiya and his niece Setsuko in Komiya's study, they discuss golf. Setsuko remarks that she was quite good but got calluses on her hands and, in addition, had too little time for it because she was studying classical voice. Komiya says, "So you sing *kiyomoto?*" (a body of music composed in the nineteenth century to accompany Kabuki), and she replies that her teacher praised her rendition of "*Ochiudo*," the name of a particular song that translates as "the fleeing warrior." Komiya is, of course, the "fleeing warrior," who will soon be fleeing from his wife and his golf game. Ozu thus moves from golf to classical music to his motif of the fleeing warrior, which will motivate the rest of the film, and back to golf as his wife, Tokiko, appears and insists Komiya play that day as the maid Fumiya readies his clubs.

Besides the obvious plot device, which has Komiya ditching his golf game for a day in the city, what exactly Komiya is fleeing depends on whom you ask. Setsuko, echoing prevalent ideology, sees Komiya fleeing his responsibility as a "warrior" to maintain his status as head of the house and keep his wife submissive, but Ozu sees him instead fleeing his responsibility to be a good husband. Instead of a "warrior" dominating his wife, he expects Komiya to simply communicate with her. After Setsuko explains to Tokiko that Komiya doesn't always want to play golf, he follows up with his own explanation of his night out, thus restoring comity.[18]

When Setsuko criticizes Komiya for not asserting his prerogative to dominate Tokiko, he explains that some men treat their wives badly, but that wives should be respected, adding, "They like to think they're in control, so it's better to let them think that, like scolding children by praising them." He calls it "the opposite approach." (Throughout this scene, Komiya is, inexplicably, wearing an apron, suggesting that his wife is actually still in control.)

This idea intrigues independent Setsuko, but she figures out that it is fundamentally patronizing. During her farewell lunch with Okada, she discusses "the opposite approach," and warns her besotted and slightly befuddled sweetheart not to "use it when we marry." If he does, she says, she will use the "opposite-opposite approach," thus giving us another variation on Ozu's fascination with the meaninglessness of direction.

During the same farewell lunch, Setsuko looks out the window and comments, "This time tomorrow I'll be in Osaka." Later, after she has taken her train home, Tokiko wonders where Setsuko is on her journey, and Komiya guesses, "around Numazu." This is the time/space/nostalgia complex that had surfaced to some extent in *Tokyo Chorus* and *A Story of Floating Weeds*, but it seems out of place in this comedy of manners with its multiple happy endings: the Komiyas remark that their house feels lonely without Setsuko but reassure themselves that she will visit often as they prepare for a night of lovemaking. Ozu's evocation of the time-space continuum combined with loss and nostalgia, however, looks forward to and would dominate the postwar films.

Events in China and Europe seem far from the concerns of *What Did the Lady Forget?*, but Ozu nevertheless serves up several oblique reminders of the fascism taking hold in Europe. In one sequence Okada tutors Fujio, son of one of Tokiko's friends. Stuck on an arithmetic problem involving the sea, Fujio fetches a globe, which harks back to the geographical and international interests of earlier films: the flags in *Walk Cheerfully* and *Tokyo Chorus*, the map in *That Night's Wife*, and the globe in the teachers' room in *The Only Son*. But here these interests darken: as soon as Fujio sits down with his globe, he points out Ethiopia. Fascist Italy had invaded Ethiopia in 1935, overcoming its poorly equipped army by 1936 and, among other tactics, deploying aerial bombardments of mustard gas, which had been outlawed by the Geneva Protocol in 1928. Although Fujio and a friend subsequently play a game that requires them to call out the names of other locations, his mention of Ethiopia stands by itself for almost three minutes—through a change of scene and back as well as through several conversations—before the later game begins.

The second reference to fascism is the magazine spread on Marlene Dietrich that Setsuko reads toward the end of the film (Figure 5.1). Like Joan Crawford, whose picture appears in *The Only Son*, Dietrich was a Hollywood actress who portrayed strong women. Emigrating from Germany to America in 1930, she refused to return to Germany to work for the Nazis and became an outspoken critic of the regime.

Figure 5.1: Marlene Dietrich's face appears prominently in shots of Setsuko reading her magazine in *What Did the Lady Forget?*

The Calm 99

While Ozu's mention of Ethiopia combines with his reference to Marlene Dietrich to suggest an anti-fascist stance, which his leftist critics would have understood as such, his censors and the general public will have understood something very different. The Japanese government and the general public embraced Italy's invasion of Ethiopia, which, like Japan's occupation of Manchuria, had been condemned by the League of Nations. By letting the word "Ethiopia" simply hang in the air for three minutes, Ozu could project an ambiguity that would satisfy everyone, a tactic he would perfect during years of war and occupation.

What Did the Lady Forget? was released in March of 1937. On July 7, 1937, the Marco Polo Bridge Incident propelled Japan into an all-out war with China. Ozu was called up almost immediately and served until 1939.

Notes

1. John Dower, "Modernity and Militarism," in Jacqueline A. Atkins, John Dower, Anne Nishimura Morse, and Frederic A. Scharf, *The Brittle Decade: Visualizing Japan in the 1930s* (Boston, MA: MFA Publications, 2012), 41.
2. Ben Urwand, *The Collaboration: Hollywood's Pact with Hitler* (Cambridge, MA: Harvard University Press, 2013), 26–30.
3. Peter B. High, *The Imperial Screen: Japanese Film Culture in the Fifteen Years' War 1931–1945* (Madison, WI: University of Wisconsin Press, 2003), 20–22.
4. High, *Imperial Screen*, 173.
5. The incident was memorialized as *bakudan sanyushi* (Three Human Bomb Patriots). Whereas many of the signs and other wall décor in Ozu's films are partially obscured and somewhat difficult to read, this sign is very large, crystal clear, and dominates the screen for about five seconds. Neither the censors nor the general public were to have any doubt about where Ozu's loyalties lay.
6. High, *Imperial Screen*, 166.
7. Such internationalist flag displays were popular in Japan at the time. See Dower, "Modernity and Militarism," 39.
8. Jacqueline M. Atkins, "Wearing Novelty," in Atkins et al., *The Brittle Decade*, 129.
9. Bordwell, *Poetics*, 270.
10. Bordwell, *Poetics*, 274.
11. See Alex Kerr, *Dogs and Demons: Tales from the Dark Side of Japan* (New York: Hill and Wang, 2001), 11, 15, 43–47.
12. https://en.wikipedia.org/wiki/Germany–Japan_relations.
13. High, *Imperial Screen*, 70.
14. Lars-Martin Sorensen, *Censorship of Japanese Films During the U.S. Occupation of Japan: The Cases of Yasujiro Ozu and Akira Kurosawa* (Lewiston, NY: Edwin Mellen Press, 2009), 252.
15. John Dower, *Embracing Defeat: Japan in the Wake of World War II* (New York: W.W. Norton & Co., 1999).
16. Junji Yoshida notes the similarity between Setsuko and the maligned *moga* in a right-wing propaganda piece entitled *Japan in Time of Crisis* (*Hijoji Nippon*, 1933). Yoshida believes the similarity is deliberate and that as late as 1937 Ozu was willing to mock the conservatism

that had been overtaking Japan since the war in China had begun in 1931. Junji Yoshida, "Laughing in the Shadows of Empire: Humor in Ozu's *Brothers and Sisters of the Toda Family* (1941)," in Choi, *Reorienting Ozu*, 159.

17. Sweet-faced Tokihiko Okada starred in six of Ozu's early films, most notably *Tokyo Chorus*. He died of tuberculosis in 1934, and, although Okada is a fairly common name—a Yoshiko Okada starred in *Woman of Tokyo*—it seems likely that Ozu named this character Okada, played by an equally sweet-faced Shuji Sano, after his former star. He riffs on Sano's good looks when he has Setsuko say she wouldn't mind being thought to have compromised herself with him "if he were at least handsome."

18. This plot device, in which Tokiko discovers Komiya's deception because it rained at the golf resort while he reported good weather, is based on Ozu's own experience when he told his mother he had gone hiking with friends in the mountains while instead sneaking off to Nagoya to watch movies. When it rained in the mountains but not in Nagoya, he was caught in his lie. Tadao Sato, *The Art of Yasujiro Ozu 5*, 84.

6
The Storm

I'm off to the front for a little bit.

—Yasujiro Ozu[1]

War with China (*The Brothers and Sisters of the Toda Family*, 1941)

Historians generally concur that Japan's war with China was an unprovoked act of aggression that targeted civilians with aerial bombardments and brutal mass killings. But for the soldiers on the front lines, it was a war like any other war: deadly, terrifying, and dehumanizing. Corporal Ozu was one of those soldiers. In accord with his earlier training, he served in a poison gas unit. The gas used was not lethal but, like tear gas, had the power to immobilize enemy units for a short time, which gave Japanese units an advantage as they tried to advance their positions.[2]

Already famous, Ozu was sought out for interviews, and, while always patriotic, many of his statements were typically contrary. Of the Chinese soldiers, portrayed as sneaky and craven in propaganda and the popular press, he said, "One would expect the Chinese to run away in the face of an all-out assault by our forces . . . but they stuck to their trenches with solid bravery."[3] He criticized writers trying to cover the front: "The troops over there are disgusted when they get a load of them."[4] He repeatedly stated that he wanted to make a war film when he returned and was scornful of the films already in circulation: "There's not much in common between the soldiers who populate the imaginations of people back home and the real soldiers at the battlefront."[5] In so saying, he echoed the thoughts of most combat veterans; and he described the process by which the combat soldier becomes alienated from the noncombatant: "One undergoes a distinct mental change. The process starts the first time you come under fire. Thereafter, the worse things get, the more profoundly you change on the inside."[6]

Ozu was ever aware of the danger he faced and often included some version of *if I come through this alive* in his remarks to the press.[7] He was deeply shaken when fellow draftee, friend, and critically acclaimed director of *jidai-geki*, Sadao Yamanaka, died of enteritis in a field hospital near the front in 1938.[8] Within a year of Ozu's return from China, 100,000 Japanese troops had died there.

Ozu was demobilized in August 1939. Although still hinting he would make a war film, he instead wrote a script with a storyline similar to *What Did the Lady Forget?* called *The Flavor of Green Tea over Rice*, which ends with the husband leaving for the war. Close to the time that Ozu returned, however, his government enacted a draconian Film Law, based on the Nazis' *Spitzenorganization der Filmwirtschaft*, which placed film censorship directly under the control of the Cabinet Propaganda Office. Whereas earlier censorship laws had forbidden certain film content—mainly communism and "lewdness"—and examined only finished films, the new law proactively prescribed content, demanding nationalistic themes and Confucian morals, and examined scripts as well as finished films. This newly restructured Censorship Office rejected *The Flavor of Green Tea over Rice* for being too "frivolous" (*fumajime*).

The working title for the *Green Tea* script was *He's Going to Nanking* (*Kare shi nankin e iku*). Nanking was the site of the most notorious mass killing of civilians in this war. Corporal Ozu and his poison gas unit were present at the siege of Nanking, and accounts of the atrocities committed there were available in Japan to those who wanted to know about them.[9] Nevertheless, the city, which had been Chiang Kai-shek's headquarters, became the administrative center for the Japanese Foreign Ministry's government in China and was sufficiently cosmopolitan to host Japan's third Great East Asia Literary Conference in 1944. Whatever Ozu intended with the reference to Nanking in his script's working title and for reasons we will probably never know, he changed it.

Despite his stated desire to make a war film, Ozu continued on a path he knew well, domestic drama. In both his script for *Green Tea* and his next film, *The Brothers and Sisters of the Toda Family*, he continued to explore the foibles of the upper class. *The Brothers and Sisters of the Toda Family*, however, would toe the National Policy (*kokusaku*) line—mostly.

To understand how Ozu and others navigated Japan's Greater East Asia War, it is helpful to understand some of the differences between a Western and a Japanese worldview. We in the West tend to see things in terms of "either . . . or." You are for us or against us, right or wrong, good or bad, left or right, Protestant or Catholic, Jew or Gentile, and so on. In a democratic system, you either win or lose.

Japanese tend rather toward "both . . . and," frequently adopting a more nuanced and ambiguous stance. For centuries Japanese have happily combined Buddhism, a world religion with a vision of heaven and hell and a clear ethical system, with Shinto, an ancient, native, animistic nature worship. Japanese find it acceptable to maintain different standards of behavior in private and in public, at work and after work, drunk and sober, at home and abroad. As a society that values consensus, people may act in concert yet harbor individual reservations.[10] Traditionally, Japanese are famous for experiencing a perpetual conflict between *giri* and *ninjo*, duty and personal feeling. After the Meiji Revolution, Japan looked to "modernize," i.e., become like the West, but struggled ever after to understand what it meant to be Japanese. If Japanese aesthetics have, by Western standards, always been "modern," their mindset has, perhaps, always been "postmodern."[11]

The Storm 103

A consensus society may seem to move in lockstep, but when consensus cannot be reached, the results can be muddled, and this muddle played out noticeably during World War II. Never a true democracy before 1945, Japan's oligarchic government consisted of a variety of actors with overlapping roles and an ever-shifting cast: the emperor and his councilors, the prime minister and his cabinet, the bureaucrats, the competing branches of the military, and the democratically elected legislators in the Diet. Admiral Tojo, who led the wartime government (for which he was eventually hanged), had less actual power than Roosevelt or Churchill, never mind Hitler.[12] Ben-Ami Shillony credits both the emperor and the bureaucracy with preventing Japan from becoming either a true democracy or a true dictatorship.[13] Eri Hotta details how Japan's highest officials dithered their way into the attack on Pearl Harbor even though most of them did not want a war with the United States, and Shillony explains how their competing stratagems and viewpoints made an efficient pursuit of the war impossible.[14] Nor when, by 1944, all concluded the war could not be won and needed to end, could they agree on an exit strategy until the nuclear bombing of Hiroshima and Nagasaki convinced the emperor to end his traditional impartiality and insist the government accept unconditional surrender.[15]

Other wartime conundrums included the 1942 symposium on "Overcoming Modernity" (i.e., Westernization), for which no satisfactory conclusion was reached, as well as the ambivalence toward English. Officials attempted to proscribe English, the enemy's language, but it was the only foreign language most Japanese knew and the only language with which they could communicate with the peoples of their conquered territories.[16]

Against this background we can better understand how censorship and other laws intended to encourage nationalism, support the war effort, and control public discourse were mutable to some degree. For example, American films were supposedly banned in 1937, yet some continued to be shown up until the attack on Pearl Harbor. Ruth Benedict notes that Americans who saw Japanese war films reported that they were "the best pacifist propaganda they ever saw."[17] Allied to Germany, the Japanese at times extolled Nazi ideology but held to Confucian principles that were often at odds with it. Propaganda Office guidelines may have appeared well defined, but their execution was less so, which made it easier for filmmakers like Ozu to create films that fulfilled National Policy objectives while at the same time reflecting the artist's individuality, personal philosophy, a continuity with prewar work, and, possibly, a hint of resistance. Scott Nygren has noted that Ozu's other wartime film, *There Was a Father* "can be read as both complicit with or resistant to the war."[18] Nygren unconsciously falls into our Western "either . . . or" mindset, beginning his phrase with "both" but concluding it with "or" instead of "and." Indeed, *Toda Family* and *There Was a Father* are both supportive of the war *and* resistant to it.[19]

Marking a break with the past, *The Brothers and Sisters of the Toda Family* was singular in several ways. Returning from the front, Ozu had to find a new cameraman as his former DP, Hideo Shigehara, had gone to another company.[20] Whether his new cameraman, Yuharu Atsuta, was responsible for some of the changes in Ozu's style—Bordwell points out that in this film Ozu codified his way of shooting the Japanese house[21]—or whether the director's increasing maturity had readied him to abandon some idiosyncrasies in his earlier style—his play with focus, for example—is difficult to say, but it was probably a combination of both. The film would, in addition, be his only story with so large and complicated a family: elder parents with five offspring, two married, one a widow, two still single, as well as two grandchildren. The film's National Policy implications, however, are what have most interested, sometimes outraged, critics in the postwar era.

Joan Mellen, in her polemical 1976 survey of Japanese film, accuses Ozu of "gently tak[ing] the unthinkable for granted," referring to making China the preferred destination for the younger Toda siblings.[22] Darrell Davis included the film as an example of "monumental style," Japanese cinema's answer to the "back to Japan" impulse of the 1930s and 1940s, in a 1989 article but omitted it from his 1996 book on the subject.[23] (Indeed, it is hard to imagine any Ozu film as an "epic, ponderous . . . celebration of the national character and heritage."[24]) However, Davis correctly describes a more rigorous, austere style in the film: "Individuating elements of each shot are pared down until only the most minute details . . . are left to graphically differentiate one shot from another," while Bordwell notes that "Ozu frames figures in long-shot and holds establishing and re-establishing shots much longer than in his previous work."[25]

Both Davis and Mellen see the patriarchal figure of father Toda as reinforcing the wartime ideology that valorized the Japanese family in its Confucian incarnation, i.e., patriarchal and hierarchic, which in turn was the declared model for Japan's relation to its colonies.[26] Adding insult to injury in Mellen's eyes, the film also references Hitler and Nordic hero Siegfried. Japan's militarist leader, Admiral Hideki Tojo, also rates a mention. (Tojo was minister of war when the film was made and later prime minister.)

Toda Family's three-pronged evocation of National Policy in terms of traditionalism, fascism, and colonialism, was not, however, consistently reverential or unproblematized, nor imposed simply to satisfy the censors, but was paradigmatically woven into the film's fabric. The Toda parents evoke traditionalism, for example. Although their villa has both Japanese- and Western-style rooms, we see the old couple only in the Japanese part of the house, where they are connected to a variety of Buddhist images. Mother Toda moves about with a caged myna bird and potted orchids, traditional hobbies. However, Father Toda, like the wealthy fathers in *Where Now Are the Dreams of Youth?* and *A Mother Should Be Loved*, dies at the beginning of the film, in this case leaving his family with large debts and his wife and youngest daughter destitute, hardly a reassuring view of patriarchy. Twice youngest daughter Setsuko looks longingly at father Toda's picture, but, rather than shoring up patriarchy, the frequency with which Toda's picture is shown only underscores his absence and failure. Junji Yoshida points out that this funerary picture of father Toda is not a normal one but has him looking back over his shoulder with laughing eyes, which adds to the slightly comic persona he presented earlier in the film while still alive.[27]

Meanwhile, the Buddhism referenced in the film is associated primarily with the father's death, his wake, and first-anniversary-after-death ceremony, as well as with the family *butsudan*, where Father Toda's picture resides. Buddhist statues are among the art objects the family is forced to sell. Consequently, the traditionalism evoked by the film—patriarchy, Buddhism, classical art—is associated with death and failure.

Japan had signed the Tripartite Pact with Germany and Italy in 1940, and, for all that Germany is mocked in *The Only Son*, it fares better than traditionalism in *Toda Family*. A poster for the 1936 Winter Olympics in Garmisch-Partenkirchen hangs on the wall in grandchild Ryokichi's room. "Germany 1936" shows up distinctly on it.[28] This gesture toward the internationalism, characteristic of Ozu's earlier films, is a pointed reminder of prewar days. If Setsuko longs for a time before her father's death, the poster with its skier reminds its audience of what has been lost to wartime austerity: a pastime so popular in the 1920s and 1930s that Ozu had made a film about it. The Japanese had been wildly enthusiastic about the Olympics, at which they had acquitted themselves extremely well in both 1932 and 1936. Leni Riefenstahl's *Olympia* (1938), which features gold medalling marathoner, Kitei Son, a Korean running under the Japanese flag, had been enormously popular in Japan.[29] In fact, the 1940 games had been awarded to Japan, but the honor was relinquished in 1938 due to wartime budget restrictions. (The games were subsequently awarded to Finland but ultimately cancelled when Europe erupted in war.)

In addition to the Winter Olympics poster, oldest sister Chizuko's home displays numerous Germanic-looking knickknacks, along with several beer steins; and all three homes with Western wings—the two oldest children's homes as well as the original Toda villa—evoke a Teutonic spirit with their ubiquitous deer antlers.

The references to Hitler, Siegfried, and Tojo, although handled humorously, constitute an apparent nod to fascism. Protesting his sister Setsuko's suggestion that he marry her friend Tokiko, Shojiro says he will marry when Hitler does; later, using shyness as an excuse, he insists that all men have a weakness: Siegfried, for example, had a weak back.[30] Earlier in the film Shojiro joked that "Father's telescope made him look like Admiral Tojo."

Unsettling as these references have been to a generation of postwar critics, they are particularly intriguing because historians record Japanese disaffection for both Hitler and Tojo. John Dower writes that "Hitler and most of his Aryan supremacists were embarrassed by their alliance with one of the *Untermenschen*," and "Privately, the Japanese ... often expressed contempt for their German allies."[31] Meanwhile, Tojo had many internal enemies and had been publically criticized as early as 1941.[32] Yet, Ozu's humorous references suggest an affectionate familiarity felt by Japanese toward both Hitler and Tojo. Very likely, the discontent historians record existed mainly within the oligarchy and less among ordinary Japanese, who were heavily propagandized by a press committed to supporting the government. Tojo's unpopularity, for example, derived from the rivalry among government officials and, after mid-1942, from Japan's losses in the war, of which the general population was told almost nothing.

At the end of Jun'ichiro Tanizaki's *Makioka Sisters* (*Sasameyuki*), Hilda Stolz, Sachiko Makioka's friend and erstwhile neighbor, writes from wartime Germany, "We are both young nations fighting our way up, and it is not easy to win a place in the sun. And yet I do believe that we will win in the end."[33] Since the novel was first published after the war, Hilda's words resonate with irony, but they capture the aspirational unity ordinary Japanese had with Germans: both were trusting in militarist governments to give them a better life.

National Policy decreed films needed to honor fathers and elder brothers, but in this regard *Toda Family* essentially trashed it: not only is its patriarch a failure, but the elder brother Soichiro proves feckless when he fails to provide a comfortable home for his mother and sister, eventually fobbing them off on older sister Chizuko. Younger brother Shojiro steps into this void, shames his older siblings, and offers to provide his mother and youngest sister, Setsuko, a home in China. Setsuko's friend Tokiko, proposed as Shojiro's future bride, will undoubtedly go with them.

Somewhat at odds with National Policy, this emphasis on the young was in keeping with the revolutionary ideals of both Nazism and communism, and, of course, a staple of American culture, where, throughout the 1940s, adults referred to one another as "kids." It was also a staple of many of Ozu's earlier films. From *Walk Cheerfully* and *The Lady and the Beard* to *What Did the Lady Forget?* the young take the lead and provide whatever hope—sometimes more, sometimes less—the films have. Those films in which the young give up, *Woman of Tokyo* and *The Only Son*, for example, are sad or tragic. Thus Ozu continued to explore his own familiar themes despite National Policy.

Tokiko, who works as a store clerk and whom Setsuko urges Shojiro to marry, serves as a foil for the married Toda children, who, despite their father's debts, are rich, pretentious, and often wasteful. By the time the film was released, Japan had been at war in China for most of three years and had paid a steep cost in both men and treasure. Scarcities plagued daily life and luxury was deemed "the enemy."[34] Ozu could get away with demeaning older brother Soichiro because he is wealthy and his wife wasteful. Hardly subtle, Ozu has Setsuko exclaim, "Tokiko would be angry," as she cleans up the barely eaten apple and cake from her sister-in-law's tea party. Though he mocks the rich in *The Lady and the Beard*, *Where Now Are the Dreams of Youth?*, and *What Did the Lady Forget?*, Ozu portrays them with a sharper, nastier edge in *Toda Family*: they are not only rude to their servants but rude and uncaring toward their indigent family members, Setsuko and Mother Toda, who eventually seek refuge in the family's run-down villa by the sea in Kugenuma, a resort town west of Kamakura. Thus the film upholds National Policy to a degree, but its main propaganda value derives from those aspects that truly concerned ordinary people: thriftiness and the opportunities presented by the colonization of Manchuria and the occupation of China.

An irresponsible youth who can't quite get in sync with his family's fortunes, *Toda Family*'s Shojiro is late to everything and has literally gone fishing when his father dies. The death shocks him into taking charge of his life by moving to Tianjin (Tientsin) in China, where he succeeds in reforming himself. This story element, which endorses

The Storm 107

the Japanese occupation of China and, by extension, the brutal war there, has troubled postwar critics most. "Shojiro returns . . . " fumes Mellen, "in Chinese clothes, as if he had indeed fully integrated himself into the Chinese environment, and as if this were a natural and morally acceptable thing to do."[35]

However, having colonies, including concessions in China's treaty ports, of which Tianjin was one, was, by European standards, still the norm in 1941. Japan had won concessions in Manchuria after the Russo-Japanese War (1904–1905) and claimed the entire territory in 1932 after the Mukden or Manchurian Incident, in which the Japanese Imperial Army deliberately sabotaged its own South Manchurian Railway and blamed it on the Chinese. The resulting puppet state, known as Manchukuo, was immensely popular with the Japanese public, reeling at the time from the Great Depression. For them Manchuria meant having a second chance, the same role that Western territories played in nineteenth-century America, the same role colonies played for Europeans, and likewise the role that Tianjin plays for Shojiro.[36] The endorsement in *Toda Family* of Japan's settlements in China is not simply an endorsement of National Policy but an expression of popular sentiment.

The way in which Shojiro describes China—the sky seems higher there and appearances don't matter—could easily be a description of the American West.[37] His assurance to Setsuko that "No one there will care about whatever you do," references the fact that Setsuko, who has no money of her own, wanted to get a job like Tokiko's but was reprimanded by oldest sister, Chizuko, who insisted that "Father [even though he's dead] would be disgraced." "Sticking to appearances, you can't do a thing," counters Shojiro, encouraging her to emigrate with him.

Shojiro's comments appear to take aim at traditional values but were very much in keeping with the Japanese government's needs of the moment. Women were needed as workers outside the home and encouraged to dress in *monpe* (baggy pants worn by female farm workers).[38] Appearances, so very important in Japanese culture, had to be set aside.[39]

Although many leftists in Japan opposed the war in China, some Marxists joined the bureaucracy there, hoping to realize their anti-capitalist ideals in much the same spirit as the Jewish leftists who settled in British Palestine, though without the same results.[40] Shojiro's liberalism, which might seem incongruent to postwar viewers, had roots in the world of leftist ideology with which Ozu identified to some extent.[41]

Although most of Ozu's films have reasonably happy endings, these are often qualified by some form of nostalgia: the pain of parting, the inevitability of growing old and dying. *The Brothers and Sisters of the Toda Family* has no such qualification. Anyone who has been an ex-patriot knows how strong nostalgia for the homeland can be, but Ozu, master of nostalgia, rarely alludes to it here, definitely not in the person of Shojiro, whose only regret is that he can't get Japanese food in China (something the film notes twice).[42] Instead, the film has one of Ozu's most optimistic endings: Shojiro running down the beach, ostensibly to escape the *omiai* with Tokiko. The audience knows he won't escape this obligation forever, but, seeing him framed against the vast, open landscape of the sea, they know he will escape the confines of Japan. As the film's final image, it testifies powerfully to the importance of Manchuria as a colony. Mellen rightly notes that "China is seen as a place of refuge and salvation" and functions in the film as much more than an unfortunate allusion to Japan's wartime status.[43] The colonization of China is central to the hope and happiness the film projects.

The image of Shojiro alone on the beach also evokes the image of the lone samurai or Hollywood's Western hero—the warrior forging his way in a new land (as China was represented to the Japanese public). Shojiro is the new samurai, heir to the armor on display in his father's home, and he will gather up the remnants of Japanese tradition—the orchids and the myna bird are also moving to China—and honor his remaining parent; for him and the strong-minded women moving with him, China promises liberation, something the film suggests is impossible in Japan.

These sentiments hit a nerve with the public, and *The Brothers and Sisters of the Toda Family* became Ozu's first box office hit. It also won "Best One" (first place) in *Kinema Junpo's* annual rankings, a distinction it shared with *I Was Born, But . . .* , *Passing Fancy*, and *A Story of Floating Weeds*.

While the propaganda value of *Toda Family* is clear, resistance, though subtle, makes an appearance. Some English is tucked into the film along with a brief mention of baseball, but it has no props of American origin, and its European artifacts are mainly Teutonic—except for the print of Goya's *Red Boy*, which appears in Shojiro's room in both his parents' home and the seaside villa. (Did Mother Toda and Setsuko travel from lodging to lodging with Shojiro's belongings as well as their own?) That the Goya print turns up a second time, however improbably, suggests its importance. Francisco de Goya was a Spanish artist active at the turn of the nineteenth century. (In 1941, Franco's Spain was neutral in Europe's war but pro-Axis.) The painting, completed in 1788, depicts a little boy, the son of a Spanish count, holding a string tied to a magpie (similar to Mother Toda's myna bird) which three cats eye hungrily. Goya was famous for the dark visions that inhabited even his most elegant paintings and particularly for his series of etchings, made after Napoleon's invasion of Spain in 1808, which came to be known as *The Disasters of War*.

This was the face of resistance in wartime Japan. Shillony points out that magazines with small circulations could be critical of the war and the government without necessarily being shut down, but "only a few knew of their existence, and only a handful of writers used them [to criticize] the government."[44] In a film that ostensibly justified the war in China, Ozu inserted a print of a painting that most people in his audience would not even notice much less recognize. But for those that did, who knew the artist and his history, there was an antiwar message.

The Pacific War (*There Was a Father*, 1942)[45]

When novelist Yoshiro Nagayo learned of the bombing of Pearl Harbor, he wrote, "Never in my life have I experienced such a wonderful, such a happy, such an auspicious

The Storm   109

day. The heavy clouds hanging over our heads . . . suddenly disappeared."[46] Ozu probably did not share those sentiments. His next film, *There Was a Father*, is one of his most somber and contrasts starkly with *Toda Family*'s optimism.

Admiral Isoroku Yamamoto, the brilliant military tactician who planned the Pearl Harbor attack, first argued against it, then warned that the war against America must be won within the first six months if it was to be won at all. Yamamoto had studied and later worked in the United States. He had seen firsthand the factories and the endless "waves of grain" that he knew would fuel any war the Americans might undertake.[47] Ozu, who had never set foot in the United States, had also seen the cities, the factories, and the farms—at the movies. He understood the degree to which Hollywood and its technology dwarfed the Japanese film industry. He had watched Harold Lloyd overcome every obstacle put in his path and Charlie Chaplin bob up like a cork from whatever difficulty he faced. After the war he joked that he knew Japan would lose after he saw *Fantasia* (among captured films in Singapore), remarking, "These guys look like trouble, I thought," but it is unlikely he needed to wait that long.[48] Mansaku Itami is famous for his assessment of what American films meant for the Japanese: "In any American movie I can hear someone crying out: Young man, be dauntless!"[49] Such dauntless Americans were not likely to give up in despair before Japanese bravado as Japan's high command had theorized, and men like Ozu and Itami must have known this intuitively.[50]

Despite having been released in April of 1942, while Japan was still winning the Pacific War, *There Was a Father* is about separation, death, duty, and sacrifice, all hardships the Japanese populace would endure in far greater measure than it had thus far in its war against China. The script for the film had first been written in 1937. Joo therefore discounts it as a National Policy film, but Richie quotes Ozu as saying that he "wrote and rewrote it over and over again," and it is clearly tailored to the times in which it was filmed.[51]

Bordwell has exhaustively cataloged the extent to which the film is all Japan all the time, including even a postcard-like shot of Mt. Fuji, seen from Lake Ashinoko in Hakone.[52] As a testament to their patriotism, directors often found ways to show Mt. Fuji—Naruse's 1934 *Street Without End*, for example—but this is the first and last time it would appear in Ozu's work (except as the Shochiku logo).[53] Another anomaly emphasizing Japanese traditions is the way in which the son, Ryohei, dresses when he is a little boy. He always wears *hakama* (pantaloons) with a kimono so that he looks like a little samurai. His classmates all dress in their school uniforms, and no one comments on or questions Ryohei's dress, which serves the dual purpose of making him stand out so that we always know which boy he is and, ideologically, evoking the image of old Japan.

One exception to the relentless focus on Japaneseness is a scene in which Ryohei and his schoolmates practice their English lesson. As noted above, officials were conflicted about the continuing use of English in Japan, and considerable controversy ensued over whether it should still be taught in schools. Ozu uses the students' confusion with their English lessons as a source of humor—"if a hen is a female chicken and a rooster is a male chicken, what is a dog?"—but there is a more serious message, i.e., English should continue to be taught in schools. Significantly, the eponymous father, Horikawa, is a math teacher and son Ryohei grows up to be a chemistry teacher, both "Western" subjects that were questioned by those right-wing, anti-modernist Japanese seeking a complete break with the West. By emphasizing math, chemistry, and English, Ozu was endorsing what the nation needed to support its wars, while eschewing anti-modernist views. Not coincidentally, the chemistry lesson we see Ryohei teach concerns the explosive TNT.

Designated a *kokumin eiga* (national film), the National Policy implications of *There Was a Father* fall into two categories: aid and comfort to the military government and aid and comfort for those affected by the war, both soldiers and families. Possibly, Ozu saw the entire film falling into the latter category, but certain aspects of its message would have been particularly helpful in recruiting soldiers, elevating their status, and eliciting sacrifices from the home front. At the very beginning of the film, for example, the child, Ryohei, complains that his shoes are worn out, but father Horikawa insists they can still be used. Later he tells Ryohei to be frugal with his spending money.

Scenes with older students show them dressed and/or filmed in such a way as to make them look like soldiers. During the school excursion at the beginning of the film, the boys are shown marching along the ancient Tokaido Highway, photographed from behind, legs wrapped in military-style leggings. They sing a song about "old warriors" defending their valley. One of the boys gets blisters but, when asked about them, remains stalwart and uncomplaining. Later, when Ryohei has himself become a teacher, his students sit on a bridge watching a train. They wear military-style hats and light-colored pants. Only their jackets belong to the traditional all-black school uniform that was standard at the time and long afterwards. In other words, Ozu suggests a seamless transition from student to soldier.

Joo notes that when Horikawa praises his son for passing his draft physical, he is resolving "a fundamental dilemma of the modern young Japanese who are caught between the filial duty to their parents and the social role to work and fight for the state."[54] The entire film, in which Horikawa and Ryohei live apart most of the time, suggests the inevitability of separated families and the necessity of sacrificing traditional family life for a greater good. In the film that "greater good" is financing/getting an education and holding down a responsible job, but within the context of the times it was, clearly, serving in the military. Permission to sidestep filial obligation to do one's duty is made particularly explicit when one of Ryohei's students, dressed, as we have seen, to look partially like a soldier, asks for permission to go home because his mother has just had a baby. "Your duty is to study hard," Ryohei tells him. "Don't worry about your parents." Later his own father admonishes him not to "worry about me."

Buddhism plays an especially large and very serious role in this film once we get past its tourist aspects: the boys have a class picture taken in front of Kamakura's giant Buddha. It is the same one Kenji and Yasue visit in *Walk Cheerfully* and plays the same

The Storm   111

role, evoking tradition through a familiar landmark. In *Father* no one makes fun of its half-closed eyes, although watching a photographer break down his equipment in front of it suggests Ozu understood that this particular Buddha was more for tourists than religion.

Immediately thereafter, however, Buddhism is associated with death and failure as it is in *Toda Family*. A shot of small stupas follows the Kamakura Buddha and precedes shots of the boys marching.[55] The boys rest in an inn on Lake Ashinoko, while several go on an unauthorized boating excursion, and one student, Yoshida, drowns. Another shot of the stupas is followed by a shot of the capsized boat, then a cut to Yoshida's funeral. As in *Toda Family*, considerable screen time is given over to the funeral service, which, with its chanting and drumming, is both seen and heard. In one shot the standard moth on a light fixture is framed with a branch of the gilded temple flowers, making explicit the connection between Buddhism, death, and the afterlife.[56]

Feeling he has failed in his duty to protect his students, Horikawa resigns his teaching post. Late in the film, his now-grown former students invite him to a reunion. During the reunion sequence, Ozu "cheats" a back-projected shot of one of the stone stupas into a medium shot of Horikawa. As they are in a large reception hall, the stupa not only never appears in any other shot of Horikawa or the room but cannot do so since there is no credible space for it in this hall. The shot occurs soon after two former students and former colleague Hirata mention the long-ago accident and the party given for Horikawa upon his resignation. The stupa reminds us of the accident but also foreshadows Horikawa's own impending death, which occurs two scenes later.

In addition to Buddhist artifacts, the film includes an actual priest as a character (not simply one presiding over a funeral or other service). He is a friend of Horikawa, who goes to stay with him after the boating accident to recover from the shock and determine how to proceed with his life. The priest, singular in an Ozu film, appears in several scenes chatting with Horikawa. He never offers profound advice or appears again in the film although, when Ryohei stays with his father toward the end of the film, he mentions having visited with the priest. The character's actual purpose, therefore, remains a mystery until the aforementioned last visit when Ryohei tells his father that he passed his draft physical. A new recruit, his head is shaven, much like a priest's. At his father's request, he goes to the *butsudan* to pray to his mother. Ozu holds a long time on the image of Ryohei praying at the family altar. In his loose-fitting suit coat, Ryohei looks like a priest, the image of which has been rehearsed for us in the form of the family friend (Figure 6.1). In prayer, head shaven, the new recruit has been elevated to a holy status. The conflation of soldier and priest is apt because Japan's war against America was often spoken of as a holy war in which the Japanese would win or die trying.

Ozu most likely thought they would die trying, but in this film about duty and sacrifice, he powerfully pictures the notion of holy war, of the cause for which one would "do [one's] best" as Horikawa continually intones, and for which one would probably die. The idea of the holy warrior was, of course, helpful to the military, but it was also a tribute to the men Ozu had served with in China and a comfort to families whose men

Figure 6.1: Praying at his mother's altar, Ryohei, a new recruit, takes on the appearance of a priest in *There Was a Father*.

and boys would serve or were already serving; much of the film, in fact, extends both comfort and sympathy to families riven by war.

For example, the film pictures the "good death." Horikawa dies peacefully, knowing he has "done what he could." Trying to comfort Ryohei, Horikawa's friend Hirata gives a long speech about what a wonderful man his father was, how he did his best and died peacefully. Doing one's best, one's duty, and working hard epitomize the good life, and, whether humble or great, the man who has done that has done all. By extension, the good soldier could die happily, knowing he had done his best, and his parents could likewise be proud.[57]

Moreover, the film expends considerable time honoring the dead generally. Initially, Horikawa's schoolboys visit, off-screen, the Yasukuni Shrine, which commemorates Japan's war dead, and there is, of course, the funeral for the dead boy, Yoshida. At the reunion Horikawa acknowledges that he still makes offerings at Yoshida's grave. As a child, Ryohei visits, off-screen, the graves of his mother and his grandfather. As an adult, he gives his father "pocket money," which Horikawa promises to put on his wife's altar. After Ryohei prays at his mother's altar (while looking like a priest) Horikawa follows him at the altar, communing with his dead wife. Finally, we see Ryohei and his new bride, Fumiko, on a train, taking the father's ashes back to Ueda, his hometown (*furusato*).

The Storm   113

Laid over this ending is the music to a naval song, "When We Go to Sea," (*Umi yukaba*).[58] It suggests both that Horikawa has, metaphorically, been a good soldier and that Ryohei will soon become a real one.

Part of the sympathy the film extends to both soldiers and those on the home front alike is acknowledging the pain of separation. When, as an adult, Ryohei suggests leaving his job in Akita to come to Tokyo to live with his father, Horikawa dismisses the idea and carries on at some length about the need to do one's duty and not give in to personal feelings. Prior to this confrontation, the two had been enjoying themselves in a hot springs bath; now Ozu shows the bath empty but still steaming. As we saw in the silent films, steam can denote strong emotion, in this case the pain of father and son not being together. The empty bath is followed by two shots of their empty room, with steam coming up from the hot spring baths, as seen from the windows. A cut to the two men fishing follows. As in *A Story of Floating Weeds*, the two men cast in perfect unison, but subsequently Ozu frames each man separately, emphasizing their apartness, holding each shot for a long time before cutting back to the empty steaming bath. Ryohei, not allowed to give in to personal feeling, cannot express his pain and disappointment, so Ozu does it for him through the steam, the empty rooms, and the long hold on him lost in thought.

For Bordwell this is an exercise in juggling shots around to confound our expectations, ending with a "cliché[d]" reference to "evanescence" (the steam).[59] It is also a long sad look at the men's incurable separation. The empty steaming bath and the empty room denote loneliness and sorrow, not generic "evanescence."

The film ends with a typical Ozu shot of the train carrying Horikawa's ashes back to Ueda disappearing in the distance, smoke billowing from its stack. Here one can speak of evanescence, i.e., Horikawa's passing and the inevitable comparison to smoke from a crematorium, but it also includes the sadness of parting/separation since a sorrowful Ryohei is on the train; in its complexity, the train's smoking stack functions much like the smoking chimneys at the end of *Woman of Tokyo*.

Significantly, when Ryohei and Horikawa first move to Ueda early in the film, the exterior shot of the train bringing them there—which moves toward the camera instead of away from it—includes no smoke. When the two subsequently eat lunch in a small restaurant, steam billows from the kitchen, correlating with the mention of the graves of the mother and grandfather.

Horikawa's death marks the final separation between father and son. Signs and parallels tie together all five critical scenes in which the separation between Ryohei and Horikawa is established and, from early on, they link separation with death. The first is a fishing scene after Ryohei has passed his junior high school entrance exams, during which his father announces for the first time that they must live apart. It links, of course, to the later fishing scene at the spa. In the earlier scene, the boy stopped his fishing to mope when told he must live in his school dorm, and this connects to the long-held shot of the adult Ryohei, framed alone with his line in the water. In addition, the scene of the child Ryohei fishing with his father is framed by shots of stupas (presumably connected to the temple where the two are living at this time) and is linked by these to the death of Yoshida.

While Ryohei is in junior high school, Horikawa announces his move to Tokyo, meaning that father and son will be even farther apart than before. The scene takes place in a traditional restaurant. Steam rises up from a chimney outside the window, linking this scene to the spa sequence that will unfold later in the film. Ryohei begins crying and stands with his back to his father; when his father asks him to come back to their table, he runs across the room instead and sits again with his back to his father. The sequence is linked to Horikawa's death in three ways. First, before Horikawa announces his intended move to Tokyo, Ryohei lies on his back, relaxing on the tatami in the restaurant where they are having lunch. Similarly, shortly before his father's heart attack, the adult Ryohei lies on his back on the tatami in his father's apartment. Second, the *fusuma* in the restaurant are painted with lotuses, a Buddhist symbol, which, as we have seen, is often linked to death. Finally, when Horikawa dies, Ryohei begins crying, then jumps up from his chair and runs into the hallway, standing with his back to the camera while his father's friend Hirata pleads with him to recognize the father's "good death," much as Horikawa had pleaded with him to understand the necessity of his going to Tokyo. Death is the final separator, and Ozu leaves little daylight between separation by distance and separation by death, the two following easily upon one another in wartime.

In the scene in which Ryohei's students sit on a bridge watching a passing train, Ozu makes clear that this pain of separation includes the whole nation. The students speak of their longing for home and their wish to be on that train going home.

When one boy asks for permission to go home, Ryohei asks sympathetically about the boy's family, knowing his older brother is in the army. The student says his parents are managing because "neighbors are kind." On the train in the final scene, Ryohei tells his new wife, Fumiko, that he wants her father (Hirata) and her younger brother to move in with them. Traditionally, the Japanese household, the *ie*, consisted of a patriarch and his wife, his male descendants, the wives who married them, and any unmarried female descendants. The relatives of those who married into the *ie* would remain in their own households and never become part of their out-marrying relatives' new family. To Westerners, Ryohei's suggestion sounds very sensible, but to Japanese at the time, it constituted a break with tradition. (In the 1939 story *Chichi to musume*, upon which Ozu's *Late Spring* was loosely based, the daughter asks her prospective bridegroom if her father can live with them, and he refuses to consider it, thus launching the plot in which the father must remarry in order to convince his daughter to marry.) Likewise, for neighbors to help one another in this very family-centric society was not something one could count on. In both these instances, therefore, Ozu is telling his audience that this war requires them to break out of their family circles and help one another.

For all that the film supports the war effort, however, there is, if not resistance, at least critique. On the back wall of the room in which Horikawa and Hirata play Go, there is a large map, connecting this film to the internationalism evidenced by maps and flags all the way back to *Walk Cheerfully* and *That Night's Wife*. The Pacific Ocean lies

The Storm   115

at the center of this map; Japan is barely visible, but the United States looms very large to the right. The map is reminiscent of a joke that was popular in wartime Germany: a schoolteacher, giving a geography lesson, points out the landmass of Russia, then the United States, and finally Germany. Alarmed by the size discrepancy between Germany and her enemies, a child raises her hand and asks anxiously, "Excuse me, does Herr Hitler know this?" Ozu's map makes the same what-were-we-thinking point.

There is also an implied critique in the incident that initiates the separation between Horikawa and Ryohei: the death of the student Yoshida while on an excursion under Horikawa's supervision. Horikawa quits his teaching job, not only out of remorse but because, in his words, he is *afraid* of such an enormous responsibility. Having failed once to keep those in his care safe, he cannot face the possibility of it ever happening again. Ozu didn't need to use this particular plot device. The film's main concern is the separation between father and son—which for Ozu was semi-autobiographical—and any number of possible storylines might have initiated it.[60] Ozu, famous for recycling his story elements, never used it again. For Horikawa, depicted as a paragon of rectitude and virtue, a single death was one too many.

What kind of a message did this send a country in wartime? What kind of fearsome responsibility did Ozu seek to pin on commanding officers or on those government officials who had just plunged Japan into an ever-deeper war? "I'll never forget Yoshida's parents . . . they raised him for many years and now he'd dead," Horikawa says. Later he will say of twenty-five-year-old Ryohei, "To me, he's still a child." In other words, every man killed in battle is someone's child.[61]

An even more pointed, if less obvious, critique comes with the mention of the artist Watanabe Kazan, an exhibit of whose paintings Horikawa suggests that the adult Ryohei visit at the Tokyo National Museum. Kazan lived at the turn of the nineteenth century when the Tokugawa Shogunate was beginning to crumble. A samurai, he served as senior councilor to a lord in the Nagoya area and is credited with saving every person in the local population from starvation during a four-year, nationwide famine in the 1830s. He was also a proponent of Western ideas about science, politics, and art at a time when Japan was still closed to the outside world. His writing on this subject eventually got him in trouble, after which he committed ritual suicide. Ozu could, obviously, identify with Kazan on many levels, his care for those in his charge, his enthusiasm for Western ideas, and his combining European with Japanese techniques in his art. His was also a cautionary tale for artists and intellectuals inclined to be critical of Japan's military government.

Bordwell contrasts Otsune in *The Only Son* urging her son, Ryosuke, to have more ambition with Horikawa in *Father* urging his son to stay in his rural outpost and do his duty, and the contrast between the two films, each with its own particular darkness, is both striking and telling.[62] Unlike Ryosuke and Okubo, Horikawa has no difficulty finding a job in Tokyo. (He would have been looking c. 1929 before the Depression deepened, but full employment also prevailed in 1942 because so many men were at the front.) But, as per Bordwell, ambition has now segued into duty. While Otsune's visit with her son is painful, every moment Horikawa and Ryohei spend together is pleasurable and precious. Whereas Horikawa dies a good death—having done his best—Otsune—who has certainly done *her* best—looks to death as her only escape from disillusion and disappointment. The two films touch at many points, but what a difference a war makes!

According to High, "By 1941 ... the total subordination of personal affairs [to the state] had become integral to the very definition of a Japanese citizen."[63] Through his depiction of the affection between family members and friends in *There Was a Father*, Ozu manages to make that subordination palatable, even preferable, to life before the Pacific War.

A substantial list of suggestions for war-related projects followed *There Was a Father*, and Ozu completed a script based on his wartime experiences in China titled *Burma Campaign: Far Motherland* (*Biruma sakusen: Haruka nari fubo no kuni*) in November of 1942. Ozu, who wrote scripts with certain actors already in mind, intended to cast Takeshi Sakamoto, star of the Kihachi films, in it—a friend suggested calling it *Kihachi Goes to War*—and to reprise the father-son duo from *There Was a Father*, Chishu Ryu and Shuji Sano, as senior and junior officers, the senior officer dying at the end as Horikawa had died at the end of *Father*. Sano, who had already served in China from 1938 to 1941, was called up again before shooting could start, and Ozu never revived the project or passed on the script for anyone else to make. "Just why the script ... was never filmed remains a mystery," according to High.[64]

While in China, Ozu kept a diary and took particular interest in the anti-Japanese propaganda he encountered. Joo records that, in 1939, Ozu gave an interview in which he recalled how Chinese prisoners were brainwashed "to believe that China was winning the war and would soon invade Japan ... 'Nothing is as dreadful as ignorance,'" he commented.[65] How must he have felt when Japan began doing the same thing?

When *There Was a Father* was released (April 1942), Japan was still piling up victories. That changed on June 4–5, when the Americans successfully defended Midway Island. The six months Admiral Yamamoto had given the navy to consolidate their victory had run out, almost to the day. By the end of 1942, the Japanese had abandoned Guadalcanal, and their fortunes grew steadily worse. Imperial Headquarters nevertheless described Midway as a victory, claiming that Japan had lost only one carrier while the US had lost two. (The real numbers were four Japanese carriers sunk to one American.) The losses on Guadalcanal were also described as victories "until in February 1943 the public suddenly learned that Japanese forces on the island had completed a 'sideward advance' (*tenshin*)," meaning all Japanese troops had left the island.[66]

Like the veterans portrayed in *Early Spring*, Ozu undoubtedly wanted Japan to win, but he probably had few illusions about the possibility of that happening, particularly by the end of 1942. The decision to make a film about Burma originated with the High Military Command (*Dai Hon'ei Rikugun Hodobu*)—not with Ozu or Shochiku—and Shochiku was assigned the task. Ozu completed the script, but by February, Shochiku announced that Ozu would instead make a documentary about Burma. Believing Ozu

The Storm   117

had really wanted to make his narrative war film, High has detailed many possibilities why he never did, but it seems fairly obvious that, complications notwithstanding, Ozu did not want his name on obvious war propaganda.[67] Akira Kurosawa has recounted how Ozu buffaloed the military censors into passing his *Sanjiro Sugata*, which suggests that the director knew how to checkmate the military authorities when he needed to.[68] *There Was a Father* would remain his only "war film."

In June 1943, Ozu was sent to Singapore to make propaganda films. He started one about Indian independence but eventually burned the footage he had shot as Allied victory became inevitable. While there, he screened more than 100 captured Allied films. When the British retook Singapore on September 12, 1945, Ozu was among 77,000 Japanese troops interned on the island until they could be repatriated. Ships for that purpose were few, and internees drew numbers to see who would go first. Ozu drew a low number but, practicing the humanism he preached, gave it to a member of his staff, stating, "I don't mind going later." He finally returned to Japan on February 2, 1946.[69]

Notes

1. High, *Imperial Screen*, 181.
2. High, *Imperial Screen*, 181.
3. High, *Imperial Screen*, 181.
4. High, *Imperial Screen*, 206.
5. High, *Imperial Screen*, 211.
6. High, *Imperial Screen*, 211.
7. High, *Imperial Screen*, 18.
8. One of Yamanaka's favorite films was *Dragnet Girl*. See Bordwell, *Poetics*, 244.
9. See Ben-Ami Shillony, *Politics and Culture in Wartime Japan* (Oxford: Oxford University Press, 1981), 131.
10. John Dower and others have objected to the characterization of Japan as a consensus society. See Mitsuhiro Yoshimoto, *Kurasawa: Film Studies and Japanese Cinema* (Durham, NC: Duke University Press, 2000), 27n44; Dower, *Embracing Defeat*, 440. But what should one call a society whose most frequently quoted aphorism is "The nail that sticks up gets pounded down," and whose chief social value is harmony (*wa*)? According to Peter High, "Don't be late for the bus," was a wartime expression indicating that it was time to get behind the war effort, and the police expended enormous energy getting people to change their leftist views to support the war (*tenko*). (See High, *Imperial Screen*, 289, 324ff.) By contrast, no one in Nazi Germany spoke of being "late for the bus." One was either for the Nazis or against them. If against, one left the country, joined some form of resistance, or put one's head down, kept one's mouth shut, and tried to survive as best one could. Resisters, if discovered, were sent to concentration camps or executed. The value the Japanese placed on unanimity is conveyed by the wartime expression "100 million hearts beating as one." It was propaganda, of course, but no one in America, Britain, or Germany would have ever thought to characterize their populations in that way.

11. I do not mean to suggest that Westerners are incapable of nuanced or multifaceted thinking or that Japanese do not hold strong opinions. We are all equally complex beings. I am suggesting only general cultural tendencies in the way people in each region approach the world. What we might deem wishy-washy and non-committal, the Japanese would see as diplomatic; what might seem dogmatic and argumentative to them we would see as "making our point" and so on.

12. Shillony, *Politics*, 30.

13. Shillony, *Politics*, 43.

14. Eri Hotta, *Japan 1941: Countdown to Infamy* (New York: Alfred A. Knopf, 2013); Shillony, *Politics*, 30ff.

15. Shillony, *Politics*, 77ff; see also Marc Gallicchio, *Unconditional: The Japanese Surrender in World War II* (New York: Oxford University Press, 2020), 157.

16. Shillony, *Politics*, 148ff.

17. High, *Imperial Screen*, 359.

18. Nygren, *Time Frames*, 150.

19. Woojeong Joo writes that "Ozu is never *either* modern *or* traditional, or *either* reactionary *or* radical." (*Ozu*, 15.) While my focus here is to explain how Ozu's wartime films could be both compliant and resistant, I agree with Joo's more general assessment.

20. Richie, *Ozu*, 226.

21. Bordwell, *Poetics*, 284.

22. Joan Mellen, *The Waves at Genji's Door: Japan Through its Cinema* (New York: Pantheon Books, 1976), 155.

23. Cf. D. William Davis, "Back to Japan: Militarism and Monumentalism in Prewar Japanese Cinema," *Wide Angle* 11, no. 3 (1989) and Davis, *Picturing Japaneseness*.

24. Davis, "Back to Japan," 16.

25. Davis, "Back to Japan," 23; Bordwell, *Poetics*, 287.

26. Davis, "Back to Japan," 24; Mellen, *Waves*, 152. See also John Dower, *War without Mercy: Race and Power in the Pacific War* (New York: Pantheon Books, 1986), 280.

27. Yoshida, "Laughing in the Shadows of Empire," 166.

28. In 1924, 1932, and 1936 the same country hosted both the Summer and Winter Olympic Games, France in 1924, the US in 1932, and Germany in 1936. Winter Olympics were first introduced in 1924.

29. High, *Imperial Screen*, 291.

30. These references to Hitler and Siegfried are not translated on Bo-ying's DVD version of the film.

31. Dower, *War Without Mercy*, 207.

32. Shillony, *Politics*, 45.

33. Jun'ichiro Tanizaki, *The Makioka Sisters* (New York: Alfred A. Knopf, 1957), 465.

34. High, *Imperial Screen*, 287.

35. Mellen, *Waves*, 155. Chinese-style clothing had become fashionable in Japan at the time because of the incursions into China, much as Egyptian and North African decoration and dress influenced Parisian fashions in the nineteenth century. See Anne Nishimura Morse, "Modern Girls in the Palace of Lyrical Elegance," in Atkins et al., *The Brittle Decade*, 84.

36. Louise Young writes that "Glossy spreads on new Manchurian cities in highbrow magazines advertised the empire as a land of opportunity for middle-class Japanese." Meanwhile, "the

The Storm 119

job market in Manchuria was a bonanza for university graduates." Louise Young, *Japan's Total Empire: Manchuria and the Culture of Wartime Imperialism* (Berkeley, CA: University of California Press, 1998), 417, 277. That Ozu would present China as a promised land in 1941 is perhaps less a question than why he didn't mention it earlier in the context of his films about jobless university graduates.

37. Text on a garment celebrating settlements in Manchuria spoke of "the opening of the 'wilderness' to provide a better life for the immigrants." See Atkins, "Wearing Novelty," 139.

38. See High, *Imperial Screen*, 255ff.

39. Isolde Standish describes Shojiro's view of Manchuria as "a meritocratic land of opportunities where the old values of class and society do not apply." Standish, *A New History of Japanese Cinema*, 127.

40. See Dower, "Modernity and Militarism," 37.

41. Louise Young writes that dreams of "economic development promised modernist utopia for Manchuria's cities and social justice for its countryside." Young, *Japan's Total Empire*, 419.

42. Ozu did not simply miss Japanese food in China but suffered real hunger. Joo, *Ozu*, 233n112.

43. Mellen, *Waves*, 155.

44. Shillony, *Politics*, 133.

45. "Pacific War" is a term that was foisted on the Japanese by the Americans at the beginning of the Occupation and conveyed the American perception of the war. The Japanese term for their war was "Greater East Asia War." (See Dower, *Embracing Defeat*, 419.) For the purposes of this narrative, however, I use the term "Pacific War" to denote the period after the bombing of Pearl Harbor.

46. Shillony, *Politics*, 115.

47. Yamamoto had also opposed Japan's wars in Manchuria and China and was hated by the radical militarists, who, the government feared, might assassinate him. Loyal to the emperor, however, he planned the successful attack on Pearl Harbor and the failed attack on Midway and remained in charge of Imperial naval operations until his death, which was specifically ordered by Franklin Roosevelt, over the Solomon Islands in 1943.

48. Bordwell, *Poetics*, 8.

49. Tadao Sato, *Currents in Japanese Cinema*, 34.

50. For more on Itami's stance on the war, see Kyoko Hirano, "Japanese Filmmakers and the Responsibility for War: The Case of Itami Mansaku" in *War, Occupation, and Creativity: Japan and East Asia 1920–1960*, ed. Marlene J. Mayo, J. Thomas Rimer, and H. Eleanor Kerkham (Honolulu, HI: University of Hawai'i Press, 2001), 212–34.

51. Joo, *Ozu*, 129; Richie, *Ozu*, 229.

52. Bordwell, *Poetics*, 8.

53. A painting of Fuji appears in the 1958 *Equinox Flower* as a riff on the Shochiku logo.

54. Joo, *Ozu*, 131.

55. The stupas have been identified as gravestones for the Soga Brothers, famous for avenging their father, so they are thematically relevant in addition to representing the darker side of Buddhism. Daisuke Miyao notes the darker lighting used to characterize them. See Daisuke Miyao, "Ozu and the Aesthetics of Shadow: Lighting and Cinematography in *There Was a Father* (1942)" in Choi, *Reorienting Ozu*, 128.

56. The insect in this case seems, for the sake of expediency, to have been pinned to the fixture instead of being alive and hovering.

57. Daisuke Miyao notes that the lighting used for Horikawa, even for his funerary urn, is almost always bright, which is thematically appropriate given his saintliness. Cameraman Atsuta remarked that he deliberately made the lighting for the death scene very bright and felt it contrasted with and heightened the scene's sadness, but it also emphasizes the "good death" that Horikawa dies. See Miyao, "Ozu and the Aesthetics of Shadow," 126.

58. High, *Imperial Screen*, 174.

59. Bordwell, *Poetics*, 290.

60. Ozu lived in Matsuzaka, away from his father, whose business was in Tokyo, for a decade during his childhood, then lost him to heart disease in 1934. Some of the scenes toward the end of *There Was a Father* were based on his own father's death. See Richie, *Ozu*, 219.

61. Since Japan had been at war since 1931, it does not matter whether the plot device involving Yoshida's death and Horikawa's anguish over it was conceived in 1937 or 1942. Its message to the military would have been the same, only heightened in 1942.

62. Bordwell, *Poetics*, 292.

63. High, *Imperial Screen*, 42.

64. Peter B. High, "A Drama of Superimposed Maps: Ozu's *So Far from the Land of Our Parents*," *Gengobunkaronshū/Journal of Language Culture* 29, no. 2 (March 2008), 5.

65. Joo, *Ozu*, 115.

66. Shillony, *Politics*, 96.

67. High, "A Drama of Superimposed Maps," 20nn11–12.

68. Akira Kurosawa, *Something Like an Autobiography*, trans. Audie Bock (New York: Vintage Books, 1983), 131.

69. High, "A Drama of Superimposed Maps," 19.

7
The Reckoning

> The authority of the Emperor and the Japanese Government shall be subject to the Supreme Commander of the Allied Powers.
>
> —Truman administration, August 11, 1945

Japan formally surrendered on September 2, 1945, and the American Occupation of Japan under the Supreme Commander for the Allied Powers (SCAP) began. With it came a reckoning. War trials were held; Tojo and others deemed to be war criminals were hanged; key players were removed from their jobs, among them Shiro Kido, head of Shochiku, who was suspended until 1950. Others in the film industry did their own soul-searching. Critic Akira Iwasaki, who spent time in jail for his leftist views, wrote, "without a doubt, every last one of them [Ozu and others] harbored strong moral qualms about the war. But once the artillery opened up in foreign fields, they rallied to support the war. It wasn't that they had been forcefully drafted into the war effort. Rather, they gave of themselves freely, feeling it their duty as subjects of the state."[1] When public debate on the subject erupted during a union meeting at the Toho studio, it was concluded that almost everyone had collaborated in some way. "In the end, no ethical stance was achieved," noted one observer. "[I]n typical Japanese fashion, everything was swept under the carpet of vagueness."[2] "In typical Japanese fashion" essentially meant rejecting "either . . . or"—guilty or not guilty—in favor of "both . . . and."[3]

The Tokyo Ozu returned to was hosting an occupying army, had been devastated by aerial bombing, suffered from acute food shortages, and was home to thousands of widows and orphans. Ozu's next two films would be about them.

Hard Times (*Record of a Tenement Gentleman*, 1947; *A Hen in the Wind*, 1948)

Record of a Tenement Gentleman and *A Hen in the Wind* were Ozu's contributions to a genre of films made in Rome, Berlin, and Tokyo amid the devastation, poverty, and squalor that characterized the defeated Axis nations in the immediate aftermath of World War II. American censors guided those made in Germany, known as *Trümmerfilme* (rubble films), and those in Japan. The censors in Germany seem to have been more liberal than those in Japan, where they were wary and sometimes arbitrary. Among the reasons for their wariness were the extreme cultural differences between Japan and the United States. Germany stripped of Nazism was a recognizable Western culture, and, while Nazism drew on certain aspects of European culture, anti-Semitism in particular, its most salient attributes, industrial-scale eugenics and genocide, were the stuff of science fiction and nightmares, easily recognized and rooted out, at least in a film script.

On the other hand, if a constellation of internal and international politics had brought on Japan's war, the toxic cocktail that had supported it was drawn entirely from traditional Japanese culture: anti-Westernization, fealty, emperor worship, Shinto, purification rites, a tolerance of suicide, and so on. The American project to disarm and democratize Japan "in order to rehabilitate it as a member of the world community" was faced with eliminating the excesses of the wartime culture while respecting traditions the Japanese held dear.[4] Accounts of film censorship under the Occupation read like a comedy of errors, but in general the two sides worked together amicably. The Japanese film community, used to accommodating decades of censorship, quickly adjusted to the new demands, and most were grateful to be out from under the Japanese wartime censors.[5]

SCAP censors, divided into two bureaucracies, the CCD and the CI&E (Civil Censorship Detachment and Civil Intelligence and Education) pushed for films that promoted democracy, individualism, sexual expression, women's liberation, and baseball. Prohibited was anything deemed to promote militarism, revenge, nationalism, xenophobia, a misrepresentation of history, discrimination, feudal loyalty, suicide, the subjugation of women, or the abuse of children.[6] In addition, the censors did not want the war, the Occupation itself, the difficulties of postwar life or the atomic bomb to be mentioned in films, nor did they want it generally known that the films had been censored! Consequently, filmmakers were required to create smooth continuity anytime a line or a scene had to be cut.[7] Japanese films were also subject to some of the same requirements as American films of the time, namely, moral probity and, as the Cold War progressed, anti-communism.[8]

Throughout his career, Ozu had had to veil his criticism of government policies, and that would continue during the Occupation, no less but no more than before. In fact, one of the more noteworthy aspects of his postwar films is the extent to which they carried on the motifs, images, strategies, and subterfuges of his prewar films.

Record of a Tenement Gentleman expanded on the idea, put forward in *There Was a Father*, that in such fraught times people need to help one another. The film begins with neighborhood denizen Tamekichi's apparently unmotivated monologue, which comes from a *shinpa* play called *Onna keizu*, based on a 1907 novel by Kyoka Izumi.[9] *Onna keizu* was filmed multiple times, once in 1942, thus only four years before *Tenement Gentleman*, so Japanese audiences may well have understood the reference if not the reason for the recitation.[10] However, the line "Even the moon is shadowed once in a while, let alone small human beings who are easily shadowed into darkness,"

The Reckoning

is particularly pertinent to this story, as Bordwell and others have pointed out.[11] The "small human beings" are, of course, the homeless children with which the film concerns itself but also the Japanese people as a whole, who were experiencing far more darkness than the film could reveal.

Another puzzling but pertinent aspect of the recitation is that the speaker is asking for a divorce. Tamekichi is alone, and we never find out for whom the speech is intended or why, but its theme, ultimately, is separation. When his roommate Tashiro appears with a lost child, Tamekichi wants nothing to do with him and suggests they dump the child on Otane, their neighbor across the street, who runs a small broom shop. She feels put upon and struggles to care for the boy, Kohei, who is at bed-wetting age. A neighborhood meeting, enhanced by sake and Tashiro's singing, starts to change the film's ethos from separation to community. Eventually, Otane comes to love her young charge just as his father shows up to claim him. In addition to changing her attitude toward the boy, she realizes she had misjudged the father, whom she supposed had knowingly abandoned him. She resolves to adopt one of the many homeless boys who populate Tokyo. The film ends with shots of homeless boys in Ueno Park, gathered near the statue of samurai hero Saigo.

Unable to distinguish between Kohei and the boy we see in full frame, sitting among the orphans beneath the Saigo statue, Lars-Martin Sorensen revives the "ambiguous ending" theory of Ozu's work, suggesting that perhaps Kohei's father really has abandoned him.[12] However, the boy at the end is not Kohei (actor Hohi Aoki), but Ozu has costumed him similarly, presumably to let his audience know that there were a lot of Kohei's out there needing to be adopted.

The problem Ozu pointed to in *Tenement Gentleman* was widespread and seemingly incurable in part because, instead of showing sympathy, Japanese tended to stigmatize "anyone who did not fall into a 'proper' social category." John Dower adds, "Many of the most pathetic Japanese war victims now became the country's new outcasts."[13] Asked why Japan did nothing about its street children, author Jiro Osaragi concluded in 1948 that "as a people, they simply lacked love toward strangers," and wondered if "Japanese were shallower than other peoples when it came to love?"[14] Even Ozu regarded his postwar subjects as "cold-hearted."[15] The message in *Tenement Gentleman* might seem simplistic, formulaic, and overly didactic, but in light of the social norms of the time, it was a radical call for Japanese to reach out to help others.

A Hen in the Wind examines the plight of women left to fend for themselves in the immediate postwar period. According to Dower, such women "were forced to support themselves and their children in an environment in which military salaries had ceased to arrive, wartime factory jobs had been abolished, and millions of men back from overseas as well as others laid off from defunct wartime industries were competing for scarce jobs."[16] For such women, prostitution often became their only means of survival.

Hen's Tokiko is not technically a widow, but her husband has not yet come home from the war, and she finds herself with no money and a sick child. To pay the hospital bill, she accepts one assignation in a house of prostitution, and, although Ozu makes sure we understand that she does not actually have intercourse with her john, she, her best friend, Chieko, and her husband, Shuichi, who eventually comes home, all agree that she was a "fool" and that she should/could have sought other means of help. But since no one she knows has money to lend, her only other choice would have been to sell her sewing machine, her sole means of support at a time when she had no way of knowing when or if her husband might return.

With an occupying army in residence, prostitution in this period was so common in Japan that children played a game called *panpan asobi*, in which they enacted procuring prostitutes for GI's with the same innocence and enjoyment that children elsewhere played "house."[17] In 1947, an interview with a woman named Otoki, in which she described the reasons women turned to prostitution and the difficulty they had extracting themselves from such a life because of the stigma that followed them, was broadcast on the radio and caught the public's attention.[18]

In *Hen in the Wind*, Ozu divides his take on prostitution into two parts. The first, involving Tokiko, is a recycling and updating of Otaka's plight in *An Inn in Tokyo*. A woman with a child, no husband, and no job—Tokiko is a seamstress but brings in little money from it—finds prostitution her best option when her child falls sick. (Even though all kinds of infectious diseases were rampant in Japan at this time—a fact Ozu acknowledges when a policeman asks Sakai, Tokiko's landlord, if he has had his typhoid shot—her child succumbs to the same illness that almost all of Ozu's young children suffer from: an inflammation of the colon brought on by too many sweets.)

The film's second look at prostitution is more in keeping with the times. Tokiko's husband, Shuichi, obsessively seeks out the location of the relevant brothel and meets one of its regular workers, Fusako. She explains that she is the sole support for her family. Instead of bedding her, he offers to find her a decent job. Like Otoki in the radio broadcast, she objects that once a prostitute, it is impossible to climb back into decent society, but Shuichi insists that her life can change and makes good on his promise.

Tadao Sato believed the film was meant to disabuse the Japanese of their claim to a unique "purity," which played such an important a role in wartime propaganda and was supposed to make Japanese soldiers superior to others and enable them to win the war.[19] But the film is also about innocence and contrasts innocence with purity. Purity in the wartime sense was comprised of those virtues of sacrifice on display in *There Was a Father*, symbolized by the hot springs bath father and son share. (Traditional bathing in Japan is a kind of purification rite that requires washing and rinsing the body before relaxing in a very hot, very deep bath intended to cleanse body, mind, and soul.) Purity meant following *bushido* (the samurai code), unconditional loyalty to the emperor, a willingness to die rather than surrender, and so on. As a soldier, Tokiko's husband, Shuichi, has been indoctrinated with these notions of purity and is disillusioned when he comes home and finds his wife has been "impure."

Innocence, on the other hand, is evoked by Chieko when she and Tokiko talk about their childhood and by the prostitute Fusako when she comments that she used to go to the school which stands, in glorious irony, right behind the brothel. But innocence also exists in the present. The sound of children singing *Natsu wa kinu* ("Summer has Come") plays over shots of Fusako's school as well as her subsequent conversation with Shuichi. The images of summer that the song describes contrast with the ugly present of the film's mise-en-scène.

The walls of Tokiko's room are covered with childlike images: pictures of *kokeishi* dolls, an Impressionist print of a mother and child, a Bobbsey Twin-like child, and a Mary Poppins-esque figure. There are also real children in the film, principally Tokiko's son, Hiroshi.

The war has compromised innocence, but it proves more resilient than "purity," and it is Shuichi, not Tokiko, who is pointedly shown to have lost his innocence when he rapes his wife. A full shot of toddler Hiroshi, who wakes up while Shuichi is browbeating Tokiko, demanding all the details of her experience, precedes the rape. As Shuichi pushes Tokiko down behind a half-closed *fusuma*, a child's paper balloon—heir to those from happier days in *Walk Cheerfully* and *Tokyo Chorus*—falls off a dresser onto the floor. The Sakai family below is shown sleeping innocently. After the rape, the paper balloon appears in the foreground behind Shuichi as he sits brooding. During this time a moth flits around the light fixture above him. Formerly indicative of a dead child or one close to death, the self-destructive insect here suggests the death of Shuichi's own innocence. That the moth symbol pertains particularly to him is made clear by the light flickering on his face, ostensibly created by the insect fluttering in front of the light. Significantly, Ozu does not include a moth in the scenes of Hiroshi in the hospital, even though a bare light bulb is clearly visible, but saves it to serve as a less clichéd, more trenchant symbol, i.e., lost innocence.

Unlike purity, which Tokiko feels she has lost irretrievably, innocence can be regained. Shuichi begins his redemption when he helps the prostitute Fusako recover hers. As in *Tenement Gentleman*, reaching out to help others is posited as the best way for Japanese to move forward and put the war behind them.

Despite helping Fusako, Shuichi still cannot reconcile himself to what feels like Tokiko's betrayal, and the symptoms he describes to his boss, Satake, are classic PTSD. Since SCAP censors did not want filmmakers to reference the war directly, Shuichi and his inability to forgive Tokiko become emblematic of the disillusion experienced by thousands of Japanese veterans, who not only felt betrayed by their government, for whom they had been ready to sacrifice everything, but came home to find themselves reviled by their fellow citizens. According to Dower, "For a great many ex-soldiers and sailors, the greatest shock of returning home lay in finding themselves treated, after all their travails, as pariahs in their native land."[20]

Hen's Orie, the brothel's cynical liaison, reinforces the idea that the veterans' sacrifices were essentially worthless when she mocks a war medal, "7th Order of Merit," that she has been given to sell. Only by committing more violence toward Tokiko does Shuichi finally accept his boss Satake's advice to forget the past and forgive her. If we wonder why it takes him so long or why Ozu shows him so frequently simply brooding in medium shots and close-ups, it is because the battle he fights is with much more than

126   *Ozu*

Tokiko's infidelity. We have seen the way in which Ozu sometimes substitutes a minor character's experience or feeling for those of a major character (Chapter 4). Here he substitutes Tokiko's particular betrayal for the country's betrayal of its veterans.

At the end Shuichi forgives Tokiko and agrees to move on. "Let's be more generous," he says. Generosity forsakes "purity" and restores innocence. Ozu ends the film with shots of Hiroshi and other young children playing outside the tenement. They are the true innocents, and they are the future.[21]

The bleak industrial landscapes from *An Inn in Tokyo* and *The Only Son* recur in *Tenement Gentleman* and *Hen* as war-shattered landscapes. In *Tenement Gentleman* the open land behind Otane's neighborhood has obviously been bulldozed, and new construction can be seen in the distance. In *Hen*, the characters live in workers' tenements attached to an abandoned, presumably bombed-out, factory. Large holding tanks encircled by spiraling lattice-like catwalks dominate every shot of the neighborhood. The more distant tanks from *Inn* and *Only Son* now loom menacingly over the landscape in this film.[22]

Drying laundry, so often emblematic of a bright new day, is now wedged, at least visually, between the tanks, its happy connotation completely lost. Following a shot of Shuichi dragging himself home after a night spent away, we see three *yukata* (cotton kimonos) hanging on laundry poles, their long sagging shapes echoing his despairing mood.

Ozu emphasizes not only the barren, ugly landscape in *Hen* but also the fact that the factory is closed and completely deteriorated. Whatever its original purpose—it undoubtedly turned out war matériel in its most recent past—it has no jobs to offer the residents, who still live in its worker-designated housing. One recurring motif, the piece of large rusty industrial pipe with an attached flange that turns up in multiple settings, typifies the ruined landscape in general and the abandoned factory in particular.

Besides joblessness, hunger, homeless children, devastated landscapes, and prostitution, other indications of the immediate postwar period include references to the black market, high prices, rationing, procuring food from the countryside—both Otane and the boy's father in *Tenement Gentleman* bring back potatoes from Chigasaki—and crowded trains. *Hen*'s Shuichi says he had to stand up all night on the train, and *Tenement Gentleman*'s Otane mentions having to climb in through the train window to get home from Chigasaki.[23]

Ozu rehabilitated the neighborhood association (*tonari-gumi*) in *Tenement Gentleman*. These associations had spied on their members during the war and coerced them into a variety of activities that supported the war effort. SCAP had ordered them disbanded, but Ozu shows this one as a positive force for the community, promoting camaraderie, mutual aid, and hope. In general, SCAP censors did not want this or any mention of postwar conditions included in films, but they specifically objected to the treatment of the boy in *Tenement Gentleman* as "too cruel."[24]

Kyoko Hirano has suggested that bribery may have allowed *Tenement Gentleman* to proceed as written.[25] Whether references to the realities of postwar life in both films

The Reckoning   127

survived because of bribery or because they were sufficiently subtle for the censors to overlook them or because Ozu simply ignored the censors' "suggestions" is unknown.[26]

Edward Fowler and Lars-Martin Sorensen have, between them, advanced the theory that *Tenement Gentleman* is constructed around a highly nationalistic, anti-American agenda.[27] To be sure, there are lots of reasons to resent an occupying army, even one professing the best of intentions, and, as we have seen, Ozu, throughout his career, was inclined to tweak the nose of whatever government and/or censorship board he and his work were subject to. But to assume the kind of wholesale rejection of the Occupation program as well as a lingering nationalistic allegiance to a defeated government, whose ambitions, lies, and fantasies had destroyed Japan, as Fowler and Sorensen do, assumes, first, a willingness to ignore the continuity in Ozu's work; second, that Ozu was no longer the subtle, nuanced thinker we have thus far seen him to be; and, finally, that, faced with a shattered country, he had nothing better to do with his public platform than inveigh against the conqueror.

Fowler's main contribution to this argument is his discovery of an approximate image of an American flag disguised in the futon that the young boy pees on in *Tenement Gentleman*.[28] Sorensen has added to our understanding of this image by noting that the pee stain, which we are shown at one point in a lengthy close-up, looks like an approximation of a mushroom cloud.[29] I accept that these hidden images exist and were probably intentional, but what they proclaim is not an all-purpose anti-Americanism but a very specific critique.

As part of an aggressor army with the opportunity to observe some of its worst excesses, Ozu well understood the devastation war brings and that Japan had reaped what it had sown, but for Japanese and for much of the rest of the world the nuclear bombing of civilian populations in Hiroshima and Nagasaki was a bridge too far. If the futon in *Tenement Gentleman* is an American flag, nuclear holocaust in particular is the stain on it, not the Occupation in general. This is the flag that Ozu showed right next to the teacher's head in the party sequence in *Tokyo Chorus* (see Figure 2.4, p. 50); this is the country he championed via Joan Crawford's portrait in *The Only Son*, while mocking Japan's new ally, Germany. This is the country whose movies he loved. But through his pee-stained "flag," Ozu draws a line at nuclear warfare.

Even if one believed that the Japanese were still highly nationalistic and felt more oppressed by a comparatively liberal occupying army than by their own wartime government, the idea that Ozu's flag image would have resonated with them seems unlikely, given that, to my knowledge, no one had ever mentioned the futon *cum* flag before Edward Fowler advanced the idea in a 1998 conference at Dartmouth College. Like the Goya portrait in *Toda Family*, few besides Ozu himself would have caught or understood the reference.

Adding to the litany of parallels Bordwell has found in *Tenement Gentleman* is a futon hanging outside a home in the Chigasaki sequence that is, atypically, all stripes.[30] This illustrates not only Ozu's "parametric" balancing but his sense of humor: one futon has the stars, another the stripes. If few viewers recognized the peed-upon "American flag" as such, fewer still would have noticed the futon supplying the missing "stripes." Ozu's joke was mainly for himself.

We have seen that *Tenement Gentleman* moves from separation to inclusion, from selfishness to community, but instead of seeing Ozu exhorting a traditionally family-centric society to broaden its concerns, Fowler perceives a move from a selfish, Americanized present back to a community-oriented Japanese past.[31] Unfortunately for this argument, the Japanese did not necessarily credit themselves with a community-oriented past. No less a patriot than Crown Prince Akihito would write privately that the Japanese had lost the war in part because of "individual selfishness" and concede that "the Americans were superior when it came to working as a group."[32] What we forget when we accept the cliché of American individualism versus Japanese group-orientation is that the latter was burdened by hierarchy, social propriety, and a disdain for outsiders, hence Otane's immediate dislike of her young charge and her assumption that his father is a bum.

Fowler also sees Tamekichi's "après-guerre" daughter, Yukiko, as an indictment of "democracy and individualism."[33] However, the après-guerre young woman, who would wend her way throughout Ozu's postwar films, is simply an updating of the prewar *moga*, who might or might not be a sympathetic figure in Ozu's films. Moreover, if Tamekichi's daughter seems selfish and rude—she visits him without bringing any food with her—so is Tamekichi! He is the one who adamantly refuses to have anything to do with the lost boy, cheats in the drawing to see who will bring the child back to his old home in Chigasaki, and helps himself, uninvited, to Otane's dried persimmons. Selfishness here is a family—not an American—affair.

Hen in the Wind makes clear that the "Americanization" of Japan did not start with the Occupation as Fowler implies when he describes *Tenement Gentleman*'s Yukiko. During Tokiko's picnic with Chieko, we learn that, as late as 1941, when she quit work, presumably to get married, Tokiko dreamed of a house in the suburbs with a lawn, an Airedale, and a Max Factor compact, the last of which her husband eventually bought for her. In this exchange Ozu makes it clear that young people like Tokiko yearned for these American embellishments in their lives right up to the attack on Pearl Harbor, despite the war on "Westernization" that intellectuals and others who molded public opinion had been waging throughout the 1930s. This conversation between Tokiko and Chieko moves from nostalgia for childhood to nostalgia, not simply for a prewar past, since Japan was deeply involved in its war with China by 1941, but specifically for a pre–Pearl Harbor past.

Other American references in *Hen* include the Mobil Gas sign on the wall in landlord Sakai's living room, the jazz club next to Shuichi's office—boss Satake tells him that "cabarets have opened everywhere"—and the movie posters in Orie's room. These, too, are cited as part of Ozu's anti-American agenda, but they are simply extensions of motifs he had been using since the late 1920s. English-language advertisements for American products were ubiquitous in his early films, particularly in *Where Now Are the Dreams of Youth?* The jazz club in *Dragnet Girl* is presumably an endorsement of

American culture—gangsters hang out there, of course, but they are *our* gangsters—and in *Hen* Shuichi's calm, sensible boss, Satake, enjoys the jazz music coming from the nearby club.

Posters for three American movies appear in procuress Orie's room in *Hen*. Sorensen insists that because she is the one who tempts Tokiko into prostitution, the presence of American movie posters are meant to send an anti-American message despite the fact that Ozu's prewar films are crammed with American movie posters.[34] Bordwell supposes that, given their titles and/or artwork, they are intended to reflect on Orie and her loose life.[35] The titles *Kiss and Tell* and *Love Letters* and the couple embracing in *The Green Years* poster certainly point in that direction, but Bordwell's assumption is only partly true, for these posters do double duty. *Love Letters* (1945) is about a woman with a dual personality, and this, of course, refers to Tokiko. Tokiko's statement "I'd sell my soul to care for my child," are the last words we hear before we see the poster, and, later in the film, Ozu revives his doppelgänger mirror shots to literally reflect Tokiko's wrenching decision to indulge in prostitution for this reason. In a six-shot sequence he cuts back and forth between close-ups of her and her reflection in the mirror as she tries to come to terms with what she is about to do (Figure 7.1).

Figure 7.1: A conflicted Tokiko gazes into her mirror as she decides prostitution is her only option in *A Hen in the Wind*.

The title of the 1945 film *Kiss and Tell* refers to the fact that Tokiko does exactly that, tells her husband about her indiscretion. However, this film is actually a comedy starring a teenaged Shirley Temple, and we see Chieko framed with the words "Shirley Temple" behind her as she talks with Orie, another indication of the childhood innocence associated with Chieko.

The poster for *The Green Years*, a 1946 Hollywood film, appears behind Orie. Although it shows a couple embracing, meant to characterize one aspect of her "business," it is actually a feel-good family film. We see the poster as Orie explains to Chieko the financial advantages of prostitution, so the title, quite divorced from the film's plot, functions to describe Orie's comfortable and profitable life as a procuress and a black marketer.

While I reject the notion that either *Tenement Gentleman* or *Hen in the Wind* is programmatically anti-American or anti-Occupation, both films contain much material, besides the futon-flags, which was either officially forbidden or that subtly resists SCAP policies. The embracing couple from *The Green Years* poster is one example. In addition to forbidding certain subjects in films, SCAP encouraged others, one of which was portraying physical affection, otherwise known as "kissing scenes."[36] Although filmmakers and audiences came to like this directive, there was considerable resistance at first, understandable in a culture where modesty and discretion were highly valued. Showing the embracing couple on *The Green Years* poster was Ozu's way of fulfilling this demand while mocking it at the same time.

One SCAP directive Ozu had no trouble following was that forbidding too much detail in rape scenes. We understand Shuichi's rape of Tokiko in *Hen* mainly in theory, and Tokiko's encounter with her john is conveyed only by shots of the empty bedroom.

SCAP policies discouraged films about the feudal past (*jidai-geki*) or references to samurai. Ostensibly Ozu included the Saigo statue in Ueno Park in *Tenement Gentleman* because it was an actual gathering place for war orphans, but Saigo himself is also the subject here. Sometimes called "the last true samurai," Saigo was instrumental in forming the new Meiji government in 1869, though he later rebelled against it. He can be thought of as the father of Japanese militarism in that he helped to establish a conscript army, wished to provoke war with Korea, and opposed both modernization and opening Japan to the West. Sorensen sees the statue as a nod to what he supposes was Ozu's abiding militarism, nationalism, and anti-Americanism, but, as we have seen, Ozu held to none of these with any consistency.[37] Saigo was a complex hero in a country with a complex history, which was entering an unprecedented new phase: foreign occupation. Ozu knew well how things had come to this—his films had documented the trajectory—but that made it no less tragic. In the film's final shot, Saigo has his back to us (Figure 7.2). The poignancy of this last sequence extends beyond the orphaned boys to Japan itself, a country that had betrayed both its past and its future.

The overtones of Christianity present in *Tenement Gentleman* and *Hen* add to the complexity of their subtexts, which are neither for nor against the Occupation. For starters, the Judeo-Christian tradition exhorts its followers to care for widows, orphans,

Figure 7.2: *Record of a Tenement Gentleman* ends with Saigo's back turned to the audience.

and strangers, just as these two films enjoin their audience to do.[38] Moreover, *Hen*'s Tokiko is an updating not only of *An Inn in Tokyo*'s Otaka but also of *Dragnet Girl*'s Tokiko—same actress, same character name, same full-length embrace at the end (only the second in the extant films). Like *Dragnet Girl*, *Hen in the Wind* employs specifically Christian references: the redemption of the fallen woman, the invocation of forgiveness, and the close-up of Tokiko's hands, clasped behind Shuichi during their final embrace, as if in prayer. Ozu works up to this last shot of Tokiko's hands by showing her intertwined fingers earlier in the film, clasped more in anxiety than prayer, but this last shot is clearly meant to suggest praying hands. Buddhists pray, at least ceremonially, with the palms of their hands held together. Hands clasped with fingers interlaced is typically Christian.[39]

Ozu would remain the quintessential "both . . . and" director, invoking humanism, even Christianity, while pining for the selfless austerity of the samurai spirit. In these two films he responds in particular ways to the strictures imposed by the Occupation censors, but overall these early Occupation films show a remarkable consistency with his earlier work: similar themes, motifs, characters, and humor, and the same subtle critiques of current government policies, some funny, some serious.

Neither *Tenement Gentleman* nor *Hen in the Wind* was successful at the box office. Perhaps the Japanese public did not want to see a milder version of the hell they were

132   *Ozu*

living through and/or perhaps they no longer wished to be lectured to. Ozu would, in any case, take a sweet story from 1939 for his next film, Kazuo Hirotsu's *Chichi to musume* ("Father and Daughter") about a single father whose only means of persuading his daughter to marry is to get married himself.

Reverse Course (*Late Spring*, 1949)

With *Late Spring*, Ozu revived his collaboration with scriptwriter Kogo Noda, with whom he had not worked since 1935. Noda had written only a third of Ozu's silent films, but he would become the director's sole collaborator from this time on. He is credited with steering Ozu away from using the impoverished classes as subject matter and back to the middle class. All of the subsequent films would deal with this comparatively affluent social milieu except for *Floating Weeds*, a remake of 1934's *Story of Floating Weeds*. Since Ozu describes his collaboration with Noda as one of almost perfect agreement, it seems likely he was already headed in this direction.[40]

Based on a Kazuo Hirotsu story, first published in *Gendai* magazine, *Late Spring* looks to instill a sense of normality in a country still under occupation and still recovering from the war. Widespread hunger had, for example, only finally abated by 1949, the year *Late Spring* was made. Father Somiya's seemingly absurd argument with his sister Masa about whether she would eat at her wedding if she were a contemporary bride—"You'd eat!" he insists—makes sense against this background. It fits with Ozu's jokes about ladies' appetites, which, in the extant films, began with *What Did the Lady Forget?* and continued through many of his subsequent films. *Late Spring*'s petite Aya wants "just a little" jam, but "a lot actually," and she is later shown with a gigantic piece of "short cake." In this film, these jokes are embedded in a harsh reality.

Concerned with a father's attempt to get his daughter married, the story assumes a 1939 normality that simply did not exist a decade later. When, after the heroine Noriko's *omiai* (meeting between prospective marriage partners), Aya advises, "Good men are rare these days. Grab him!" she echoes a cliché that could have come from Rosalind Russell or any number of women in any number of time periods, but in 1949 Japan it was no cliché. An inordinate number of "good men" were dead and families in such disarray that local governments arranged *shudan miai*, marriage markets intended to help large numbers of young men and women find partners simultaneously. John Dower writes, "young women of marriageable age . . . found themselves in the most desperate circumstances, for the demography of death in the recent war had removed a huge aggregation of prospective husbands . . . A large cohort of women, most of them born between 1916 and 1926, [Noriko would have been born in 1922] confronted the prospect not merely of coping with postwar hardships without a marriage partner, but of never marrying at all."[41] The 1948 *shudan miai* illustrated in Dower's book took place at the Hachiman Shrine in Kamakura, the same shrine that Somiya and Masa visit to pray that Noriko will accept the man they've proposed for her. Certainly a disconnect existed between the cozy world portrayed in the film and the postwar hardships many Japanese still faced, but that was in large part the point of the film: to restore a sense of normality.

Joo quotes Tadao Sato as concluding that *Late Spring* "completely wiped out all these postwar phenomena [as if] there had never been a war."[42] However, the war is mentioned—Noriko has suffered from anemia because of food shortages and her wartime labor—but with a popular postwar interpretation: "She was a victim!" says friend Onodera when Somiya describes Noriko's wartime hardships. Critics have noted the way in which postwar Japanese almost immediately cast themselves into the role of victims, thereby relieving themselves of responsibility for the suffering they had caused so many others.[43] Within its first twenty minutes, *Late Spring* echoes this popular sentiment.

Meanwhile, the presence of the occupying army is, despite censorship prohibitions, referred to obliquely. Exterior shots of the train Somiya and Noriko take into Tokyo clearly show the car reserved for Occupation personnel with its wide white line painted on the side (Figure 7.3). When Noriko bikes near the beach with her father's assistant, Hattori, they pass over a small bridge with instructions in English as to the maximum miles per hour and tonnage allowed, clearly meant for American military drivers. (The speed is also posted in Japanese for the benefit of Japanese civilians, particularly those who would have been driving trucks for the US military.)

Figure 7.3: In *Late Spring*, exterior shots of the train Somiya and Noriko take into Tokyo show the white stripe on the car designated exclusively for American Occupation personnel.

The Coca-Cola advertisement the couple subsequently passes has more to do with Ozu's longstanding fascination with American products and advertising graphics than with exposing the Occupation, but barely visible below it is an arrow pointing the way to Hiratsuka Beach, which is not far from Chigasaki, where Hattori and Noriko are headed. Hiratsuka had been the site of an ammunition arsenal for the Imperial Navy and a military aircraft factory, both of which were destroyed by American bombing in 1945. It had been considered an ideal landing beach for the planned US invasion of Japan, and, given that the words on the arrow below the Coca-Cola sign are written in English, it was presumably being used by the US Navy in 1949.

Despite its attempts to convey normality, *Late Spring* is as much an "Occupation film" as *Hen in the Wind* and *Tenement Gentleman*, but many of the analyses that purport to show this are misdirected or overblown. David Bordwell and Kristin Thompson feel that Noriko's father's sweetness, his refusal to order Noriko to marry, and his lack of regard for the continuity of his *ie* (family line) constitute an affirmation of Occupation reforms, which elevated the status of women and abolished the *ie* and Family Registry.[44] The latter had been highly touted by Japan's wartime government, but, in fact, the *ie* had lost its relevance for most urban Japanese by the end of the 1930s, if not earlier, and has no relevance whatever in any of Ozu's films, except perhaps *Toda Family*, where it is clearly falling apart. Moreover, a daughter cannot perpetuate an *ie* unless her family adopts her husband, which is not Somiya's intention in *Late Spring*.

Somiya as a sweet, caring father is simply an extension of the father in *There Was a Father*, not some new invention inspired by the Occupation. Where Horikawa exhorts his son to accept the necessity of their living separately and sacrificing their mutual happiness in the name of "duty," Somiya likewise pushes his daughter to separate from him, in this case because that is how life and the human race are able to continue. Both fathers cherish their offspring, and neither is overbearing.

If Japanese families ordered their daughters to marry particular men prior to the Occupation, that notion is not borne out by popular literature. In Hirotsu's *Chichi to musume* the father marries his secretary in order to relieve his daughter of her sense of responsibility for him; and in Tanizaki's *Makioka Sisters* (*Sasameyuki*), written during the war about the 1930s, the family demonstrates enormous patience with sister Yukiko, enduring endless *omiai*, until she finally finds the perfect partner.[45]

This raises the question of Noriko's *omiai*. Occupation authorities tried to promote the idea of "love marriages" based on young people's own preferences and discouraged *miai* marriages both in real life and on celluloid, but Japanese families continued the practice, which they found sensible and convenient. In *Late Spring* Ozu gets around the censors, first, by never showing the *omiai* and, second, by letting Noriko voice her disapproval of "arranged marriage." Aya, whose own "love marriage" has failed, takes the other side, insisting that Noriko is much too reticent to find a husband in any other way. (She has indeed missed the opportunity to begin a courtship with her father's assistant, Hattori, a man she is clearly attracted to.) Thus Ozu frames a debate, which, while not new, was raging in Japan at the time because of Occupation decrees.

The Reckoning   135

I will write about Ozu's liberated women in a later chapter, but suffice to say here that he had previously depicted female heroines who were strong and self-directed. Setsuko in *What did the Lady Forget?* is played in large part for laughs, but, as the quintessential *moga*, she is smart, accomplished, and determined to chart her own course—Americanized long before the Occupation.

On the other hand, Alastair Phillips has pointed out that the schoolchildren that we see visiting the Kiyomizu temple in *Late Spring* are, uncharacteristically, girls, and this may indeed have been a nod to the Occupation.[46] Children always indicate the future, and Japan's future would elevate women in a way its past had not.

Another obvious element that marks *Late Spring* as an Occupation film is baseball. Introduced in the Meiji era, baseball had been enormously popular in Japan and never died out completely during the war years even though banned in 1943 as the "enemy's game." Forced underground until the Occupation, it was not only reintroduced by the Americans but heavily promoted as a democratizing force. *Late Spring* shows a children's baseball game from which Noriko's cousin has withdrawn because he has, for unspecified reasons, painted his bat red and now has red paint all over his glove. Aya uses baseball metaphors when describing how her next marriage will be a "home run," and Noriko's groom supposedly resembles Gary Cooper in "that baseball film." (*Pride of the Yankees* [1942] was released in Japan in 1949 amid great publicity, which included RKO giving away baseball bats and gloves, supposedly as presents from Gary Cooper.[47])

By 1949, the Occupation had changed direction. The reforms of the early years gave way to greater economic pragmatism along with growing anti-communism, characterized by crackdowns on the Japanese Communist Party, on organized labor, and by other "Red purges." Large companies, slated to be broken up, were left intact, and individuals once sidelined for their connection to the wartime militarists were rehabilitated. The Japanese press referred to these changes as "reverse course." Dower writes, "Driven by Cold War considerations, the Americans began to jettison many of the original ideals of 'demilitarization and democratization' that had seemed so unexpected and inspiring to a defeated populace in 1945. In the process, they aligned themselves more and more openly with the conservative and even right-wing elements in Japanese society, including individuals who had been closely identified with the lost war."[48]

Eric Cazdyn sees *Late Spring* reflecting the "reverse course" in a variety of ways, but his arguments are both abstruse and unconvincing.[49] He is not wrong, however, to suppose "reverse course" found its way into the film, very specifically when Onodera asks the location of various landmarks in Kamakura.

ONODERA: Is the ocean near here?

SOMIYA: A 15-minute walk . . .

ONODERA (*pointing over his shoulder*): Is it this way?

SOMIYA (*nodding in another direction*): No, this way.

ONODERA (*gesturing left*): Is the shrine over this way?

SOMIYA (*pointing in the opposite direction*): No, that way.

ONODERA: Which way is Tokyo?

SOMIYA (*pointing to his right*): Tokyo's that way.

ONODERA (*pointing in front of himself*): That means east is that way . . .

SOMIYA (*pointing in the opposite direction*): No, east is that way . . .

ONODERA: Has it always been that way?

SOMIYA: Of course it has!

Kristin Thompson has pointed out that the conversation plays into Ozu's obsession with direction, which indeed it does, that obsession inevitably touching on his use of a 360° cutting space and his frequent violation of the 180° rule.[50] But, as we have seen in *That Night's Wife*, Ozu sometimes used his obsession with direction to mock public entities, in that case the police, and this prolonged and confused conversation about direction, along with the accompanying gestures, would surely have brought the Occupation's "reverse course" to mind for a contemporary audience.

As with *Tenement Gentleman*, Lars-Martin Sorensen analyzes *Late Spring* as anti-Occupation and anti-American. He dismisses the commonly held belief that the Japanese made a "180° turn" from wartime nationalism to accepting the Occupation government and its reforms, but the 180° turn in the 1930s from an infatuation with Western lifestyles and Western-inspired liberties to embracing hyper-nationalism and militarism appears to him both credible and complete.[51] If the deprivations of the Depression rendered the Japanese ripe for militarism, wouldn't the extreme suffering brought on by the war have made them open to something new? John Dower has amassed copious evidence not only of Japanese willingness, often eagerness, to cooperate with the Occupation authorities but of their disillusion with their wartime leaders, including the emperor.[52]

Sorensen details the changes censors asked for in the *Late Spring* script but draws dubious conclusions from this evidence. For example, censorship records indicate that Ozu had wanted to stage the boys' baseball game on a burned-out field, but the burned field did not make it into the film.[53] No further notes on this exist, but we know that the SCAP censors objected to showing war damage, which a burned-out field would suggest. However, we don't know why Ozu wanted to show the burned-out field. Sorensen insists Ozu wanted to show this American game against the backdrop of "war damage" to mock the SCAP censors and their predilection for baseball scenes.[54] But it is just as likely that Ozu had wanted to show baseball and the young people playing it rising, phoenix-like, from the ashes of war. (In 1984, Masahiro Shinoda would dedicate an entire film, *MacArthur's Children*, to this idea.) Not only does *Late Spring* contain other, positive references to baseball—comparing a successful marriage to a home run, for example—but Ozu's prewar films contain many references to college baseball, including the famous Waseda-Keio game. SCAP did not need to twist anyone's arm, least of all Ozu's, to revive baseball or to get it included in postwar films. According to

The Reckoning 137

those who worked with him, Ozu loved baseball so much that he not only encouraged his crew to form a team but called an early halt to shooting on days when they had a game.[55]

In another instance, Ozu had wanted to show a war-damaged landscape in *Late Spring* immediately after the Noh performance, in which Noriko glimpses her father nodding to Mrs. Miwa and becomes consumed with jealousy. The censors wrote: "Is this necessary?" and Ozu dropped the idea.[56] Sorensen believes that showing the war damage was intended as an anti-American indictment and that Ozu instead showed metaphorical "war damage" by having Noriko treat her father very rudely after the performance, which "achieves the subversive effect he had in mind," the presumption being that Noriko's rudeness was the fault of the Occupation because it had liberated women.[57] Noriko's rudeness is, indeed, an issue in the film, but Ozu does not lay it at the feet of the Americans. Setsuko in *What Did the Lady Forget?* and Setsuko in *The Brothers and Sisters of the Toda Family* are rude to their elders. We don't know, of course, what Ozu had in mind by wishing to include "war damage" in this scene, but his intention was more likely to illustrate Noriko's shattered psyche than to stoke anti-American sentiment.

We also don't know why, in both instances, Ozu dropped the idea of showing war damage. As we have seen with other films, he was inclined to ignore the censors' suggestions when he felt strongly about particular scenes. I would argue that showing war damage in a film that was trying to restore a sense of normality might have defeated that purpose. I suspect the decision to respect the censors' suggestions was driven as much by Ozu's own thematic and aesthetic purposes as by fear that the finished film would not be approved.

Ozu does, in fact, refer obliquely and not very sympathetically to "war damage" when he has Onodera complain about the "horrible people" in Ueno Park, where he and Noriko have just visited an art exhibit, one of whom was trying to shoot a pigeon off the head of "the statue." The statue, of course, is Saigo, where the war orphans were seen congregating in *Tenement Gentleman*. Apparently many were still there, two years older, and they had no doubt been joined by homeless veterans.[58] (Sorensen has noted that the censors objected to mentioning the name "Saigo," hence "the statue."[59])

Fundamental to the flaws in Sorensen's approach to Japanese film and history is his dogmatic, Western "either . . . or" mindset: if Ozu supported the war effort in the early 1940s, he could not have tolerated the Occupation; if the Japanese were indoctrinated with nationalism, they could not have turned around and embraced the Occupation, and so on. His analysis of *Late Spring* pushes this bifurcation to absurdity by asserting that the film is neatly divided between East and West. Everything associated with the Occupation—including anything of Western origin and characters with Western leanings, like Aya, the updated *moga*—was dirty and bad. Everything "Japanese"—including Somiya, Noriko, Aunt Masa, the many shrines, temples, ancient cities, tea ceremony, and so on—was clean and good. Yet all of the characters are patently a mixture of Japanese and Western tastes and characteristics. Somiya is a member of PEN, an international organization dedicated to creating a "world community of writers," and Aya, the modern girl, voices Buddhist notions of fate when she says, "Everything is divine providence." Both Aya and Noriko have a predilection for Western-style tea, and even Aunt Masa has evidently seen "that baseball movie" (*Pride of the Yankees*). In addition, there is a cuckoo clock in the hall outside Noriko's room and a European peasant doll in her room, remnants perhaps of Japan's infatuation with Teutonic artifacts.

I have detailed some of the ways in which Ozu subtly indicates the American presence in Japan, and I owe the observation of the restricted railway car to Sorensen, but he adds to this list the Hattori Building in downtown Tokyo, which at the time housed not only the American censors' offices but the military Post Exchange (PX).[60] The Hattori Building is a famous landmark that stands in and for the Ginza, Tokyo's famed shopping district. It is framed, for example, next to the heroine's face at the end of Naruse's *Street without End*. Early in *Late Spring* Noriko is headed to the Ginza, so showing the Hattori Building is typical Ozu shorthand for indicating that she has arrived. His Tokyo audience would have been aware of its contemporary use as the conqueror's PX, and Ozu may well have intended the shot to double as a famous landmark as well as an indicator of the Occupation.

Later, in one of his visual puns, Ozu cuts from a discussion of the character Hattori, Somiya's assistant, to the Hattori Building to a sign for the Balboa Tea and Coffee shop, obviously located in the Ginza, to Hattori himself inside chatting with Noriko. Sorensen believes the Hattori character was given that name because the Hattori Building housed SCAP activities. The Hattori character, he surmises, belongs to the Westernized, "dirty" side of the story, "somehow in league with the occupiers," because, while they are inside the aforementioned Balboa Tea and Coffee shop, Hattori tries to lure Noriko on a date even though he is engaged to another woman. The coffee shop is also suspect because it is Western.[61] Needless to say, this is not the usual view of either the Hattori character or the building.

The original Hattori Building was built in 1894 by Kintaro Hattori, founder of the Seiko watch company. That building was torn down and a new building known as the Wako Building with the Hattori Clock Tower was completed in 1932. Famous as one of the few buildings in the area to survive the war, it was consequently an obvious choice for the Americans to commandeer for their PX and offices. That it was used as such would hardly have negated its rich history and miraculous survival for a Japanese audience. If Ozu indeed named his character after the building (or more accurately its clock tower), it would have been because of its distinguished history, not its temporary use as a PX. The Hattori character is, after all, Somiya's trusted friend and fellow scholar.

Sorensen writes that "The sadness of the ending [of *Late Spring*] consists of Somiya falling victim to modernization [i.e., Westernization]," but "modernization" had been disrupting Japan for a very long time and was hardly a postwar phenomenon.[62] The sadness of Somiya alone at the end of *Late Spring* is the same as the sadness of Otsune alone at the end of *The Only Son*, except that, under different circumstances, Otsune could have expected her son to take care of her in old age. Without a son, Somiya was

The Reckoning   139

destined to be alone if his daughter married, modernity or no modernity. The sadness at the end of both films simply reflects the human condition: we are each of us alone, ultimately, and each of us will die. That is one reason these films continue to resonate over time and beyond national borders.

Late Spring was made in the first year that postwar Japanese finally had enough food to eat but at a time when young women still had difficulty finding husbands. A large number of biracial babies were being born—I agree with Sorensen that this may be the scandal Aya whispers to Noriko while they are having tea[63]—and a lot of young women, many from good families, married young Americans whose backgrounds and prospects they had no real way of assessing. Against this backdrop and in contrast to his earlier postwar films, Ozu's *Late Spring* presents an oasis of calm carved out of a still troubled country. His original synopsis for the film, which was submitted to the censors, states that he intended to depict "a pure and beautiful world," but having debunked the wartime notion of purity in *A Hen in the Wind*, we have to assume that his idea here was a good deal broader than Sorensen credits him for.[64]

Ozu included many famous temples and shrines in *Late Spring* along with scenes of tea ceremony and Noh drama. According to Marius B. Jansen, "The amuletic terms of the postwar era were 'peace,' 'democracy,' and 'culture.' Japan had vowed to reorient itself as a 'nation of culture.'"[65] The pile-up of ancient "culture" in the film thus corresponds to the nation's new orientation, but less widely noted is Ozu's inclusion of contemporary art and artists. Onodera and Noriko visit the Artist Associations' Joint Exhibit in Tokyo's Metropolitan Art Museum. (Significantly, the exhibit takes place between May 14 and June 5, i.e., late spring.)

In addition, Hattori attends a violin concert performed by Mari Iwamoto. A musical prodigy, Iwamoto was the product of an American mother and a Japanese father and thus represented the confluence of America and Japan Ozu had so idealized in his early films. Her grandparents were Christians, and both were involved in women's education during the Meiji era, advocating for exactly the kind of gender equality that the Occupation mandated. Growing up in 1930s Japan as a biracial child, Iwamoto had been bullied so badly at school that her parents decided to educate her at home. At a time when a prodigious number of mixed-race children were being conceived and born in Japan, Iwamoto, who had toured Japan tirelessly during the war years, stood as an example of how beautiful, brilliant, and patriotic such children could be.

Beyond the liberal history that Iwamoto represented, she and the Artist Associations speak to a vibrant contemporary art scene in 1949 Japan, complementing the ancient art that figures so prominently in the film. According to Peter B. High, during Ozu's internment in the Jurong prison camp immediately after the war, he was "selected as the [camp newspaper's] titular 'editor' and he held the same title with the camp 'culture' magazine (*Bunka Shuho*) . . . His name also appears on the program of the Jurong Art Society (*Jurong Bijutsu-kai*), with the title of 'Head of the Culture Division' (*bunka-cho*) at its first meeting in January 1946."[66] Clearly an active art world was important to Ozu even in prison, and, far from simply clinging to a long dead past, he embraced that contemporary world in *Late Spring*.

The film ends with a reprise of the shot of waves on a beach, first seen as a prelude to Noriko and Hattori's bicycle trip along the coast near Kamakura. The waves suggest the eternal cycle of life—birth, maturity (marriage), and death—with which this film and many that followed it were preoccupied, as the following chapter will demonstrate. Bordwell has connected the waves to the pretend waves, the gravel raked around the "island" stones, in the Zen temple Ryoanji, where Somiya and Onodera discuss the pros and cons of daughters.[67] In this sense, the waves betoken Japan itself, a nation of islands, where waves lap on countless shores. *Tenement Gentleman* ends with the samurai Saigo's back turned to its audience, *Hen* with children, Japan's future, and *Late Spring* with the nation itself, lately risen literally from the ashes, its rich heritage and customs intact, its arts community thriving, its beloved baseball restored; a nation not stuck in a glorious or a shameful past but, like Noriko, moving forward to an unknown future, determined to make it a happy one. This is the "normality" Ozu hoped to reify in *Late Spring*.

Economic Recovery (*The Munekata Sisters*, 1950; *Early Summer*, 1951)

After its surrender in August of 1945, Japan lost control of the Korean Peninsula, which it had annexed in 1910. That territory, an independent nation once again, was divided, as postwar Germany had been, into two states: a Communist North and an anti-Communist South. In 1949, green-lighted by both Stalin and China's newly victorious Mao Tse-tung (Mao Zedong), the North invaded the South. Fearing a Communist takeover in a country next door to Japan, the United States, under the auspices of the United Nations, went to war once again in June of 1950.

The Korean conflict extended the Occupation because Japan was needed as a staging area, but it marked the end of Japan's economic woes. Procurement orders for a wide variety goods, including light armaments, which Japan was, officially, not supposed to be making at all, poured in from the American military. In addition, Japanese workers repaired heavy equipment, built bases for additional troops, and provided food and recreational opportunities for soldiers and their families. The war and the economic lift it provided would continue beyond the end of the Occupation.

Ozu's *Munekata Sisters* was released in August of 1950. Although the Korean War went unacknowledged, several of the film's characters enjoy prewar levels of affluence. If *Late Spring* sought to establish a degree of "normality," *The Munekata Sisters* willingly debated the effects of the Pacific War on this particularly genteel slice of Japanese society.

"The war changed many things," says the sisters' father. The pairing of two women, often sisters, representing tradition and modernity, had been popular in fiction since the 1920s, but here the women represent, specifically, a prewar and a postwar mentality.[68]

The Reckoning

The older sister, Setsuko, like her father, loves temples, and, as the father lives in Kyoto, they have many opportunities to visit them. Both state that those who dislike traditional art are "ignorant," which was no doubt Ozu's own sentiment, as was Setsuko's admonition to younger sister Mariko, "Things that are really new never get old."

Mariko, on the other hand, dislikes temples and Buddha statues enough to repeatedly tell us so. "Why are there so many temples in Kyoto," she asks (in contrast to the characters in *Late Spring*, who are delighted by Kyoto's serenity). She dislikes traditional pottery and mocks the samurai armor in one character's foyer.

Many years later Wim Wenders would shed light on Mariko's reaction to traditional culture when he talked about growing up in occupied Germany where he gravitated to rock music as "the only alternative to Beethoven . . . because I was very insecure about all culture that was offered to me, because I thought it was all fascism."[69] Ozu probably did not understand Mariko in quite this way; yet he faithfully recorded a phenomenon present in both Germany and Japan, where a lost war coupled with a friendly occupation that offered alternatives—Wenders listened to rock music on [US] Armed Forces radio—served to alienate the young from their own culture.

Besides not liking temples, Mariko wears Western clothes, smokes, reads fashion magazines, and frequently makes faces. Setsuko, in contrast, always wears a kimono, reads books, and projects a serenity that belies her troubled life.

Both Setsuko and her father warn Mariko against simply following fashion as an alternative to "temples and statues," but Mariko herself is far more creative in her rebellion. Described by her father as a "tomboy," who can't help sticking out her tongue, she burlesques traditional storytellers in an ongoing performance for family friend Hiroshi, detailing the old romance she imagines between him and Setsuko.

She also mocks Maejima, her sister's bartender, for having been a kamikaze pilot, repeatedly addressing him as "Propeller!" (The war ended before many designated kamikaze pilots could fly their missions.) Drunk, she echoes Setsuko, stating: "No matter how much time passes, things that are new don't get old," and asks if Maejima understands. Both young people confess that it makes no sense to them.

Earlier Setsuko had criticized Maejima for wanting to "dance and play" even though he was once a kamikaze pilot. Today we understand better the escapism inherent in his desire for frivolous amusement after coming within inches of death, but Ozu may again have been recording a phenomenon he didn't completely comprehend.

Into this mix of conservative and modern, Ozu adds Hiroshi, who is an example of a prewar internationalized Japanese. He lived in France throughout most of the war, has a European-style apartment filled with French dolls, German beer steins, and a Buddha head. He always wears Western clothes, drinks Coke with Mariko, shares her enthusiasm for baseball, and makes "*fanicha*" (furniture), i.e., tables and chairs, in contrast to Japanese-style furniture (*kagu*). He lives in Kobe, one of the first ports to welcome foreign shipping in the Meiji era, famous for its international ambiance. (The sisters live with Setsuko's husband in Tokyo, but Mariko loves Kobe in preference to Kyoto.)

The focus of the film is Setsuko's early romance with Hiroshi and her present, unhappy marriage to Mimura. The sisters' radically different reactions to this situation go beyond merely prewar-conservative/postwar-modern, however, and venture into the weird, where husband Mimura is permanently situated.

Mimura, characterized by the graveyard near his house and later by the skeleton of a war-ravaged tree, is obsessed with cats. A drunkard, he abuses his wife on the excuse that he has lost his job. Maejima describes him as having looked like a ghost when he came into the bar on a previous night. Toward the end of the film, he enters Setsuko's bar again, looking almost like a specter; then, standing near Mariko, he throws his glass at the Don Quixote quote on the wall behind the bar (borrowed from *What Did the Lady Forget?*): "I drink upon occasion, sometimes upon no occasion." Mariko responds by throwing glasses at the wall as well.

When Mariko learns of the romance between her sister and Hiroshi, which took place fifteen years earlier, she throws herself at Hiroshi, insisting he marry her as a substitute for her sister. Later she seeks out Hiroshi's female friend Yoriko and repays her hospitality with rudeness and hostility. (Yoriko has her own designs on Hiroshi but treats Mariko with good humor and patience.)

Fed up with Mimura's abuse, Setsuko agrees to divorce him and marry Hiroshi but is instead relieved of her marriage when the intemperate Mimura drops dead of a heart attack, as predicted cinematically by the graveyard, the dead tree, and his ghostly presence. Consumed with guilt, Setsuko refuses to marry Hiroshi, feeling she will always be haunted by Mimura's death. The film thus pushes conservative vs. modern to an extreme that betrays the "everydayness" Woojeong Joo sees as Ozu's most salient characteristic in his Ozu book, subtitled *Histories of the Everyday*.

While I have challenged the notion advanced by Bordwell and others that Ozu's stories are ambiguous, parts of *The Munekata Sisters* truly are so. We do not really know, for example, why Mimura is such a sour character. Is it because he has lost his job or because, as Mariko theorizes, he has read Setsuko's diary and knows she once loved Hiroshi, or is he simply a self-centered, misogynistic, alcoholic louse? The film never clarifies this, but Ozu probably modeled Mimura on disillusioned, jobless vets in an indirect reference to the war. The war-blasted tree that introduces Mimura's last drinking scene ties him to such veterans, but exactly what he did in the war is never mentioned.

The romance between Hiroshi and Setsuko also lacks clarity. Toward the end of the film, he tells her that her suffering has made her "a great woman," but what the two have remotely in common at this point in their lives is not clear. Setsuko is highly repressed, dedicated to the past and its mores, while sweet Hiroshi is totally Westernized and casual. Although the gulf between them suggests they won't get together at the end, it nevertheless seems sad when they don't, and Setsuko's brave assertion that she will be fine living alone rings hollow.

Hiroshi's sojourn in France, which interrupted his mid-1930s romance with Setsuko, is another indirect reference to the war. Although ostensibly unrelated to it,

The Reckoning 143

his long absence recalls those of men who went to the front and came back, if they came back at all, to young families that barely knew them, women who had married someone else, parents who had passed away, among other tragedies and disappointments. "We had high hopes then," Hiroshi tells Setsuko when they return to the Yakushi temple in Nara for the first time in fifteen years. Any middle-aged person given to nostalgia can recall unrealized youthful dreams, but in this case a war intervened to help subvert those dreams.

Direct references to the war and Occupation are few but include Maejima's service as a would-be kamikaze pilot, the blasted tree that precedes one scene with Mimura, and a shot of the "Tokyo General Hospital Annex," whose prominent sign is all in English. There is also the fact that all of the major characters—the Munekata family, Hiroshi, and Mimura—lived and knew each other in Manchuria at one time. We learn that father Munekata worked for the South Manchuria Railway, but what Mimura and Hiroshi did there is not clear.

Early in the film father Munekata returns a book to Hiroshi with the comment that he had read it before in Manchuria, and, although it was popular at the time, he didn't like it, but he does now. This throwaway comment appears to speak to Ozu's own change of heart regarding Manchuria and the occupation of China. In *The Brothers and Sisters of the Toda Family*, China was the Promised Land. In *The Munekata Sisters* and *Tokyo Twilight* (1957), the film that most closely resembles it, Manchuria is the backdrop for Ozu's most unhappy characters' personal tragedies: Hiroshi travels from there to France, leaving Setsuko to marry Mimura; in *Tokyo Twilight*, the mother has abandoned her family in the late 1930s and immigrated to Manchuria with her lover.

Both films contrast an older and a younger sister, the older trapped in an abusive marriage and the younger searching for her identity in a changing world. *Tokyo Twilight* borrows its central plot device from Elia Kazan's *East of Eden* (1955)—which Ozu corroborates when, toward the end of the film, the estranged and stricken mother enters a sake bar across the street from a "Bar Eden"—but both films use Manchuria as the site of those prior events which have caused the difficulties the characters face in the films' present.[70]

Ozu's attitude toward Manchuria faithfully tracks the Japanese experience in the former colony. After the Russian invasion on August 9, 1945, many former settlers were trapped there, unable to make their way back to Japan, and many suffered abuse from Russian soldiers as well as from the retreating Japanese army. Hundreds of thousands of Japanese soldiers and government personnel were taken prisoner, and many died in Soviet camps.[71] Those who survived were repatriated slowly, most by 1951, but some as late as 1956.[72]

The Munekata Sisters, like the later *Tokyo Twilight*, did not succeed at the box office. One reason may have been the film's ambiguities, which the viewer experiences more as confusion than artistry. Part of the problem arose, no doubt, from the fact that Ozu, moonlighting for a new studio, Shintoho, was required to adapt a novel not of his choosing (Jiro Osaragi's *Munekata kyodai*). In addition, Ozu and Noda appear to have faithfully captured the thoughts and experiences of different types of people in the postwar period but dropped them into the familiar trope of conservative versus modern instead of looking for other, better explanations.

Ozu returned to Shochiku for his next film. *Early Summer* marked his first conscious effort to "show a life cycle" and "depict mutability,"[73] topics I will address in a subsequent chapter, but the film also attempted to resolve the question posed in both *Late Spring* and *The Munekata Sisters* of what it meant to be a liberated woman in postwar Japan and how such a woman should approach marriage.

In *Early Summer*'s Noriko, Ozu created his ideal woman. (According to Shizuo Yamanouchi, one of Ozu's producers, Shochiku objected to his using Setsuko Hara to play Noriko in *Early Summer* because she had already appeared in *Late Spring*. When Ozu threatened to drop the film rather than make it without Hara, the studio relented.[74])

Early in the film Noriko asserts, "We [women] are finally the way we should be," when brother-in-law Koichi mutters about women having become impossible after all the postwar reforms. This Noriko helps to support her family, has, as a schoolgirl, admired Katharine Hepburn, and eventually shocks family and friends by agreeing to marry her widowed neighbor, Yabe, raise his child, and move with him to northerly Akita. Asked why she has chosen this less financially secure and socially acceptable match, when her boss and family had proposed a wealthier if older man, she replies that she trusts a man with a child more than one who is still "drifting around" at forty. (All Yabe has done since his wife died is "read books," according to his mother.) "Poverty doesn't worry me like it does other people," Noriko asserts and assures her sister-in-law that she has no qualms about loving another woman's child.

As in *There Was a Father* and *Tenement Gentleman*, Ozu endorses opening up the family circle to include outsiders. To Westerners, a stepchild or a wife's father are hardly outsiders, but in Japan at that time, they were, and Occupation reforms could only do so much to change such attitudes. One recalls the difficulties that arise in *A Mother Should Be Loved* because the two brothers have different mothers. Noriko's willingness to meet this challenge marks her depth of character.

In a scene devoted entirely to Noriko's father, he sits to wait for a passing train on his way to buy birdseed. A sign near the tracks—in English because this is still the Occupation—reads: "Caution, automatic alarm is out of order," which suggests that traditional values are no longer automatic. Young people like Noriko have to figure out what their values will be, and her decisions point to those values Ozu thought worthy.

The film endorses women's postwar liberation—Noriko is never shown wearing a kimono—but doesn't rest there. Liberated, Noriko has choices, and Ozu is as concerned with those choices as he is with her liberation. In a nation "revaluing all values," Ozu is careful to distinguish between truly liberated values and Western bourgeois values as empty as their Japanese counterparts.[75] Noriko's friend Aya names the latter: a Western-style house with a picket fence, a flower garden, a covered porch and a tiled kitchen, a refrigerator full of Coca-Cola, as well as a white sweater and a terrier. Noriko should, Aya imagines, be listening to Chopin and flaunting her English. Noriko's forty-year-old

The Reckoning

prospect, meanwhile, comes from a prosperous family that "keeps their home in the best traditional style." She shuns both sets of values, offering instead to raise a motherless child and compete with her sister-in-law in thriftiness. Yabe, her groom, embraces the opportunity to go to Akita, not simply to advance his career, but to pursue his medical research "on local problems." In accompanying him, Noriko tacitly supports this worthy purpose.

Explaining her sudden realization that Yabe would make a good husband, Noriko echoes Dorothy in the *Wizard of Oz*: "You look for something all over the place and find it was right in front of you all along." For the second time she is identified with a strong American film heroine.

After the rather dreary justifications for marriage in *Late Spring* and *The Munekata Sisters*—marriage is hard work but necessary to create the next generation—this film examines a variety of motivating factors for women to get married: sex ("real happiness," which Aya disputes, comparing it to the anticipation of winning at the racetrack); status (Noriko's married friends flaunt it); wealth and social position (Noriko's mother always supposed her daughter's charm and beauty would lead to this); and "love." Love as a socially acceptable and preferable basis for marriage had been pushed by the Occupation, and Noriko's friends embrace it enthusiastically, but Ozu questions the American version of love (as conveyed by Hollywood), namely, romance. Noriko has opted instead for trust and friendship.

(Ozu mocks Noriko's friends, who discretely if smugly discuss their sex lives, by placing the young women at a restaurant table directly in front of a huge, unlovely Picassoesque painting of eros: a buxom female sits between Pan playing his pipe and a goat.)

As noted earlier, arranged (*miai*) marriage remained popular in Japan despite the Occupation's objections to it. This film does not debate its merits but illustrates a new and radical version of it that may have been as shocking for Ozu's audience as it is for Noriko's family. Without consulting them, Noriko accepts a proposal from Yabe's mother, who has not yet consulted her son!

We are told Yabe is happy about the arrangement; beautiful Noriko would, after all, make any man an ideal wife, but this groom, who seems to fly under everyone's radar—the story's characters and film critics alike—is pointedly contrasted to Noriko's brother Koichi. In one scene he lovingly greets his little girl, Mitsuko, at the door, and he subsequently helps Noriko look for her runaway nephews. Koichi, by contrast, does not get along well with his sons and inexplicably plays Go with his neighbor instead of looking for the boys when they run off.

Yabe is also associated with a constellation of positive, even sacred, references in a scene in which he and Noriko converse in a coffee shop. First, the two look out the window at the domes of the Nikolai Cathedral while music sounding vaguely liturgical plays on the soundtrack. This Russian Orthodox cathedral became a repository for the bodies of the dead during the incendiary bombing of Tokyo toward the end of World War II.[76]

Yabe notes that he often came to the coffee shop with Noriko's missing-and-presumed-dead brother Shoji and reveals to Noriko that he has always kept a letter with a stalk of barley that Shoji sent him from the China front. He was, he tells her, reading *Wheat and Soldiers* (*Mugi to heitai*) at the time. (The word *mugi*, translated into English here as "wheat," actually means barley.) *Wheat and Soldiers* (1939) is the day-to-day account of a soldier's life, written by Katsunori Tamai (aka Hino Ashihei), who was serving in China at the time.[77] The book became a bestseller, conveying the truth about soldiers' lives that Corporal Ozu had accused popular films and novels of being unable to capture.[78]

Over Yabe's shoulder we can just make out the word "Garfield," out of focus in what appears to be a giant movie poster. John Garfield was the celebrated antihero in movies like *The Postman Always Rings Twice* (1946) and *Body and Soul* (1947). On April 23, 1951, Garfield, whose wife had been a member of the Communist Party, testified before the House [on] Un-American Activities Committee (HUAC) and was subsequently blacklisted for refusing to name names. *Early Summer* was released on October 1 of the same year. Referencing Garfield here comports with the Christian allusions in this scene as well as the memory of the war dead. Martyrdom is strongly associated with Christianity in Japan, and both Garfield and the bombing victims could be seen in that light.

The barely readable word "Garfield" is the strongest rebuke Ozu would direct at the Occupation government, which was similarly busying itself with communist purges. Although SCAP's censorship division was phased out after 1949, General Headquarters itself became ever more antagonistic to the political left. After the outbreak of the Korean War, "Red purges spilled over into the private sector and, among many other fields of activity, swept through publishing and film making, as well as public radio."[79] This, not the reforms of the early Occupation, provoked the anti-Americanism in Japan that led the way to the Japanese New Wave, which began in the late 1950s. Ozu, in contrast to those later filmmakers, who worked in a fully democratic era, could only signal his opposition to government oppression subtly and slyly, but did so throughout his career. Doubtless aware of Garfield's integrity and sacrifice, he put the actor's name up on the screen, associating him with his ideal heroine's ideal mate.

If Yabe is associated with a constellation of positive actions and references, Manabe, the groom proposed by Noriko's boss, Satake, is not. His family is from Zentsuji, a town on the island of Shikoku and site of one of Japan's most notorious POW and slave labor camps. While the Manabe family presumably had nothing to do with the camp, Koichi's friend, another doctor, was stationed there during the war. Was he there as a medical doctor? Did his duties involve the camp in any way? We are never told, but Zentsuji's actual camp doctor was hanged for war crimes.[80]

Did the reference to Zentsuji resonate with Ozu's audience, little given to introspection regarding war crimes, or was this Ozu's own private reckoning? That he simply pulled this city out of a hat with no regard to its history seems unlikely, for why would he place Manabe's highly respectable, traditional family on faraway Shikoku if not with

The Reckoning

147

the specific intent of invoking Zentsuji's recent history?[81] Combined with Koichi's comparative indifference to his children and his hostility to Noriko's choice of Yabe for a husband, the reference to Zentsuji casts a further shadow over him and his preferred groom.

For the younger family members, the war is in the rearview mirror as they reminisce about 1946: the railway station was crowded and Fumiko was still wearing *monpe* (the baggy pants women were encouraged to wear during the war years). Nevertheless, Noriko's mother listens daily to the "Missing Persons Hour," hoping to hear of her missing son although her husband has advised her to give up hope. (One reason for his pessimism is that most soldiers, even those captured by the Russians, had been repatriated by 1951, the year the film was made.) Great Uncle has had to sell one of the family's heirloom paintings to survive the postwar inflation, and, although they have enough, the family is very sensitive to the cost and value of food, hence Koichi's anger when his son Minoru kicks a loaf of bread.

Still, recovery is palpable. Looking out his window, Noriko's boss, Satake, invites her to have a last look at Tokyo, which, he notes, "is not so bad." In *Late Spring*, Tokyo was "dusty," in contrast to pristine Kyoto, because the censors would not allow Ozu to say that it was still a war-ravaged mess.[82] Although *Early Summer*'s Aya contrasts Tokyo unfavorably with peaceful Kamakura, which escaped Allied bombing, Tokyo is judged "not so bad" by the end of the film.

Like *The Munekata Sisters*, *Early Summer* celebrates old Japan, but it belongs mostly to the older generation. Noriko's father tends caged birds, a traditional hobby, but old Japan converges mainly around the great uncle, who has brought the family an antique scroll, an heirloom. He adores the Kabuki performance he can barely hear, and Noriko takes him and the children to Kamakura's *Daibutsu* (Great Buddha). He sits on the steps below the Buddha with a similar look of serenity on his aged face.

Great Uncle lives in the family seat in the Yamato region near Nara, Japan's ancient capital, and, after Noriko's marriage, her parents join him there. "Yamato" is the name for Japan's earliest period of recorded history and signifies a culture thought to be purely Japanese before Japan's rulers adopted Chinese clothing, art, religion, and governmental structures. "*Yamato-e*," for example, refers to a unique style of Japanese painting that does not derive from China. In the run-up to war in the 1930s, everything "Yamato" was considered the ideal, and the "Yamato race" implied Japanese superiority to other Asians and other races. *Yamato* was also the name of a legendary aircraft carrier, the flagship at the Battle of Midway, which was sunk by the Americans during the Battle of Okinawa. A source of great pride for the Japanese, its loss came to be equated with the loss of Japan's empire.[83]

Lyrical shots of Yamato's ripe barley fields accompany the final sequence in which Great Uncle and Noriko's parents watch the bridal procession of a country wedding pass by. The procession substitutes for Noriko's unseen wedding and reminds us that she, too, will be living, at least for a time, in rural Japan.

148   *Ozu*

Echoing critic Masasumi Tanaka, Joo argues that the tracking shot over the barley fields that ends the film suggests the soldiers' march through barley fields at the battle of Xuzhou described by Hino in *Wheat and Soldiers* and can thus be interpreted as a "funeral march."[84] As we will see in Chapter 8, Ozu often identified weddings with funerals, so this interpretation comports with what is evident in a number of his other films. The film's serene ending contrasts with the memory of war and loss that both the barley and the term "Yamato" betoken. Loss here is both national and personal, caused by war but also by the inroads of time, the life cycle Ozu wished to portray. The parents have lost their son to war, their daughter to marriage, and their home in Kamakura. Moreover, they and Great Uncle are in the last phase of their lives.

The Japanese title for the film is *Bakushu*, meaning "time of the barley harvest," which occurs in late May and June. Like the art show poster in *Late Spring*, the ripe barley in the final scene time-stamps the story, but, more than that, barley is the lynchpin that holds many of the story elements together. It links Noriko to Yabe and both to the lost brother. It links the brother to other soldiers who fought and died in China and these, ironically, to Noriko and Yabe's wedding. Along with the references to Zentsuji and the Nikolai Cathedral, it constitutes the dark cloud that drifts below the surface of this story—intimations of a war whose scars remain—in a film which is otherwise about liberation and recovery.[85]

Early Summer invokes Ozu's prewar films in several instances. The pair-of-brothers motif from *I Was Born, But . . .* is reintroduced and would appear again in *Tokyo Story*. Eventually, they would be featured once more in a film of their own, *Ohayo*. Additionally, a calendar surrounded by international flags is posted in the boys' room. It is similar in spirit to the globes, maps, and decorative flags that appeared in the early films, as though, the continuing Occupation notwithstanding, Japan had once again taken its place in the community of nations. Finally, Katharine Hepburn joins the roster of strong women like Joan Crawford and Marlene Dietrich celebrated in the prewar films.[86] Ozu's next film, *The Flavor of Green Tea Over Rice*, would create an even stronger link to his prewar cinema.

Many critics accuse Ozu of making the same film over and over, but, in fact, between those signature postwar films that recycle story elements and deal directly with multi-generational families and the cycle of life, he and Noda inserted films with very different stories. *The Munekata Sisters* was one, and *The Flavor of Green Tea Over Rice* would be another.

The Occupation Ends (*The Flavor of Green Tea Over Rice*, 1952)

With *The Flavor of Green Tea Over Rice*, Ozu would come full circle. The script was an updating of his rejected wartime script of the same name and follows the same contours as his 1937 *What Did the Lady Forget?*: a wife with a coterie of female friends has a rebellious, modern niece named Setsuko, whose behavior scandalizes her aunt and exposes underlying discords between the woman and her husband when he indulges

The Reckoning   149

his niece's whims. Meanwhile, he has a young protégé with whom the niece forms a romantic attachment. At the end, husband and wife reconcile, the female friends gossip about it, and the niece meets her new beau for a date.

Although not as snappy, well-structured, or funny as *What Did the Lady Forget?*, *Green Tea* was nevertheless a box office hit, perhaps because it continued to debate the merits of modern love versus arranged marriage.[87] Setsuko not only rejects the idea of arranged marriage but ditches an *omiai* that her parents have arranged and begins a relationship with Non-chan, the young friend of her uncle Motoki. Current wisdom, reiterated by Non-chan at one point, holds that within an arranged marriage, husband and wife will learn to love each other, and Motoki and his wife, Taeko, demonstrate this, if rather late in their relationship. Taeko explains to her friends that she has finally realized that the most important thing about a husband is reliability and that women don't realize all the reliable things their husbands do because they only see them loafing at home.

Advised of this conversation, Non-chan applies its wisdom to himself, telling Setsuko, "If you detest it [his "cheap but good" clothing], you'll repent later." She, however, rejects his condescension, and the film ends with him chasing her in and out of the old, empty guardhouses outside the Akasaka Palace. This exchange is similar to the final meeting between Setsuko and Okada in *What Did the Lady Forget?* where Setsuko explains to him "the opposite approach," her uncle's theory that indulging wives makes them think they're in control, but warns him not to "use that when we marry." Neither Setsuko wishes to be patronized. Arranged marriage or love marriage, equality is the ideal.

Like *What Did the Lady Forget?*, *Green Tea* begins with the view from a moving car, possibly a conscious homage to the earlier film, although it is a view shot from inside the car, not the running board. Much longer than the running board shot in *Lady*, however, the ride in *Green Tea* extends for ninety seconds. Taeko and Setsuko sit in the back of a taxi while it drives along one side of the Imperial Palace moat. (SCAP headquarters can be seen opposite the palace gate.) As it approaches the Ginza, Taeko directs the driver to turn left at the "PX," i.e., the Wako/Hattori Building, which we immediately view in close-up through an office window. As noted above, the film ends with Non-chan chasing Setsuko outside the wrought-iron fence of the Akasaka Palace, an opulent, Neo-Baroque building, sometimes referred to as the Japanese Versailles. Once the property of the Imperial Family, ownership was transferred to the state in 1946. Are the film's imperial palace bookends intended to remind Ozu's audience of its cultural heritage, or are they tokens of an emperor demoted from a god to a man, whose European-style palace now belongs to the democratized state, all through the agency of a conquering power, referenced when Taeko mentions the "PX"? Or both? In either case, we watch modern courtship unfold on the ruins of imperial privilege.[88]

Ending with the "Japanese Versailles" ties into a French theme that runs throughout the film. One character in *The Munekata Sisters* had actually been to France, but French culture is cited more often in *Green Tea*. During their taxi ride, Setsuko tells

Taeko that she is going to see a Jean Marais movie although she never says which one. Classically handsome Jean Marais was best known for his work with Jean Cocteau, of which *Beauty and the Beast* (*La Belle et la Bête*, 1946) is the most famous. Of all Ozu's heroines, Michiyo Kogure's Taeko, with her French-style beauty mark, is the most glamorous, and the beauty-and-beast story reflects, in a general way, on Taeko's discovery that the husband she finds common and dull is actually a gem. Meanwhile, her childishness, preciousness, and patrician snobbery are reflected in the china figurines in eighteenth-century costume that inhabit a shelf in her Western boudoir-style room and in the couple's kitchen calendar, which reproduces Watteau's c. 1717 painting "The Dance." This painting depicts children playing at being adults: a young girl in the foreground, dressed in upper-class finery, prepares to dance while little boys play pipes for her. A medium shot of Taeko frames her together with Watteau's Rococo maiden. Humbled in this scene in which she and Motoki prepare green tea over rice together, Taeko nevertheless remains the Beauty.[89]

In addition to debating arranged marriage, *Green Tea* takes on a postwar craze in Japan at the time, pachinko. The characters debate whether pachinko is "indecent," a waste of time, a sign of societal decay, or simply fun. Oddly Hirayama, the owner of the pachinko parlor (a Chishu Ryu cameo), insists that the pachinko rage won't help "the world improve." Motoki, new to the game, sums up its appeal by saying, "You can be alone in a crowd, just you and the balls." Non-chan admits that it is "no match for bicycle racing." (He and Motoki subsequently attend a bicycle race.)

Hirayama turns out to have been under Motoki's command during the war and invites his former corporal along with Non-chan into his living quarters for some sake. It is the first of several reunions of old war buddies in Ozu's films and testifies to a nostalgia for war as a time out of time, overlain by the exoticism of the tropics. In *Tenement Gentleman* Tashiro (also played by Ryu) sang about the first Sino-Japanese War, 1894–1895; here Ryu as Hirayama updates us to the recent war as he sings about a comrade killed in battle. Yet the very real hurt of war is still present in this film: Non-chan's older brother, Motoki's contemporary, has died, presumably in the war, and his mother "got old fast" after that.

Occasionally characters sing in Ozu's films, particularly if they are played by Chishu Ryu. *Green Tea* is exceptional in that five characters sing a total of three songs, which serve to define national tendencies and gender roles in 1952 Japan. Early in the film Non-chan, a recent graduate, sings *Gaudeamas igitur*, a collegiate drinking song with *carpe diem* sentiments. It confirms Japan's connection to the West, particularly in education, i.e., science and technology, as well as the fact that men go to college so that they can get "reliable" jobs working for companies. (Taeko's friend Aya works but in her own dressmaking business. A company would not have given her a managerial position.)

Later Aya, Taeko, and their friend Takako sing a song about flowers from the "Girl's Opera," aka the Takarazuka Revue. The Revue is an all-female song and dance troupe, which, founded in 1913, acquired the Takarazuka Theater in 1924. Having taken its cue from Western song and dance revues, the Takarazuka Revue stands as a counterpart and contrast to Kabuki, whose singing can be heard off-screen in *Green Tea* in the failed *omiai* sequence, which takes place in Tokyo's famed Kabuki-za. Where Kabuki is ancient and completely Japanese, the Revue is modern and based on Western sources; whereas men play both male and female roles in Kabuki, women play all roles in the Revue. This opposition between the all-male world of Kabuki and the all-female world of Girls' Opera underscores the battle of the sexes that plays out in *Green Tea*.

Finally, pachinko parlor owner Hirayama sings an old-style battle song about Japan's Greater East Asia War, characterizing his generation of men and the war that would always haunt it. Like *Gaudeamus*, Hirayama's song embraces a world known only to men.

The story climaxes when Motoki leaves on a business trip to Uruguay aboard a Pan American "Stratocruiser" while headstrong Taeko is away on a trip of her own and telegrams have failed to bring her home. We may wonder why Ozu has Motoki fly Pan American (PAA) to Uruguay when Northwest Orient dominated air travel in Asia in the decades immediately after the war. (A poster for Northwest appears in *Early Summer*.) One likely reason is the crash in the Amazon of a Pan Am Stratocruiser after stops in Montevideo and Rio on April 29, 1952, knowledge of which would have heightened the audience's perception of the danger surrounding Motoki's travel and the gravity of Taeko's selfish and irresponsible behavior. Boeing's Stratocruiser was known to have temperamental engines, and the crash of Pan Am 202 was considered the worst in the plane's history. Motoki's return the same night because his plane had engine trouble is, therefore, entirely credible; the fact that he will be leaving the next day in a presumably equally problematic aircraft endows the couple's green-tea-over-rice midnight meal with some of the same urgency that it had in Ozu's original script, in which the meal takes place the night before the husband leaves for war.

Another reason to choose a Pan Am route over those run by Northwest, which also flew Stratocruisers, was the logo emblazoned on the tails of Pan Am planes. In contrast to Northwest's solid red tail, Pan Am planes had an American flag at the top of theirs. As Motoki's plane pulls away from the gate, Ozu's camera declines to follow as the aircraft slowly leaves the frame (Figure 7.4). Consequently, the American flag on its tail slowly disappears from the screen. The Occupation was over. (Five shots of the enthusiastically waving crowd follow this last view of the American flag. They are ostensibly waving to those taking off on the plane, but, like so much in Ozu's work, one can read a double meaning here.)

With the exception of the Ryukyu Islands, the American Occupation of Japan ended on April 28, 1952 (one day before the crash of Pan Am 202). *The Flavor of Green Tea Over Rice* was released on October 1. The film ends with Non-chan and Setsuko scurrying away from the camera, down the sidewalk in front of the Akasaka Palace. One other extant Ozu film and one fragment end similarly with a character running away from the camera into the distance: *The Brothers and Sisters of the Toda Family* and *I Graduated, But* . . . This burst of energy at the end of all three films speaks to an exhilaration missing from and inappropriate to most of Ozu's other work. In *I Graduated,*

Figure 7.4: The American flag on the Pan Am Stratocruiser's tail moves slowly out of the frame as onlookers wave in *The Flavor of Green Tea Over Rice*.

But . . . the wife, delighted that her husband finally has a job, runs away from the train station, where she has seen him off to work, toward home. In *Toda Family*, Shojiro runs along the beach, ostensibly to avoid meeting the woman his sister wants him to marry but at the same time conveying the thrill of starting life anew in occupied China. In *Green Tea* Setsuko and Non-chan frolic down the sidewalk in a democratized Japan, endowed with new freedoms, and lately liberated from its liberators.

* * *

Woojeong Joo has subtitled his Ozu monograph *Histories of the Everyday*. That "everyday" included current headlines much more than previous authors have recognized. To the extent that Ozu had strong opinions about those headlines, he often hid them, frequently among the props on his sets.

Having come of age in the liberal, Westernizing Taisho era, Ozu never lost his liberalism, his resonant humanism, or his belief in internationalism. If his infatuation with the United States ever dimmed, it will have been during that country's rabid

The Reckoning

anti-communist phase, less than during the Pacific War or the subsequent Occupation. Even so, he would continue to reference Hollywood films in his late work.

As Bordwell and others have pointed out, Ozu forged the style of his classic films with *The Brothers and Sisters of the Toda Family* and made two of them, *Late Spring* and *Early Summer*, during the Occupation. He would continue to explore their themes, marriage and the life cycle, in much of his subsequent work.[90]

Notes

1. High, *Imperial Screen*, 334.
2. High, *Imperial Screen*, 507.
3. For more on postwar attitudes, see Hotta, *Japan 1941*, 291–92.
4. Kyoko Hirano, *Mr. Smith Goes to Tokyo: Japanese Cinema under the American Occupation* (Washington, DC: Smithsonian Institution, 1992), 261.
5. Hirano notes the case of a pro-war Daiei film called *Separation is Also a Pleasure* that was in mid-production when Japan surrendered. It was reshot "without regret," turned into a "harmless musical," and released in mid-September 1945. See Hirano, *Mr. Smith*, 148.
6. Hirano, *Mr. Smith*, 44–45.
7. Hirano, *Mr. Smith*, 46.
8. For an account of SCAP censorship generally, see Dower, *Embracing Defeat*, 405ff.
9. Edward Fowler, "Piss and Run," 274.
10. Tamekichi's unexplained recitation parallels Tashiro's recitation based on the *Tragedy of Hototogisu*, also known as *Namiko*, adapted from a novel by Kenjiro (Roka) Tokutomi.
11. Bordwell, *Poetics*, 301.
12. Sorensen, *Censorship*, 133.
13. Dower, *Embracing Defeat*, 61.
14. Dower, *Embracing Defeat*, 63.
15. Woojeong Joo, "Rethinking Noriko's Marriage Narrative as Historical Allegory in Ozu Yasujiro's *The Moon Has Risen* and Other Occupation-Era Films," *Screen* 56, no. 3 (Autumn 2015): 341.
16. Dower, *Embracing Defeat*, 64.
17. Dower, *Embracing Defeat*, 111f.
18. Dower, *Embracing Defeat*, 124.
19. Bordwell, *Poetics*, 302f.
20. Dower, *Embracing Defeat*, 60.
21. Kate Taylor-Jones, also subscribing to the notion that Ozu's films are open-ended and ambiguous, believes the ending of *Hen in the Wind* "raises a sense of unease and confusion" because it shows one of the neighborhood's ever-present gas tanks dwarfing the people walking near it. In fact, this last shot, which follows the shot of the children playing, is comparatively upbeat for a film that has focused on postwar ruin and destruction. Two identical figures in traditional peasant dress walk down the road together in Ozu's signature *sojikei* style, indicating the persistence of both tradition and balance. Meanwhile, an amiable dog trots toward the camera. Far from unease and confusion, these signs reinforce the positives we have just witnessed in the couple's reunion and the children at play.

Taylor-Jones's premise that *Hen in the Wind* illustrates a "post-colonial moment" seems generally misconceived. *Hen* describes a country on life support, not a "post-colonial moment." Moreover, Japan quickly embraced victimization as its operating mindset during this period. The "post-colonial moment" within Ozu's oeuvre came in *The Munekata Sisters* and, especially, *Tokyo Twilight*. The ruptured personal relationships in these films appear to correlate, in one way or another, with time spent in Japan's colonies. Coincidentally (or not) both films were made at or close to a time when European countries were losing their colonies in Asia. See Kate Taylor-Jones, "Rhythm, Texture, Moods: Ozu Yasujiro, Claire Denis, and a Vision of a Postcolonial Aesthetic," in Choi, *Reorienting Ozu*, 215–31.

22. A 1929 print by Koizumi Kishio, *Senju Town with Storage Tanks*, a stylistic cross between *nihonga* and German Expressionism, shows these tanks looming over tiny residents as they make their way down a shadowed street. Ozu's use of this imagery thus had precedent. See Frederic A. Sharf, "Showa Sophistication" in Atkins et al., *The Brittle Decade*, 146, pl. 141.

23. Crowded trains were so notorious that Dower records one teacher's account of children playing "train" games, which included three kinds of trains, the "repatriate train," in which the children "shook and trembled," pretending to be returning veterans; the "special train," modeled on railway cars reserved for Occupation personnel, on which only "pretty people" were allowed; and the "ordinary train," in which everyone got on, shoving and pushing and crying for help. The teacher noted that the children had gone "from playing war to playing at utter confusion." Dower, *Embracing Defeat*, 112.

24. Hirano, *Mr. Smith*, 75.

25. Hirano, *Mr. Smith*, 74n82.

26. The American censors always presented their ideas as "suggestions," but studios understood that the Americans controlled their supply of raw film. Hirano, *Mr. Smith*, 177.

27. Fowler, "Piss and Run," 278; Sorensen, *Censorship*, 128ff.

28. Fowler, "Piss and Run," 283–85.

29. Sorensen, *Censorship*, 131.

30. For Bordwell's list of parallels, see *Poetics*, 129.

31. Fowler, "Piss and Run," 282–83.

32. Dower, *Embracing Defeat*, 291.

33. Fowler, "Piss and Run," 282–83.

34. Sorensen, *Censorship*, 134.

35. Bordwell, *Poetics*, 303.

36. Hirano, *Mr. Smith*, 154ff.

37. Sorensen, *Censorship*, 132.

38. Buddhism stresses compassion and care for the poor, but this conflicted with Confucianism, which emphasized family ties. Although Buddhist organizations in Japan engage in social activism today, it was unusual in Ozu's time.

39. Ozu's understanding of this difference is illustrated by *End of Summer's* culturally ambiguous Yukiko when she takes leave of Manbei's corpse: first she bows her head with her palms held together in Buddhist fashion; then she crosses herself and holds up clasped hands, fingers intertwined, in a sign of Christian reverence.

40. Joo, *Ozu*, 153.

41. Dower, *Embracing Defeat*, 106–7.

42. Joo, *Ozu*, 153.

The Reckoning   155

43. See Dower, *Embracing Defeat*, 29ff.

44. Thompson, *Breaking the Glass Armor*, 321–22; Bordwell, *Poetics*, 307.

45. *Late Spring* deviates considerably from Hirotsu's original story, where, after a successful *omiai*, the prospective groom refuses to agree to having the father live with them after their marriage. The daughter then cancels the engagement, but eventually the father agrees to marry his secretary, his daughter returns to her fiancé, and everyone is happy. Unlike *Late Spring*, there is no deception, no jealousy, no missing out on the man the girl really loves, and the father is not left alone at the end. Ozu's film is more complex and considerably darker.

46. Alastair Phillips, "Pictures of the Past in the Present: Modernity, Femininity and Stardom in the Postwar Films of Ozu Yasujiro," in *Screening World Cinema*, ed. Catherine Grant and Annette Kuhn (New York: Routledge, 2006), 96.

47. Hirano, *Mr. Smith*, 175

48. Dower, *Embracing Defeat*, 525.

49. Eric Cazdyn, *The Flash of Capital: Film and Geopolitics in Japan* (Chapel Hill, NC: Duke University Press, 2002), 228ff.

50. Thompson, *Breaking the Glass Armor*, 347.

51. Sorensen, *Censorship*, 15ff.

52. Dower, *Embracing Defeat*, 65ff; for disillusion with the emperor, 304ff.

53. Sorensen, *Censorship*, 153.

54. Sorensen, *Censorship*, 153.

55. Igarashi, *Ozu's Films from Behind the Scenes*. In Igarashi's film, Takashi Kawamata, assistant cameraman on *Late Spring*, also recalls that during the Kyoto shoot, "Mr. Ozu wanted us to find the best baseball team in Kyoto, and the next day we played a game on the field of the botanical garden." Shinnosuke Kometani confirms Ozu's love of baseball (*Chasing Ozu*, 104–5). The author also supplies the specifics for the baseball game shown on TV in *An Autumn Afternoon*.

56. Sorensen, *Censorship*, 153.

57. Sorensen, *Censorship*, 153.

58. Onodera concludes his remarks about the man with the air gun shooting at the pigeon, saying "just like William Hart," referring to the American silent screen cowboy. (Subtitles on every copy of the film I have seen translate this erroneously as "just like William Tell.") Ozu would complement this nod to American Westerns four years later in *Tokyo Story* when one of the boys whistles the theme from John Ford's *Stagecoach*.

59. Sorensen, *Censorship*, 154.

60. Sorensen, *Censorship*, 164.

61. Sorensen, *Censorship*, 164

62. Sorensen, *Censorship*, 171.

63. Sorensen, *Censorship*, 157.

64. Sorensen, *Censorship*, 149.

65. Marius B. Jansen, *The Making of Modern Japan* (Cambridge, MA: Harvard University Press, 2000), 705.

66. High, "Drama," 20.

67. Bordwell, *Poetics*, 311.

68. Bordwell, *Poetics*, 313.

69. Kathe Geist, *The Cinema of Wim Wenders: From Paris, France to Paris, Texas* (Ann Arbor: UMI Research Press, 1988), 12.

70. So Yamamura, who plays Mimura in *The Munekata Sisters*, has a cameo in *Tokyo Twilight* as the family friend from whom Akiko borrows money for her abortion, a further link between the two films. Yamamura had more substantial roles in *Tokyo Story* and *Early Spring*, the two films that preceded *Tokyo Twilight*.

71. Of the 223,000 settlers—Japanese farmers who had been induced to move to Manchuria to establish farms in the "wilderness"—living in Manchuria at the end of the war, approximately one-third died, mostly of illness and starvation, trying to evacuate. Over 11,500 died violently, more than a third of these by suicide. See Louise Young, *Japan's Total Empire*, 410–11.

72. See Elyssa Faison, "Tokyo Twilight: Alienation, Belonging and the Fractured Family" in *Ozu International: Essays on the Global Influences of a Japanese Auteur*, ed. Wayne Stein and Marc DiPaolo (New York: Bloomsbury Academic, 2015), 60.

73. Richie, *Ozu*, 237.

74. Igarashi, *Ozu's Films from Behind the Scenes*.

75. Dower, *Embracing Defeat*, 245.

76. Joo, "Rethinking Noriko's Marriage," 352.

77. A commemorative towel (*tenugui*), designed by Ozu to commemorate the war in China, shows a toy-like tank with a Japanese flag negotiating barbed wire. In the lower-right corner, there is the head of a stalk of wheat or, more probably, barley. No doubt a nod to Hino's book, it recognizes the common soldiers Ozu served with in China. The towel is owned by the Koishibu Cultural Center in Tokyo. See Hidenori Okada, "Ozu Yasujiro ni okeru kaiga to dezain" [Ozu Yasujro's painting and design], in *Ozu Yasujiro Taizen*, ed. Kanji Matsuura and Akiko Miyamoto (Tokyo: Asahi Shinbun Publications, 2019), 136.

78. For all its realism, *Wheat and Soldiers* (*Mugi to heitai*) was nevertheless subject to strict censorship rules regarding its portrayal of the war. See Haruko Taya Cook, "The Many Lives of Living Soldiers: Ishikawa Tatsuzo and Japan's War in Asia," in Mayo et al., *War, Occupation, and Creativity*, 186n13.

79. Dower, *Embracing Defeat*, 437.

80. See http://www.mansell.com/pow_resources/camplists/osaka/zentsuji/zentsuji.htm.

81. Ofuna, location of the Shochiku studio, itself contained a secret POW camp operated by the Imperial Navy, used mainly to interrogate Allied officers before moving them on to other prison camps. Similar to the black sites used by the CIA during the Iraq War, it was so secret that no one in the surrounding neighborhood knew of it, and as such it was illegal by the terms of the Geneva Conventions. Like the doctor from the Zentsuji camp, one medical orderly who worked there was sentenced to hang although the sentence was eventually commuted to thirty years of hard labor. The camp commander was similarly sentenced to twenty-five years of hard labor. That such a camp had been operating right under their noses throughout the war must have shocked the Shochiku community. Ozu's mention of Zentsuji in *Early Summer* may well have been inspired by revelations about the Ofuna camp, a typically oblique reference to a painful subject. See https://en.wikipedia.org/wiki/Ōfuna_prisoner-of-war_camp.

82. Hirano, *Mr. Smith*, 54.

83. The *Yamato* was sent on a suicide mission with only enough fuel for a one-way trip to Okinawa; out of 3,332 crew members, only 256 survived its sinking. See Gallicchio, *Unconditional*, 4–6.

84. Joo, "Rethinking Noriko's Marriage," 352.

85. Joo comes to a similar conclusion, writing "The postwar is waiting ahead for the newly-weds, but they will not be entirely free from this vision of the past in which the memory of war remains." Joo, "Rethinking Noriko's Marriage," 352.

86. Criterion's subtitles for its 2004 DVD release of the film wrongly identify the "Hepburn," whose pictures Noriko collected, as "Audrey" instead of "Katharine." Audrey was still a child, living privately with her family, when the fictional Noriko was collecting her "Hepburn" pictures. This mistake was no accident but was promulgated by Donald Richie, who worked on the DVD with Criterion and had already insisted that the relevant "Hepburn" was Audrey in his Ozu monograph (p. 12). Artist Daryl Chin has explained that Richie believed the reference was to Audrey because Audrey Hepburn had become very popular by the time *Early Summer* was made. (See: https://www.youtube.com/watch?v=3SfR09O1qIg.) Although ultra-feminine Audrey makes no sense as independent Noriko's ideal, never mind the time discrepancy, Ozu's script may well have alluded only to "Hepburn" in deference to Audrey's contemporary popularity.

87. Joo, *Ozu*, 166.

88. A painting of the Akasaka Palace gate decorates the office of the sewing school where Akiko teaches in *Late Autumn* (1960).

89. Actresses in Japanese films were sometimes offered roles that corresponded with their off-screen lives. The scandal-ridden Yoshiko Okada, for example, appeared in three of Ozu's films as a woman who prostitutes herself (*Until the Day We Meet Again,* 1932; *Woman of Tokyo,* 1933; *An Inn in Tokyo,* 1935; see Wada-Marciano, *Nippon Modern,* 95–97). Michiyo Kogure, who plays Taeko in *Green Tea*, was perceived as a happily married actress and even wrote an advice column for wives in a popular film magazine. See Jennifer Coates, *Repetition and the Female Image in Japanese Cinema, 1945–1964* (Hong Kong: University of Hong Kong Press, 2016), 99. The story of Taeko reconciling with her husband at the end of the film suggests the kind of advice Kogure likely gave in her column.

90. Bordwell, *Poetics*, 284.

Afterword Part II: "Then it's good we lost."

The Greater East Asia War continued to be referenced in Ozu's films right up to the end. In *Tokyo Story*, the Hirayamas have lost one son (with the same name and MIA status as Shoji in *Early Summer*). Their friend Hattori has lost two sons. The Imperial Navy's *Gunkan* March, banned during the Occupation, plays in a red-lantern bar. War casualties pile up in *Early Spring*, where Masako's friend Sakae has lost her husband, Sugimura's friend Miura has lost a brother, and war buddies meet and lament the loss of a man in their unit named Nishijima.[1]

Characters in *Equinox Flower* comment on their friend Mikami, once a naval officer based in Kure (from which the famous battleship *Yamato* was launched). They imply that this was the high point of Mikami's career. Later he leads the singing of once-banned patriotic songs about samurai heroes that were valorized during the war. *An Autumn Afternoon*'s Hirayama, played, like Mikami, by Chishu Ryu, seems to have had a similarly distinguished naval career only to end up in a job a friend found for him.

Apart from Masako's sarcastic comment in *Early Spring*—after meeting her husband's drunken war buddies, she opines that "with soldiers like them it's no wonder Japan lost the war"—*An Autumn Afternoon* is the only film to treat the war humorously: Hirayama meets his former petty officer, and the two pantomime shipboard discipline while a bar hostess plays the *Gunkan* March. The former sailor remarks on the hard times after the war then offers some absurd speculations on what might have happened if Japan had won, to which Hirayama responds dryly, "Then it's good we lost." Later, in the same bar, the hostess plays the march again for Hirayama, and two other patrons mock their former shipboard duty: "At 5:30 hours, Imperial Navy units engaged the enemy," says one, "And lost!" rejoins the other.

In these films we learn tidbits about the home front: what women wore, where families sheltered during bombing raids, or to where they evacuated. Several men comment on their dislike of the arrogant militarists who swaggered around at the time (very likely Ozu's own view).

The films also provide a virtual tour of the Greater East Asia Co-Prosperity Sphere. The men in *The Flavor of Green Tea Over Rice* have served in Singapore, those in *Early Spring* in Thailand. As noted in Chapter 7, *The Munekata Sisters* and *Tokyo Twilight* mention Manchuria while the father in *Tokyo Twilight* was away in Korea when his wife

Afterword Part II

left him. In *Equinox Flower* a map of Indonesia hangs on the wall of the guest waiting room of Hirayama's company.

As in *Green Tea*, however, the war's main role in these late films is one of nostalgia. In *Early Spring, Equinox Flower*, and *An Autumn Afternoon*, wartime service, whatever its terrors at the time, is remembered fondly as a time of greater purpose, adventure, and patriotism than the present can offer. The older men in these films were in their prime during the war, so nostalgia for the war is also nostalgia for their youth. *An Autumn Afternoon* makes this point with particular poignancy as a drunken Hirayama continues to sing the *Gunkan* March as he prepares for bed in the film's final scene.

Knowing as we do the cruelty Japan visited upon its Asian neighbors as well as upon captured British and American soldiers and civilians, the utter foolishness of engaging the United States and the "war without mercy" that ensued, which ended in nuclear holocaust, it is hard to fathom, much less appreciate, the enthusiasm the Japanese felt about the prospect of new colonies and conquests in Asia or their dedication to the holy war against the United States.[2] Ozu's two wartime films, *The Brothers and Sisters of the Toda Family* and *There Was a Father*, capture that excitement and that sense of sacrifice and dedication. His subsequent films allude to the letdown: secure and at peace but more or less a satellite of the United States, Japan would never again experience the exhilaration of its headlong drive to catch up to the West in the prewar and, disastrously, the war years. A particular generation of men would miss the intensity of that era.[3]

Notes

1. In 1983, I wrote an article, based on films shown at the Japan Society of New York's 1982 retrospective of Ozu's work, in which I recorded this conversation between two veterans in *Early Spring*: "'We were forced to fight and fought reluctantly,' says one. 'But I didn't want to lose,' counters another." (See Geist, "Notes on a Retrospective," 8.) In his 1999 *Giants of Japan*, Mark Weston recorded this exchange between the same veterans: "There are a lot of pretentious guys nowadays who go around saying, 'I opposed the war.' They're all frauds and fakes." "Yeah, big fakes . . . If we'd said something like that, we would've been shot on the spot." See Mark Weston, *Giants of Japan: The Lives of Japan's Most Influential Men and Women* (New York: Kodansha International, 1999), 306–7. None of these sentiments, which were undoubtedly Ozu's own, are spoken in the Criterion or British Film Institute DVD versions of the film, nor do they occur in my notes from 1987, which were based on New Yorker's 16mm copy of *Early Spring*. This leads me to suspect that these lines and the corresponding footage were removed from those versions of the film intended for widespread distribution in the United States and Europe. By whom is not clear.
2. *War Without Mercy* is the name of John W. Dower's account of the war in the Pacific.
3. Textile historian Jacqueline M. Atkins chronicles the perspective of ordinary Japanese regarding the prewar and war years in her jaw-dropping study of *omoshirogara*, textiles that commemorated the fads, wonders, and historical events that Japanese found "interesting" (*omoshiroi*) during this time. (See Atkins, "Wearing Novelty," 91–143.) Along with

skyscrapers, zeppelins, biplanes, subways, cartoon characters, baseball, radio, and various incarnations of the Olympics, these textiles were also decorated with tanks and battleships as well as events the Anglo-American West viewed as infamous: Japan's exit from the League of Nations, Italy's invasion of Ethiopia, the fall Nanjing, and the bombing of Pearl Harbor. According to Atkins, "None of the omoshirogara textiles was commissioned or ordered by the government or its military branches. The soft propaganda message implicit in these [images of Manchuria] and other designs is one that the textile producer or artist picked up as patriotic motifs that would sell." (Atkins, "Wearing Novelty," 140.)

While historians usually view Japan in the 1930s as being pulled by competing factions: modernization, internationalization, and liberalism vs. nativism, militarism, and repression, the textiles tell a different story, one in which modernization merges seamlessly into a war for colonies and international recognition as a great power. As Louise Young writes, "[I]n Manchukuo the culture of Japanese modernity became the culture of imperialism." See Young, *Japan's Total Empire*, 430.

Part III

Religion, Sex, and Other Matters

Ozu's late films, 1953 to 1962, focused ever more resolutely on the life cycle, ephemerality, and nostalgia. The most famous, *Tokyo Story*, was the first of these. Four others involve the marriage of a daughter, like the Occupation-era films *Late Spring* and *Early Summer*, and two, *Ohayo* and *Floating Weeds*, were remakes of two critically acclaimed silents, *I Was Born, But . . .* and *A Story of Floating Weeds*.

The two remaining films from the late period handle themes that are somewhat unusual among Ozu's extant films. *Early Spring* examines the disintegration of a marriage while *Tokyo Twilight* looks at the disintegration of a young girl's emotional stability. Understated *Early Spring* succeeds as a classically balanced Ozu film and would become the basis of Masayuki Suo's immensely successful *Shall We Dance? Tokyo Twilight*, in contrast, tried to combine a highly charged, emotional drama with Ozu's normally resigned and elegiac treatment of disappointment and death and was not well received.

Rather than treating these films either singly or as a group, Part III takes up five distinct topics that potentially concern all of Ozu's films although the first of these, "Narrative Strategies in the Late Films," discusses this group in particular, along with *Late Spring* and *Early Summer*. The next three chapters concern the extent to which religion imbues Ozu's films, his attitude toward a variety of gender issues, and his films' relationship to other two-dimensional art forms in Japan. To some extent these chapters revisit and elaborate upon topics that have come up earlier in this book, tying them to Parts I and II.

Part III's final chapter looks at the specific influence Ozu's work, both early and late, has had on particular films and filmmakers, two German, two American, two Japanese. In addition to noting particular borrowings from Ozu's films, this chapter details the ways in which each filmmaker understood Ozu, which were far from uniform and not necessarily in line with my own understanding of him. I have, in the course of this book, discussed studies of Ozu with varying perspectives, some of which I agree with and others with which I disagree, at least in part. Chapter 12 gives us insight into how other filmmakers viewed Ozu and how each one's particular understanding of Ozu's work informed his own.

Most readers will, generally, be more familiar with Ozu's late films than with his earlier ones, but those less familiar with some or all of these films are urged consult the Plot Synopses on pages 253–269 as needed.

8
Narrative Strategies in the Late Films[1]

> Rather than tell a superficial story, I wanted to go deeper to show the hidden undercurrents, the ever-changing uncertainties of life.
>
> —Yasujiro Ozu[2]

Noël Burch, dazzled by the spatial/pictorial inventiveness of Ozu's early films, has called the late films a "final fossilization" of his style; their imagery and diegesis "a senile mannerism."[3] Woojeong Joo sees them showing signs of "diffidence and fatigue."[4] In fact, Ozu had, in his late period, so refined the cinematic "transgressions" that characterized his early films that they flow logically, seamlessly, and ever more complexly, revealing an unorthodox master of both style and narrative.[5]

The films Burch found so distasteful are characterized by scenes made up of perfectly composed, relatively static shots with little or no camera movement; flat lighting; cryptic "empty shots" (empty of identified characters) often used as transitions between scenes; and an even, stately, unhurried rhythm. These films eschew drama, and their plots unfold over a unified time and in locales that are predictable from film to film: the upper-middle-class house, the lower-middle-class apartment, the restaurant, the bar, the office, the train station, the temple, the scenic pilgrimage spot, elements that were present to some extent in *The Brothers and Sisters of the Toda Family* and even more so in *Late Spring*. Beginning with *Early Summer*, Ozu indicated that he was consciously striving to reflect the life cycle, mutability, and ephemerality.[6] As such, the films depict families, composed generally of young children and their parents, young people of marriageable age, and elderly people, some of whom die.

In Chapter 4, I mentioned Bordwell's contention that Ozu's stories were banal in order to accommodate his odd style, but, as we have seen, Ozu's style is frequently, if not always, an integral part of the narrative process and a necessary guide to his narrative and thematic meanings. His frequent use of repetition and ellipsis do not "impose their will" on his plots: they *are* his plots.[7] By paying attention to what has been left out and to what is repeated, one arrives at Ozu's essential story.

The End of Summer, which chronicles the end of a family-owned brewery business when the patriarch, Manbei Kohayagawa, dies, has the most complex narrative structure of all the late films. It opens with two shots of Osaka at night. In the second of these a large neon sign beams the words "New Japan." They prelude a scene in an Osaka bar where an uncle discusses a possible marriage arrangement for Akiko, widow of Manbei's only son. Akiko arrives at the bar to meet the prospective suitor but quickly excuses herself to telephone home to see if her sister-in-law, Noriko, the younger Kohayagawa daughter, is waiting for her. Photographed from behind, she walks up the passageway between the bar stools and the booths. The camera cuts back to the men waiting for her. Smitten, the suitor, Isomura, orders three gin fizzes. Instead of seeing Akiko return through the aisle in the bar, however, we next see her walking down the hallway outside her own apartment. She enters and chats briefly with Noriko, who is indeed waiting for her. Noriko wants to discuss a proposed *omiai*, and the scene ends with a shot of Noriko from behind as she walks down the same hallway that Akiko came up at the beginning of the scene.

These opening scenes violate a number of narrative norms. First, Ozu suppresses what Akiko learned from her telephone call; only when she is already home do we know its content. We anticipate her return through that passageway in the bar and are momentarily confused to see her in a different but similar passageway. Finally, Ozu includes a gratuitous shot of Noriko walking down the same passageway that Akiko came up. We seem to have both too much and too little information, yet reading what we are given as *information pertinent to the narrative* instead of reading it as deformity allows us deeper insight into Ozu's story.

By not telling us what Akiko learned from her phone call or what excuses she made to her uncle and his prospect, Ozu establishes her rejection of the suitor even though no formal proposal has been made. He does what his character in all politeness cannot: he cuts out the suitor. Figuratively she never returns to him; this becomes literal in a later scene in the same bar in which the suitor waits for her, but she never shows up.

The closing shot of Noriko walking down the hallway outside Akiko's apartment functions thematically. First, it identifies the two women with one another, showing them in especial sympathy since neither wants the marriage arrangements proposed for them. Second, it creates a completed cycle. Like all the films under consideration in this chapter, *End of Summer* deals with the life cycle and is particularly rich in circle imagery, created through both editing and graphic patterning.[8] Circle imagery also relates to Buddhist design and ontology and will be discussed in that context in the following chapter. Finally, it allows Ozu to show the passageway once more. Passageways in houses, corridors in office and apartment buildings, and alleyways through neighborhoods abound in Ozu's films. They can be read as symbolic of the passages in human life from one state to another; or, if that seems too literal, they can be seen as the "go spaces" (*michiyuki hashi*) in *ma*, the Japanese concept of time-space continuity, which connects one time to the next.[9] In either case, they belong specifically to Ozu's vision of an ephemeral world in flux.

The confusion we feel when we expect to see Akiko in the bar only to find her at home contributes to one of the film's major paradigms: things never happen as expected. Its main story event suggests this structure; patriarch Manbei becomes ill

Narrative Strategies in the Late Films

and is feared dying in the middle of the film but recovers only to die suddenly and unexpectedly at the end.

Between the fourth and fifth scenes, another transition occurs in which Ozu deliberately misleads his viewers. Gathered in their living room, members the Kohayagawa family discuss marriage prospects for both Akiko and Noriko. Brother-in-law Hisao remarks that Noriko's *omiai* will take place in the New Osaka Hotel. Soon after the scene ends, a new one begins with a shot of tall office buildings, an indication that we are in Osaka, the business and industrial center of southern Honshu. To remove all doubt, Osaka Castle, an iconic landmark, appears in the background of the following shot, which has been taken out the window of one of the buildings. Surely Noriko's *omiai* will be the subject of this scene. Instead we see an unknown woman talking on the telephone, presumably inside the office building whose window we just looked out of. After hanging up, she sits down at a desk beside Noriko. The telephone call has been an invitation to a party for a fellow employee named Teramoto, who will soon be leaving for a job in Sapporo, capital of Hokkaido. Noriko seems disappointed, and we soon learn that she is in love with Teramoto. Using a sound bridge (the Japanese version of "My Darling Clementine"), Ozu cuts to a restaurant where the farewell party is underway, showing first the hallway outside the party room and then the party itself. The next scene takes place in a train station, where Noriko and Teramoto converse awkwardly while waiting for their separate trains.

Earlier Ozu had led us to believe that we would see Noriko's *omiai*. Instead he showed us Noriko at work. The substitution was not merely a trick, however, for instead of the *miai*-suitor, we meet the man Noriko really loves and will eventually marry. Although Noriko later reports on the formal *omiai*, Ozu does not waste time on the wrong man. But having promised us an *omiai*, he gives us one in the form of the train station scene. Although attracted to one another, Noriko and Teramoto are obviously not in close contact because she first learns of his final decision to move to Sapporo from her officemate. Thus the scene in which they sit on the station platform bench speaking shyly to one another has the character of an *omiai*: each feels pressured by the impending departure and the distance that will separate them to reach a decision about marrying on the basis of relatively little familiarity. Here Ozu substitutes the unexpected for the expected, but, in doing so, he jettisons the unimportant for the important, thus keeping his storyline right on track. (Although Noriko does not make a final decision to marry Teramoto until the end of the film, Ozu includes a spoiler alert in the form of an advertising poster for Fuji Bank, visible to the left of the couple, which announces: "your bright future.")

The film climaxes when Manbei collapses from a heart attack. Noriko runs to telephone a doctor. From Noriko telephoning, Ozu cuts to two empty shots of the Hirayama Clinic, over which the phone keeps ringing. He then cuts back to the corridor, now empty, where Noriko had been telephoning, to the empty living room, to the empty passageway between the living room and the garden, and finally to the bedroom where a doctor is treating Manbei. Again we have been deliberately misled.

The unanswered telephone ringing in the clinic suggested that the doctor was out and that Manbei would die from lack of medical attention.[10] Yet here again the narrative structure does not simply disrupt our conventional expectations; it tells a different story. In addition to the sound of the phone ringing over the shots of the empty clinic, we hear a clock ticking, and in the second of the clinic shots we see this clock. Over the shot of the empty corridor in the Kohayagawa house and repeatedly thereafter, we hear a train whistle; in the empty living room a coil of insect-repelling incense sends up a plume of smoke. Smoking coils appear in every room of the house. Of the three shots inside the house, two are of passageways. Thus, at the moment Manbei appears to be dying, Ozu montages a series of visual and aural symbols of passage and transience. The empty rooms indicate the void Manbei will leave if he dies. (Ozu uses this same void structure in *Late Spring* and *An Autumn Afternoon* when he shows the empty room of the daughter/bride after she has left for her wedding ceremony.) In addition to these symbols of transience and absence, Ozu has placed a stupa in the garden outside Manbei's bedroom. We see the stupa behind the doctor every time the camera cuts to him. It seems unlikely that the Kohayagawas have a stupa in their garden since such figures are generally used to honor saints in a Buddhist temple. Like the stupa that was cheated into shots inside the banquet room in *There Was a Father*, this one's positioning is completely unrealistic and functions solely to suggest Manbei's death.

The sequence following that of the doctor treating Manbei contains two brief scenes with Noriko cut between seven empty shots, which show the living room, the brewery, and the cemetery at dawn. In this manner we wait with the family and view the anticipated void. Bordwell has pointed out that the sequence echoes that in the earlier *Tokyo Story* in which the family waits by the grandmother's bedside through the night until she dies toward dawn.[11] Thus we are given every indication that Manbei will die.

The dawn sequence ends with a conversation between two clerks at the brewery. "Did the Old Master have a bad heart?" the younger asks. "No, a bad liver," the older man replies. In this way Ozu reminds us to expect the unexpected in this film, and, indeed, in the following scene Manbei astounds his family by getting out of bed fit and chipper.

In the next scenes Akiko visits the family, tells Noriko that she does not want to remarry, and pries from her sister-in-law the secret of her love for Teramoto. Manbei plays hide-and-seek with his grandson and uses the occasion to sneak off to visit his mistress, Tsune. This is his third visit to Tsune in the course of the film, and we expect to see him at her house once again, but we see them at the bicycle races instead. However, before we see them, Ozu uses eleven shots to establish the location of the scene. The first three are typically cryptic; a stone post tells us we are near Saidaiji in Nara, but Tsune lives in Kyoto, not Nara. Finally, we see the stands and the racers and remember that the couple, whose relationship underwent a nineteen-year hiatus, recently renewed their acquaintance while Manbei was returning home from a bicycle race.

Such a long, uncharacted sequence is unusual even for Ozu. Part of the explanation lies in the associative and symbolic content of the shots. The cyclers race in a circle, again the completed cycle. Some win and some lose; Manbei's racers lose. So do those of an anonymous individual who throws his worthless stubs in the air in the shot immediately preceding that of Manbei, who subsequently does the same. An empty shot after the dialogue sequence between Manbei and Tsune shows torn stubs floating to the ground like confetti. Someone must have won this race, but Ozu tells us only about the losers, which thus suggests Manbei's impending death. In fact, this scene is the last in which we see him alive. His conversation with Tsune seems trivial enough, and we wonder why Ozu inflates the bicycle races to the status of a major scene by using such a lengthy introduction. Only later do we realize that it was important because it was the last time we would see Manbei alive; yet Ozu told us the scene was important at the time, just as he told us early in the film that Akiko would not marry her suitor and that Noriko would marry the man she loves and not her *miai*-suitor.

At the end of the short dialogue at the races, Manbei insists they go to Osaka. The shot of torn stubs falling behind the empty bleachers follows; then the shot of Osaka's neon lights flashing "New Japan" is reprised. Using conventional logic, we anticipate finding Manbei and Tsune in Osaka, but instead we return to the film's opening scene: Akiko's uncle and her suitor, Isomura, in the bar. Again Ozu has brought us to Osaka with the expectation of meeting one set of characters only to have us meet another. Formally, however, he is consistent, for the "New Japan" sign also preceded the earlier version of this scene. Thematically, too, the sequence makes sense. Manbei's loss at the races is followed by Isomura's loss of Akiko, for she doesn't show up at the bar this time and thereby signals her rejection of his proposal. Meanwhile, Isomura's loss of Akiko substitutes for Manbei's loss of life, which occurs in the story at about the same time as the second bar scene.

In short, Ozu's plot in *End of Summer* unfolds with relentless logic. Although it confounds our expectations, it provides a rich and accurate description of the characters, themes, motivations, and events in Ozu's story and never deviates from nor clutters that story with irrelevant information.

A similar logic operates in *An Autumn Afternoon*. A scene between the protagonist, Hirayama, and his friend Kawai ends with Kawai declining an invitation to dinner on the excuse that he cannot miss his baseball game. A shot out of Hirayama's office window is followed by six more uncharactered shots: three of the stands during a night baseball game, one of the game on a television set, and two of men we don't know watching the television in the bar section of a restaurant. Finally we are shown Hirayama, Kawai, and their friend Horie having dinner in the same restaurant. Again we have been deliberately misled. Kawai's comment, followed by the shots of the stands at the baseball field, suggests we will find him there. Instead he has changed his mind and joined his friends for dinner, information we are denied until we actually see the three men together. In an early article on Ozu, Bordwell and Thompson called this sequence Ozu's "most transgressive transition," one in which he moves "through spaces between scenes independently of any narrative demands."[12] Stephen Heath has objected to the suggestion that the transition is "transgressive," forcing a split between space and narrative. "Certainly," he writes, "there is a play of difficulty in finding the men, but that play—irony and revelation . . . is not transgressive of the terms of the narration given."[13]

In other words, Ozu narrates on his own terms, but *narrates* nonetheless. Moreover, what may seem like an elaborate joke on the director's part also points to a serious subtext in the film. By taking us to the baseball game, Ozu does not simply show us where Kawai is not; he shows us what Kawai is missing. Later in the restaurant Kawai protests Horie's early departure by pointing out that he gave up his baseball game for this meeting, thus underscoring his missed opportunity. Throughout the film, characters have missed, do miss, or might miss a variety of opportunities. "Gourd," the old teacher, has neglected to marry off his daughter, and now it is too late. Kawai fears that Hirayama will do the same with his daughter, Michiko. Having insisted she was not ready to marry, Michiko misses the opportunity to marry the man of her choice. Near the end of the film, Kawai and Horie tease Hirayama by telling him that since he waited too long to give an answer on the *miai*-match Kawai arranged for Michiko, the young man is no longer available, although this is only a joke. Throughout the film, Hirayama's son Koichi agonizes over a set of MacGregor golf clubs that his friend is selling at a bargain price, an opportunity not to be missed. Even Hirayama's former seaman speculates about the dubious opportunities Japan missed by losing the war.

An Autumn Afternoon is Ozu's third film on the subject of a daughter deciding to marry and leave a single parent, but neither of the others, *Late Spring* or *Late Autumn*, treats the subject in terms of missed opportunity. Neither exhibits the baleful example of a middle-aged old maid. In fact, in all of Ozu's "marriage films" except *Autumn Afternoon*, the heroine has an unmarried, highly independent female friend who is doing very well on her own. Although, as I will argue shortly, *Late Spring* suggests that the heroine misses out on marrying the man she knows and is attracted to, the film's actual text makes little of it. Thus "missed opportunity" is uniquely central in *Autumn Afternoon*, and the baseball game is our first indication of it.

Late Spring is another case in which reading Ozu's "transgressions" considerably amplifies one's understanding of the film. The first of the marriage films, it begins with two shots of the Kita-Kamakura train station and proceeds to a teahouse where Noriko, the heroine, learns tea ceremony with her aunt and a Mrs. Miwa, who will later be put forward as a possible marriage prospect for Noriko's father, Professor Somiya. Noriko returns home to find Somiya working with his handsome assistant, Hattori. The next sequence begins with two shots of a station platform, shots of a train going through a tunnel, and views inside the train where we find Noriko and Somiya. The presence of the train here, as in the opening shots of the Kita-Kamakura station, suggests the idea of passage, with which the film is concerned. Richie has noted that Ozu was careful that the locales through which we see the train pass in this three-minute sequence all occur in correct order; such attention to detail is not gratuitous but sustains the parallel between a train journey and the life cycle insofar as each follows a fixed order.[14]

However, the sequence also contains far more explicit references to marriage or at least to coupling. The first shot shows an unknown woman standing alone on the

Narrative Strategies in the Late Films   169

platform. The next shot, taken farther down the platform, shows a man and a woman standing together, and in the next shot the train goes through the tunnel. A coupling process seems to be implied here, as though Ozu were labeling this train sequence with the particular kind of passage with which this film will be mainly concerned.

For Ozu, station platforms invite coupling. In *Early Summer, Early Spring, Ohayo, End of Summer*, and *An Autumn Afternoon*, would-be lovers wait together on station platforms. Prior to *Late Spring*, the newlyweds in *Where Now Are the Dreams of Youth?*, the young married couple in *There Was a Father*, and the reunited couple in *A Story of Floating Weeds* are shown riding on trains in the films' final sequences, the last couple having reunited on the train platform. In addition, the young lovers in *A Story of Floating Weeds* meet near the train tracks and watch a passing train.

In *Floating Weeds*, the 1959 remake of *A Story of Floating Weeds*, the inn where the young couple consummates their love affair and agrees to stay together is near the train station. Between shots of a sign for the inn and its front hallway we see two trains in their shed, one of them puffing away, ready to go. Sounds of the puffing train punctuate the beginning and end of the sequence. As the lovers kiss toward the end of it, we hear the train leaving and gathering speed. This is Ozu's most explicit rendering of the connection between trains and coupling (in keeping with this film's comparative heavy-handedness overall).

Given these associations, one is perhaps surprised to find Noriko and her father on the train in *Late Spring*. Yet the twist makes perfect sense, for the film's central emotional tension arises from Noriko's oedipal feelings for her father. Although we're not to suppose there is an actual physical relationship between Noriko and her father (which would seriously deform Ozu's story), oedipal psychology is straightforwardly described by Somiya at the end of the film when he tells Noriko she must transfer her love for him to a new man because that is how life goes on.

The train ride ends in Tokyo, where Noriko accidentally meets Somiya's friend Onodera. He suggests that they go to an art exhibit in Ueno, but Noriko says she has to buy needles. Ozu then cuts to a close-up of the poster for the exhibit, a shot of the same poster with the museum steps behind it, a close-up of a lantern outside a restaurant, then Noriko and Onodera sitting at the restaurant's bar. No mention is made of the exhibit, but Noriko says how much she enjoyed going to Ueno Park, implying that they went to the exhibit after all. Onodera tells her that he has remarried, which Noriko finds distasteful.

Instead of introducing a scene in the museum, the two shots of the exhibition poster stand in for the trip there. As we saw in Chapter 7, the poster has significance for the "culture" theme that runs through the film but not for the story itself. In eliding the visit in the museum, Ozu omits what is unimportant for his story. By including the conversation in the bar, however, he introduces a critical theme, Noriko's distaste for the idea of an older man remarrying.

As with the twin bar scenes in *End of Summer*, *Late Spring*'s is paired with another in the same bar at the end of the film, in which Somiya confesses to Noriko's friend Aya that he never intended to remarry but lied about it to push Noriko into marrying. Thus the debate over the propriety of remarriage, which began in the first bar scene and over which Noriko has expended so much emotional energy, is closed in the second bar scene.

Noriko brings Onodera home with her, and he remarks to her father that she should be thinking about marriage. The scene ends with Onodera, apparently on a whim, asking the direction of the ocean and making several incorrect attempts to point in the right direction. We have seen in Chapter 7 that this pointing sequence has political significance aside from the film's story, but it also cues a cut to a shot of the ocean, which begins a lengthy sequence in which Noriko and Hattori bicycle by the sea. They appear to be on a date, and on a narrative level Onodera's concern that Noriko should marry links this scene to the one before it. Later, upon hearing of the bicycle trip, Noriko's father asks if she wouldn't like to marry Hattori, whereupon she informs him (and us) that Hattori is already engaged.

At this point we wonder why Ozu has wasted so much time on the wrong man. The bicycling scene by the ocean appears totally superfluous—Kristin Thompson calls it "inessential"—yet a closer look reveals it as central to the film.[15] For one thing, it establishes an important aspect of Noriko's character: she tells Hattori she is "the jealous type," a trait neither he nor we are inclined to credit since she appears to be a paragon of good nature. Subsequent events prove her right, however, for she reacts angrily to her father's admission that he plans to remarry. Her jealousy and disappointment goad her into her own marriage and is thus the pivot on which the plot turns.

When her father suggests Hattori as a match, Noriko bursts out laughing. The joke is on him and on us and is reprised toward the end of the film when Hattori brings his wedding picture to the Somiya house. Not finding the family at home, he leaves it with the maid, who remarks to her husband, the gardener, "I thought he was going to marry Miss Noriko." The humor has a darker side, however, because Ozu makes it clear that Hattori *should* have married Noriko. She admits to her father that Hattori would make a good husband, and subsequent to the bicycling scene, she meets him in a coffee shop, where he asks her to accompany him to a concert for which he has already purchased two tickets. Beginning to find their friendship awkward, she declines. He goes to the concert alone, placing his hat on the empty seat beside him. The camera holds on a close-up of the hat for about four seconds, then cuts to Noriko walking down the sidewalk, alone and disconsolate.

The man Noriko marries never appears in the film, although he is "represented" by the meter man, whose voice we hear early in the film, for Noriko tells Aya that her suitor looks like their meter man (*denkiyasan*). Significantly, however, it is Hattori who helps the man find a stool and Hattori whom we watch, while the meter man remains largely off camera. Noriko's actual wedding is elided, but, as Somiya's friend, Hattori is present during the wedding preparations, standing in for the groom he will never be.

Ozu is not simply teasing by always showing us the wrong man. Hattori is the right man. That he and Noriko miss each other is meant to be seen as lamentable. Ozu was

Narrative Strategies in the Late Films

less subtle in *An Autumn Afternoon,* where both young people express deep disappointment at having missed the opportunity to marry one another.

Equinox Flower is the fourth film in Ozu's "season cycle" (films with seasons indicated in their titles) and the third concerned with marrying off a daughter. In it a conflict breaks out between a father and daughter over whether she should be allowed to marry a man of her own choosing. Forced to concede, ostensibly because of a trick his daughter's friend plays on him, the father, Hirayama, heads toward a reconciliation with his daughter in the film's last moments.

Ozu has said the film is principally about the parents, and indeed the daughter, Setsuko, appears in only six of the film's twenty-five scenes, and in one of these she merely waves from a rowboat in extreme long shot. Young women as a group, however, constitute a major force in the film and counterbalance the weight given to Hirayama. Three young women, in addition to Setsuko, have major roles, and all play opposite Hirayama most of the time: Hisako, Hirayama's younger daughter who, too young to marry, insists she will want to choose her own husband; Yukiko, Setsuko's friend from Kyoto, who seeks Hirayama's advice on marriage and tricks him into consenting to Setsuko's marriage; and Fumiko, the daughter of Hirayama's friend Mikami. Unable to obtain her father's consent to marry the man she loves, Fumiko lives with him out of wedlock, and Hirayama visits her as a favor to Mikami.

The film's title refers to both Hirayama and the young women he must contend with. *Higanbana,* literally translated as "equinox flower," is a red amaryllis that blooms in September at the time of the autumnal equinox. As in *Autumn Afternoon* and *Late Autumn,* the season refers to the parents' generation.[16]

The color red of the amaryllis, however, refers to the four young women. In Japan red is a color associated with festive occasions and with children, but most specifically with girls, whose holiday kimonos are red and pink, in contrast to the blue, green, and brown that boys wear. Young unmarried women continue to wear red and pink freely, and red appears in the headdress of the bride's traditional wedding garb and in the lining of the outer wedding kimono. At the time Ozu made this film, red was still considered inappropriate for married women to wear, at least as an outer garment. (Hirayama's wife has a red lining in one of her kimonos.) The color red appears throughout *Equinox Flower*—most prominently via the Hirayamas' red teakettle—presumably in reference to the quartet of young women. (Ozu was very fond of red and used it extensively in his color films but most extensively in *Equinox Flower.*)

Like a number of Ozu's late films, *Equinox Flower* opens with references to trains. A shot of Tokyo Central Station from the front is followed by a long shot of the station from the back, taken from across the many tracks that converge there. Next we see a close-up of one platform's time-and-destination sign as the numbers flip over to indicate that a train has just left, then an unidentified wedding party sending off the bride and groom on their honeymoon. Next two station workers discuss the large number of brides they have seen that day. The connection between trains and marriage is made

172 *Ozu*

particularly obvious here. The train taking the bride on her honeymoon literally takes her into a new life, a journey from childhood to adulthood.

Equally obvious is the close-up which ends the sequence: a track sign reading "Warning: Strong Winds Expected." The station workers comment on the predicted bad weather, but two scenes later a character says, "I'm glad the weatherman was wrong," indicating that the storm held off. The storm that comes, however, is Hirayama's outrage at his daughter's engagement. In typical fashion, Ozu suggests one thing, then seems to reverse it (as in *Late Spring* when we learn that Hattori is not available after all), only to have it fulfilled in another way (Hattori *should* have been the groom).

Equinox Flower's next scene begins with a view of the station from an open window, then one down a long corridor (or passageway). A bridal party crosses at the end of the corridor on their way to another room, associatively connecting this scene to that in the train station. Over these shots and those that follow, we hear a traditional wedding song, similar to Noh-like chanting. We cut to guests at a wedding banquet, the bride and groom, and three principal characters, Hirayama, his wife, and their friend Horie. A shot of the traditional singer and more guests follows, then one of Hirayama, then Kawai, friend of Hirayama and father of the bride. They remark that Mikami is missing, and later we find out why. Hirayama is asked to make a speech, and he notes appreciatively that this is a love match.

The scene functions in several ways. It introduces Hirayama and his cohort and, by introducing them well before we meet the younger set, establishes them as the film's main focus. This wedding banquet serves further as a substitute for Setsuko's eventual wedding, which takes place at the end of the film but which we never see. That this wedding has resulted from a love match links it even more closely with Setsuko's wedding and helps to set up Hirayama's hypocrisy, which is revealed in due time.

Substitution works on other narrative levels as well in *Equinox Flower*. Yukiko substitutes for Setsuko, not metaphorically but literally. Hirayama has heart-to-heart talks with her that he ought to be having with his own daughter, and at the end she represents Setsuko's problem of parental opposition to marrying the man she loves to Hirayama as though it were her own—and getting, as anticipated, a much more sympathetic response.

Equinox Flower appears to climax when Hirayama, tricked into consenting to the wedding, also agrees to attend it, having vowed not to. Setsuko bursts into tears at the good news, but the scene does not end there. Rather, it ends with Hirayama still voicing his doubts: "I never thought she'd defy me," he says to his wife when they are alone. "She made this vital decision without letting her parents know. It's not right."

We then cut to Hirayama's class reunion in Gamagori, which Kawai has mentioned earlier in the film. The reunion scene is a long one, and a full three minutes of it are devoted to Mikami singing part of an epic poem. In his lengthy essay on *Equinox Flower*, Edward Branigan dismisses this scene as irrelevant to the plot, while Donald Richie intuits that it "seems to suggest an importance beyond itself, as though it were somehow commenting on the film as a whole," but he fails to find the connection.[17] In fact, this scene is the film's emotional center, the point at which we come to understand and sympathize with Hirayama.

Previous to this, our assessment of Hirayama has been largely negative. He seems distant from his family, unjust to Setsuko, hypocritical in his standards, and stubborn. His jocularity with Yukiko is appealing, but it further underscores his unfairness to Setsuko. When his wife accuses him of inconsistency, he fumes, "Then everyone is inconsistent except God!"

The scene at Gamagori centers on the poem about Masatsura Kusunoki that Mikami recites. The Kusunoki family were fourteenth-century samurai who remained loyal to their emperor against the Ashikaga shogunate. Masatsura was the son of Masahige, who, in 1336, though vastly outnumbered, obeyed when the emperor insisted he join battle with the opposing forces. His troops eventually vanquished, Masahige committed suicide rather than face capture.

Behind Mikami, visible as he recites the poem, is a scroll with the portrait of Kamatari Fujiwara and his sons. Kamatari, a seventh-century statesman, was the founder of the powerful Fujiwara clan, whose reforms consolidated imperial power in Japan. The Kusunoki family, commemorated in the poem, fought and failed to shore up the emperor's power against the encroaching shogunate. Thus both the poem and the painting honor imperial power.

The poem begins, "The precepts of my father lie buried deep in memory. The edicts of the emperor I will follow faithfully." It then describes what the edicts are: to fight for the emperor and to die to the last man if necessary. Ancient though the poem may be, it describes the ethical standards with which this generation of schoolboys grew up. Remembering that during World War II most Japanese expected to die by suicide rather than surrender, one realizes that the inconsistencies Hirayama's wife accuses him of are embedded in the Great Inconsistency of twentieth-century Japan: after the bombing of Hiroshima and Nagasaki, the emperor reversed the centuries-old edict and told his people that Japan would surrender unconditionally but that they should *not* commit suicide. Significantly, the young man Setsuko marries has been transferred to Hiroshima. The bombing of Hiroshima forever changed Japan and its emperor, and, in order to be reconciled with Setsuko, Hirayama must travel to Hiroshima, i.e., acknowledge that Japan has changed.

David Bordwell sees the reunion scene as part of an ongoing schema of nostalgia that is present in most of Ozu's postwar films.[18] While this analysis comes closer than any previous one to appreciating the significance of the scene, it fails to justify the scene's length or recognize its centrality to the story. After this scene, Mikami tells Hirayama that he has reconciled with Fumiko. The reconciliation has taken place earlier in the story, but only when the men talk on the Takeshima Bridge in Gamagori do we learn about it.[19] At the film's end, we understand that Hirayama will likewise be reconciled with Setsuko. Meeting with his cohort to celebrate outdated values apparently frees Hirayama to accept and accommodate the present.

The Gamagori reunion scene is also deeply poignant. When Mikami finishes his recitation, the group sings a popular ballad, *Sakurai no ketsubetsu*, supposedly Masahige's farewell to Masatsura: "Twilight is a time of sorrow and grief: the warrior ponders what the world is coming to." The image here describes Hirayama, as epitomized by the previous scene's last shot in which he ponders, confused and perplexed, how Setsuko could have flouted his authority. He is entering his twilight (autumn) years and, played by Shin Saburi, best known for his samurai roles, he is very much the disillusioned warrior described in the song. Even as he travels to be reconciled with Setsuko, he sings the *Sakurai* ballad softly to himself. Once again, Ozu's apparent "transgression"—a static scene with little seeming relevance—turns out to be the pivot on which the film's dramatic and thematic structure turns.[20]

As we know, *Tokyo Story* is about the decline of the Japanese family, and, since even Ozu characterizes it as such, it must be so.[21] Ozu's endorsement notwithstanding, this view requires qualification. For one thing, the film's family has, by traditional standards, disintegrated long before the film opens. Two sons have left home to work in large cities, and a third, who also left home for Tokyo, has been killed in the war.

Two female characters are contrasted in the film, the daughter Shige and the daughter-in-law, Noriko. Shige finds her parents' visit burdensome and is insensitive and rude toward them. Noriko, who has far less means, welcomes them and treats them kindly. Ozu intends us to understand that their differing treatment of the parents arises from their different characters. (The plants on Shige's roof deck are all cacti, which, if her dialogue weren't enough, define her well.)

However, in some respects the two women's behavior corresponds to what was expected in the traditional Japanese family more than it deviates from it. Certainly Shige lacks filial piety, always deviant by traditional standards, but as a married daughter she is no longer part of her parents' family and has few obligations toward them. This is why a girl's marriage was, traditionally, so traumatic for a Japanese family and why only daughters' marriages are at issue in Ozu's films. When the father comments that "a married daughter is like a stranger," he is restating a cliché of traditional family life. On the other hand, a daughter-in-law, even a widowed one, is more obligated to her husband's family than to her natal family, and Noriko fulfills these traditional obligations. That the parents are truly touched by her kindness indicates that they really don't expect the standards of traditional family life to apply anymore.

More than the decline of the Japanese family, *Tokyo Story* is about the inroads time makes on human relationships and, finally, on human life itself. Time and distance have caused the children to grow apart from their parents. Ultimately they are as disappointed as the parents to find that the filial bonds have stretched so thin. "No one can serve his parents beyond the grave," mourns the youngest son, Keizo, at his mother's funeral. Their regret is not merely conditioned by a culture that has idealized these bonds but is one that most children who live far from their parents experience.

Even Noriko cannot dam time with tradition. She tells the father, "Sometimes I feel that I just cannot go on like this. Sometimes at night I lie and wonder what will

Narrative Strategies in the Late Films

become of me if I stay this way [unmarried, faithful to the dead son]." (When Noriko borrows items from her neighbor with which to entertain her in-laws, the neighbor's baby under its baby tent is foregrounded each time Noriko comes in the door, emphasizing what her life is missing and what she still might have should she remarry.) She tells the unmarried daughter, Kyoko, who still lives at home and can't understand her siblings' selfishness, "I may become like that. In spite of myself."

The parents experience disillusionment not simply because they are victims of a particular social problem, the decline of the Japanese family, but because in Ozu's films disillusionment is a condition of old age. In *Tokyo Story*, not only the protagonists Tomi and Shukichi are disappointed in their children; Shukichi's friend Numata is disillusioned, too. In *Early Spring* and *Ohayo*, retirement has disappointed the old men. The old teacher in *An Autumn Afternoon* has had neither a successful retirement nor a successful child. "Children don't live up to their parents' expectations," says Shukichi in *Tokyo Story*. "Let's think they are better than most." He echoes the parents in *Early Summer*, who insist that they have been really happy, that their lives have been better than average, and yet look sadly out over the fields that surround the ancestral home to which they have returned. And, of course, the mother of all of Ozu's disappointed parents is Otsune from *The Only Son*.

Like many of the late films, *Tokyo Story* begins with a montage of symbols for passing time, but unlike other films, which generally use only one symbol in the opening montage—the train station in *Late Spring* and *Equinox Flower*, smokestacks in *Autumn Afternoon*, the ocean in *Early Summer*—*Tokyo Story* incorporates trains, boats, the sea, and smoke all in the film's five opening shots, which run as follows:

1) The sound of a boat chugging over a close-up of a stone lantern with Onomichi's harbor in the background.
2) Chugging continues over a shot of children walking to school.
3) A train moves through town, seen through the rooftops of Onomichi.
4) CU of the train.
5) LS of the temple with the stone lantern; smoke comes out of a chimney; a train whistle sounds.

Finally we join Tomi and Shukichi, who are packing for their journey to Tokyo—by train, of course. They talk about the train schedule, and over the scene we hear a ticking clock. The next scene, which introduces Tokyo, begins with a shot of smokestacks, a train whistle over it, and two shots of a station platform.

The symbols are insistent and seem to be most closely associated with Tomi's death, for shots of the harbor recur just before and after her death. As she lies dying, Ozu cuts to a shot of the boats in the harbor, then to a moth fluttering around a light, well-worn symbol of impending death. In the scene that follows, the oldest son, a doctor, tells the family that Tomi will not live much longer. A montage paralleling the opening sequence follows:

1) An empty pier in the harbor.
2) The stone lantern from shot #1 in the opening sequence.
3) Sailboats tied up.
4) The sidewalk from shot #2 in the opening sequence.
5) The train tracks from shot #4 in the opening sequence.

Back at the house, Tomi has died. Ostensibly, the harbor, the tracks, and the sidewalk are empty and the boats tied up because it is daybreak; but their emptiness tells us that the transient life they signaled at the beginning of the film has ended, at least for one person. Shots showing the harbor active once again are reprised at the end of the film, intercut with Noriko taking the train, perhaps to a new life, and Shukichi left to carry on alone. Throughout much of the Onomichi footage, including at the very end, we hear boats chugging in the harbor, like a clock or a heartbeat, ticking away the time.

As in many of Ozu's films, train symbolism is central to *Tokyo Story* and is most prominently displayed in the scenes right before Tomi's death when the family waits in the Tokyo train station with the old couple and in the sequence that follows when the couple stops over in Osaka. The younger son works for the railroad in Osaka, so that stopover, occasioned by the onset of Tomi's illness, is filled with references to trains. The trains associated with marriage in *Late Spring* and *Equinox Flower* are here associated with death, a different "passage."

Bridging the marriage and the death films, *Early Spring*, a very long, very dense film, describes the disintegration and resurrection of a couple's marriage. In contrast to the other films under discussion in this chapter, the tension here is between the husband and the wife rather than between parents and children. In 1958, Ozu expressed disappointment in American critics who applauded *Tokyo Story* but failed to appreciate *Early Spring*. "Foreigners . . . only follow the story. They cannot understand the life of salaried men, ephemerality, and the atmosphere outside of the story at all."[22] The story in *Early Spring*, in which Sugiyama, an office worker bored with the monotony of his life, has an affair with a fellow commuter, is narrated more straightforwardly than are most of the late films, but the narration is filled with references to passing time: "ephemerality and the atmosphere outside the story."

Many of *Early Spring*'s story events refer to disillusionment, old age, and death—uncharacteristically the death of the young. The Sugiyamas' only child has died some years before the film opens, war buddies recall a fallen comrade, and a young man, Sugiyama's friend and fellow worker, dies after a long illness. His older brother has died in the war. The death of the young correlates with the stultifying life of salarymen, of which both young and old workers complain throughout the film. Two older men, one who has retired and opened a bar and one who still works for Sugiyama's company, discuss the disappointment that lifelong service to a big company brings. The Sugiyamas' resolve to repair their marriage, which began as a love match, comes from recognizing that love and fidelity are their only hedge against ephemerality, the only comforts in a world that brings mainly death and disappointment, even to the young.

As in his other films, Ozu makes many visual references to passing time: bridges, smoke, steam, and empty corridors. Again trains are central. Sugiyama's girlfriend, Goldfish, is one of a group of young workers who commute together. Thus the train is literally the vehicle which, over the course of time, erodes the marriage. At the end of the film, Sugiyama is transferred to a small industrial outpost where tall smokestacks and the railway running past the factory are major motifs. His wife joins him there, and after explaining why she decided to come back to him, she points out a passing train. The next shots are the train with a smokestack in front of it, a two-shot of them standing and looking outside, a shot of them from behind, still looking out, a long shot of many smokestacks with the train disappearing in the background, taken above the rooftops of the village where the couple lives, and finally a medium shot of a single smokestack. Helpless against time's passing, they can at least help one another.

As the Sugiyamas watch the train here, they speak longingly of an eventual return to Tokyo: passing time can also bring good things. One young couple is expecting a baby. However, the implications of passing time in this film are mainly negative and link it to the "death films"—*End of Summer* and *Tokyo Story*. The smokestacks at the end of *Early Spring* return at the end of *End of Summer* as those of the crematorium.

Balanced thematically between the marriage and death films, *Early Spring* is a reminder that Ozu connects marriage and death in obvious and subtle ways in most of his late films. One strategy is linking weddings and funerals. During the wedding scene at the beginning of *Equinox Flower*, a traditional wedding song dominates the soundtrack. Although ostensibly a happy song, it is nevertheless reminiscent of the chanting that figures prominently in the funeral service in *Tokyo Story* and in the seventh anniversary [after death] memorial service in *Late Autumn*. (We also hear chanting in the funeral and memorial services in the wartime films, *Brothers and Sisters of the Toda Family* and *There Was a Father*.) Ozu underscores the connection when, after this wedding reception, Hirayama tells his wife not to put away his formal clothes because he needs them the next day for a funeral. "Wedding one day, funeral the next," she says (so that we won't miss the point). Similarly, at the end of *Autumn Afternoon* the father enters a bar after his daughter's wedding and is asked if he's just come from a funeral. "Something like that," he replies. *Late Autumn* begins with the seventh anniversary ceremony for the dead father and ends with the daughter's wedding. The wife/mother wears a black kimono to both.

The comparison between weddings and funerals is not purely Ozu's invention but is so fundamental a concept in Japanese culture that these ceremonies as well as those surrounding births have built-in similarities. Both new babies and corpses are dressed in pure white kimonos, and, correspondingly, the bride in a traditional wedding wears a pure white kimono under her heavily embroidered outer robe. The symbolism indicates that she dies to her natal family—the wedding *is* like a funeral for that family—and is reborn into a new family. Falling between birth and death, marriage, according to anthropologist Joy Hendry, is "the vital link in the sequence, at once associated with the birth of the next generation and the death of the previous one."[23]

The melancholy Ozu evokes at the end of *Late Spring*, *Late Autumn*, and *An Autumn Afternoon* arises only partly because the single parent has been left alone. The father in *Autumn Afternoon*, for example, is not entirely alone; his younger son still lives with him. The sadness arises because the marriage of the younger generation inevitably reflects on the mortality of the older generation. Somiya in *Late Spring* says as much when he tells Noriko she must look to her husband for her future happiness because his own life is entering its last phase. The final, elegiac shot of him slumping forward after peeling an apple gives way to the final shot of Hirayama in *An Autumn Afternoon*: frail, drunk, he sits on a stool in his kitchen with a glass of water, photographed in the far back of a long shot—mankind in all its helplessness. Although Ozu did not intend *Autumn Afternoon* as his last film, mortality was clearly more real and less theoretical to him than it had been thirteen years earlier.

Of Ozu's many symbols for passage, evanescence, and passing time, bridges play a particularly conspicuous role in the late films. If time creates an inevitable bridge between marriage and death, that bridge is shown literally in film after film as a familiar and scenic landmark: Seta Bridge on Lake Biwa in *Early Spring*, Gamagori's Takeshima Bridge in *Equinox Flower*, Tokyo's Kiyosu Bridge in *Late Autumn*, Arashiyama's Togetsukyo Bridge in *End of Summer*. (In the Kyoto section of *Late Spring*, Somiya mentions that, in the course of their first day, they visited Kodaiji. Kodaiji is the temple featured in many tourist posters with a long covered bridge that crosses a stream and a pond to connect to two other buildings.)

A shot of the Kiyosu Bridge brackets *Late Autumn* and is followed each time by a corridor with a painting of what appears to be Tokyo's ancient Ryogoku Bridge. The painting hangs in the restaurant favored by the three gentlemen whose plot to get their deceased friend's daughter married motivates the story. Thus the bridge shots bring us twice from one scene to the next and, appearing toward the beginning and end of the film, span a story that moves from a memorial service to a wedding. (The men meet at this restaurant after each event.) These bridge shots, therefore, function both metaphorically as a symbol of passage and literally as a "bridge" within the film's structure.

A deep identification with the life cycle inheres in Japanese culture as well as in Ozu's films and accounts, perhaps, for the inherent "Japaneseness" many viewers sense in them. But whether or not his late films are inherently Japanese, they are deeply philosophical, built around an awareness of the give-and-take of the life cycle and mankind's inability to do anything about it. Their subject matter is not "banal"; nor are they empty of meaning and full of immobilized "codes," *tabulae rasae* on which Ozu performed artistic feats at the expense of narrative coherence.[24] Rather, the narratives unfold with an astounding precision, in which no shot and certainly no scene is wasted, and all is overlayered with an intricate web of interlocking meaning.

Notes

1. An earlier version of this chapter appears in Nolletti and Desser, *Reframing Japanese Cinema*, 91–111.
2. Quoted in Inoue, *I Lived, But . . .*
3. Burch, *To the Distant Observer*, 276.
4. Joo, *Ozu*, 194.
5. Bordwell was not among those who dismissed the artistry of Ozu's late films. In the final sentence of his Ozu monograph, he calls *An Autumn Afternoon*, Ozu's last film, "a young man's work." Bordwell, *Poetics*, 376.
6. Richie, *Ozu*, 237.
7. Bordwell, *Narration in the Fiction Film*, 288.
8. Bordwell describes the circle motif in *End of Summer* in great detail but insists that its only interest for Ozu was formal patterning. Bordwell, *Poetics*, 368.
9. See Cooper-Hewitt Museum, *MA: Space-Time in Japan*, exhibit catalog (New York: n.d.); and Gunther Nitschke, "MA: The Japanese Sense of Place," *Architectural Design* 36, no. 1 (March 1966): 143.
10. When Father Toda collapses in *Brothers and Sisters of the Toda Family*, there are three shots: Setsuko telephoning, the empty clinic, and a closer shot of the clock in the clinic. By the next shot Father Toda has died, so we never know if a doctor came or not or if his absence was an issue. In *End of Summer*, Ozu expands this three-shot sequence to play a trick on his audience.
11. Bordwell, *Poetics*, 368.
12. Thompson and Bordwell, "Space and Narrative in the Films of Ozu," 51.
13. Stephen Heath, *Questions of Cinema* (Bloomington, IN: Indiana University Press, 1981), 61–62.
14. Richie, *Ozu*, 165–66.
15. Thompson, *Breaking the Glass Armor*, 343.
16. The Japanese title for *An Autumn Afternoon* is *Samma no aji* (the taste of *samma*). *Samma* (Pacific saury) are a fish that migrates from north of Hokkaido south to the coast of Chiba Prefecture in the autumn and are typically caught and eaten at that time.
17. Edward Branigan, "The Space of *Equinox Flower*," *Screen* 17, no. 2 (Summer 1976): 82; Richie, *Ozu*, 44.
18. Bordwell, *Poetics*, 346–47.
19. This bridge, which leads to an island shrine, is supposed to bring luck to couples, so it is appropriate that Hirayama and Mikami stand on the bridge when they discuss the young couples that have lately distressed them but with whom they have been or will be reconciled.
20. Cf. Joo, *Ozu*, 197, for a complementary analysis of the reunion party scene. The song the men sing, *Sakurai no ketsubetsu*, was popular during the war and banned during the Occupation. Masahige Kusunoki was the particular hero of kamikaze pilots. Joo, *Ozu*, 240n40.
21. "Ozu on Ozu: The Talkies," *Cinema* (USA) 6, no. 1 (1970): 4.
22. Kikuo Yamamoto, "Postscript," trans. Kyoko Hirano from Paul Schrader, *Seinaru eiga: Ozu, Bresson, Dreyer* (Tokyo: Firumu ato sha, 1981), 282. This quote originally appeared in Shinbi Iida, "A Talk with Ozu," *Kinema Junpo*, June 1958.
23. Joy Hendry, *Marriage in Changing Japan* (London: Croom Helm, 1981), 235.
24. Branigan, "The Space of *Equinox Flower*," 81ff.

9
Religion

> Though I am no Ishidomaru, the brevity of human life, fleeting as a bubble on water, presses through my abstracted gaze.
>
> —Yasujiro Ozu[1]

Scholars, critics, and fans have long discerned a religious component in Ozu's art, most famously Paul Schrader, who labeled it "transcendental"; others have pointed out the influence of Zen.[2] Wim Wenders consistently refers to Ozu's films as "sacred." Still others insist, to the contrary, that Ozu was not religious, that such assertions are too general, and that the twentieth-century practice of Zen and its arts are too far removed in time from their historical practice to be relevant to Ozu.[3]

Ozu himself scoffed at the suggestion that his films reflected Zen, but there is some evidence that he and his family had a connection to Renzai, a Zen sect of Buddhism.[4] There is also the oft-told anecdote of Ozu asking a Buddhist priest in China to write the word *mu*, the Buddhist concept of "void," for him, calligraphy he kept all his life. Although Ozu dismissed the idea that his films were indebted to Zen, he admitted they were about "ephemerality," a Buddhist preoccupation. About cinema itself he would say, "I believe that the attractive thing about a film is this transience, its mist-like vanishing quality."[5]

Religion, in fact, occurs in many guises in Ozu's films, not the least of which is iconography. Usually Buddhist, but sometimes Christian, architecture, altars, statues, photographs of deities, gravestones, temples, and religious paintings appear as props, motifs, signs, and sometimes symbols. Moreover, aspects of Ozu's style and content invite comparison with both Zen aesthetics and Buddhist philosophy, which, however far removed from their origins, were still present in 1950s Japan. Finally, the films are informed by an overarching sense of morality, derived from the various religious and ethical systems that touched Japan: Buddhism, Confucianism, and Christianity. This chapter will examine the many ways in which religious belief and practice touch Ozu's films.

As we have seen, references to Christianity surface in a handful of Ozu's films, usually in the context of personal relationships: a gangster couple feels their way toward commitment and reform in *Dragnet Girl*; a couple rededicate themselves to

Religion 181

their marriage, shattered by wartime hardships, in *A Hen in the Wind*; and a couple's marriage, based on mutual affection and respect and requiring the woman to forego wealth and prestige, is blessed before it becomes a reality in *Early Summer*. In each case, parts of Christian buildings, tropes like the redemption of the fallen woman, or graces like sacrifice, reformation and redemption create a Christian context. (See Figure 1.2, p. 16.)

Equinox Flower, likewise, references Christianity in repeated shots of the tower of St. Luke's International Hospital, topped by a very prominent cross, where Akiko Sasaki's mother stays while the pair visits Tokyo. Located in Tsukiji (where the boys fish in *Tenement Gentleman*), St. Luke's was founded in 1902 by Rudolf Teusler, under the aegis of the American Episcopal Church. Recruiting a dedicated Japanese staff, which would succeed him, Teusler made the hospital's mission improving public health for the poor.[6] As such, it became a famous and venerated institution. The building we see in Ozu's film was built in 1933 (Figure 9.1).

Bells ring on the *Equinox Flower* soundtrack when we are first introduced to St. Luke's and again over a concluding shot of the tower after the sequence in which Mrs. Sasaki is treated at the hospital. Liturgical-sounding choral music plays behind shots of her in the hospital; this sequence concludes with Akiko and Setsuko looking at the building from the inn where Akiko is staying, while the choral music continues.

Figure 9.1: St. Luke's International Hospital in *Equinox Flower*

Christianity was outlawed during Japan's Tokugawa period and suppressed in the 1930s and in wartime Japan. In *Equinox Flower*, Setsuko's father, Hirayama, is a product of the wartime era, which, as we see in the reunion sequence, harkened back to feudal times. His samurai-like stubbornness, however, is opposed by a quintet of women: his wife, his daughters, and the Sasakis, who counsel flexibility and forgiveness. He eventually accedes to their prodding, attending Setsuko's wedding, of which he does not approve, and later agreeing to visit her in Hiroshima.

Forgiveness, change of heart, and reformation are specifically Christian virtues, alien to Buddhism, which holds that character does not change until, after many incarnations, enlightenment is attained. Consequently, the cross atop St. Luke's tower connects to Hirayama's change of heart at the end of the film. Among all the women in the film, the Sasakis are most responsible for the change in Hirayama, Akiko by convincing him to approve Setsuko's marriage and her mother by proposing the trip to Hiroshima. Consequently, they are the ones associated with the hospital and its cross.

One may wonder where and how Ozu came into contact with Christianity to the extent that its images and ideas appear in his films in such specific ways. One answer is through Western movies and literature, but, as the example of St. Luke's Hospital illustrates, Japanese Christians also exerted considerable influence on prewar Japanese society. In the rush to embrace Western culture in the Meiji era, Christianity became popular among intellectuals, who saw it as modern and enlightened, particularly with regard to freedoms for women. Prominent Japanese Christians became intellectual leaders, writers, and activists who championed women's rights, pacifism, and even communism. Many had been educated in the West and advocated maintaining good international relations with Western countries, particularly the United States. The books of Toyohiko Kagawa, a Christian reformer and pacifist who for many years voluntarily shared in the miseries of the poor, were particularly popular with women.[7] Other activists include Mari Iwamoto's grandparents, Yoshiharu Iwamoto and Shizuko Wakamatsu, who founded a school for girls, a women's magazine, and mentored other Christian educators seeking to empower women. Sen Katayama co-founded the Japanese Communist Party. Michi Kawai established Keizan University for women, and Tadao Yanaihara published a small Christian pacifist magazine throughout the Greater East Asia War (World War II), changing its name every time the military government tried to shut it down.[8] Japanese Christians were frequently as radical as Christianity was intended to be and in many instances were the face of liberalism and modernity in prewar Japan. Ozu, as we know, was attracted to both in the 1930s.

In advocating that the Japanese start caring for their war orphans, Ozu's *Tenement Gentleman* also advances a Christian mandate (James 1:27), but the film references no Christian iconography.[9] Repeated shots of boys fishing off a bridge in Tsukiji instead show the Tsukiji Honganji, an unusually structured Buddhist temple, built in 1934 and inspired by South Asian Buddhist architecture.[10] St. Luke's Hospital is in spitting distance of the Hoganji but is never shown, even peripherally, presumably because by 1947 St. Luke's iconic building had been commandeered by the Americans and

Religion 183

was being used as a military hospital. (By contrast, the Honganji is visible in *Equinox Flower*'s second shot of St. Luke's.)

Tsukiji itself, however, was the site of prewar foreign settlements and Christian missionary activity, and the Hoganji, if not Christian, is international in its architecture and decoration. (It has stained glass windows, for example.) Referencing Tsukiji, therefore, suited a film advocating an essentially foreign (in this case Christian) agenda.[11]

Moral reform occurs in a number of Ozu films and often has a religious, though not always Christian, context. Criminals reform in all of Ozu's gangster films as well as in *The Lady and the Beard*. In *Walk Cheerfully* and *Lady*, it happens in proximity to Buddhist icons, although, in terms of the narrative, love is the motivating factor. Likewise in *That Night's Wife*, Hashizume reforms for the same reason he stole: out of love for his daughter. Love as the basis for morality is, of course, a Christian notion, but Ozu did not create a Christian paradigm in any of the crime films until *Dragnet Girl*.

In *Dragnet Girl* the path to love and reform is more complicated than in the other crime films and at times mysterious. Tokiko is motivated to reform in part because she wants to be more like the girl Jyoji has a crush on, but her feelings for the young woman change suddenly from antipathy to affection as if by divine inspiration. Jyoji agrees to reform in part to appease Tokiko but, having been pulled back into criminal activity, is not willing to surrender his freedom for her. His heroism in saving Hiroshi and Kazuko from ruin notwithstanding, he is completely humiliated at the end of the film, and only in this state of humiliation does he fully surrender to his love for Tokiko. (See Figure 1.1, p. 13.) This is not quite Saul on the Road to Damascus, but it tends in that direction. The simplicity with which reform is effected in the early crime films becomes much more complex and is given Christian overtones in *Dragnet Girl*.

Of course, Buddhism has a much larger presence in the films than Christianity because Japan is a predominantly Buddhist country. Japanese Buddhism does not separate out native Shinto or China-derived Confucianism, but all combine into a traditional religious practice. Bordwell suggests that Ozu's approach to religion reflected society's attitude at the time, from frivolous (1920s) to serious (wartime), but this does not account for the development of the director's own thought and aesthetic practices nor, as we have seen in his invocation of Christianity, for the needs of his stories.[12] Nor was his attitude toward religion linear. Gags at the expense of religion occur most frequently in the early films but recur in *Ohayo*. We encounter irreverence in both the wartime *Brothers and Sisters of the Toda Family* and *Late Autumn*. Nor do gags and irreverence imply disbelief in traditional Japanese religion. Once again a "both . . . and" ethic applies. Meanwhile, death, with its religious implications, hovers over half of the extant films from the mid-1930s on.

Ozu was a moralist and at times connects virtue, or the lack of it, to religious objects, even while using the object to create gags. In *The Lady and the Beard*, a talisman from Naritayama, probably from the Shinshoji, its most prominent Buddhist temple, protects Okajima's virtue. We see it first in the film's opening kendo match, where it is symptomatic of Okajima's good luck, i.e., success in the match, and of his old-fashioned ways. We see it next in association with Hiroko, where it is connected to his luck in finding her.

The talisman figures in two of the film's gags. In one, Okajima turns away from the camera to zip up his fly, then turns away again, this time confounding our expectations when, instead of checking his fly, he gets out the talisman for luck in his job interview. Later, upon visiting Hiroko's home and attempting to utilize his long underwear as socks, the talisman's long cord gets tangled and is eventually caught in the door.

The talisman appears again when Okajima is tempted by the criminally inclined Satoko, who spends the night in his apartment and declares her love for him. After he removes the trousers he wears over his lumpy long underwear, we can see the talisman hanging prominently from his waist (Figure 9.2). Rejecting Satoko's advances, he sleeps in his kendo armor, which, significantly, is designed to protect his genitals as well as his chest. Thus the talisman is reunited with the kendo motif and works, with the armor, to protect him again, this time from temptation. The result is a happy reunion with Hiroko, the embodiment of the good luck that the talisman brought him earlier in the film.

In *Walk Cheerfully* true love blossoms beneath the gaze of Kamakura's Great Buddha even as Kenji, Yasue, and her little sister play at imitating the Buddha's half-closed eyes.

Figure 9.2: Okajima's talisman hangs prominently from his waist in *The Lady and the Beard*. A poster for *The Rogue Song* appears behind him.

In *Passing Fancy* both Kihachi and Tomio wear talismans, but they prove as ineffectual as Kihachi himself, which suggests that faith without virtue is useless.

In *Days of Youth*, Watanabe parks his chewing gum on Yamamoto's statue of the Buddhist poet Saigyo. Bordwell cites this as "skepticism [regarding religion] among 1920s youth," but it rather shows how truly awful Watanabe's personal behavior is.[13] Intentionally satiric, however, is the pseudo-Buddhist aphorism Okajima displays above his door in *The Lady and the Beard*, which reads: "If the spring arrives, I accept it; if it goes away, I do not chase it." As soon as we are able to read this, Hiroko comes in that door, and, of course, Okajima chases her. Based on what Gregory Barrett calls the "Chaste Warrior," Okajima's pose is exposed here in all its ridiculousness.[14]

Christian practice is likewise spoofed when the boys in *I Was Born, But . . .* make the sign of the cross as part of their "resurrection" ceremony for those they have "killed" in their children's games. While Ozu appears to have taken the moral aspects of Christianity seriously, he was not above mocking the resurrection story.

A Story of Floating Weeds is saturated with religious references, both in image and belief, perhaps because Japanese theater has its roots in Shinto and Buddhism and because the film is intended to evoke an image of "old Japan." The theater itself has little shrines, *kamidana*, and a statue of Jizo, a protecting deity in priests' robes, thought to be effective in preventing fires but also attentive to the concerns of women. When Kihachi sends Otoki away after upbraiding her for having seduced Shinkichi, she passes the Jizo figure and pats it absently on the head. Is it comforting her, or is she comforting it?

Otsune has a very large daruma figure on a shelf in her sake shop. Plump, legless, and usually red, the daruma is a tribute to Bodhidharma, founder of Zen Buddhism, but is generally regarded as a good luck charm related to achieving certain goals in one's life. Daruma are often sold with blank eyes, and the owners fill in the eyes as they achieve their goals. Otsune's large daruma has blank eyes. Her goal is to give Shinkichi a good education with its attendant middle-class life, but, in light of his involvement with Otoki, the film leaves everyone uncertain that this goal will ever be realized. The daruma's eyes may never be filled in.

Little prayer flags have been planted under the tree where Otoki stations herself to attract Shinkichi's attention. Bordwell has suggested that there is irony in Otoki waiting beneath a prayer tree to seduce Shinkichi, but Shinto is not Christianity.[15] It is rather an animistic folk religion that celebrates fertility, so there is, in fact, a correspondence between the sacred tree and the carnal attraction between Otoki and Shinkichi.

Bordwell's misunderstanding of Japanese religion goes further when he has his hypothetical "interpretive critic" suggest a possible "battle" between Shinto and Buddhism in *A Story of Floating Weeds*, when, in fact, both coexist happily within Japanese culture.[16] Each fulfills complementary functions, which conduct the believer through life from birth to death as well as providing talismans for luck and festivals and ceremonies that placate demons and restless gods, comfort the sorrowful, encourage fertility, and so on.

Bordwell is equally mistaken when he suggests that the scene in which Kihachi and Shinkichi fish together has something to do with "purification by water."[17] Neither of these characters is in any way "pure." In the wartime *There Was a Father*, where, given the timeframe and the exaggerated purity of both father and son, the water they fish in and especially the bath they share can be seen as symbolizing purity or purification. In *A Story of Floating Weeds*, however, the stream that father and son fish in, far from suggesting purification, initiates the series of losses that Kihachi experiences throughout the film, for it bears away his wallet. The idea of loss in connection with a river is consistent with "the use of river imagery to symbolize the Buddhist negation of human desire and attachment," however.[18]

Tadao Sato notes that the river in *Hen in the Wind* where the Shuichi encounters the prostitute Fusako eating her lunch and the river in *Early Spring* where Sugimura has his heart to heart with Onodera have to do with cleansing in the sense of unburdening one's inner thoughts and sorrows, which makes sense in both cases.[19] However, the idea of cleansing is not consistent with the plotline in *A Story of Floating Weeds*. We have seen that Ozu's use of symbols was neither narrow nor necessarily consistent. One reason may be that Japanese culture itself endows certain images with a fairly wide range of meaning.

A Story of Floating Weeds makes prominent use of circular shapes. Dozens of large containers wrapped in roping made from rice stalks are piled on one another in front of a restaurant near the theater, visible when Kihachi sets off to visit Otsune. The bottoms of these containers face the camera, all with perfect wheel shapes, including "spokes" formed by the rope thongs that crisscross them.

A large wheel stands outside Shinkichi's room on the second floor in the foreground, screen left and, moved around presumably by the director, appears in several subsequent shots taken from inside or outside Shinkichi's room. A wheel (perhaps the same one) is apparent when Kihachi goes down the stairs, and it appears again inside Otsune's front entryway. It reappears outside to the left in medium shots of Kihachi in the scene in which he and Otaka argue in the rain from opposite sides of the alley outside of Otsune's shop. More dramatically, a very large wagon wheel stands in front of Otaka during this argument, forming a barrier between them, while another very large wheel shape stands behind and to the left of her, close to the camera and out of focus (Figure 9.3).

Ozu was famous for moving props around to create the perfect composition or, as we saw in Chapter 4, to make a thematic point. If the huge wheel between Kihachi and Otaka were not enough to convince us of its significance, the fact that Ozu moved the other wheel or spool around his sets should do so.

The circle or wheel is significant in Buddhist tradition as *samsara*, the "suffering-laden, continuous cycle of life, death, and rebirth, without beginning or end." It can also mean a "cycle of aimless drifting, wandering or mundane existence."[20] The idea of aimless wandering is certainly relevant to *A Story of Floating Weeds*, and, although this film does not concern itself with the life cycle in particular as would later Ozu films,

Figure 9.3: A large wheel stands between Kihachi and Otaka as they argue in *A Story of Floating Weeds*. A larger wheel appears out of focus to the right.

Kihachi's comings and goings from this village as well as his inability to create a different life for himself—planning instead to form a new acting troupe with the same mistress at the story's end—evoke the idea of endless cycle. The concentration of wheels, described above in the sequence in which Otaka visits Otsune's shop, suggests that Kihachi's deception cannot change his son's fate, that Shinkichi does not, as Kihachi insists, "belong to a better world" than his and Otaka's, something Otaka is determined to prove.

Circle imagery occurs in other Ozu films as well. The second shot in *The Only Son*, an exterior in Otsune's village of Shinshu, and almost every sequence in Otsune's home include wheels or spools of some sort, not to mention the automated spinning wheels in the silk factory where Otsune works. The Tokyo sequences have fewer wheels, but a cart by the noodle shop near Ryosuke's home displays a very large wheel, and tubular cement pipes create a wall of circles near one of the large holding tanks Otsune and Ryosuke pass on their way to visit Okubo. The film itself comes full circle, ending where it began, with the spinning wheels in the silk factory. In the final sequence we see Otsune in medium shot with large circles prominently displayed on the towel around her head. Although Ozu would not explicitly state that he wanted to make films about the life cycle until he made *Early Summer*, *The Only Son* not only includes three generations of a family but emphasizes the suffering and the inability of individuals to escape from a cycle of poverty (an escape that education was supposed to facilitate)—hence the film's emphasis on wheels and circles in its ultimately fatalistic appraisal of modern life.

Most of the postwar films specifically related to the life cycle do not make prominent use of the wheel/circle motif—it lends itself less well to depicting city life—but the motif returns in the form of the ubiquitous red hula hoop in *Ohayo*. The hula hoop, together with the grandmother's prayer beads and *butsudan*, with and at which we see her pray, form generational ends of Buddhist tradition. Both evoke humor, but that does not diminish their truth: three generations interact, and, towards the end of the film, the Hayashis begin to worry about retirement. Humorous or not, the cycle keeps turning.

The circle motif returns with a vengeance in *The End of Summer*. The family crest is composed of a large circle surrounded by eight small circles, while tipped-up tubs and vats form more circles. One shot includes a bicycle wheel juxtaposed to one of the vats. In another, the upturned tubs are joined by the circular shapes of two traditional (bamboo and oilpaper) umbrellas bearing the circles of the family crest. Just before his death, the patriarch Manbei Kohayagawa attends a bicycle race: two-wheeled vehicles race around a large circle. *The End of Summer* is the starkest of the life cycle films in the sense that it ends not only with a death but against the backdrop of the crematorium, and its setting, an old family business outside Osaka, lends itself to an amplification of the circle motif.

Although Buddhism extends to many aspects of Japanese life and culture, its funerary aspects are its most prominent in the lives of ordinary Japanese.[21] Ozu dramatizes parts of funeral or memorial services in five films: *The Brothers and Sisters of the Toda Family*, *There Was a Father*, *Tokyo Story*, *Late Autumn*, and *The End of Summer*. *Early Spring* includes a wake. In addition, small stupas, memorials for priests and others worthy of commemoration, appear several times in *There Was a Father*, and stupas associated with Jodoji reintroduce Onomichi after Tomi gets sick in *Tokyo Story*. Ghostly stupas also appear where a stupa would not normally occur in *There Was a Father*, *The End of Summer*, and in the reunion sequence in *Equinox Flower* (Plate 1B). While the stupa cheated into the reunion scene in *There Was a Father* predicts Horikawa's impending death, as does the one that appears in Manbei Kohayagawa's garden in *End of Summer*, its presence in *Equinox Flower* relates not to a specific death but to the death of the culture Hirayama and his contemporaries came of age in, which they are remembering and celebrating. It also serves as a kind of *memento mori*: this generation, too, will pass on in time. There is even a miniature stupa-like figure in the alcove along with the famous vase in *Late Spring*. Noriko's mood change during the time we look at the vase indicates her sorrow at separating from her father, but the tiny stupa figure suggests the more permanent separation that lies ahead, and this, too, may have occurred to her as she contemplates the future.[22]

If *Equinox Flower* is structured around a Christian paradigm and *A Story of Floating Weeds* around *samsara* and other Buddhist constructs, *Tokyo Story* is structured around

Religion

a contrast between Tokyo and Onomichi, part of which inevitably involves the role of religion in Onomichi. The hills of Onomichi, from which the frequent shots of the harbor were photographed, are filled with more than thirty temples and shrines. The film opens with a shot of a large stone lantern that overlooks the harbor. A subsequent shot in toward the hills shows the Jodo temple, an Onomichi landmark founded by Prince Shotoku, who in the seventh century fostered the growth of Buddhism in Japan.

The Hirayamas apparently live near this temple because after Tomi's death, Shukichi stands in front of Jodoji in an open area flanked by other stone lanterns and looks out at the sea. This view from Jodoji is remarked on in one of the Tokyo sequences by former Onomichian Mrs. Hattori, who says, "We used to enjoy the view from the temple." That the elderly couple lives next door to it is confirmed by a later shot of Shukichi tending his garden with Jodoji in the background. The small building surrounded by stupas, which sits behind a retaining wall and appears in the fifth shot of the opening montage, is also part of Jodoji, and Jodoji is the site of Tomi's funeral.[23]

In addition to images of the temple, tablets with small Buddhist figures are set just inside the garden wall of the parents' house and appear in every shot in which the garden serves as background. In the final shots of Shukichi sitting alone in his house, these images hover in the background like the guardians they are no doubt intended to be.

Shots from the garden into the Hirayama house show three gourds hanging in the room just inside. Gourds are associated with Zen Buddhism but are commonly thought to simply be symbols of good luck.

The emphasis on Buddhist icons contrasts Onomichi to Tokyo. While Ozu prefaces his Tokyo sequences with industrial smokestacks, Onomichi is prefaced by Jodoji's stone lantern. Such lanterns were often associated with the souls of the dead. Because Buddhist temples cater to the cult of ancestors, "it is the household which is the traditional and fundamental social unit of Buddhism."[24]

If family ties are neglected in Tokyo, so, it seems, were Buddhist observances, particularly by newcomers. "Since we've moved here we haven't bothered to get a new *butsudan* or new *ihai* [mortuary tablets] or anything . . . I'm ashamed to say," replied an informant in Ronald Philip Dore's classic study of a Tokyo ward.[25] The authors of the 1959 *Village Japan* wrote of their subjects, "The people of Niike are sober, responsible, and religious: their religion does not bring about their sobriety, but it comforts and reassures them of order in the world."[26] Onomichi may be a provincial backwater, but it stands for what is good, stable, and ongoing in the Japanese tradition, which includes not only ancestor worship but close family ties, precisely what is lost in Tokyo.

In his study of city life in the 1950s, Dore found three elements of Buddhist thought that were "so thoroughly absorbed into Japanese culture that they no longer depend on Buddhist institutions for their perpetuation." Among these were "the high value placed on the state of non-self," certain aesthetic values related to Zen, and a "fatalistic determinism emphasizing the necessity of resigned acceptance of one's lot."[27] All of these are present in Ozu's films.

From *I Was Born, But...* to *An Autumn Afternoon*, many of Ozu's characters express the "fatalistic determinism" that Dore describes, particularly those in *Tokyo Story*. "I suppose I should be happy. Nowadays some young men would kill their parents without a thought. Mine at least wouldn't do that," says Numata, Onomichi's former police chief. "Children don't live up to their parents' expectations . . . Let's think that [ours] are better than most," Shukichi tells Tomi. "Life is like that," explains Noriko to sister-in-law Kyoko, "Everyone looks after their own affairs." "Isn't life disappointing?" asks a disillusioned Kyoko. "I'm afraid so," Noriko responds.

Like Buddhist iconography, Zen arts appear whole cloth in some of Ozu's films, *Late Spring* in particular, which features: tea ceremony, Noh drama, the Kiyomizu-dera with its Noh stage, and Ryoanji's stone garden. We have seen that these inclusions were probably inspired by Japan's desire to reinvent itself as a nation of "culture," although Ozu is said to have been particularly fond of Noh drama.[28]

Less tangible are the Zen concepts of *mu* (void), *ma* (a moving version of *mu*; time and space as one), and *hashi* (bridging the void), which are present in Ozu's mise-en-scène and editing, whether or not he consciously set out to bring them into his art. Scenes, particularly in the late films, often begin and end with unpeopled, therefore "empty," shots, which invite comparisons with the concept of the "void." Ozu himself explained them this way: "Instead of constantly pushing dramatic action to the fore, I left empty spaces, so viewers could have a pleasant aftertaste to savor."[29] This is as good an explanation of *mu* as any other. The controversial vase shots in *Late Spring* function in this way: not a point of view but a space, empty of people and action, time in which we can reflect on Noriko's dilemma, time in which Noriko, too, reflects and moves from cheerfulness to sadness.

Ma is a kind of moving *mu*, a void pregnant with possibilities, time defining space and vice versa. The traditional Japanese house is the best illustration of *ma* because it is empty space without fixed barriers which is constantly being shifted and adapted to the needs of the moment—a living room, a dining room, a bedroom, a porch open to the garden can all be the same room, depending on how the family chooses to use it, time defining space. During and after the war, as Ozu focused more on Japaneseness and less on Japan's Western adaptations, the Japanese house became increasingly central to his stories.

Hashi means "bridge," but in Zen terminology, it is bridging the void. I have discussed the idea of passages and bridges as related to the life cycle at length in Chapter 8, and I pointed out the many famous bridges Ozu cites in his films. These are the tip of the iceberg, for many other less distinguished bridges populate his films, and these, too, can be seen as bridges from one nexus of time and space to another.

Sometimes the rooms and passageways in Ozu's films are empty of people, and sometimes we see people moving through these modular spaces, defining them by their movements. Often the camera will hold on a room into which people come and go, as this sequence from *Tokyo Story*, in which the older son's wife gets ready for the parents' visit, illustrates:

Religion 191

1) Fumiko sweeps the upstairs tatami rooms; she goes out and comes back while the camera waits; she goes out again.
2) Match cut to the hallway as she comes in; she cleans and starts to go out right.
3) Shot of another bedroom; Fumiko comes into camera range from the right then goes out again.
4) Shot of the downstairs hallway; the camera remains static as Fumiko comes in, goes out, comes back again.

Susabi, the empty place where "phenomena appear, pass by, and disappear," describes that coming and going from otherwise empty rooms and hallways that we see so often in Ozu's films.[30]

Susabi also means "to play," and there are indications that this tendency in Ozu's films may have its roots as much in Japanese religion as in Ozu's own psychology.[31] In Chapter 4, I discussed his play with direction, of which his frequently crossing the 180° line is part. We have seen how he invariably renders the concept of direction meaningless. Alan Watts has pointed to the *hossin*, a type of *koan* or Zen riddle posed to students that begins by sending them off "in the direction exactly opposite to that in which they should look."[32] "Breaking the rules" is an honored tradition in Japanese art, and we know that from an early age Ozu loved breaking rules.[33] Did his contrariness mature into a *koan*-inspired or, at least, a *koan*-analogous art form? It seems likely.

The last Buddhist concept Dore cites as still present in 1950s Japan is *muga*, the non-self. Although the ontology behind the idea of non-self is abstruse and opposed to the Christian notion of the soul, in common usage it means selflessness or self-renunciation, which is not that different from the Christian notion of selfless loving-kindness except for the extremities to which it may be taken. *Tokyo Story*'s Noriko, for example, is selfless in caring for her in-laws, in contrast to the other siblings, but her willingness to forego remarriage for the sake of traditional, Confucian-inspired values (even though she lives too far from her father-in-law to be of service to him) goes beyond simple kindness to a form of *muga* or self-renunciation. Shukichi rejects her gesture, urging her to remarry—she is still of childbearing age—but the noblest of Ozu's older widows and widowers do not remarry, and those that do are ridiculed. Shukichi achieves a level of sublimity as he sits alone at the end of *Tokyo Story*. *Muga* is considered inseparable from wisdom, and it seems to envelop him. Less satisfying is Setsuko's refusal to remarry at the end of *The Munekata Sisters*, but this, too, is supposed to be understood as being in keeping with *muga*. Setsuko calls it being true to herself, but in fact she is renouncing herself by not fulfilling her emotional desires.

The famously onerous demands Ozu made on his actors required from them a degree of *muga*, which most found difficult to achieve. However, Chishu Ryu, the actor most associated with Ozu, has said that he approached his Ozu roles as "an empty page" that Ozu filled.[34] While shooting *There Was a Father*, Ozu told him to act as if he were wearing a Noh mask, and that helped him to achieve this state of non-self that Ozu required. (It also accounts for the slightly glazed stare one frequently catches on Ryu's

192 *Ozu*

face in Ozu's films.) Ineko Arima, who played Setsuko in *Equinox Flower*, had a hard time with Ozu's directions, but added that when she saw the final film, she realized that he was trying "to reduce things to their . . . essence, free of all excess."[35] That freedom from excess is the ultimate goal of Zen art.

Samsara, the wheel, can also refer to enlightenment. Fifteenth-century Noh master Zenchiku Komparu insisted that "extreme enlightenment looks just like non-enlightenment. In the end Noh art returns to its original starting point."[36] Ozu would echo this typically contradictory, enigmatic statement, saying at one point, "The end of a film is its beginning."[37]

The religious aspects of Ozu's films are subtle and varied but abundantly present— from overtly Christian paradigms to an echoing of Zen aesthetics to a conscious effort to reduce actions to their essence. They include an overarching moral vision that emphasized purity and selflessness and balanced itself between Christian and Buddhist ideals. Most fascinating, though, is the extent to which Ozu saw cinema itself in its circular and transitory nature as the embodiment of certain essentially religious, i.e., Buddhist, notions.

Notes

1. From a poem written on the occasion of bringing his mother's ashes to Mt. Koya, translated and recorded in Inoue, *I Lived, But . . .* Ishidomaru is a legendary Buddhist saint (Bodhisattva) who studied at Mt. Koya.
2. See Paul Schrader, *Transcendental Style in Film: Ozu, Bresson, Dreyer* (Berkeley, CA: University of California Press, 1972); Marvin Zeman, "The Serene Poet of Japanese Cinema: The Zen Artistry of Yasujiro Ozu," *Film Journal* 1, nos. 3–4 (Fall–Winter 1972): 62–72; and Ruth Vasey, "Ozu and the Nō," *Australian Journal of Screen Theory* 7, no. 80 (1988): 88–102.
3. Bordwell, *Poetics* 26–30; Nygren, *Time Frames* 148ff. See also Darrell W. Davis, "Ozu, the Ineffable" in Choi, *Reorienting Ozu*, 33–43.
4. Richie, *Ozu*, 256n21. Part of the evidence for a connection to Renzai is that Ozu used a Renzai temple (Tozenji) for the Buddhist rites in *Late Autumn*; Engakuji, where Ozu is buried, is Renzai; Ozu's mother's funeral services were held in a Renzai temple (Jochiji), and she is buried at Yogakuji in Fukugawa, which is also Renzai. See Kensuke Masakiyo, "Ozu eiga ni okeru okyo," in Matsuura and Miyamoto, *Ozu Yasujiro Taizen*, 371–77.
5. "Ozu on Ozu: The Silents," 24.
6. By the turn of the twentieth century, Japan had caught up to the West in terms of medical knowledge and practice, but health care was expensive (a plot point in so many Ozu films!) and public health neglected. St. Luke's worked to fill those gaps. "Rather than occupying himself with the objective of converting large numbers of Japanese to Christianity through medicine . . . Teusler sought to 'Christianise' the Japanese health care system." Garrett L. Washington, "St. Luke's Hospital and the Modernisation of Japan, 1874–1928," *Health and History* 15, no. 2 (2013): 28.
7. Barbara Sato, *The New Japanese Woman: Modernity, Media, and Women in Interwar Japan* (Durham, NC: Duke University Press, 2003), 135.

Religion   193

8. Shillony, *Politics*, 131.
9. Throughout the Bible, strangers, widows, and the "fatherless" are groups to whom adherents are expected to offer special consideration, aid, and justice.
10. Owing to its large size, the Tsukiji Hoganji was the site of Ozu's funeral as well as that of one of his leading ladies, Kinuyo Tanaka, in 1977.
11. Tsukiji was also part of the *shitamachi*, the working-class part of Tokyo, hence a place one could expect to find homeless boys, but in 1947 there were undoubtedly many such places.
12. Bordwell, *Poetics*, 28.
13. Bordwell, *Poetics*, 28.
14. See Barrett, *Archetypes in Japanese Film*, 43ff.
15. Bordwell, *Poetics*, 258.
16. Bordwell, *Poetics*, 258.
17. Bordwell, *Poetics*, 258.
18. Tadao Sato, "Japanese Cinema and the Traditional Arts: Imagery, Technique, and Cultural Context," in *Cinematic Landscapes: Observations on the Visual Arts and Cinema of China and Japan*, ed. Linda Ehrlich and David Desser (Austin, TX: University of Texas Press, 1994), 168.
19. Sato, "Japanese Cinema and the Traditional Arts," 168.
20. Quoted in https://en.wikipedia.org/wiki/Saṃsāra; see also Wayne Stein, "Afterword: The Samsara of Ozu Cinema—Death and Rebirth in Our Daily Struggles" in Stein and DiPaolo, *Ozu International*, 173ff.
21. Hendry, *Marriage in Changing Japan*, 63, 232.
22. For the many interpretations of the vase itself, see Abé Mark Nornes, "The Riddle of the Vase: Ozu Yasujirō's *Late Spring* (1949)," in *Japanese Cinema: Texts and Contexts*, ed. Alastair Phillips and Julian Stringer (New York: Routledge, 2007), 78–89.
23. Although there are few shots that might positively identify the temple in the funeral scene, Keiko McDonald believed the funeral temple is the one seen from the harbor in the opening montage, i.e., Jodoji, on the basis of the Japanese script. See Keiko McDonald, *Cinema East: A Critical Study of Major Japanese Films* (East Brunswick, NJ: Associated University Presses, 1983), 205. The Tourist Department in the Onomichi City Hall confirmed this identification in a letter to me dated June 27, 1995.
24. Hendry, *Marriage in Changing Japan*, 63.
25. Ronald Phillip Dore, *City Life in Japan: A Study of a Tokyo Ward* (Berkeley, CA: University of California Press, 1958), 362.
26. Richard K. Beardsley, John W. Hall, and Robert E. Ward, *Village Japan* (Chicago, IL: University of Chicago Press, 1959), 470.
27. Dore, *City Life in Japan*, 362.
28. Nornes, "The Riddle of the Vase," 87.
29. Inoue, *I Lived, But...*
30. Cooper-Hewitt Museum, *MA: Space-Time in Japan*.
31. Bordwell cites numerous instances of Ozu's "ludic" instincts. See *Poetics*, 109ff.
32. Alan Watts, *The Way of Zen* (New York: Pantheon Books, 1957), 160.
33. Richard B. Pilgrim, *Buddhism and the Arts of Japan* (Chambersburg, PA: Anima Books, 1981), 54.

34. Wim Wenders, *Tokyo Ga*, (Berlin and New York: Wim Wenders Produktion, Chris Sievernich Filmproduktion, Gray City, Inc., 1985).
35. Quotes from both Arima and Ryu recorded in Inoue, *I Lived, But* . . .
36. Pilgrim, *Buddhism and the Arts of Japan*, 55.
37. Inoue, *I Lived, But* . . .

10
Gender Issues

Ozu's vivid depictions of multidimensional women belie the authenticity of stereotypical Japanese female images.

—Barbara Sato[1]

David Bordwell and others have written at length about the humiliation most of Ozu's men suffer at the hands of the state, the economy, and their families.[2] Ozu often played this for laughs—deflating the privileged is a comic device dating back to Greek comedy and the court jester—but Bordwell sees it more as a commentary on the failure of the Japanese state to live up to the promises of middle-class prosperity fueled by education and science implicit in the Meiji Reformation. Woojeong Joo has summarized this trend succinctly: "[I]f patriarchy was shown [in Ozu's films] to be facing a crisis, it indicated a failure of the whole modernization process rather than a weakening of traditional Japanese values, a symptom of which I think Ozu was well aware."[3]

The perceived failure of patriarchy in interwar Japan mingled with dismay at rampant Westernization and a remilitarization program that exalted masculine values. Ozu's films record these trends as well as the gradual liberation of Japanese women. Much has been written about women in Japanese films generally, but few authors have specifically analyzed Ozu's attitude toward them. Those that have often try to fit Ozu's women into a larger political context and, at times, misread Ozu's actual intentions.[4] Joo discusses the women in Ozu's silent films and draws some insightful conclusions, particularly regarding female bonding, but discusses them mainly in terms of the clichéd *moga* vs. *ryosai kenbo* (good mother/good wife) dichotomy, which, while certainly a Japanese trope at the time, somewhat hobbles his discussion.[5] Robin Wood's "Noriko Trilogy" is one of the few close analyses of women in Ozu's films, but, highly tendentious, it suffers from Wood's ignorance of Japanese culture.[6] This chapter will analyze Ozu's handling of a range of gender issues—patriarchy, feminism, sex, marriage, abuse, and same-sex bonding—that touch on the mitigation of patriarchy and the rise of women's status in Japan over his career.

Although Western feminists of the 1970s would decry chivalry as just another means of denying women true equality, it nevertheless played, from the Middle Ages on, an important role in elevating the status of Western women, according them greater respect and influence than most of their Asian counterparts enjoyed. Chivalry originated in the worship of the Virgin Mary, who, as the mother of Jesus, assured Western women of an esteemed if secondary status in society. Confucian morality, by contrast, denied Asian women similar respect or status, subjecting them to absolute male authority (father, husband, son). While their consequent suffering was celebrated in literature as an expiation of the sins of patriarchy, no thought was given to alleviating it. The frequent references to women's suffering that occur in films and other forms of Japanese storytelling are nothing more than a reification of a status quo that had been in place for centuries, not feminist and not a change-agent.[7]

In *Early Summer*, Ozu's Occupation-era film most concerned with women's liberation, Noriko and her sister-in-law, Fumiko, enthusiastically discuss the newly introduced "*etiketto*," much to brother Koichi's chagrin. *Etiketto*, their word for the twentieth-century version of chivalry, i.e., particular male courtesies toward women, was clearly seen as raising the status of Japanese women. (Although fraternization between Japanese nationals and Occupation personnel was discouraged on both sides, many respectable Japanese women dated and married Americans, invariably disarmed by their *etiketto*.)

What can be called "Ozu's feminism" did not need to wait for the Occupation, however, but began in the 1930s. *An Inn in Tokyo*, in fact, displays a startling evocation of chivalry: its Kihachi character steals in order to save his friend Otaka from prostituting herself and then turns himself in to police. In a culture with no tradition of chivalry, he gives up his job, his children, his good name, and his freedom just to keep her pure. This gesture differs vastly from that of Omitsu's husband in Naruse's *Every Night Dreams* (*Yogoto no yume*, 1933). That man is an unstable weakling, who robs to keep his wife from working in a bar when their child is hurt. (She had worked there earlier because he had deserted her.) His concern is less for her than for his own reputation, and having lost that reputation because of the robbery, he commits suicide. Although Ozu's Kihachi would like to marry Otaka, he must forego that dream, too, in his attempt to protect her.

Ozu's feminism was part of a larger project to disarm patriarchy by those who championed Japanese modernism and women's rights. While patriarchy was an ancient feature of Japanese society, the Meiji Civil Code had rendered it one of the most oppressive aspects of the Meiji state. According to Irene González-López and Michael Smith, "For hundreds of years, the regulation of the family . . . [was] based on . . . varying local administrative regulations . . . [which] meant that there were great differences across geographical regions and social classes. The promulgation of the Meiji Civil Code in 1896, however, changed this reality for ever. [W]omen 'were not legally recognized persons and therefore enjoyed no rights.'"[8]

Women's groups and other activists worked to change the Civil Code, educate women, and raise their status, but one of the most active sites of change was in the realm of popular culture. Beginning in 1902, girls' magazines began to appear, which created a consciousness in young women of their individuality and worth outside the patriarchal family.[9] The reality of small numbers of middle-class women entering the labor force,

Gender Issues

including film actresses in 1919, gave rise to the image of the *modan garu* (modern girl or *moga*), which "became the corporeal expression of the destabilization of traditional ideologies of gender."[10]

Ozu's boss, Shiro Kido, who led the way in promoting American-style films, also saw a market for films that would appeal to women. For both reasons, he preferred "sprightly, brave, optimistic forward-looking" girl stars over the suffering women in *shinpa*-derived melodramas.[11] "[T]he old moralistic [Confucian] ideas have a repressive stranglehold on women," he insisted.[12]

While Ozu's feminism was neither consistent nor thoroughgoing, at times it streaked across his films with meteoric brilliance, never more so than in his depiction of the equal relationship that is established between Jyoji and Tokiko in *Dragnet Girl*. In the beginning of the film, Jyoji expresses male privilege in a number of ways: he asserts that he is "living off a woman"; he flirts with Misako at the jazz club dance, and, when the foursome return to his apartment that evening, he leads the way. The fact that Tokiko follows with Misako at her side somewhat disguises the fact that Japanese men at the time always walked six to ten feet ahead of their women, the latter following along behind, usually hobbled by their kimonos. (We see this demonstrated later in the film when Jyoji leads Kazuko to the boxing club.)[13]

When, after the jazz club dance, Jyoji admonishes Tokiko for encouraging her boss's advances, she challenges him, laying bare the difference in their status, and reminding him of his attentions to Misako that evening. In response, Jyoji teases her, and they begin a playful banter, seen in long shot, in which Jyoji touches her cheek three times in quick succession as if to make up for touching Misako. In other words, she refuses to submit to his authority, and he placates her.

The two are portrayed as complementing one another. Jyoji, his gangsterism notwithstanding, is strong, brave, and noble while Tokiko is the idea-person, if a little scatterbrained. Most of her ideas are bad, of course, letting Hiroshi into the gang, threatening Kazuko with violence, and robbing her boss, but she has one good idea— that they should go straight—and Jyoji ultimately goes along with all of them. When she sets off to meet Kazuko with a gun, he objects but doesn't try to stop her physically even though her rashness threatens to doom them both.

When, having been converted to "domesticity," she makes him hold her yarn while she tries to wind it into a ball, he rebels and throws the yarn away angrily. An earlier film, *Days of Youth*, helps us to understand the full significance of his action here. In that film, Chieko, the boys' love interest, has Yamamoto hold her yarn while she winds a ball, and the situation is clearly emasculating. Jyoji goes along with most of Tokiko's ideas but refuses to be emasculated in the process.

This leads to a fight, however, with Jyoji refusing to imagine Tokiko in the role of the "good woman" she aspires to become. In response she says to him twice, "I'm just a delinquent anyway!" inviting him to contradict her. When he doesn't, she says, "You comparing me to that girl [Kazuko]? No thanks!" and leaves, asserting her right to define herself. When that evening her boss, Okajima, suggests a serious liaison, she asks him, "Do you think I'm worthy?" The question of her worth clearly preoccupies her.

She soon returns to Jyoji, however, and begs him to love her more, but, instead of pouring out her passion for him, says, "You're the only one I can count on." On the surface this statement seems extraordinary. She has just left a man with money and position, who is completely infatuated with her, yet she credits Jyoji, the as yet unreformed gangster, as the only one she can count on.

In contrast to Okajima, who is obviously disloyal to his wife, Jyoji is strong and noble, and he exhibits that nobility a short time later when, having just agreed to go straight, he insists on helping Kazuko's punk brother, Hiroshi, after Hiroshi has gotten himself in trouble. This is something Jyoji cannot easily do as the honest man he has just pledged to become, but here too he defends his manhood, insisting on the Japanese version of "a man's gotta do what a man's gotta do" against Tokiko's wish that he "forget about them." Thus each character gives way to the other in matters that are very important to the partner.

At this point in the story, the lovers renounce their extracurricular love interests. Jyoji is rude to Kazuko, severing the sympathy that had existed between them, and Tokiko proposes robbing Okajima, a much more definitive break than simply walking away from him.

Tokiko's rashness plays out one more time at the end of the film and again underscores her instinct for equality: when, during their escape, she refuses to go any farther, Jyoji hits her, and she, in response, shoots him. (Men who hit women in Ozu's films are often shamed but rarely shot!) Although Jyoji is hurt and humbled at the end of the film, he is not humiliated in same sense that Ozu's men often are (by the oppressions of the workaday world) but is further ennobled by his tears of repentance and the reconciliation that the couple achieves right before the police arrive. (See Figure 1.1, p. 13.)

That Ozu creates this equal relationship using gangsters is no accident. Such relationships may have existed in some instances in the literary and artistic worlds he inhabited but not in conventional middle-class Japanese society. Gangsters, like artists, were outside the mainstream, and such a relationship could thus be imagined only within that largely fantasy world.

In *Dragnet Girl*, Ozu moreover gave voice to the *moga*, the modern girl, who scandalized conservative society yet displeased the left with her seeming vacuity. "Hers was a voiceless existence surrounded by ambivalence—the ambivalence of class and occupation, ambivalence presented and represented through the media."[14] Tokiko's quest for validation throughout the film reflects the ambivalence with which society regarded the *moga*, who was often seen as a delinquent (*furyo shojo*) and is, in fact, presented as such in Ozu's earlier films *Walk Cheerfully* and *The Lady and the Beard*.[15]

Within the body of Ozu's extant films, we encounter only two other truly liberated heroines, Setsuko in *What Did the Lady Forget?* and Noriko in *Early Summer*. As noted in Chapter 5, Setsuko in *What Did the Lady Forget?* is Ozu's last *moga* and the most upscale. To her aunt's dismay, Setsuko consistently appropriates male privilege

Gender Issues

by drinking, smoking, expecting to come and go as she pleases, and fraternizing with her uncle as though he were a contemporary. She wins the heart of her uncle's student Okada, and, in the penultimate scene, assumes they will marry and live on equal terms.

As we have seen, *Early Summer*'s Noriko has, as a teen, idolized Katharine Hepburn, holds down a good job as a private secretary, and, at twenty-eight, is still unmarried despite being an acknowledged beauty. Not waiting for either an *omiai* or a man to chase her, she chooses her own husband, offering to marry her next-door neighbor, Yabe, an idealistic, widowed doctor with a young child, whom she has known since childhood. The whole point of an arranged marriage in Japan was for the family to choose a man, preferably from a good family, free from obvious defects, with a stable background, able to provide for a wife and children. To her family's chagrin, Noriko makes all these calculations for herself, noting that her groom's outstanding qualification is that she can trust him.

Another sign that these two women are liberated over and above the usual Ozu heroine is that we never see either of them sewing. With a few exceptions, almost all of Ozu's women are shown sewing, knitting, or with dress forms and sewing machines in their homes. Two of the working women, Akiko in *Late Autumn* and Aya in *The Flavor of Green Tea Over Rice*, are variously employed in the dressmaking industry, and Tokiko in *Hen in the Wind* sews for a (meager) living.

The "sprightly, brave, optimistic" girls in Ozu's early films all sew (or knit), which is sometimes developed as a plot device. Oshige in *Where Now Are the Dreams of Youth?* shows her preference for Horino by sewing up a tear in his shirt, and Hiroko in *The Lady and the Beard* demonstrates her fitness for love and marriage when she sews up Okajima's kimono, a task both Okajima himself and bad girl Satoko have attempted in vain. In *Dragnet Girl* Kazuko knits, and, taking this as the obvious sign of a decent woman, Tokiko tries to emulate her. The baby sock hanging on the fence toward the end of the film suggests she has succeeded.

By the time he got to *Ohayo*, Ozu would present a more jaundiced view of the good woman as seamstress or knitter. In one gag, the boys' mother, Mrs. Hayashi, is knitting while wondering if she should put rat poison on their pumice stone—which, unbeknownst to her, the boys have been gnawing on to help them fart better—because she thinks that perhaps rats have been chewing on the stone: the good woman is about to poison her children! In *An Autumn Afternoon*, daughter Michiko is shown winding a measuring tape around her fingers as she absorbs her disappointment at the news that the man she prefers is already engaged: the good woman is still not free to follow her heart (Plate 1A).[16]

In his "Noriko Trilogy," critic Robin Wood looked at Setsuko Hara's three "Noriko" roles in *Late Spring*, *Early Summer*, and *Tokyo Story*, along with the fact that Ozu never married and had once written a romantic letter to a fellow (male) student, and concluded that Ozu was subversively suggesting that marriage is a trap, to be avoided if at all possible. Because the Noriko of *Tokyo Story* does not remarry in the course of the film, Wood assumes she never will and that she alone has escaped the trap.[17]

Wood's analysis suffers from an insufficient knowledge of Japanese culture and, possibly, a biased perspective, given that he was a gay man. (Before the age of marriage equality, marriage for a gay man meant marrying a woman to hide his homosexuality, a trap indeed.) Wood is right, of course, that marriage for a Japanese woman meant subjugation to a husband, but, as we have seen in Chapters 7 and 8, Ozu had definite ideas about marriage, and, while they showed a degree of enlightenment, they were hardly subversive.

We don't know why Ozu never married. He liked women, but his interest seems to have been more romantic than lustful.[18] If he was bisexual, that has never surfaced as a fact beyond the one letter, and, in a school with only boys, an attraction to a pretty one could as easily be a sublimated longing for a girl. We know that at the same time this letter was written, Ozu routinely carried a picture of Pearl White in his pocket, which suggests he liked adventurous girls who acted like boys.[19] In *The Munekata Sisters*, Setsuko justifies her decision not to marry Hiroshi by saying, "I have to be true to myself." This may have been Ozu's rationale as well, but on what grounds we don't know. Perhaps he *was* bisexual and didn't want to hide behind a wife, although he apparently asked at least one actress to marry him.[20] Perhaps he was too immersed in his work to give a family the time he thought they deserved. Perhaps he thought his habits too irregular, although Kogo Noda's wife seems to have put up with them.[21] Perhaps in middle age he was in love with Setsuko Hara but thought himself too old for her. ("You don't want [your kids] finishing middle school when you're fifty," Hirayama counsels his son in *An Autumn Afternoon*.) Or perhaps he simply didn't want to grow up in that sense, leaving the responsibility for "the order of human life and history," as Somiya describes marriage in *Late Spring*, to his characters.[22]

Ozu's films, reflecting Japanese culture generally, see marriage as life's inevitable middle stage. While Robin Wood laments Noriko's loss of freedom in *Late Spring*, Ozu created in *An Autumn Afternoon* an ugly, unforgiving portrait of what happens to a woman who doesn't marry.[23] He nevertheless acknowledges that marriage, particularly arranged marriage, was frightening for women, who might barely know their prospective grooms and could look forward to being subservient to them. (On the topic of remarriage, the widowed Akiko in *Late Autumn* says, "I don't want to climb that mountain again.") Robin Wood is right that marriage in Ozu's Japan would curtail a woman's freedom, but in Ozu's universe there is no alternative. Marriage was a train one had to hop on before it left the station altogether, and this is made particularly clear when he portrays individuals missing out on their preferred marriage partner.

Oshige in *Where Now Are the Dreams of Youth?* agrees to marry sad sack Saiki when Horino disappears from her life, assuming this is the best she can hope for. Bordwell ascribes her fate, i.e., the fact she doesn't throw Saiki over when Horino reappears, to Horino's loyalty to his *batsu* (male school friends).[24] But a promise of marriage was, among other things, a contract between families; hence, we are introduced to Saiki's mother. Saiki's willingness to give Oshige up reflects his weakness while Horino and Oshige's insistence that she honor her promise reflects their virtue.

Gender Issues

In *An Autumn Afternoon*, Michiko misses the chance to marry her brother Koichi's friend Miura, but it is Miura's reaction that underscores the need both sexes felt to marry in a timely fashion. When Koichi approaches him, Miura explains that he has already become engaged. Although his fiancée is someone he knows and likes, not an arranged partner, he expresses profound disappointment that he has missed out on Michiko, saying he didn't think she was ready to get married. This is hardly flattering to Miura's fiancée! A Western man would not be expected to think "It's time to get married; I'd better see who's available" but to pursue the woman he liked best. Similarly, a running joke in *Late Autumn* is that the entire *batsu* of older men is still in love with Akiko, who chose the now-deceased Miwa, and their wives know and laugh about their continuing infatuation. None of these men waited to find someone he admired as much as Akiko because marriage was a contractual obligation that involved whole families and a particular timeframe.

In his prewar films, Ozu's women invariably marry, live with, or become engaged to men they know, like, and choose. Oshige misses out on marrying Horino, but she has always been friends with Saiki. Even in Ozu's wartime films the young people marry or expect to marry people they or their siblings already know. However, when this situation was codified by Occupation reforms and a new constitution, which decreed that young people should choose their own partners and not be forced to marry against their will, a debate raged in Japan over whether "love marriages" or arranged (*miai*) marriages were best, and this debate consumed over half of Ozu's postwar films.[25]

Young women in these films who are expected to marry are confronted with a choice between marrying a total stranger or a man that she knows and likes. In those cases where the preferred partner is no longer available, she marries the stranger. While the films as a whole favor marriage with a friend or boyfriend over *miai* marriage, someone in them is sure to opine that either situation will result in happiness if the partners work at it.

In keeping with Japanese tradition, Ozu does not see romantic infatuation or sexual attraction as particularly good foundations for marriage and mocks both in *Early Summer* in the persons of Noriko's friends from her school days. The shattered union in *Early Spring* began as a love marriage, but six or seven years in, it requires a major overhaul. (See Chapters 7 and 8.)

One reason for the comparative indifference to love marriage vs. *miai* marriage is the rigid separation of the sexes in Japan, particularly in Ozu's time. Traditionally, women had their domestic world, and men had their work world. These were expected to intersect far less than they do in the West—women did not socialize, for example, with the husband's officemates. As a result, there was often less communication between husband and wife than we expect in the West and consequently less mutual companionship. *Early Spring* depicts this situation clearly. Although wife Masako is invited to what turns out to be the fateful excursion to Enoshima Island with her husband's fellow commuters, she prefers to visit her mother, and throughout the film, her husband, Sugimura, socializes with his friends while she visits with her mother or a girlfriend.

Although the couple becomes increasingly estranged, the separate socializing that we see was and to a certain extent remains typical of Japanese marriages, even happy ones.[26]

The second reason love marriage seems less important in Ozu's Japan is, as Somiya tells us in *Late Spring*, that marriage is for continuing "human history," i.e., bringing the next generation into the world. Women were expected to have children, and the children, more often than the husband, became their source of emotional fulfillment. That is why marriage, in Ozu's eyes, is reserved for the young and why he mocks older men who remarry for either companionship or sexual fulfillment. Contrary to what Robin Wood projects, *Tokyo Story's* Noriko will remarry because she is not only very beautiful but young enough to have children (in addition to which both of her late husband's parents urge her to remarry). Ozu connects her to babies when he shows the neighbor's infant in the foreground of every long shot of Noriko coming in or going out of her neighbor's apartment and, at one point, has her inquire about the baby.[27] For Japanese women at that time, the companionship of a child was considered essential and those without one pitiable. Wood may be right when he writes, "Whatever it is that Noriko can't help yearning for . . . we can take it that it is not another husband," but she is undoubtedly yearning for someone to love.[28]

Ozu's films also deal with marriages that have deteriorated (*The Flavor of Green Tea Over Rice* and *Early Spring*) and those that are genuinely bad and abusive (*The Munekata Sisters* and *Tokyo Twilight*). A large dose of humility heals the troubled marriages, but the disposition of the abusive ones is more problematic. Takako in *Tokyo Twilight* goes back to her terminally self-absorbed husband because she wants her daughter to grow up with two parents. When the abusive Mimura drops dead in *The Munekata Sisters*, his wife is so guilt-ridden that she refuses to pursue her earlier plan to marry the man she truly loves, and we, the audience, are expected to see this renunciation as noble. Spousal abuse, therefore, is not held to be either dangerous or reprehensible in any absolute sense. (In all fairness, this is the era when, even in the United States, couples remained married "for the sake of the children," and public awareness and condemnation of spousal abuse was minimal.)

Ozu demonstrates greater sensitivity to abuse in *A Hen in the Wind*, in which he condemns Tokiko's rape by her husband, characterizing it, via his symbolism, as a kind of death for the rapist. (See Chapter 7.) There is no on-screen discussion of his action, however. This (1948) was a time when non-consensual sex within marriage was viewed throughout the world as a man's right even though feminists had been inveighing against it since the nineteenth-century. Ozu at least condemned it.

He likewise called out sexual harassment in the workplace long before it was widely recognized as a problem. In the two similar gangster films, *Walk Cheerfully* and *Dragnet Girl*, the heroines are courted by their bosses, who hope to make them their mistresses, and the women's jobs depend on some degree of acquiescence. The situation in *Walk Cheerfully* escalates into skullduggery, which, when foiled by hero Kenji, results in heroine Yasue getting fired. Tokiko in *Dragnet Girl* calls accepting her boss's advances "job insurance."

More subtle is Noriko's boss, Satake, in *Early Summer*, whose constant sexual innuendo constitutes harassment.[29] Even would-be feminist Robin Wood misses this, calling Satake "always helpful and benevolent."[30] By the end of the film Satake makes it clear that he has always been attracted to Noriko, speculating on whether she would have married him had he been available, which suggests a motive for the harassment. He is not seen as evil in the sense that the boss in *Walk Cheerfully* is evil, but, as detailed in Chapter 7, he is grouped, along with Noriko's brother, Koichi, with those characters vaguely associated with the infamous Zentsuji prison camp.

Satake is similar to Ozu's older men who remarry or seek to do so: funny in a compromised way. In *Late Autumn*, for example, Horie says to Mamiya, "At our age [sexual desires] are embarrassing." He leaves, trying to scratch the center of his back—the itch you can't scratch, i.e., a widower's desire for sex. Similarly, the jokes made by the older male *batsu* companions in *Equinox Flower, Late Autumn* and *An Autumn Afternoon* at the expense of the stout waitress highlight male obnoxiousness even as the films revolve around the men's foolishness and vulnerability.[31]

Ozu's mocking of older men's sexual needs points to a puritanism that runs through his films.[32] One of the reasons critics so often misinterpret *Woman of Tokyo* is that they suppose Ozu condones Chikako's involvement in prostitution, reasoning that a modern, adult woman ought to be able to earn money as she chooses; but in this film Ozu characterizes prostitution, again via symbolism, as dirty. (See Chapter 4.) Kihachi's accusation in *An Inn in Tokyo*, "You want to live an easy life," when he discovers Otaka is prostituting herself, is harsh given that Otaka's has a sick child for whom she must pay medical bills, but it could more justly apply to Chikako, who does not need to indulge her brother to the extent she does and apparently has enough education to moonlight in a respectable occupation.

That said, Ozu understands that the commodification of sex requires buyers, and he doesn't let men off the hook for consuming it. When, in *A Hen in the Wind*, Shuichi asks the prostitute Fusako why she is involved in this dirty business, she throws it back at him: "Why did you come here?" she asks. Once he understands her economic distress, Shuichi finds her an honest job. As noted earlier, once Kihachi in *An Inn in Tokyo* learns why Otaka has prostituted herself, he steals to save her.

Men, in Ozu's mind, have a responsibility to save women from prostitution, not simply to condemn them, and certainly not to purchase their services, even though patronizing prostitutes of varying social degrees had always been deemed a male privilege in Japan and was famously celebrated in art. When Isomura, Akiko's suitor in *The End of Summer*, admires the bar hostess's compact and says, "Someone bought you a nice gift," implying she does sexual favors for the bar's patrons, she retorts, "I bought it myself!" Shiro Kido's "sprightly, brave, optimistic, forward-looking" women were not intended as men's playthings.

Ozu's films also distinguish between the ugliness of prostitution and the ways in which men view impropriety on the part of women as a reflection on themselves, as in Naruse's *Every Night Dreams*. Thus *Woman of Tokyo*'s Ryoichi is right to condemn his sister's involvement in prostitution but wrong to take it so personally that he commits suicide. When Nomoto in *I Graduated, But . . .* discovers his wife is working in a bar, he is mortified even though she is not granting any kind of sexual favors. She not only defends her work by their need for her income but insists, "I'm happy working." Nomoto is forced to reassess his pride on several levels and ends by accepting his less than perfect job offer. Women, Ozu suggests, are not extensions of the male ego.

In addition to its jaundiced view of marriage, Robin Wood's "Noriko Trilogy" addresses female bonding. Wood sees in the *Tokyo Story* relationship between Noriko, mother-in-law Tomi, and sister-in-law Kyoko a "continuity between women across time and space" that constitutes "female bonding, for mutual support and strength within a male-dominated culture."[33] This he links to radical feminism. When discussing *Early Summer* earlier in his article, he indicts the institution of marriage for intruding on Noriko's group of former schoolmates, in which the married women have grown apart from the singles.[34] For Wood to single out these specific instances to support his theory that Ozu was a proto-radical feminist is problematic to say the least. For one, female bonding, which occurs and has always occurred in every culture in every age, cannot be attributed specifically to radical feminism. As for Noriko's gradual alienation from her school friends, Ozu's characters continually lament the inroads that time makes on relationships, those between friends and particularly those between family members. That is, after all, the major premise of *Tokyo Story*. Ozu is not suggesting marriage is evil because it causes friends to drift apart but rather that such erosion is as inevitable as marriage itself.

Moreover, both female and male bonding are abundantly present in Ozu's films, and both are common and ritualized in Japan, which, again, speaks to the comparative separateness of the sexes there. In fact, it is the male bonding in Ozu's films, particularly that of school-derived groups, that will seem unusual to Westerners, whose same-sex bonds among heterosexuals tend to be casual and are rarely prescribed by custom. Among Ozu's films, the greatest outcry over the erosion of same-sex bonds due to time and fortune occurs in *Where Now Are the Dreams of Youth?* where Horino is dismayed to find that his position as president of his family's company has changed the carefree relationship he once had with his old college friends, now his employees.

Male bonds dominate *Passing Fancy*. After three films in a row focused on women (*Until We Meet Again*, 1932; *Woman of Tokyo*, 1933, and *Dragnet Girl*, 1933) Ozu ended 1933 with *Passing Fancy*, as if his spate of women's films called for an equal and opposite reaction. Its main characters are Kihachi, a man incapable of growing up, his younger friend Jiro, and his son Tomio, males at different stages of life, and the film employs an array of signs and symbols related to masculinity, militarism, and duty. Most noticeable is the carp *noren* (curtain) hanging over the doorway to Otome's restaurant, which the men frequent (Figure 10.1). Associated with men, particularly boys, carp symbolize strength and endurance. Traditionally, carp windsocks were flown on Boys' Day (May 5) by families with sons, and the second of Tomio's calligraphy exercises, which hang beside his desk, makes reference to these Boys' Day carp and the pinwheels that accompany them.³⁵ From the end of the twelfth-century, Boys' Day (*tango no sekku*) had been associated with a martial spirit.

Militarism makes its way into *Passing Fancy* elsewhere. Jiro has been a soldier and wears a soldier's cap throughout the film (in contrast to Kihachi's more internationally conceived beret). Tomio shows ingénue Harue a photograph of Jiro in uniform as well as other renderings of soldiers that he has collected. A movie poster in Jiro's room refers to the differing fates of a brother and a sister, the brother clearly in uniform. There is a poster in Otome's café for a period film that is anachronistically titled *Manchu no musume* (Maid of Manchuria), a reminder of Japan's then-current war in that territory. Also posted in Otome's café is the schedule for an upcoming sumo competition (*basho*).

Harue, smitten with Jiro, is archetypically passive and wears traditional dress, including the *shimada* hairdo. Even after she has won Jiro's affection, she seems perpetually sad. Jiro's treatment of her ranges from callous to imperious and is in line with contemporary Japanese notions of male purity and devotion to duty.³⁶ Ozu via Kihachi criticizes Jiro's behavior, but, given the uptick in militarism and traditional values Japan was experiencing at the time, he may have felt he could criticize Jiro's stance only by speaking through a fool. Despite its all-maleness and obvious nod to militarism, *Passing*

Figure 10.1: Tomio, with a patch on his eye, stands in front of the carp banner that hangs in the doorway of Otome's restaurant in *Passing Fancy*.

Fancy is not about restoring patriarchy but is essentially a buddy film, a genre concerned with men hoping to escape the world of females, in essence not growing up.

In *Passing Fancy* and eleven other extant films, a father-son or mother-son relationship is important if not central to the story. This ended in 1949. Robin Wood makes much of the fact that in *Tokyo Story* Tomi's large pocket watch is passed on to Noriko, a gesture generally reserved for men when a pocket watch is passed from father to son.[37] In fact, Ozu inverts the traditional father-son/mother-son relationship into a father-daughter/daughter-in-law relationship in eight of his films beginning with *Late Spring*. The father-daughter relationship is not always central in each of the eight films, and sons are not entirely absent, but the role of the daughter, sometimes daughters, is always the central focus.

Depicting a father-daughter relationship was rare in both Japanese and Hollywood movies, although three Spencer Tracy films from the early 1950s (*Father of the Bride*, 1950; *Father's Little Dividend*, 1951; *The Actress*, 1953) paralleled Ozu's move in that direction. But whereas the Spencer Tracy character often feels sidelined by the women in his family, Ozu's fathers are responsible for seeing their daughters married properly and, in most of the films, are the only parent left in this parent-child relationship.

Juxtaposing the most valued member of the traditionally conceived Japanese family to the least valued member furthered Ozu's critique of patriarchy and shined a spotlight on that aspect of the Occupation reforms that the Japanese found most controversial, i.e., the liberation of women.[38] Having already portrayed a tentatively liberated woman in *Dragnet Girl* and a fully liberated, if somewhat bratty, one in *What Did the Lady Forget?*, Ozu was ideally prepared to respond to the controversy. The comedy of the cheeky niece/henpecked uncle duo from *What Did the Lady Forget?* (reprised in *The Flavor of Green Tea Over Rice*) would morph into relationships between sympathetic, dignified fathers and daughters who were, for the most part, vibrant, kind, and responsible—ideal women for a new age.

If Ozu was a radical in terms of film style, he was, in the stories he told, a liberal and humanist throughout his career. Leftist critics in the 1930s felt his critiques of society didn't go far enough, and New Wave filmmakers in the 1960s considered him conservative and old-fashioned. But neither the far left nor the avant-garde necessarily had a more enlightened view of women and their challenges. Ozu defended women against sexual violence, exploitation and harassment, against forced marriages, infidelity, and bullying. He mocked female characters who were frivolous or superficial, but, with the exception of Akiko in *Tokyo Twilight*, he never pictured women as victims—the legacy perhaps of his early infatuation with Pearl White.[39]

Notes

1. Sato, *The New Japanese Woman*, 2.
2. Bordwell, *Poetics*, 37, 43–44 and throughout.
3. Joo, *Ozu*, 46.

Gender Issues

4. For example, Standish in *A New History of Japanese Cinema*, 61–62. (See Chapter 4.)
5. Joo, *Ozu*, 86–94. Joo provides an interesting analysis of the women in the lost *Until the Day We Meet Again* (1932), but without the actual film, it is hard to know exactly how these portrayals would come across.
6. Robin Wood, "The 'Noriko Trilogy': Three Films of Ozu with Setsuko Hara," *Cineaction* 26/27 (1992): 60–81.
7. Catherine Russell notes that Tadao Sato and others see the suffering woman trope, particularly in Mizoguchi's films, as part of a *feminisuto* tradition, i.e., their suffering is so bad that men must feel guilty. (See Russell, "Insides and Outsides," 75–80.) The problem, of course, was that men never felt guilty enough to change.
8. Irene González-López and Michael Smith, "Introduction: Onna Monogatari," in *Tanaka Kinuyo: Nation, Stardom and Female Subjectivity*, ed. Irene González-López and Michael Smith (Edinburgh: Edinburgh University Press, 2018), 2.
9. Tamae K. Prindle, *Women in Japanese Cinema: Alternate Perspectives* (Portland, ME: Merwin Asia, 2016), 442.
10. Standish, *A New History of Japanese Cinema*, 53.
11. High, *The Imperial Screen*, 13.
12. Catherine Russell, *The Cinema of Naruse Mikio: Women and Japanese Modernity* (Durham, NC: Duke University Press, 2008), 40.
13. One author, writing in 1924, opined, "If I were to take a survey of the younger generation's likes and dislikes in girls, we would find that young men prefer girls who walk side by side and are in step with them rather than girls who trail behind like sheep." (Sato, *The New Japanese Woman*, 58.) However, the custom of women, particularly those in kimono, walking behind their men would persist throughout Ozu's lifetime.
14. Sato, *The New Japanese Woman*, 48.
15. Sato, *The New Japanese Woman*, 118.
16. In Inoue's *I Lived, But . . .* actress Shima Iwashita describes the direction Ozu gave her in exactly how to wind the tape measure around her fingers. Iwashita's gestures as Michiko are at the core of Shigehiko Hasumi's "Ozu's Angry Women," a talk given at the conference "Yasujiro Ozu: International Perspectives," put on by Columbia University and the Film Society of Lincoln Center in October 2003. See Shigehiko Hasumi, "Ozu's Angry Women," http://www.rouge.com.au/4/ozu_women.html.
17. Wood, "Noriko Trilogy," 60–81.
18. Richie, *Ozu*, 196–97.
19. Inoue, *I Lived, But . . .* Pearl White starred as the action-adventure heroine in a number of serials, the most famous being *The Perils of Pauline* (1914). She performed many of her own stunts.
20. Richie, *Ozu*, 196.
21. Inoue, *I Lived, But . . .*
22. Shinnosuke Kometani lists additional reasons Ozu may not have married in *Chasing Ozu*, 77–78.
23. Wood, "Noriko Trilogy," 71–72. Lest readers think *Autumn Afternoon*'s portrayal of Japanese women in that era who never married is accurate, those I know have had rich, fulfilling lives.
24. Bordwell, *Poetics*, 235.

25. Even before the war, families debated the practicality of love marriages. According to Barbara Sato, "Even parents [in the 1920s] who intellectually recognized the progressiveness of a marriage that considered the couple's emotions were reluctant to consent to such a marriage for their own daughters." (Sato, *The New Japanese Woman*, 146.) For love marriages to be legislated by an occupying foreign power, however, made the demand seem not only risky but obnoxious, and *miai* marriages continued. A UNESCO report from 1961 found that "many young couples accepted arranged marriages . . . relations between husband and wife within the home remained unequal, and that the tradition of male inheritance was upheld by many families." Coates, *Repetition and the Female Image*, 57.

26. Companionship as the motivation for marriage still figures far less into the calculations of Japanese men and women than it does in the West. See Motoko Rich, "Craving Freedom, Japan's Women Opt out of Marriage," *The New York Times*, August 3, 2019.

27. Wood's observation that the neighbor "keeps her baby under what looks like the kind of cover used to keep flies off cheese" underscores his cultural obtuseness. Wood, "Noriko Trilogy," 78.

28. Wood, "Noriko Trilogy," 77. Cf. Benedict, *Chrysanthemum and Sword*, 255–56.

29. When I asked a friend who had worked in Japan in the 1950s if such harassment was common, she confirmed that it was.

30. Wood, "Noriko Trilogy," 75.

31. Yoko Tsukasa, who played Ayako in *Late Autumn* and Noriko in *The End of Summer*, supposed these men were modeled on Ozu and his friends and collaborators Kogo Noda and author Ton Satomi. Kometani, *Chasing Ozu*, 213.

32. In the prewar years, strict censorship imposed on the Japanese film industry forbid the overt depiction of sexual relations. (See Barrett, *Archetypes*, 202ff.) In *Dragnet Girl*, Ozu used a fallen shoulder strap, foreplay in long shot, and embraces that were continually interrupted to deftly and convincingly suggest a sensual relationship between two people that is not present in any of his other extant films.

33. Wood "Noriko Trilogy," 79.

34. Wood, "Noriko Trilogy," 75.

35. Boys' Day was changed to Children's Day in 1948, but it took several decades for Japanese to actually stop thinking of it as Boys' Day.

36. See Benedict, *Chrysanthemum and Sword*, 288.

37. Wood "Noriko Trilogy," 79.

38. See Coates, *Repetition and the Female Image*, 21ff.

39. Ozu's niece recalled him saying to her father, "From now on, there will be many women who will work hard and determine their own paths in life." See Komentani, *Chasing Ozu*, 79.

11
A Two-Dimensional Art Form

I am like a painter who keeps painting the same rose over and over again.

—Yasujiro Ozu[1]

The plastic arts touched Ozu's life and influenced his art in multiple ways. Biographers emphasize his youthful naughtiness and his early passion for movies but generally fail to mention that he demonstrated a talent for drawing from an early age or that this interest continued in later life.[2] A critic who visited his home in 1932 found "paints and paint brushes scattered around," (the inspiration, perhaps, for the artist's studio *cum* dwelling in *That Night's Wife*).[3]

According to Tadao Sato, "Ozu came from a family that had deep ties to the traditional arts."[4] His parents were descended from samurai families, and Ozu apparently enjoyed visiting his maternal grandmother in Tsu, even writing his friends about it. Sato notes "how deeply he loved the exquisite life in [his grandmother's] old and noble family."[5]

Throughout Ozu's life, exhibitions of traditional art were available to the Japanese public, and, as demand grew for exhibits of pre-Meiji art, national museums were founded to showcase it. In the Taisho period, in which Ozu came of age, even department stores regularly hosted exhibits of traditional art, which "often helped stimulate the latest artistic fashions."[6]

In later life Ozu would surround himself with his own fine art, and pieces from his collections often appeared in his films.[7] Whether from his own collections or not, Ozu's films abound in fine art whenever it is appropriate to the setting, i.e., in homes whose families are wealthy enough to afford it, in upscale restaurants, and offices. This art is eclectic and includes traditional painting, ceramics, and Buddhist sculpture as well as modern painting in both the *yoga* (Western-style) and *nihonga* (Japanese-style) traditions. In other settings, prints and posters with traditional art, often *ukiyoe*, appear. As we have seen, he knew enough about European art to place reproductions of famous paintings, Goya's *Red Boy* and Watteau's *The Dance*, in sets not only as decoration but as commentary.

Ozu had an almost fanatic obsession with turning his sets into perfect compositions, moving props around freely and causing his assistants constant worry about continuity.[8] We have seen that he was frequently more concerned with the impact of his individual shots for their thematic or symbolic content than with continuity, and this same indifference held as he attempted to perfect the composition of each shot.[9]

In two of his films, *There Was a Father* and *Late Spring*, Ozu's characters visit (or are advised to visit) art exhibits. He also created a commentary on art in several of his films. In *I Was Born, But . . .* the boys argue about whether a zebra has white stripes on a black background or vice versa, a reference to positive versus negative space in any kind of black-on-white art: photography, printmaking, or Japanese *sumi-e* (ink brush painting). In *The Munekata Sisters*, Setsuko insists, "Being new means not getting old; things that are really new never get old," meaning that the beauty and perfection to be found in traditional art can never be considered old-fashioned but is always fresh and amazing. In several films (*There Was a Father, The Munekata Sisters*) characters opine on the beauty of traditional Japanese art.

In *Passing Fancy*, Tomio is shown making art, i.e., drawing his alarm clock. This always struck me as odd until I learned of Ozu's own childhood interest in drawing. He would say of this film that he wanted to "draw an *ukiyoe* on a copperplate," meaning he wanted to show traditional Japanese life in a modern, Western manner.[10] That he used two printmaking methods, one Japanese, one European, as his metaphor suggests the extent to which he conceived of his filmmaking in terms of fine art.

The following chapter examines Ozu's work in the context of traditional two-dimensional art in Japan, both classical and contemporary to his time. The first part will examine Ozu's indebtedness to spatial constructs found in traditional art while the second part examines the parallel struggles on the part of Ozu and contemporary *nihonga* artists to be both "modern" (i.e., Western) and Japanese, a struggle that, as we have seen, engaged the whole nation in a variety of contexts.[11]

Although David Bordwell reminds us that we cannot simply link Ozu's work to the "outer circle" or broadest configurations of Japanese history and culture but must contextualize these within the periods in which Ozu worked, he nevertheless compares the director's lifelong study of Tokyo to Hiroshige's *One Hundred Famous Views of Edo* (1857).[12] Indeed, traditional art remained pervasive in twentieth-century Japan, is a valid source of comparison to Ozu's work and a possible influence on it.

In a 2005 publication, Bordwell continued to insist that Japanese plastic arts had little influence on Japanese cinema beyond directors' self-conscious efforts from the 1920s on to incorporate pictorial elements from traditional arts in order to create a veneer of Japaneseness that would distinguish their product from that of other nations. He admonishes those who would see deeper connections between traditional Japanese art and cinema, stating, "We are not in the habit of explaining contemporary Hollywood style by reference to northern European Renaissance painting, so why should ancient aesthetic traditions be relevant to twentieth-century Japanese film?"[13] However, if we *were* "in the habit" of comparing classical Hollywood cinema to Renaissance painting, we would more deeply understand the meaning of "classical" and the extent to which certain aesthetic preferences have persisted over centuries in Western culture. That the same may hold true for Japanese painting and Japanese cinema should not be dismissed out of hand.

We know that Ozu and twentieth-century Japanese artists were generally conversant with both Japanese and Western concepts of how to render space on a two-dimensional surface. The idea of an inviolable narrative space developed in the West during the Renaissance, primarily in response to the invention of one-point perspective, which made classical illusionism possible. But one-point perspective was merely a symptom of an underlying philosophy that caused artists in the West to approach pictorial space quite differently from their counterparts in China and Japan. Since, for the Greeks, the human being was the measure of all things, space was something to be dominated by humans. This philosophy worked itself out not only in the expansionist imperative of both Greece and Rome but in two-dimensional design as well. In temple friezes, vase painting, mosaics, and wall painting, Greek and Roman designs were geometrical, centered, and symmetrical. A tendency to fill up all available space was dubbed *horror vacui*; but where empty space remained, it was evenly distributed, no more in one place than in another. Pictures usually contained human figures, and these were generally placed at the center of the composition.

European medieval art continued these design strategies. God was now the measurement and the measurer, the subject of most painting, but God generally appeared in a manlike form or, conveniently, as his son, Jesus Christ. With some notable exceptions, nature was a secondary subject in Western painting, usually rendered with Aristotelian, scientific scrutiny. This collaboration between science and art led, during the Renaissance, to the development of one-point perspective, which soon replaced multipoint perspective systems, through which narrative space up to that time had been less convincingly created.

By contrast, the Taoist (Daoist) and Buddhist traditions of China and Japan viewed the human being as merely an element in nature; they concentrated on the void (*mu*) and saw space and time as relative, interdependent intervals (*ma*) rather than fixed measurements that could be pinned down and controlled. As a result, the Japanese painter approached space very differently from the Western painter. Nature rather than the human being was the dominant subject matter and was rendered impressionistically rather than exactly. There was no *horror vacui*. Nature contains a lot of vacant as well as unseen spaces, and traditional painters apparently felt no need to either lay bare or fill up all this space when rendering it two-dimensionally. Instead they used empty space as an active design element. Moreover, the Japanese painter seldom treated narrative space as a unified whole, separate from the surface on which it was rendered, but generally acknowledged the surface of the screen or scroll containing the painting. A single scene, for example, might be painted over several folding screens and would, therefore, be broken into segments, often separated by lacquer frames. Confronting a similar problem (in altarpiece or fresco painting, for example), Western painters would almost always paint separate scenes within each framed area to preserve the unity of their narrative space.

The means of creating one-point perspective was never discovered in Japan but was introduced by the Dutch in the seventeenth century and had found its way into traditional Japanese art by the late eighteenth century. Traditionally, narrative space was constructed using various intuitive perspective systems much as in Western medieval painting; but it was never an inviolable space, for writing in the form of calligraphy frequently shared the space, rendering the two-dimensional surface obvious. Japanese painters became increasingly sophisticated in exploring and exposing the contradictions inherent in creating an illusion of three dimensions on a two-dimensional surface. A similar exploration would not take place in the West until the advent of modernism.

Since the Meiji period, two distinct schools of painting have coexisted in Japan: *yoga* (Western-style painting) and *nihonga* (Japanese-style painting). Despite the popularity of *yoga* in the Meiji period and Japan's fascination with Western modernism in the 1920s, traditional painting maintained a strong presence in Japanese society. Works from previous centuries were frequently on exhibition, and new works, *nihonga*, were created by artists who founded vital schools, clubs, and publications.[14] Bordwell's insistence that *nihonga* "could never be confused with the works of centuries past" is both overstated and irrelevant.[15] In most instances, *nihonga* preserved both the style of rendering and the spatial constructs of traditional art, and those works without contemporary references (e.g., Takata Biichi's screens [*byobu*] with cormorants in Boston's Museum of Fine Art) come very close to looking like traditional art.[16]

The traditional *tokonoma* alcove in Japanese homes required a Japanese-style painting (*kakemono*). A *nihonga* scroll, a copy of a famous painting, or a family heirloom placed there insured a continued consciousness of traditional painting. Discoveries in the late Meiji period of art objects from pre-Edo times, housed in tombs and temples, fed a growing interest in earlier schools of Japanese art. As Japan turned inward and nationalism increased in the 1930s, interest in classical Japanese art increased.

Traditional Spatial Strategies

In creating narrative space in his films, Ozu was clearly conscious of traditional two-dimensional art forms in Japan, for he frequently extrapolated the implications of traditional renderings of space into the time-medium of cinema. Of the many ways in which he imitated traditional spatial constructs, the most obvious and most obviously conscious is the view into deep space framed by objects in close-up. For example, a high shot from *End of Summer* is framed on the left and above by an extreme close-up of a tree and looks down on the tiny figures of two women walking by the Katsura River (Figure 11.1). It is similar to the composition of Hiroshige's *Kinryusan Temple* (1856), which is framed on the left and above by an "extreme close-up" of the temple gate with its huge lantern, then shoots into deep space along a snowy path to the main temple building (Figure 11.2). (The shot from *Walk Cheerfully* which Bordwell compares to a Hiroshige print is based on the same compositional strategy.[17] These examples from

A Two-Dimensional Art Form 213

Figure 11.1: Akiko and Noriko walk next to the Katsura River in *The End of Summer*.

Figure 11.2: Utagawa Hiroshige, *Kinryusan Temple, Asakusa*, from the series *One Hundred Famous Views of Edo*, 1856. Woodblock print, ink and color on paper. Courtesy of the Brooklyn Museum of Art, Frank L. Babbott Fund; photo by the Brooklyn Museum of Art.

Hiroshige employ one-point perspective more for drama than illusion, an exercise in comparing close with far away.)

These compositions also use empty space as a positive compositional element (*mu*). Apart from the large, off-center lantern and gatepost, nothing appears in the fore- or middle-ground of Hiroshige's print. Similarly, Ozu's composition makes generous use of empty space, the two small figures displacing only a small amount of it. By Western standards, Ozu's composition is not as radical as Hiroshige's, for his figures are centrally placed, not relegated to the edges like Hiroshige's temple visitors. However, Ozu's figures are not anonymous bystanders but two of the film's central characters. Although the shot is set up as Fumiko's point of view, it is nevertheless unusual to introduce an intimate conversation with an extreme long shot as Ozu does here. In this he was flouting conventional film style while imitating traditional Japanese pictorial style.

Ozu's use of empty space as a compositional element is not confined to the single shot but expands into the edited sequence where "empty shots" appear as transitions between scenes. The empty shot is not, of course, completely empty, but in terms of classical film style it is empty of reference: no characters from the film appear in them, and the location and/or purpose of these shots is not always clear to the viewer, although they almost always refer in some way to the scene just ended or the one about to begin. As we have seen, Ozu described them as pauses that allow the viewer "to have a pleasant aftertaste" (see Chapter 9) and, in this sense, they are related to the empty spaces in traditional Japanese painting that draw us to the images and ask us to imagine what lies beyond what we can see.

The *mu* concept implies that empty space contributes actively to a composition, and in traditional painting empty space is used to suggest a world lying beyond what the painter shows us. In Sesshu's famous splashed ink (*haboku*) landscape in the Tokyo National Museum, in which mountains rise out of the mist behind rocks in the foreground, the mist is represented by empty space. Horizontal washes suggest the river, but no shoreline is shown, and we are left to imagine the point at which the river touches land. A few brushstrokes represent housetops, and the same is true of the little boats in the lower right.

In *The End of Summer*, the youngest daughter, Noriko, accompanies the man she loves to the local commuter station in downtown Osaka. They have come from a farewell party; in a few days he will be leaving for Sapporo. The two sit on a station bench, too shy to express their feelings for one another. The sequence ends with a shot of the empty station platform. Although we see no train, its presence is obvious from the shadows it throws against the wall and the sound effects that accompany the shot. Like Sesshu's brushstrokes that suggest houses and boats, the implied presence of the train tells us that the two young people will now take their separate trains. This in turn points to the much greater distance that will soon separate them. The empty platform suggests the impending absence of the young man and the emptiness or loneliness that both he and Noriko will feel.

A Two-Dimensional Art Form 215

The ringing-telephone-over-the-empty-clinic sequence in *End of Summer* (see Chapter 8) likewise indicates the positive power of emptiness. Using no overt drama whatsoever, only sound over empty though identifiable space, Ozu employs emptiness—literally in the sense that the clinic is empty but also as a lack of information—to suggest a multitude of dramatic possibilities.

In addition to utilizing the power of empty space, Ozu frequently evoked the tendency found in Japanese prints and paintings to flatten a space rendered three-dimensionally, and he often used the same devices as the painters to achieve this flattened effect. Noël Burch, who views traditional Japanese painting as tending toward a flat-surface design, sees Ozu's filmic techniques as likewise augmenting the flattening of space.[18] This is far too simplistic a view, however, for both traditional painters and Ozu frequently worked with deep space and, when they flattened space, they were usually interested not merely in the flat surface but in the play between the flat surface and the illusion of depth.

Traditional painters flattened space by using white, gold, or gridded backgrounds, which emphasize the painting's flat surface and deprive the three-dimensionally rendered figures in the foreground a three-dimensional space to inhabit. Such backgrounds appear most frequently in screen (*byobu*) painting or in woodblock prints (*hanga*). In Hiroshige's *Wild Geese Alighting by Moonlight*, three geese plunge earthward in front of a huge white moon. Although the clouds below the moon suggest depth, the moon itself pushes forward and denies the geese the space suggested by their energetic movement. Screens with gold backgrounds create a similar effect: objects painted three-dimensionally, such as the bird in Kano Sanraku's *Plum Tree and Pheasant*, seem to have no space in which to exist. In Harunobu's *ukiyoe* print *Climbing Temple Steps*, the three-dimensionally rendered stairs, instead of suggesting space, create a grid, which flattens the geisha against the surface plane of the painting. The flattening, grid-like effect of the stairs is enhanced by the high, raking angle from which they and the geisha are viewed. High angles with similar flattening effects had a long history in Japanese painting and were most notably used by the twelfth-century painters of narrative scrolls (*emakimono*).

For his shots inside his characters' houses, Ozu frequently utilizes all of these visual devices to flatten the space. Bordwell glosses over the reasons Ozu's frames often appear flat, saying it is "simply because they *look like pictures*"; however, some "pictures" look flat and others achieve the illusion of depth.[19] Ozu was adept at creating flattened space, deep space, and ambiguous space.

Seventeenth-century artists of the *Rinpa* school seemed particularly intrigued by the tension between a two-dimensional surface and a three-dimensional rendering. In his *Tale of Ise (Ise monogatari)* scroll, Sotatsu copied the twelfth-century *emaki-e* style. In several scenes he completely flattened the dollhouse-like space of the earlier *emaki-e*, creating a patterned grid against which the figures interact. In *End of Summer*, Ozu created a similarly patterned grid as background for the office assistant, Rokuro, who is caught spying on his boss, Manbei.

Implicit in these examples of flattened space is an ambiguity created by the presence within each composition of objects and figures which are rendered three-dimensionally and yet are denied a three-dimensional space in which to exist. With the exception of Sotatsu's figures, which are themselves rather flat, these subjects tend simply to be pushed forward, almost into the viewer's space. The tension between two- and three-dimensionality becomes more pronounced when something recedes into a space denied by a flattened background, in which case it is no longer possible simply to push the object forward. In Korin's famous *Red and White Plum Blossoms*, for example, a blue stream filled with highly patterned gold eddies recedes into space, that is, gets narrower as it goes "back" (actually up). The space into which this stream recedes, however, is denied by the flat gold background of the screen and the decorative patterning on the stream's surface. The receding stream cannot simply be pushed forward and still be read as a stream receding into space. Instead, the viewer alternates between seeing a stream receding into the background and seeing a two-dimensional design. A push-pull effect is created, in which we read space first one way and then another. Such an effect was also evoked by Ozu in a number of ways.

Similar to those of the traditional painters, Ozu's flattened spaces are articulated by the individuals that move through them. A *ma* sense of space not existing in its own right but as the creation of time, of the action that takes place within it, is thus created. But Ozu moves beyond this to play deliberately with our perception of flat versus deep space. In *End of Summer*, he shows the front door and backdoor of a noodle restaurant in succession, followed by the shot of an alleyway. Deliberately matched, the shots are all very similar: a light area in the center surrounded by grid patterns belonging to the walls and doorways of traditional Japanese architecture. The space in the first two shots is quite shallow, however, while in the third it is deep. Yet because of the matches, we tend to read all three shots as flat until suddenly old Manbei walks into the back of the third shot and our eye is pulled into a space several houses deep. Just as in the Korin painting, surface design dictates one reading of these shots while spatial cues (i.e., the old man) dictate another (Colorplates 2A, 2B, 3A, 3B).

The confusion experienced by a viewer wondering whether to read two-dimensional space as being flat or as conveying depth was carried to great extremes by *ukiyoe* artists, who created ambiguities regarding size and distance relationships. In Torii Kiyonaga's *Woman After a Bath* we see a woman coming out of the bath while another woman continues bathing. If we look at the bottom of the print, the woman on the left clearly stands in front of the cubicle in which the second is bathing. If, however, we look at the middle of the print, we become insecure in this knowledge and find it difficult to tell exactly how far from one another the two women are. The confusion arises from the flattening of space via the grid lines and the white background, from the parallel perspective systems used in the print, and from the fact that the women are the same size.

Ozu created a similar composition in *End of Summer* in a shot of Manbei visiting his mistress, Sasaki. The Ozu frame is not as difficult to read because the two figures are clearly of different sizes—which tells us that one is farther back—and there is, of course, the camera's single-point perspective. Nevertheless, the distance between the two figures is somewhat difficult to judge for several reasons. First, the woman stands behind a transparent curtain, which blurs her figure slightly and makes her seem farther away than she actually is. Second, space has been flattened via the grid lines, the gold tones in the background, the low camera angle, and the size discrepancy in the plants. The small plants in the foreground appear to be the same size as the much larger plants in the background, and this tends to bring the back plane forward and squeeze out the middle ground.

Deliberate, playful ambiguities can be found in the early work of Ozu and in that of *ukiyoe* artists. In Torii Kiyonobu's *Courtesan Painting a Screen* (Figure 11.3) the courtesan appears to be painting on a screen, but a closer look at the artist's rendering of the floor indicates that the lady's lover lies between her and the screen, and, that being the case, she could not possibly be reaching the screen with her brush.

A similar playfulness occurs in a sequence of Ozu's *Dragnet Girl* in which the student Hiroshi wanders through the record shop where his sister works, which is decorated with RCA Nipper dogs of various sizes. In one shot we see a dog that looks quite large, but we do not know if it is a small dog that has been foregrounded and sits well in front of the boy or a large dog standing next to him. When he finally reaches out and touches the dog, we realize that, in contrast to the other dogs, this one stands about four feet high.

Figure 11.3: Torii Kiyonobu I, *Courtesan Painting a Screen*, c. 1711. Hand-colored woodblock print. Courtesy of the Art Institute of Chicago, Clarence Buckingham Collection.

Kristin Thompson has described this Nipper-dog sequence as an example of Ozu's modernism, defined as an interest in space for its own sake.[20] Certainly Ozu was modern in flaunting the fact that film is a two-dimensional medium in contrast to the dominant Hollywood film tradition, which, like Renaissance painting in the West, demands a coherent illusionism. But in challenging the spatial assumptions of the dominant film tradition, Ozu had no need to look to Matisse or Picasso, for he had in traditional Japanese painting an alternative model to classical illusionism. Centuries before Matisse and Picasso explored the tension between a flat, two-dimensional surface and illusionistic, three-dimensional space, Japanese painters had done so intuitively and deliberately.

Bordwell has noted that Ozu's play with space and image seldom intrudes upon or interrupts the narrative flow of his films.[21] Unlike the modernism of Jean-Luc Godard or even Sergei Eisenstein or Jean Cocteau, Ozu's films, while they often tease the audience, nevertheless flow undisturbed by a need to forcibly break with tradition. Similarly, traditional Japanese painting is always accessible, sparing us the broken distorted images of Picasso, while at the same time probing related issues, i.e., the relationship between two- and three-dimensional space. Ozu was familiar with Western modernism just as he knew both classical and modern modes of cinema. But insofar as his assaults on classical Hollywood concepts of space were inspired by, or similar to, two-dimensional media other than film, those media could as easily have been Japanese and traditional as Western and "modern."

Similarities to *Nihonga*

Many of the spatial strategies of traditional Japanese art were carried over into *nihonga*, Japanese painting in traditional styles. Ozu knew some of these artists personally as well as their work.

Continuing to dabble with watercolors through the 1930s, Ozu named Miyake Katsumi (1874–1954) as an artist with whom he identified.[22] Although considered a *yoga* painter, Katsumi worked in watercolors, which had a long tradition in Japanese painting, and he was thus frequently associated with *nihonga*. After the war, Ozu is said to have been friends with a number of *nihonga* artists, including Hashimoto Meiji (1894–1991), Higashiyama Kaii (1908–1999), and Yamaguchi Hoshun (1893–1971).[23] All three have work in the Imperial Palace.

Nihonga, like Japanese filmmaking, was one nexus in the struggle for a "modern cultural identity" during the 1920s and 1930s.[24] How, these artists wondered, "could one be both Japanese and modern if modernity is defined as Western?"[25] For filmmakers, of course, the question was even more acute, for the medium itself and the accepted language of cinema were Western.

Artist Takamura Kotaro (1883–1956) identified three tasks of the modern artist: 1) "to find an authentic means of individual expression"; 2) to understand one's status as a "Japanese artist"; and 3) to have "the courage to experiment."[26] In other words,

A Two-Dimensional Art Form

219

the *nihonga* artist did not simply sit on his hands and copy the past but struggled with authenticity, synthesis, and experimentation, exactly the tasks Ozu set for himself.

Kotaro did not wish to be squeezed into a box that produced only "local color," but many *nihonga* artists embraced genre painting, a tradition best exemplified by the pre-Meiji *ukiyoe* painters and printmakers.[27] Ozu, too, would become famous for his depictions of the "everyday," particularly his portraits of the working and lower-middle classes.

Another commonality between Ozu and *nihonga* artists was the camera. In creating space, *nihonga* artists sometimes went all the way back to the *yamato-e* style, with its high point of view and cutaways of roofless houses, but they might also zoom forward in time to depict a camera-eye's view of the world. Yamamoto Shunkyo, who had studied photography, produced an ink brush image of the Rocky Mountains, but, instead of using the traditional "climbing perspective" of Chinese painting, used a one-point, camera's perspective in this work, which was commissioned by the Takashimaya department store.[28]

The Meguro Gajoen, a sprawling entertainment complex in the Meguro district of Tokyo that began construction in 1931, became home to over 1,000 *nihonga* paintings, which were eventually sold off to other collections, including Boston's Museum of Fine Arts.[29] These include large panels and folding screens depicting young women in pairs that play on a traditional Japanese interest in pairing and contrasting, seen most often in pairs of folding screens with the same subject matter, varying subtly but surely from screen to screen. *Nihonga* artists continued this tradition, for example, Takata Biichi's cormorant screens in the Boston collection, in which two cormorants fly above foaming waves while one rests on a rock sticking up from the surf.

Similar repetitions and variations occur with the paired women in five large Boston paintings by three artists: Saeki Shunko, Tateishi Harumi, and Miki Suizan. Two panels by Shunko show identically dressed pairs of women, one pair in a tearoom (Colorplate 4), waitresses in perky yellow and red uniforms, the other a pair of kimono-clad women standing under an umbrella. Looking at them closely, we notice one of the tearoom girls is a little taller, has bangs, arms at her side, and one foot slightly in back of the other while the shorter girl holds her arms behind her with her feet somewhat turned out, a ribbon in her hair.[30] The umbrella women have nearly identical faces, kimonos, and permed hair, but one wears a raincoat, which allows only small parts of her kimono to show, and she carries a red purse with gray trim that both contrasts with and echoes the gray purse her companion carries.

Harumi's women contrast more obviously. A piece entitled *Clover* shows a uniformed young schoolgirl lying in the grass on her stomach, her head to the frame's left, while her companion, a young woman in an old-fashioned, Edwardian-era dress, lies on her back with her head toward the right. A second painting, entitled *Orchids*, shows two women standing on either side of an orchid plant. The woman on the right waters the plant with an atomizer while the other holds a terrier, considered emblematic of Western sophistication. (In Ozu's *Early Summer*, Noriko's friend Aya imagines her living a chic, Western-style life, complete with a terrier.) Both women in *Orchids* wear kimonos, one striped, one with a *kasuri* design. The *kasuri* kimono is bound with a striped *obi* (sash) that echoes the companion's striped kimono. The woman holding the terrier has short hair, appropriate to the fashion statement she makes with the dog; the one with the atomizer has long hair done up in a bun behind her neck. Unlike the Shunko women, who are virtually identical, Harumi creates entire, contrasting personae for his women and hints at their relationships: the schoolgirl with her older sister or a tutor, both Westernized but conservative; the women hovering over the orchid are possibly sisters, one younger and more Westernized than the other. As I noted in Chapter 7, the pairing of sisters, one conservative, one modern, was a theme that cut across many genres and anchored Ozu's *Munekata Sisters*, but the pairing we see in *nihonga* goes beyond such conventional distinctions and illustrates a sheer love of subtle contrasts.

Another Boston pair, two young women on a sailboat by Miki Suizan, wear stylish, contemporary dresses and cloche hats, but one stands and points while the other sits, holding an umbrella. One has a white hat and a red dress while the other has a salmon-colored hat and a beige dress. One has long sleeves, the other short. One wears a necklace while the other does not, and both sport a prominent decoration around low-cut necklines: gold embroidery for one and a lacey white insert for the other. Beneath their stylish hats, the women have idealized, oval faces, reminiscent of *ukiyoe*, and the swirls of water and foam around their boat are traditionally rendered, much like the water around the cormorants on Biichi's screens.[31]

Ozu is famous for his *sojikei* (similar figure) staging, the fishing scenes in *A Story of Floating Weeds* and *There Was a Father*, for example, in which father and son cast their lines in unison but contrast with one another in age and dress. Bordwell considers it "a unique feature of Ozu's performance style."[32] *Sojikei*, as used by film scholars, can apply to any number of figures acting in unison: the boys dancing in *Days of Youth*, the unemployed students beating out time with their propped-up feet in *I Flunked, But...*, or the cheerleaders in that film and *Where Now are the Dreams of Youth?* The contrasting pairs in *nihonga* painting, studies in compare-and-contrast, cousins of the similar but different panels in screen painting, constitute a more specific exercise in *sojikei* which I call "twinning." It also features in Ozu's films.

In *A Story of Floating Weeds*, the two actresses, Otoki and Otaka, one very young and the other somewhat older, are likewise paired and contrasted throughout the film. This pairing serves dramatic as well as pictorial ends when the younger woman, Otoki, runs off with Shinkichi, the young man of the fishing episode, and the older woman becomes estranged from his father, Kihachi, her boss and lover. Otaka's estrangement is foregrounded when Ozu frames her alone, not only sitting apart from the other actors but without the younger woman, with whom she has heretofore almost always been visually associated.

What Did the Lady Forget? makes use of this specific form of *sojikei* in shots of niece Setsuko walking first with Okada, the young man she likes, and later with her uncle

A Two-Dimensional Art Form

Figure 11.4: Komiya and niece Setsuko walk together in *What Did the Lady Forget?*, demonstrating the "twinning" prevalent in Ozu's films and in *nihonga*.

Komiya. Early in the film we watch two figures, unidentified at first and seen waist down from the back, walking down the street. Both wear trench coats, one black, one gray. Only the shoes identify one figure as a woman and the other as a man. The trench coat promenade is reprised late in the film when Setsuko and Komiya, photographed from the front, walk in sync. Both wear black coats with scarves tucked inside, their hat brims pulled forward toward their faces, a spoof on gangster films (Figure 11.4). Later, shot from behind, they enter the Komiya house, two figures in black, again evoking the gangster genre. These promenade sequences emphasize the modern girl's independence to the point of manliness. The "twinning" in the promenade shot with Komiya serves to emphasize the alliance between niece and uncle.

Like pre-Meiji painting, *nihonga* plays with space, sometimes creating flat backgrounds that deny three-dimensional figures the space they ought to occupy, sometimes creating a vague *ma*-like space, defined by the action that occupies it, and sometimes opting for very deep space. In Morii Koha's *Children Fishing*, for example, land, stream, and atmosphere are vaguely rendered with white and yellow washes, a single line delineating the hill the children sit on, while a few natural objects—flowers, a butterfly— further suggest ground and sky. By contrast, in Kafu's *Two Girls by the Sea* the children sit on a sand dune next to the ocean, which is depicted in deep space with mountains and a tiny steamship in the background.[33]

In Harumi's *Clover* the field of clover becomes a flat pattern of clover flowers, allowing little space for the two women to exist in. Only a patch of grass in the upper-left corner gives a hint of perspective. In Shunko's *Tearoom* (Colorplate 4) the girls stand in front of a columned archway. A tall étagère filled with plants separates them from the actual tearoom, where we glimpse part of a chair. However, the patterned floor on which they stand, the floral decoration created by the plants on the plant stand, and the patterned wainscot-level wallpaper directly behind them all work to create a flat decorative background, which denies the space the chair is supposed to occupy. Meanwhile, the girls appear to be flat cutouts against this flat space.

In Shunko's *Rain* the women stand on a vaguely delineated sidewalk while a misty rain falls behind them, creating a flat, gray background. In Enomoto Chikatoshi's *Snow Mountain*, which depicts the head and torso of a female skier, a flat, traditionally rendered pattern of silver squares behind the figure appears to represent snowflakes. In contrast, the deep space of a mountain landscape appears behind Matsushima Hakko's full-length skier, Suizan's boaters, and in Shoda Kakuyu's national park scroll, the last being a somewhat vertiginous version of the traditional climbing landscape featured in Chinese scrolls.[34] All these spatial devices have roots in traditional Japanese painting and printmaking.

I have cited examples of Ozu flattening space in his postwar color film *End of Summer*, but he had already done likewise in films contemporary to the *nihonga* art cited here. In *What Did the Lady Forget?* he framed a shot of several Japanese-style rooms in the Komiyas' house so that they appear entirely flat. Two sets of open *fusuma*, each with a different polka dot pattern along the bottom quarter, frame closed sliding doors with *shoji* on top and glass on the bottom. Through the glass we see the wall in the room behind. A brazier with a steaming teakettle and a table have been placed in the room with the *shoji* doors, but, photographed from slightly below, neither furnishing gives depth to the shot. Thus the space appears flat even though we are looking into three successive rooms with yet another room visible behind the *shoji* doors. Later, characters will walk through this space, demonstrating a depth not at all apparent when the rooms are empty. The confrontation between Komiya and his wife occurs in this particular space. At the end of the scene, Ozu holds the camera for about five seconds on the empty space, which, recently articulated by action, once again appears flat, dominated by the patterns in the *fusuma* and *shoji*.

These shots that flatten space contrast with the deep space of hallways in both the Japanese and Western portions of the Komiyas' home. In some cases, Ozu exploits the deep space dramatically, as when niece Setsuko paces up and down a hallway outside the Western-style room in which her enraged aunt first confronts her husband about his perceived misdeeds. Ozu plays at combining deep and flat space in the film's final shot, which begins with the camera looking down a long hallway in the Japanese portion of the home. One by one lights go out in various rooms; only the farthest doorway still has light around it. Komiya, having reconciled with his wife and anticipating a night of lovemaking, paces in front of the darkened doorway. Mrs. Komiya emerges from it with

A Two-Dimensional Art Form 223

a tray, and as she, following Komiya, exits the space, the camera holds on the doorway, a dark rectangle framed by light in the middle of an otherwise dark screen. Only a patch of shadow on the wall reminds us that we are looking down a darkened hallway.

The Shinto/Zen notion that people are part of nature and not necessarily the center of the universe finds frequent expression in Japanese art, and *nihonga* is no exception. In her striking *Waiting for the Moon* (1926), Uemura Shoen poses a kimono-clad woman, perhaps a geisha, looking up at a moonless sky from a balcony. We don't see her face or even all of her body because she stands behind a pillar, which blocks all but part of her back. We see mainly her *obi*, her round fan (*uchiwa*), and her head, turned toward the empty sky.[35] In keeping with the figure's own obscurity, the moon, the drama she waits for, has not yet risen.[36]

Shimomura Kanzan also plays with anonymity in his 1916 *Spring Rain*, two panels containing four Edo-era women. Three women with umbrellas, faces turned away from us, gather on the left side of the left-hand screen. They look back, however, toward the right-hand screen, whose far right side contains a single woman, whose face is visible, walking away from them. The obscure, enigmatic drama, the anonymity, the empty space all feature prominently in Ozu's films.[37]

Ozu's "empty shots," which contain no human figures, relate to the story and its various locales but often leave the viewer guessing as to how. In his prewar films, Ozu used a number of techniques that evoke a similar sense of anonymity and enigmatic drama: an emphasis on objects, a tendency to show characters from the waist down, and the use of an out-of-focus camera on significant figures (see Chapter 4). A favorite technique was tracking over a series of objects to an as-yet-unknown and usually minor character. In the *Tokyo Chorus* office sequence, we are introduced to the hero Okajima's office via a long tracking shot over several empty desks to an electric fan, followed by cuts to a typewriter with uneaten food next to it, to a pair of white shoes drying after a polishing, to an uneaten glass of jello, and finally to a sign announcing that bonuses will be given that day—the reason no one is at his desk—which solves the mystery and humorously asserts that nothing matters more than money. This resolution notwithstanding, Ozu has kept us puzzled for thirteen seconds, long by movie time. Although we suppose it is Okajima's office since he has previously mentioned the bonus to his wife, another minute and a half elapse before we finally see him.

Similarly, in *Passing Fancy*'s opening sequence, the camera tracks over the audience at the *naniwabushi* performance, then cuts from listener to listener. The main characters exchange brief dialogue, but the cuts continue and the camera pauses on a lost change purse, which passes from character to character as each decides what to do with it. Subsequently, a flea passes from listener to listener to the storyteller himself, causing a kerfuffle. The storyteller finishes his performance, the main characters exchange more brief dialogue but are lost again as the audience gets up to leave. Cuts of the theater banners and the empty auditorium precede a cut back to the main characters making their way home, at which point the film's actual drama begins. Although Ozu has signaled their importance through their brief dialogue, the main characters remain simply part of the two gags involving the entire *naniwabushi* audience until we are over five minutes into the film.

One short sequence in *Tokyo Chorus* is particularly noteworthy for its use of both the out-of-focus camera and framing characters from the waist down. Okajima enters his house and converses with his daughter, Miyoko, who sits with her baby brother in an adjoining room. Although cuts to Miyoko are in focus each time Okajima speaks to her, she remains out of focus for most of the sequence while Okajima, shown mainly from the waist down, crosses back and forth in front of the room where she sits. It is a peculiar sequence, in which we are well aware of who populates it but in which neither character is shown fully or clearly during most of it.

Later in the film, a shot tracking over ground filled with discarded papers ends at the feet of a man shown only from the waist down; he is wearing a sandwich board, whose lower edges are only just visible. A full shot of the sandwich board shows a man passing out leaflets (the discarded papers) but only from the back. Not until there is a cut to a frontal shot do we recognize the elderly worker, Yamada, on whose behalf Okajima has gotten himself fired, reduced to passing out advertising leaflets. Sixteen seconds elapse from the time we first see the discarded papers to the time we see Yamada's face.

Ozu also had a habit in his early films of showing actions carried out by legs and arms only, for example, the late sequence in *Tokyo Chorus* where erstwhile schoolmates gather in their former teacher Omura's restaurant for a reunion. We see an arm and hand scooping rice onto plates. A cut to Mrs. Okajima reveals her as the owner of the arm. Ozu then cuts back to her arm and another hand taking the plates away, then to a full shot of her helper, Mrs. Omura, holding the plates. Later we see a man's folded garments on tatami mats next to which an undershirt drops. A hand reaches for the garments, and then we cut to hands passing plates of rice to other hands that are pouring curry sauce on the rice. In this sequence Ozu never shows us who is dressing or who is handling the plates and curry sauce, although we know this from the previous scene. While this technique does not diminish these people's importance as human beings, it decenters them and denies them the centrality accorded humans in Western art.

A similar impulse to decenter the human being is present in *nihonga* painting, and it fights with the Western-oriented inclination to make humans central to the work. In the large Boston paintings, where human figures are not only central but huge, a similar impulse to reduce their importance is at work in the titles of the paintings, which are named after the background, atmospherics, or other minor, non-human elements. A panel with a full-length skier is named *Snow;* two women standing beside an orchid is called *Orchids;* two women lying on a field of clover is called *Clover;* two women standing under an umbrella is dubbed *Umbrella;* a *moga* seated before her dressing table is named *Fragrance* after her bottle of perfume, while the scene of two women boating is named *Fair Wind.* None, in other words, is named for the people who are pictured even though all are rendered large and dominate the space. Kobayakawa Kiyoshi's traditionally rendered *Listening to the Rain* pictures two geisha in a golden room, but no rain.[38]

A Two-Dimensional Art Form

While Ozu adapted traditional aesthetic concerns to film, the *nihonga* artists in turn took contemporary subject matter, often icons of modernity, and rendered it in traditional media. Kakuyu's 1933 scroll of a lush, green mountain landscape, titled *Green Shade*, looks traditional enough except for a group of hikers in one corner. No longer kimono-clad sages, poets, or peasants, the humans wear 1930s hiking gear and are not in an imaginary landscape but in one of twelve national parks, which opened in 1936, in imitation of the United States' national park system.

The Boston paintings include two of skiers and a hanging scroll by Kobayakawa Kiyoshi with that ubiquitous icon, the *moga*, who sits, tweezing her eyebrows, bare breasts showing above a wrap that covers the rest of her torso.[39] Ozu's early films, of course, include similar subject matter (minus the bare breasts).

Tokyo, rebuilt after the Great Kanto Earthquake in 1923, became a hub of modern consumerism, and *nihonga* itself was indebted to the trend. Department stores like Mitsukoshi and Takashimaya, as well as other commercial establishments, hosted art exhibits, bought, and even commissioned paintings.[40] The new commercialism found its way, in turn, into *nihonga* painting, for example, Shunko's *Tea Room* (Colorplate 4). The tearoom was the public space most associated with the *moga* and modernity.[41]

One of the more bizarre tributes to both Western influence and consumerism in *nihonga* is Boston's Kasuda Tetsu's silk painting mounted on a panel showing the upper body of a kimono-clad beauty standing next to a Christmas tree. Nothing epitomizes Western aesthetics with its *horror vacui* more than the Christmas tree, its many bright ornaments set in a tangle of branches. Nevertheless, in this c. 1933 piece, Tetsu composed along traditional diagonal lines, piling (with some difficulty) the tree and the woman into the lower-left portion of the picture and leaving the requisite empty space in the upper right corner.

Another nod to consumerism is Yamakawa Shuho's large painting of industrialist-turned-politician Fusanoke Kuhara's three daughters, posed in and around a big expensive automobile. Given a typical theme and variation treatment, the young women, with almost identical faces, all wear pastel kimonos. One, in pink, looks out the car's back window; the second, in blue, is seen through the car's open door, and the third, in beige, stands beside the car, holding a 35mm camera in a leather case, indicating both her wealth and her modernity.[42]

Well aware of these consumerist trends, Ozu pays back-handed tribute to them in *What Did the Lady Forget?* The film opens with the affluent Chiyoko arriving at the Komiyas' house, wearing a fox stole. The camera lingers on a close-up of her back, prominently and comically featuring one leg of the fox and the tail. The fox tail bounces along as she walks up to the house. Inside, her friends appraise her garments, commenting especially on the fox stole, which, she tells them, came from Mitsukoshi.[43] Soon one woman gets up to leave, off, she says, to the Ginza, Tokyo's most famous shopping district. Soon after, the Komiyas' niece Setsuko is introduced by a shot of the fashionable Western clothes she has left strewn around her room.

At the end of the film the same three women friends visit over tea at tables in something like a haberdashery. Chiyoko again wears her fox stole, but now Tokiko (Mrs. Komiya) has one as well. She goes to the counter to pick out a tie for her husband. (Apparently their reconciliation has resulted in her getting a fur stole and him a tie. From this we understand who drives the consumer revolution.) Chiyoko briefly examines the stole Tokiko has left on her seat, then joins her at the counter to find a tie for her own husband. Thus the friendly consumer rivalry continues. Tokiko mentions that niece Setsuko is shopping with her boyfriend, and we cut to them having lunch in a downtown department store restaurant, high above the city.

Ozu and *nihonga* painters were on parallel tracks, seeking to create a "Japanese" art, not simply for commercial advantage but to cultivate a native identity in a world mostly defined by Western tastes and inventions.[44] In doing so, they adopted similar aesthetic strategies and subject matters. While aesthetic strategies derived from traditional art might be thought natural for the *nihonga* artists to adopt, it was less natural for a filmmaker to translate them into cinema. Conversely, while filmmakers could be expected to cover contemporary subject matter, that painters working in traditional media did likewise is also remarkable.

The affinity between Ozu's work and Japanese painting, old and new, is evident not only from an examination of his compositions and subject matter but from his own inclination to befriend painters, admire their work, and incorporate it into his films. Already in 1936, Ozu was considered "the film director who is most like an artist."[45] In 1962, he was the first filmmaker admitted to the Art Academy of Japan (*Nihon Geijutsu-in*).

Notes

1. Quoted in Yoshida, *Ozu's Anti-Cinema*, 14.
2. See Kanji Matsuura, "Shonenki no kaiga" [Childhood drawings], in Matsuura and Miyamoto, *Ozu Yasujiro Taizen*, 130–34.
3. Sato, *Art of Yasujiro Ozu 6* (1975), 94. See also Richie, *Ozu*, 219.
4. Sato, "Japanese Cinema and the Traditional Arts," 182.
5. Sato, *Art of Yasujiro Ozu 5*, 90.
6. Thomas Rimer, "Teiten and After, 1919–1935," in *Nihonga, Transcending the Past: Japanese-Style Painting 1868–1968*, ed. Ellen P. Conant (St. Louis, MO: Saint Louis Art Museum, 1995), 46.
7. Nornes, "The Riddle of the Vase," 87.
8. Inoue, *I Lived, But . . .*
9. Sato, *Currents in Japanese Cinema*, 189.
10. Joo, *Ozu*, 76.
11. The bulk of this chapter derives from two previously published articles: "Playing with Space: Ozu and Two-Dimensional Design in Japan," in Ehrlich and Desser, *Cinematic Landscapes*, 283–98; and "Seeking a Japanese Modernity: Ozu and Nihonga Painters in the Pre-War Era," *Journal of Japanese and Korean Cinema* 2, no. 2 (2010): 97–108.

A Two-Dimensional Art Form   227

12. Bordwell, *Poetics* 17, 49.
13. David Bordwell, *Figures Traced in Light: On Cinematic Staging* (Berkeley, CA: University of California Press, 2005), 98.
14. National Committee of Japan on Intellectual Cooperation, *The Yearbook of Japanese Art, 1927* (Tokyo, 1928).
15. Bordwell, *Figures Traced in Light*, 97.
16. For an analysis of *nihonga*'s debt to traditional painting, see Paul Berry, "The Relation of Japanese Literati Painting to *Nihonga*" in Michiyo Morioka and Paul Berry, *Modern Masters of Kyoto: The Transformation of Japanese Painting Traditions* (Seattle, WA: Seattle Art Museum, 1999), 34ff.
17. See Bordwell, *Poetics*, 49, Fig. 14.
18. Burch, *To the Distant Observer*, 44–52.
19. Bordwell, *Poetics*, 88.
20. Kristin Thompson, "Notes on the Spatial System of Ozu's Early Films," *Wide Angle* 1, no. 4 (1977), 17.
21. Bordwell, *Poetics*, 74.
22. Sato, *Art of Yasujiro Ozu 6*, 94.
23. Okada, "Ozu Yasujiro ni okeru kaiga to dezain," 135.
24. Sharon Minichiello, "Greater Taisho: Japan 1900–1930," in Kendall H. Brown and Sharon A. Minichiello, *Taisho Chic: Japanese Modernity, Nostalgia, and Deco* (Honolulu, HI: Honolulu Academy of Arts, 2002), 9.
25. Kendall H. Brown, "Flowers of Taisho: Images of Women in Japanese Society and Art, 1915–1933," in Brown and Minichiello, *Taisho Chic*, 17.
26. Rimer, "'Teiten' and After," 49.
27. See Conant, *Nihonga*; examples include Kawai Gyokudo, *Bracing Breezes, Cool Waves*, 1901 (pl. 48) and *Spring Light*, 1948 (pl. 125); Murakami Kagaku, *Season of Rice Planting*, 1912 (pl. 132); Kobayashi Kohei, *Weaving*, 1926 (pl. 134), and Yamaguchi Hoshun, *Scenes from Modern Life* (pl. 135). The Hoshun work is part of a series produced by Matsuoka Eikyu with eleven other artists 1922–1928; Eikyu's atelier was famous for genre works with an urban theme.
28. Conant, *Nihonga*, pls. 42, 44. Early in his career, Ozu bought a Leica and became an enthusiastic amateur photographer who developed his own prints and sent them to photo contests. (See Richie, *Ozu*, 257n20.) For more on Japanese photography as it relates to Ozu, see Alastair Phillips, "The Salaryman's Panic Time: Ozu Yasujiro's *I Was Born, But* . . . (1932), in Phillips and Stringer, *Japanese Cinema: Texts and* Contexts, 31–32.
29. The Meguro Gajoen purchased these paintings from the yearly Imperial Academy of Fine Arts Exhibitions, known as "Teiten"; the Boston paintings date from the 1930s. I was able to examine many of these while they were on exhibit.
30. This particular image by Shunko has been designated a "machine-ist" painting by Asato Ikeda, who sees it and other Japanese paintings from the 1930s as having been influenced by Japan's militarist climate. While overt propaganda is discernable in Japanese films and even textiles (Atkins, "Wearing Novelty"), this study is one of the first to suggest a change in the style of *nihonga* due to a rise in militarism. See Asato Ikeda, "Modern Girls and Militarism: Japanese-Style Machine-ist Paintings, 1935–1940," in *Art and War in Japan and*

its Empire, 1931–1960, ed. Asato Ikeda, Aya Louise McDonald, and Ming Tiampo (Leiden: Brill, 2012), 91–109.

31. For Harumi's "Orchids" and "Clover," see Atkins et al., *The Brittle Decade,* pls. 69, 71; for Suizan's boaters, pl. 56. This publication includes additional examples of paired female figures in pls. 76, 77, 81, and 85. Pl. 83 contrasts a woman in a Chinese dress with one in a kimono. Brown and Minichiello's *Taisho Chic* includes additional examples of paired women: pls. 5, 15, 21, and 30.

32. Bordwell, *Poetics,* 84.

33. See Brown and Minichiello, *Taisho Chic,* pls. 15 and 30.

34. The Chikatoshi, Hakko, Suizan, and Kakuyu paintings are reproduced in Atkins et al., *The Brittle Decade,* pls. 55, 56, 163, and 165.

35. Conant, *Nihonga,* pl. 83. Uemura Shoen was the first female artist to practice *nihonga.* She made several paintings of women with their backs to the viewer, including *Summer Evening* (c. 1900). See Morioka and Berry, *Modern Masters of Kyoto,* pl 27.

36. Additional examples in which a geisha's face is obscured by her fan or elbow include Seiho Takeuchi's *Sudden Shower* (1909) and Bakusen Tsuchida's *Hair* (1911). See Conant, *Nihonga,* pls. 76 and 77.

37. Conant, *Nihonga,* pl. 80.

38. Atkins et al., *The Brittle Decade,* pl. 81.

39. The framing and intimacy of Kiyoshi's presentation, the mirror and other objects associated with his *moga's* toilette, her beauty-enhancing activity and partial nakedness clearly make her heiress to the *ukiyoe* geisha. For this and additional *nihonga* images of modern women, see Atkins et al., *The Brittle Decade,* pls. 12, 13, 66, 70, and 80; also Brown and Minichiello, *Taisho Chic,* pls. 5, 9, 10, 12, and 14. All date from the 1930s.

40. For details on Mitsukoshi's specific involvement in collecting and exhibiting art, see Chiaki Ajioka, "The Lure of the City" in *Modern Boy, Modern Girl: Modernity in Japanese Art 1910–1935,* ed. Jackie Mezies (Sydney: Art Gallery of New South Wales, 1998), 43.

41. Brown, "Flowers of Taisho: Images of Women in Japanese Society and Art," 19.

42. Brown and Minichiello, *Taisho Chic,* pl. 5. Fusanosuke Kuhara was a conservative politician who supported a hard line against China. The Americans designated him a Class A war criminal, but in 1952 he was again elected to the Diet and, ironically, played an important role in restoring Japan's relations with both China and Russia.

43. Japanese place so much importance on where items are purchased that gifts, which Americans would rewrap in festive paper, are left in their plain store-wrap so that the recipient will appreciate their source.

44. Bordwell notes the commercial advantage that culturally specific flourishes afforded filmmakers in his "Visual Style in Japanese Cinema, 1925–1945," *Film History* 7 (1995), 14ff.

45. Raine, "A New Form of Silent Cinema," 106.

12
The Ozu Touch: Influencing Others

> Ozu's austere yet ludic style comprises his distinctive sensibility that is rarely
> emulated by any other director.
>
> —Jinhee Choi[1]

David Bordwell has noted the extent to which Ozu began influencing other Shochiku directors early in his career.[2] And while we commonly think of Ozu as a stylist, we need only look at his execution of that most basic directorial duty—eliciting good performances from actors—to understand why, from his earliest days as a director, he commanded a following. Two actors from his early films appear in Mikio Naruse's *No Blood Relation* (*Nasanu naka*, 1932), Joji Oka and Ichiro Yuki. Under Ozu's direction both gave indelible performances, Oka as *Dragnet Girl's* gangster-in-love and Yuki as the infuriatingly incorrigible Watanabe in *Days of Youth*. In Naruse's film the two appear as antagonists: Oka as a lawyer defending a helpless woman and Yuki as a gangster; yet both performances are lackluster and bland and give no hint of what these two actors were capable of.[3] On this basis alone, it is not difficult to understand why Shiro Kido indulged Ozu's eccentricities and others looked to him for inspiration.

In the postwar years, however, Ozu's caché as an influencer in Japan waned as a new generation of directors rejected his quiescent cinema of little drama. In time, however, his films would be discovered in the West and rediscovered in Japan, and disciples and imitators would multiply. To date there has been considerable analysis of Ozu's influence on late twentieth- and twenty-first-century directors in the West, Asia, and the Middle East.[4] This chapter will look at six directors and/or films with a specific connection to Ozu. In each case, Ozu's influence will vary depending on how the filmmakers perceived Ozu's work and/or from which sources their understanding derived.

Hollywood

The first American film (and probably the first in the West) to channel Ozu was Hollywood's *Escapade in Japan* (Arthur Lubin, 1957). It was one of several dozen Hollywood films from the 1950s and early 1960s to be set in and actually filmed in Asia; a substantial subset involved Japan. These were often big budget films, some of which won Academy Awards; for example, Marlon Brando's *Sayonara* (Joshua Logan, 1957) was nominated for ten Oscars and won four. At the time, tens of thousands of American soldiers and their dependents were rotating in and out of bases in Japan and Okinawa, the latter still under US occupation. Sandwiched between the Korean and Vietnam wars, the films and their goodwill messages had a ready audience.

Hollywood's "Asia films" were a form of what Christina Klein, writing about Rodgers and Hammerstein's Asia trilogy (*South Pacific, The King and I,* and *Flower Drum Song*—all of which were made into movies) has dubbed "Cold War [American] Orientalism."[5] They embraced the erstwhile enemy and reified Japan's own reinvention of itself as a nation of culture. At a time when nearly half the United States still had anti-miscegenation laws on their books, the Asia films pushed interracial relationships and were, on the surface, anti-racist. A significant use of yellow-face undercut these good intentions, however. That and an underlying sexism—Asian women are superior to Western women because they know how to please men—make many of the films difficult to watch today.

Neither of these problems plagued *Escapade in Japan*, however, a road movie that follows two little boys, played by Roger Nakagawa and Jon Provost (just prior to his creating the role of *Lassie*'s Timmy on TV), as they flee from the Japanese police. Victim of a plane crash, young Tony has been picked up at sea by a Japanese fishing family. Kuniko Miyake and Susumu Fujita play the parents, whose son, Asahiko, misunderstands their intention when he overhears them talk about turning Tony over to the police. Supposing the police will put Tony in jail, Asahiko masterminds an escape. (The film is famous in some quarters because Clint Eastwood, an Arthur Lubin protégé at the time, has a bit part as the only rescue pilot with lines to perform.)

Like all of the Japan films, this one gives us a tourist-eye view of Japan as it follows the boys from the Inland Sea through the countryside to Nara by way of Kyoto, and, while the sites and cultural experiences chosen are somewhat unusual for this subgenre, it includes the two that were de rigueur in every Hollywood Japan film: geisha and the Japanese bath. These two conventions fascinated and titillated Americans. In *Escapade*, women in a geisha house take the boys in for a night, pop them in their private home-style bath (less sensational than the communal or spa baths featured in other Japan films), and treat them like little men, hinting at the virtues of Japanese women that were extolled more broadly by other films in the genre.

Given the two-little-boys story line, one thinks of Ozu, and this impression is enhanced by the cast: Kuniko Miyake, long-suffering mother of two boys in *Early Summer* and *Tokyo Story*, plays Asahiko's mother; Tatsuo Saito, the dad in *I Was Born, But...*, plays a schoolteacher who lets the boys join his school trip; and a silver-haired Ureo Egawa (*Where Now Are the Dreams of Youth?*) plays Kyoto's chief of police. According to Donald Richie, Shochiku co-produced the film, although this fact, if true, does not appear in the film's credits.[6]

According to its lobby card, the movie was "filmed entirely in the seldom-seen corners of the <u>real</u> Japan!" [*sic*] which suggests guidance of some sort from *real* Japanese.

A number of the sites the children visit are theatrical productions, a vaudeville-like strip show, a Takarazuka-style extravaganza with traditional dance and music, an intimate dance performed by geisha in the geisha house, and a temple dance performed by children. Lubin had a background in theater, so it was natural for him to include as many varieties of Japanese theater as he could.[7] Other sites, the Golden Pavilion (*Kinkakuji*), the *Sanjusangendo* (temple of the thousand-armed Kannon) and the tame deer in Nara Park, are typical tourist stops.

However, there are numerous sites, sets, and situations familiar from Ozu's films: views of the Inland Sea, children singing, views of a pachinko parlor, the way in which the city policemen pass information from one to the other, a sequence in the crowded third-class car of a train along with considerable footage of station platforms, a sequence with the schoolchildren in the Kiyomizu-dera, and numerous references to baseball. (We are told early in the film that Japanese boys love baseball; Asahiko wears a New York Yankees cap; and the geisha do a baseball dance—truly!) All of this raises questions that I do not have answers for: how extensive was Shochiku's role in choosing locations and shooting the film? (Daiei is the only Japanese company to receive a screen credit—for lending Miyake, who was apparently working there at the time.) Was Lubin shown Ozu's films? Did he and his team meet the great director? Was casting Miyake based on her Ozu roles as the mother of young boys?

To what extent anyone was thinking about Ozu when this film was made is an entirely open question. Nevertheless, aspects of his films are present in this story about little boys much more than in any of Hollywood's other Japan films. Two years later Shochiku would release *Ohayo*, also about little boys and starring Kuniko Miyake as the mother of the two principal youngsters. Ozu has said he had the idea for *Ohayo* in mind for a long time and pitched it to other directors, who liked the idea but weren't willing to follow up on it, so he finally made it himself.[8] One has to wonder if *Escapade in Japan* prompted that decision. Perhaps the influence went both ways.

Wim Wenders

Wim Wenders is to my knowledge the first Western director to vehemently proclaim his admiration for Ozu, calling him his "only master."[9] Wenders saw his first Ozu films on a trip to New York in 1973, shortly after Dan Talbot of New Yorker Films had acquired the American distribution rights to most of the postwar productions plus *I Was Born, But...* Wenders was making *Alice in the Cities* (*Alice in den Städten*, 1974) at the time, and he felt that Ozu's work gave him permission to not be overly concerned with plot. "My characters... are not very bound to the plot... [They] are inventing the plot... so they are much more able to show their personalities."[10] In *Kings of the Road* (*Im Lauf der Zeit*, 1976), Bruno tells Robert, "No need to tell me your stories." "What do you want to hear?" asks Robert. "Who you are," Bruno replies.

Donald Richie has described how Ozu disliked plot and how he and screenwriter Kogo Noda wrote their characters' dialogue before deciding where they would speak it in order to develop their characters free of the plot.[11] Similarly, Wenders has described how, in making *Paris, Texas* (1984), he had his actors practice their lines together before deciding how he would shoot each scene. He has also said that he creates his characters based on the actors he has chosen.[12] Ozu likewise wrote scripts based on the actors he had in mind to play various parts. When the studio balked at his choice of Setsuko Hara to play Noriko in *Early Summer*, he refused to make the film without her.[13]

Early on Wenders would say, "The importance of Ozu for me . . . was to see that somebody whose cinema was also completely developed out of the American cinema, had managed nevertheless to change it into a completely personal vision."[14] Of course, the French New Wave directors had done as much, and Wenders had encountered their work most of a decade before he encountered Ozu (though he would admit the influence Godard had on him only much later).[15] That said, the point at which Wenders encountered Ozu was critical. By 1973, he had made only two full-length commercial features: a film adaptation of Peter Handke's novella *The Goalie's Anxiety at the Penalty Kick* (*Die Angst des Tormanns Beim Elfmeter*, 1972) and a television adaptation of Hawthorne's *The Scarlet Letter*. Wenders's script for *The Goalie* had followed Handke's novella, a kind of anti-murder mystery, very closely; he was then confronted with trying to make a more conventional film with *The Scarlet Letter* (*Der Scharlachrote Buchstabe*, 1973). Neither his experience making *Scarlet Letter* nor the film itself turned out well. With *Alice in the Cities*, he was embarking on the first feature he would create entirely by himself, and it was in the midst of this process that he first encountered Ozu and felt reassured that he could trust his own instincts.

Ozu's actual influence on *Alice in the Cities* is minimal, though it does exist. The Amsterdam tour boat was probably influenced by the city bus tour in *Tokyo Story*, the first Ozu film that Wenders saw. In addition, the film is punctuated by a repetitive, orientalizing pentatonic guitar motif, reminiscent of a Japanese *koto*. According to independent filmmaker Allison Anders, who assisted Wenders on *Paris, Texas*, it was intended as an homage to Ozu.[16]

Kings of the Road also contains items lifted from Ozu's films. The hula hoop that Robert finds and demonstrates in the abandoned army hut recalls the ubiquitous hula hoop in *Ohayo*, with which the younger brother shimmies once the coveted television set has been procured. More obvious are the two railroad-crossing sequences that transpire in the town where Robert visits his father. In the first of these Robert signals the gatekeeper to open the crossing gates for him so that he can cross just ahead of the train. When, the next day, Bruno catches up to Robert, he has to wait while the train goes by. These recall the two railroad-crossing sequences in *I Was Born, But . . .* , which trace the devolution of the boys' respect for their father. (Robert's contempt for his father is likewise an issue in *Kings*.)

Meanwhile, Ozu and Wenders share certain predilections that stand out precisely because their films are not driven by highly involved plot lines. These include an interest in modes of transportation, particularly trains; an evocation of the life cycle, of passage, and, within that context, of death; an interest in empty space, even *ma* space; an interest in not only citing film history, which they share with the French New Wave, but in photography; also, a contempt for television. In *Ohayo* Ozu opines, via the father, that television will produce 100 million idiots while in *Alice* Philip complains constantly about television and even destroys a set in his motel room.

Many of these similarities were already in place in Wenders's *Goalie*. For example, Ozu and Wenders often use comparatively lengthy introductory sequences that take their time finding the main character(s). Both *The Goalie* and *Alice* begin this way. Wenders has noted the sequence in *The Goalie* in which title character, Bloch, rides a bus at night. "It doesn't have very much importance in the film, it's a five-minute sequence, perhaps less . . . the train is accompanying the bus and it's getting dark—that's the scene where I felt, even while I was shooting it, that this was the way it was going to go on for me."[17] Wenders cuts between Bloch inside the bus and exteriors of the train that travels at about the same speed in close proximity. It is reminiscent of Ozu's cuts between characters inside a train and the train's exterior as it travels along or the sequence in *Walk Cheerfully* in which Kenji's car races along next to a train.

In Ozu's films, as we have seen, trains, bridges, and other means of going from one place to another often refer to passage from one stage of life to another while the life cycle became the basis of most of his late films. Wenders evokes the life cycle in *Kings of the Road* when Robert drives his Volkswagen into the Elbe, then climbs out the top of the womb-like vehicle soaking wet, an obvious image of birth. The story ends when the two men come back to where they started, the border with East Germany. "Shit!" says Bruno, "We're at the border; we can't go any further!" They have come to a *dead* end. In this case, birth and death refer to the men's friendship. In *Lightning Over Water* (1980), shots of bridges in New York Harbor and over the East River are used to symbolize Nick Ray's passage from life to death.

Trains and the other modes of transportation depicted in their films have, of course, varied over time in terms of what they signify for each director. Wenders has said quite clearly that for him these signify travel and that he always feels best when he's traveling. He was a young man when he made *Alice* and *Kings* and still comparatively young when he made *Paris, Texas*. A youthful Ozu likewise saw trains mainly as travel, adventure, escape, and sometimes separation in films like *Days of Youth*, *Walk Cheerfully*, and *A Story of Floating Weeds*. Only later when he began to focus on the life cycle would they come to signify passage.

From the sky, empty except for a distant airplane, at the beginning of *Alice* to the vast empty landscapes in *Paris, Texas*, including Travis's picture of Paris, Texas, Wenders has shown an interest in empty space, much as Ozu likes to show empty rooms. While Ozu's empty rooms function narratively and symbolically, Wenders's empty spaces function less concretely; nevertheless, both directors have an interest in emptiness. Alice comments on one of Phillip's Polaroids, "That's a lovely picture; it's so empty." Wenders probably knew nothing of *mu* or *ma* space at this time but seems to have had an innate feeling for it. In *Kings* he shoots a landscape in which the men's truck is very far right, drives past the camera and out of the shot, which is then held for a few seconds

234 *Ozu*

more. In *Paris, Texas*, he evokes Ozu's use of *ma* space more consciously in several instances, once when he has Travis walk in long shot through a landscape and right on out of the frame and later, on the journey to find Jane, when, again in long shot, Travis drives his vehicle out of the frame then backs back into it and turns right. In both *Alice* and *Kings*, Wenders's camera seeks out rivers, the Rhine and the Elbe. This is partly a political statement—these formed the borders of West Germany—but there is also that *ma*-like feeling of endless flow.

That Wenders's sensibilities should in some ways converge with Ozu's is not surprising, given that Western modernism—and Wenders is a modernist—was greatly influenced by Japanese art. Both directors were painters, Ozu as a hobbyist and Wenders as a serious art student in the 1960s when he studied painting in Paris with Johnny Friedlaender. Friedlaender was a concentration camp survivor who had studied with Otto Mueller in the 1920s and immigrated to Paris to escape the Nazis. His abstractions, mainly etchings, make use of fortuitous design and empty space.

Bordwell calls Ozu "the most cinephiliac major director before the New Wave."[18] And Wenders, of course, following the New Wave directors as both critic and filmmaker, not only pays homage to his predecessors but makes cinema his subject in *Kings of the Road*. He illustrates how films are projected (or were before the digital era), explores what they mean for those in the business of showing them, and bemoans the deplorable state of the German film industry in the 1970s.

Beyond movies, however, both Ozu and Wenders devote considerable footage to photography. Besides the funerary photographs prominent in a number of Ozu films and the wedding photograph in *Late Spring*, the director shows the process by which formal photographs are shot in *There Was a Father, Brothers and Sisters of the Toda Family, Early Summer*, and *Late Autumn*. In *Tenement Gentleman* an entire sequence unfolds in a portrait studio and ends with what is supposed to be the view from inside the camera in which we first see the subject upside down and then blackness when the shutter supposedly closes.

For Wenders, certain photographs in *Alice* drive the plot (such as it is) while Philip makes Polaroids throughout much of the film. In *The American Friend (Der amerikanische Freund*, 1977), Ripley takes multiple Polaroids of himself while lying on a pool table. The photomat also looms large in Wenders's films. Philip and Alice take their pictures in a photomat, and in *Paris, Texas*, Travis gives Hunter the sequence of photomat images he made with Jane years before.

"The Yanks have colonized our subconscious," Robert says famously in *Kings of the Road*, and this is illustrated by both Wenders and Ozu in, among other things, many references to Coca-Cola. Although Ozu included ads for a variety of American products in his early films, references to Coca-Cola specifically begin with the famous sign in *Late Spring* and continue throughout the Occupation-era films, thereby documenting the influence of American troops.[19]

Mark Betz has argued that the monologue speeches delivered by Travis and Jane to one another in *Paris, Texas* are derived from the valedictory speeches Somiya and

The Ozu Touch   235

Noriko make during their second night in the Kyoto inn (the sequence that ends with the famous vase shots) in *Late Spring*.[20] On the surface this seems far-fetched, mainly because everything in *Paris, Texas* is so much more extreme than anything in an Ozu film; but Betz's arguments are interesting and compelling, particularly when one considers that neither Wenders's nor Ozu's films contain many lengthy speeches: Ozu's dialogue is generally pared to its essentials, and Wenders's barely exists.

One can, moreover, point to other specific instances in *Paris, Texas* where Ozu's work, particularly that in the silent films, which Wenders had evidently seen by this time, is invoked.[21] For example, Travis's brother, Walt, is a sign painter like the protagonist in *That Night's Wife*; sign-painting is not a profession one finds many other film protagonists pursuing. Walt's family, including Travis, watch a home movie, and this becomes a pivotal moment in the story in which the child Hunter understands that Travis and Jane are his real parents and becomes curious about them. Similarly, the home movie in *I Was Born, But . . .* is the pivot that generates the young boys' rebellion and eventual reconciliation with the realities of adult life.

In several instances in Walt's home, Wenders frames his shots to cut off heads and other body parts in a nod to Ozu's early films, particularly *Tokyo Chorus*. The eleven-shot sequence that introduces Travis to Walt's family in Los Angeles unfolds as follows:

1) Walt's unpeopled living room; Walt and Travis enter; Anne joins them and greets Travis; camera moves to a medium shot of Travis and Anne with Walt standing screen right.
2) A shot from the stairway in which part of the second floor landing cuts off the heads of Travis, Anne, and most of Walt; Travis and Anne continue to converse then stoop to look up the stairway, and Anne calls Hunter.
3) Reverse shot of Hunter coming down the stairs.
4) CU of Travis and Anne
5) CU Hunter
6) CU Walt
7) Repeat shot #4; Anne leaves the frame.
8) Repeat shot #5 (Hunter)
9) Repeat shot #7 (Travis)
10) Repeat shot #8 (Hunter); Anne comes into the shot, but the camera does not reframe and her head is cut off above the nose.
11) Four pairs of legs and feet under the dining table.

Ozu was famous for his love of red, which pops up frequently in his color films, especially *Equinox Flower*, where even the title refers to a red amaryllis. Red is prominent in *Paris, Texas* but is used somewhat more thematically than in Ozu's late films. It coheres mainly around Travis, who from the very beginning wears a red baseball cap, and it intensifies as he reconnects with his family. After he arrives at Walt's house, for example, there is a close-up of a pair of red shoes. (Dorothy's "There's-no-place-like-home" ruby slippers.) Although Travis and Hunter both wear red when they begin their search for Jane, neither she nor Hunter wears it in the film's penultimate scene in which the two of them reconnect, and the final shot of them embracing is framed to eliminate the red highlights in the hotel room. It thus remains Travis's color, one he takes with him at film's end.

Betz suggests that this last scene of Travis driving off, after restoring the relationship between mother and son, was inspired by the end of *Equinox Flower* in which Hirayama travels by train to Hiroshima to restore his relationship with Setsuko.[22] Several arguments can be made against any direct connection here, however. First, quite a few characters in both Wenders's and Ozu's films travel on trains. Ozu's honeymooning couples, for example, travel toward a new life much as Hirayama travels to restore a familial relationship. By contrast, Wenders's characters travel toward uncertain destinations that leave them untethered to family bonds. Driving away, Travis, in this instance, evokes Ethan Edwards of *The Searchers* (John Ford, 1956)—leaving the family with which he is too uncivilized to remain—more than Hirayama in *Equinox Flower*. The search for Jane itself echoes the search for Debbie in *The Searchers*, and once the young woman is restored to her family, the man who facilitated that restoration must leave.

Betz also argues a connection between the father-daughter farewells in *Late Spring* and the speech that Marion makes to Damiel, the fallen angel in Wenders's *Wings of Desire* (*Der Himmel über Berlin*, 1987), and Damiel's subsequent interior monologue referencing his love for Marion. He also posits a connection between the twin bar scenes in *Late Spring* and the twin concert/bar scenes in *Wings of Desire*.[23] This, too, seems credible. Wenders ends *Wings of Desire* with a dedication to Ozu (as well as to Francois Truffaut and Andrei Tarkovsky) and includes a *nihonga*-esque print above the heroine's bed.

I agree with Betz's assertion that *Paris, Texas* is the "more complete of Wenders' reworkings [of Ozu's films]," which makes sense because it is the Wenders film most focused on family.[24] In one of his earliest interviews Wenders praised the families he encountered in Ozu's films. They are traditional, he says, but not repressive; "because they all deal with the disintegration of the family, everybody is able to breathe."[25] Later he would credit Ozu with portraying "the universal family," which, he insists, "has become imaginable and understandable through Ozu's films."[26] *Paris, Texas* has one of those "universal families," alternately disintegrating and recombining throughout the course of the film.

Ozu's films served as a refuge for Wenders. In one interview he says that they "heal . . . the eyes," and they clearly served as a kind of second home.[27] Like his alienated characters, Wenders grew up in a city leveled by Allied bombing, in a Germany that was occupied by four of the Allied powers, was subsequently host to just under 400 American military bases, and would remain divided between East and West until the director was in his mid-forties. In addition, it was responsible for unspeakable crimes (and in Wenders's youth Germans who had lived through the Nazi period did *not* speak about the Holocaust). American culture filled this cultural void for Wenders, particularly rock and roll and American movies. But as he matured he began to resent the United States' hegemony in nearly everything, particularly filmmaking and film distribution.

To Wenders, Ozu's Japan was a place to refresh one's soul. Japan had also suffered militarism, war, occupation, and hosted innumerable American military bases, but you wouldn't know it from Ozu's late films, which, beginning with *Late Spring,* consciously portrayed a Japan that had survived intact. In his 1985 *Tokyo-Ga,* Wenders searches in vain for Ozu's Tokyo. "I had . . . a longing for Tokyo like for no other city . . . No other city and its people has ever felt so familiar and so intimate." His plaintive narration suggests the loss of a home that he had imagined from Ozu's films.

In his discursive, five-hour *Until the End of the World* (*Bis ans Ende der Welt,* 1991) Wenders recreates that home, filming a lengthy sequence in a Hakone *ryokan* (inn), whose beauty, peace, and traditional architecture evoke Ozu's Japan. Mr. and Mrs. Mori, who own the inn, are played by Ozu veterans Chishu Ryu and Kuniko Miyake (Figure 12.1), both of whom passed away the following year. Within this "paradise" (Wenders's word), the hero regains his sight, reveals his real name, turns out to be an idealist instead of a crook, and reciprocates the heroine's love. As an additional Ozu touch, two naughty boys are caught spying on the lovers, played by William Hurt and Solveig Dommartin.

The working methods of these two directors were, of course, completely different: Ozu, studied, meticulous, dictatorial, versus Wenders' freewheeling spontaneity. In *Tokyo-Ga,* cameraman Atsuta describes how everyone crept around Ozu's sets so as

Figure 12.1: Chishu Ryu and Kuniko Miyake play innkeepers in Wim Wenders's *Until the End of the World.*

238   *Ozu*

not to disturb the camera once it was locked in place for a shot. In contrast, Ryu notes wryly that Wenders "shoots as if he's really savoring the moment."[28]

Peter Handke

Wim Wenders and Nobel laureate Peter Handke have been friends since Wenders's film school days and have collaborated on a number of feature films: *The Goalie's Anxiety at the Penalty Kick*, *Wrong Move* (*Falsche Bewegung*, 1975), *Wings of Desire*, and, more recently, *The Beautiful Days of Aranjuez*, (*Les beaux jours d'Aranjuez*, 2016). After discovering Ozu's films in the early 1970s, Wenders introduced Handke to them, and Handke enthusiastically peppered his 1977 film *The Left-Handed Woman* (*Die linkshändige Frau*) with references to Ozu. He begins the film with a train station and a train passing through it and ends it with a train rushing past the camera, a hold on the grass rippling in the wind, created by the passing train, followed by a shot of the train from behind as it disappears down the track.

Handke's most obvious homage to Ozu is based on the famous vase sequence in *Late Spring*. His heroine, Marianne, sits on the floor in her ironing room, her head buried in her knees and covered by her arms. The camera pans from her to a poster-sized photograph on the wall, holds on the photograph, then pans back to Marianne, who now sits with her head raised and face resolute. Like Noriko in *Late Spring*, her mood changes in the time that we are shown an object in the room, in this instance the photograph. In case we have any doubt that Handke means to quote Ozu here, the photograph on the wall is that of the Japanese director. And it is not just any shot of Ozu but the one that appears on page 192 of Donald Richie's *Ozu*. Handke quotes not only the vase sequence in *Late Spring* but Richie's interpretation of it. Although Ozu cuts to the vase twice, Richie mentions only one shot of the vase. Handke, who pans instead of cuts, likewise shows the photograph only once, creating a neat package of Marianne/ photograph/Marianne that clearly shows her change of mood. Ozu's sequence is much less concise; it goes: Noriko/vase/Noriko (mood has changed)/vase/cut to Ryoanji.

The ending of *Left-Handed Woman* appears to have been based on the ending of *Tokyo Story*, where the director cuts between shots of Onomichi, Kyoko in her classroom, Kyoko looking out the window as Noriko's train passes, Noriko on the train and final shots of the train, the father at home, and Onomichi harbor. Noriko is traveling to a new life, tied nevertheless to the two women in Onomichi with which she is/was in sympathy: sister-in-law Kyoko and her dead mother-in-law. Meanwhile, her father-in-law contemplates life alone without his wife. At the end of *Left-Handed Woman*, there are numerous quick cuts showing the woman at home finishing her translation of Flaubert, views of her Paris suburb, her son swinging in the yard, her house, the street corner where she lives, the local train station, and the passing train. These shots tell us that she is forging ahead with her new life, alone but whole.

At the center of the film's story is the heroine Marianne's existential desire for her husband to leave her so that she can live alone. There is nothing in particular wrong

The Ozu Touch   239

with the marriage; she simply wants to be alone and independent. Handke sees this quest for self-sufficiency in heroic terms and, consequently, what he borrows from Ozu is used for purposes that are, essentially, opposite to Ozu's, for whose characters living alone is incredibly sad. Handke fills the film with Ozu-like "empty" shots and portentous silences—Marianne rarely speaks—that take on a larger-than-life heroic aspect rather than the measured quietude of Ozu's films.

Marianne's house (in reality beyond the means of her middle-manager husband) is large and sparsely but exquisitely furnished. It renders beautifully stark, architectonically perfect still-life compositions that enhance her mystique but overshoot the aims of Ozu, poet of the everyday, about whom Wenders would say, "[N]othing tried to be bigger or more beautiful or more important than it was."[29]

When Handke places Marianne and her father on a railed-in bluff overlooking Paris, they discuss the dangers (hence the heroism) of living alone. The scene recalls a number of Ozu setups where characters stand against a railing or bridge: the family outing in *Equinox Flower*, the fathers on the bridge in Gamagori in the same film, Noriko standing against the railing in Kiyomizu-dera while apologizing to Onodera in *Late Spring*. In the Ozu films, these scenes involve personal relationships being repaired, but in Handke's film the subject is the heroism of living alone.

The Left-Handed Woman had other mentors besides Ozu: Wenders himself, whom Handke had initially hoped would direct the film; John Ford, whose "mythic" images he hoped to emulate; Andrew Wyeth, whose paintings Handke and cameraman Robbie Müller studied; as well as Walker Evans, a book of whose photographs is included in the film.[30] If Wenders and Ozu celebrated the ordinary, Wyeth and Evans elevated it to the heroic, to which Ford added the "mythic." *The Left-Handed Woman* attempts to synthesize these competing attitudes and attractions. It acknowledges Ozu without actually subscribing to the spirit of his films or that of the devices in his films that it copies.[31]

Kohei Oguri

Kohei Oguri's *Muddy River* (*Doro no kawa*, 1981) looks back at the postwar years, whose style of cinema Oguri wished to emulate, specifically the films of Ozu. Filmed in black and white, its story centers on ten-year-old Nobuo, whose father, Shinpei Itakura, a veteran, has tried to reboot his life after the war by leaving his first wife and marrying the much younger Sadako, Nobuo's mother. Itakura dotes on Nobuo, his only child, but suffers from both survivor guilt and guilt for abandoning his first wife.

Nobuo befriends two other children, Kiichi and Ginko, who live on a houseboat that has, shortly before the film's story begins, tied up across the river from the Itakuras' restaurant. The children's mother, Shoko Matsumoto, is a prostitute, who sequesters herself in one half of the boat while her impoverished children take care of her and fend for themselves in the other half. The seaminess of their lives falls away when they play with Nobuo, however, and he remains clueless about their mother's profession until one unfortunate evening, which effectively ends the friendship. The next day the houseboat pulls up anchor and departs. Nobuo runs along the riverfront, hoping to get a last look at his friend, but Kiichi, understanding what has transpired, remains out of sight.

A film about little boys, *Muddy River* suggests elements from a number of Ozu films: the children's play on display in *I Was Born, But . . .* and *An Inn in Tokyo*, the disillusionment of the sons in *I Was Born, But . . .* , and the child neglect foregrounded in *Passing Fancy* and *Tenement Gentleman*. Like Kohei in *Tenement Gentleman*, Nobuo is a bed-wetter, and a long shot of futons hanging out to air is reminiscent of both *Tenement Gentleman* and the laundered underpants hanging out to dry in *Ohayo*.

After admonishing Nobuo not to wet his bed, Itakura muses that it will be eleven years before the boy is twenty. "Will I live that long?" he asks, echoing grandma Hirayama in *Tokyo Story*. A shot of an older neighbor praying to her *butsudan* recalls the grandmother in *Ohayo* praying to hers. The humor inherent in the *Ohayo* grandmother's actions is evoked by the same neighbor in *Muddy River* when she announces that Nobuo's bed-wetting means he's "a tree growing in water," who will one day be strong and flourishing.

The Itakura restaurant is reminiscent of the restaurants owned by the Choko Iida characters in Ozu's early films. A scene in which Nobuo sneaks cold drinks out of the restaurant's refrigerator to take to Kiichi appears to be modeled on similar kitchen thievery in both *I Was Born, But . . .* and *Ohayo*. Another in which Ginko reminds Kiichi to say "good evening" (*konban wa*) instead of the all-purpose "good day" (*konnichi wa*) when they first visit Nobuo's parents is reminiscent of the focus on the greetings associated with "small talk" in *Ohayo*, particularly when Kiichi immediately forgets and blurts out "*konnichi wa*" upon his arrival. A sequence on a train is also reminiscent of Ozu.

Stylistically, *Muddy River* has little in common with Ozu's work. The second half of the film contains considerable night photography and many high-angle shots. In several instances, Oguri uses flashbacks of words or images Nobuo has seen or heard earlier in the film. At one point he has Kiichi remembering, in flashbacks, his school days before his father died, which has occurred before the film's story begins. Unlike Ozu's films, which were mainly shot on studio sets, this one was shot mainly on the eponymous river, which itself becomes a character.

Muddy River opens with a close-up of pebbles splashing in water, followed by a cut to Nobuo throwing the pebbles from a bridge. While this recalls the cart-before-the-horse editing that was typical of Ozu's early films, it occurs only here, during the opening credits; by 1981 such opaque introductions were not unusual in mainstream films.

In Nobuo's home an insect-repelling incense coil, Ozu's ubiquitous symbol of transience, is shown in extreme close-up, framed by a window, through which we see the houseboat in extreme long shot. The Ozuesque coil may be intended to suggest the transience of life on the houseboat and/or the fragility of the children's friendship.

Muddy River is more melodramatic than Ozu's work but less so than Mizoguchi's and less pessimistic than Naruse's, drawing on the ethos of many postwar directors but reaching its own conclusions. Whereas Ozu was inclined toward universals and

The Ozu Touch   241

generalities—life is short, children are disappointing, salarymen have no autonomy and thus lead frustrating lives, marriage is important because it insures that human life continues, and so on—Oguri, looking back on a bygone era, is more specific. Itakura, taking as examples his friend Shinoda, the carter, rolled over and killed by his cart when he hauled too heavy a load, and Kiichi's dead boatman father, forced to carry cargo in a storm, indicts the period: "Japan renounced war; now it got rich using America's war in Korea, but we're left to die poor like during the war." None of Ozu's characters is as bitter or conflicted as Itakura; yet, Ozu-like, he remains affable and kind. Later, a newspaper announces, "The postwar period is over," but not, Itakura believes, for those that the war chewed up and spat out.

Like Ozu's older men, those in *Muddy River* have suffered in the war and yet are oddly nostalgic for it. In a pivotal plot point, Itakura disappears and is unable to take the boys to the local Tenjin festival as promised, which ultimately leads to Nobuo's discovery of Kiichi's mother with a customer. Itakura apologizes to his son, explaining that he had a sudden desire to see the sea at Maizuru, the port where he landed on his return from Siberia. (Maizuru was a major disembarkation port for Japanese soldiers repatriated from China.)

Nominated for an Academy Award, *Muddy River* is a beautiful and deeply affecting film that recalls Ozu in its sweetness, simplicity, and concern with the lower classes. Although set in 1956, it draws on Ozu's pre- and postwar work while generally capturing the look of Japanese cinema from the 1950s.[32]

Wayne Wang

Like Wenders and Ozu himself, Wayne Wang had a background in painting when he decided to go into filmmaking.[33] (Both Wang and Wenders had intended to study medicine when they became interested in the arts as undergraduates.) Wang's *Dim Sum: A Little Bit of Heart* (1985) incorporates more Ozu references into its eighty-eight minutes than do any of the other films documented in this chapter. The narrative itself is based on "an old Japanese movie where the widow parent pretend to get to remarry so the daughter won't have to keep sacrificing herself" (i.e., *Late Spring* or *Late Autumn*) as Uncle Tam, one of the characters, explains. The story concerns a mother, Mrs. Tam, and her daughter, Geraldine, who live in a residential neighborhood outside San Francisco's Chinatown. The daughter has a boyfriend, Richard, but hesitates to marry him. The mother, who, because of a fortune-teller's prediction, believes she will die soon, wants to see her daughter married but fears being left alone. Uncle Tam, her brother-in-law, offers to marry her, but she refuses to consider his offer.

Dim Sum references at least four other Ozu films in the dialogue, mise-en-scène, or story elements. Uncle Tam, for example, owns a bar like Kawai in *Early Spring*. He accuses Mrs. Tam of being inconsistent in her desire to both keep Geraldine with her and marry her off, much as the mother in *Equinox Flower* accuses her husband of inconsistency in his attitude toward their daughter's marriage. A shot of Uncle Tam and Geraldine sitting on a sea wall echoes the Atami seawall sequence in *Tokyo Story*. The most extensive copying of story elements and dialogue, however, occurs when Geraldine's friend Julia returns from visiting her mother in Hong Kong. Her family had gathered because the mother was thought to be dying, but she recovered, and the children returned to their homes. Sometime later Julia receives notice that her mother has in fact died. "She should have died when we were there. She was stubborn, always did as she pleased," laments Julia, who then sobs, "She was alone when she died." Both the sentiments and the circumstances are drawn from *The End of Summer* where the aunt from Nagoya comments, somewhat callously, on her brother Manbei's death, "He should have died when we were all gathered earlier [when Manbei collapsed and was feared dying]. He did as he pleased his whole life," she says, proceeding to elaborate, then suddenly dissolves into tears. Manbei has died in his mistress's house, not alone like Julia's mother, but away from his family.

Wang's attempt to imitate Ozu is most obvious in his use of empty shots or shots which start out "empty" into which characters move. These number well over sixty. Many of these are within Mrs. Tam's home. As with Ozu, we understand shots of outdoor spaces as being proximate to locations we have just left or are about to enter. As with Ozu, some of these shots are freighted with meaning. Four are of the family's shoes, left at the bottom of the stairs near the front door. According to Roger Ebert, Wang sees this image of Western-style shoes left at the door as summarizing the conundrum of Chinese-American life: characters with Western values and accouterments entering "a home . . . still run according to Chinese values."[34]

Most of the film unfolds in Mrs. Tam's house, where a large dining table serves as the anchor around which many scenes unfold. In addition to actual action around the table, there are sixteen empty shots of this table and an additional six of the birdcage (with or without the surrounding plants) located behind the table at one end of the dining room. Often the empty table simply begins or concludes a scene that takes place there, but it and other empty shots sometimes follow Ozu in indicating absence. When Richard, the fiancé, has left after a weekend visit, we see the empty table in the dining room, the empty living room, and the empty stairway.

Mrs. Tam is also associated with a large, professional-grade sewing machine, of which there are four empty shots. One, when she is away in China, is used to indicate her absence.

Wang incorporates many other Ozu-isms. A profile in close-up of an old man drinking at Uncle Tam's bar echoes shots of Chishu Ryu sitting at a bar in a number of Ozu films. Meanwhile, a baseball game plays on the soundtrack as in *An Autumn Afternoon*. An unknown family in Chinatown taking a group photograph recalls the many instances of group photos taken in Ozu's films. David Bordwell has pointed to the *sojikei* (acting in unison) compositions in the film, of which there are at least six.[35] There is one very obvious 180° cut during the New Year's dinner in which the characters seated around the table flop from one side of the screen to other as we cut from a long

The Ozu Touch   243

shot of the mother at one end of the table, passing out gift money, to Uncle Tam at the other end, doing the same.

Wang uses "*ma*-space" shots, in which characters come into what has started out as an empty space multiple times, particularly in connection with the stairway in Mrs. Tam's house. The stairway begins as an empty shot seven times, and in each of these a character comes into the frame going up or down the stairs. A shot of the empty living room into which Geraldine enters vacuuming is reminiscent of Fumiko cleaning her house in *Tokyo Story* (see Chapter 9). Particularly creative are several shots in Uncle Tam's bar. One is a close-up of the Wurlitzer jukebox, from behind which Geraldine, who has been changing the records, suddenly emerges. Another is a close-up of candles, which are burning in front of the bar's seated Buddha. Uncle Tam's face comes into the shot as he blows them out, and then withdraws, leaving the smoking candles.

Wang also uses Ozu's cart-before-the-horse editing, i.e., moving from a close shot, which obscures context, to a longer shot that reveals it. After the close-up of the candles in Uncle Tam's bar, for example, an extreme long shot shows the entire bar with Buddha and the blown-out candles at the very back. Prefacing shots of the family's New Year's dinner are a succession of close-ups indicating New Year's festivities: the bird cage decorated for the celebration, fake plum blossoms in a vase with candies in a dish in front of it, and firecrackers going off. In numerous other instances Wang employs this style of editing, in which the viewer is left guessing at what will follow.

Bordwell and others have read much more ambiguity into Ozu's stories than I believe exists, as I have argued in Chapter 4. Wang, too, may have believed Ozu's stories were ambiguous, for *Dim Sum* is redolent with ambiguity. (Like Ozu and Wenders, Wang is not very interested in plot.) Some of the film's ambiguities seem to be just poor storytelling, however. Why, for example, does Mrs. Tam have an industrial-grade sewing machine, and why does she always seem to be carrying around some sewing project? Is she a piece worker? We are never told. Why, after insisting she doesn't want to get married and leave her mother alone, does Geraldine suddenly move in with Julia? This development is entirely unmotivated.

There are, however, what appear to be deliberate ambiguities. After Richard's weekend visit, Geraldine comes down the stairs and, encountering her mother, asks if it wasn't a nice weekend. The mother says nothing and walks off. Is this because she found Richard and Geraldine in bed together and she disapproves? Or is it because she feels like a "third wheel," as her neighbor Mary suggests? Or is she worried that the couple's marrying may come sooner than she thinks? We are left to contemplate all these intersecting possibilities. Likewise, at the film's end, the mother announces that the fortune-teller has said she will not die at sixty-two after all. She tells Geraldine that there is no rush for her to get married just as Geraldine tries to tell her that she has made [marriage] plans with Richard. Is Geraldine crying at the end because she's relieved to see her mother happy or because her mother's desires are continuing to impinge on her wedding plans? Does Geraldine actually get married and leave home? Are her shoes still among those at the bottom of stairs at the end of the film? Though subtle, Ozu never left such gaping ambiguities, but Wang may have felt he was following the master in creating these in his own film.

In adapting Ozu's eccentric style to his own story of family relationships, Wang at times demonstrates great creativity, but Ozu's style does not an Ozu film make. Bordwell characterizes *Dim Sum* as an example of the "leisurely and loose plotting that characterized independent film of the period" without the "elaborate variations and minute adjustments" that comprise Ozu's parametric style.[36] Vincent Canby, who reviewed the film at the time, was less generous, insisting that it had "no spine."[37] It was, nevertheless, one of the first to explore the Asian-American family in a realistic way—its predecessor having been *Flower Drum Song* (Henry Koster, 1961)—and if the Ozu-isms seem overdone and lacking their progenitor's prowess, it was, nevertheless, fitting that Wang should have based this Asian-American film on an Asian director's work.

Masayuki Suo

The paucity of communication between men and women in Japan as compared to that in Western nations, described in Chapter 10 and which Ozu took for granted, had, by the 1990s, reached the point of absurdity. Enough Japanese wives had, in protest, ceased having sex with their husbands for it to be considered a trend, earning the moniker "the second virginity." And with Japan's birthrate plummeting, it was frontpage news.[38] Masayuki Suo begins his film *Shall We Dance?* (*Shall we dansu*, 1996) with this assessment of 1990s couples: "In Japan, ballroom dancing is regarded with much suspicion. In a country where married couples don't go out arm in arm, much less say "I love you" out loud, intuitive understanding is everything. The idea that a husband and wife should embrace and dance in front of others is beyond embarrassing."[39]

Suo, who studied with Ozu scholar Shigehiko Hasumi, is famous for reworking Ozu's films, first as softcore pornography in *An Abnormal Family* (*Hentai kazoku: Aniki no yome-san*, 1984), which referenced a number of Ozu's postwar father-daughter dramas, particularly *Late Spring*, and later as student comedy in *Sumo Do, Sumo Don't* (*Shiko funjatta*, 1992).[40] *Shall We Dance?* reimagines Ozu's salaryman film *Early Spring*, in which an attractive, young married man seeks relief from his boring job by having an affair with a flirtatious fellow commuter. In both films, the handsome hero is named Sugiyama.

In *Shall We Dance?* Sugiyama is drawn to the sad, longing face of a beautiful young woman staring out the window of a ballroom dance studio, which he passes each night on his commute home. One night he gets off the train at this stop and begins dancing lessons. The young woman, Mai, rebuffs his advances, but in dancing he finds the liberation and excitement he has longed for. He fails, however, to communicate any of his enthusiasm for dancing to his wife, who, rather than ask him why he is suddenly buoyant and happy, hires a private detective to follow him.

Sugiyama's dance class illustrates well the separation of the sexes in Japan: three men must dance with one another much of the time because in general the only women

The Ozu Touch 245

at the studio are the teachers and the loud, obnoxious Toyoko. Toyoko eventually becomes the diffident Sugiyama's partner and proves to be a loyal friend but not before her taunts cause two male characters to burst into tears, after which they confess to having been rejected by other women.

If male humiliation is a common thread in Ozu's films, Suo takes it to a new level. Sugiyama himself suffers complete humiliation, stumbling during a dance competition when he realizes his wife and daughter are in the audience. Thus men's humiliation in this film arises mainly from the rift between the sexes.

Suo continues the broad comedy of *Sumo Do, Sumo Don't* via the antics of Sugiyama's classmates, his rumba-consumed officemate Aoki, and Toyoko.[41] At the same time, he takes a deeply felt, compassionate look at middle-class Japanese life: its expectations, repressions, conformity, and the separation of the sexes. Like the couple in *Early Spring*, Sugiyama and his wife reconcile. She has felt left out and injured by his secreted dance obsession, and, at his daughter's insistence, he agrees to teach her to dance. (The intervention of the daughter in prodding an older generation toward a more liberated view of marriage is similar to the role played by the young women in Ozu's *Equinox Flower*.)

However, the film does not climax here. Rather, having given up his pursuit of dancing after his wife discovers it, Sugiyama must reconcile with his dancing friends and most of all with Mai, who, in helping him learn to dance, has confronted her own self-involvement and repression and decided to resume her stalled performance career in England. In essence Sugiyama must acknowledge his longing for more than a life in the suburbs and continue to pursue the liberation he has found in dancing.[42]

Where Ozu's characters usually reconcile with the status quo, Suo urges his to break out of the limitations of Japan's postwar world, which lingered in society despite the opportunities afforded by greater "internationalization," the catch phrase of 1990s Japan. With its blend of comedy and pathos and its spot-on depiction of middle-class Japanese caught between convention and fulfillment, *Shall We Dance?* is a tour de force worthy of Ozu.

Suo knows Ozu's films well and makes numerous nods to the fabled director in *Shall We Dance?* particularly early on in the film, which begins with a close-up of water splashing into a puddle, after which the camera rises to show the feet and legs of several people and finally the bodies and faces of Sugiyama and his fellow accountants as they return from a bar in the early evening. In an exchange that involves a 180° cut, Sugiyama explains to his drunken female officemate that he never thinks about whether he likes or dislikes his job; it's simply his job.

The film then cuts to an overhead shot of an elevated commuter train and then to Sugiyama on his train (the Seibu–Ikebukuro line). Like the commuter trains in *I Was Born, But* . . . , which do not signify passage but rather the back and forth of going nowhere, Sugiyama's train shuttles him back and forth from home to office, but at the same time it affords him a glimpse of Mai in her studio and thus an escape. *Early Spring's* Sugiyama also finds diversion via his daily commute, but an illegitimate one, whereas

Suo's Sugiyama, who hoped for an extramarital affair with Mai, instead finds real healing in his pursuit of dance.

In one early sequence, Sugiyama looks out his office window at the river with its boats and bridges, a train far in the background; these do not signify passage in the sense of Ozu's life cycle, but they do so in the sense of going somewhere (in contrast to the going nowhere of the commuter train). Watching them, Sugiyama seems to long for an escape he cannot quite yet imagine.

Bridges also appear when Sugiyama is repeatedly shown riding his bike across a series of small ones either to or from his train. The bridges here, like the commuter trains, do not signify passage but rather the separation of home and work and, by extension, of men and women. The first time we see him ride across the bridge, an "empty shot" of the front of his house, with the bicycle parked beside a small red car, follows. It signifies both the home in the suburbs he has worked so hard for and the fact that he has arrived there. Ozu-like, Suo elides his hero's actual arrival and next shows him taking off his shoes in the entryway while being greeted by his wife.

Quoting the first scene in *Early Spring*, Suo shows Sugiyama waking to the sound of his alarm clock. However, the wife rises first in *Early Spring* while her husband lingers in bed; in *Shall We Dance?* Sugiyama gets up and makes his own breakfast. Women have made some progress in Suo's Japan, but *etiketto* and considerateness do not equal adequate communication between the sexes.

In another Ozuesque shot, Suo hints at how his hero's fate will differ from that of *Early Spring*'s Sugiyama. In his films involving salarymen, Ozu frequently showed close-ups of office buildings whose rows of windows fill the screen with a flat, rectilinear, prison-like grid. Suo includes a close-up of the upper stories of office buildings in downtown Tokyo but transforms Ozu's grid into a mélange of buildings going in many different directions. Whereas Ozu's workers are trapped, Suo's will find a way out.

As the film progresses, Suo's style departs increasingly from Ozu's. His comedy becomes very broad, dancers whirl across the screen, tracked by an ever-moving camera, and he makes use of voice-over, not only in the opening monologue but in a long letter from Mai to Sugiyama in which she explains the self-knowledge coaching him brought her. Suo uses montage sequences and flashbacks, and at times his characters confess their feelings to one another much more extensively than Ozu's ever do.

In a particularly poignant exchange, the older dance teacher, Tamako, describes how, as a child, she fell in love with the film version of *The King and I*, which, more broadly, points to the love affair with American movies that Ozu, Suo, Wenders and others have, across the decades, found to be both liberating and inspiring. Similar to Ozu, who skipped school to watch mainly American movies, Suo has confessed to watching films instead of studying for his college entrance exams. "Whenever I saw an Ozu film," he says, "I felt completely happy from beginning to end. I didn't want to leave the world that Ozu had created."[43]

The films described in this chapter have little in common, yet all have a direct, obvious, and, in most cases, proclaimed connection to Ozu. Their plots involving little

The Ozu Touch   247

boys, marriageable daughters, and unfulfilled salarymen derive from Ozu, as do certain stylistic idiosyncrasies like 180° cuts, long holds on empty rooms, the evocation of *ma* space, or cart-before-the-horse editing. Wenders and Suo both have a sustained relationship with Ozu's films, but Suo, being Japanese, has internalized Ozu's ethos in a way that Wenders never could. If Ozu's films made him happy, Suo does not seem to regard them as "sacred," as Wenders has described them, but as objects of study, reflection, and adaptation. He has moved from burlesquing Ozu's films, to milking them for comedy, to creating a masterpiece derived from Ozu's appraisal of middle-class life. One hopes that Ozu would be pleased to know that at least one of his imitators had come close to reaching his own level of creativity, skill, and understanding of the Japanese everyman.

Notes

1. Jinhee Choi, "Ozuesque as a Sensibility Or, on the Notion of Influence," in Choi, *Reorienting Ozu*, 79.
2. Bordwell, *Poetics*, 25.
3. Ozu was notorious for the demands he placed on his actors. Choko Iida recalls sitting around with other cast members after a day's shooting and wishing Ozu "would die or something by tomorrow." Richie, *Ozu*, 144.
4. See Choi, *Reorienting Ozu*; Stein and DiPaolo, *Ozu International*; also David Desser, "Space and Narrative in *The Makioka Sisters*," in *Kon Ichikawa*, ed. James Quandt (Toronto, ON: Cinematheque Ontario, 1998), 373–83.
5. Klein sets her discussion of the trilogy against the background of the Eisenhower era people-to-people programs, aimed at fostering goodwill for the United States in its postwar battle against communism. *Flower Drum Song*, third in the trilogy, is the only one of Hollywood's Asia films to feature an entirely Asian/Asian-American cast (with the exception of Juanita Hall, who was African American) and the only one no part of which is set in Asia! It riffs on what it means to be Chinese American, much like the independent film *Dim Sum*, instead of charting the reactions of Westerners confronting the exotic East as do Hollywood's other Asia films. See Christina Klein, *Cold War Orientalism: Asia in the Middlebrow Imagination, 1945–1961* (Berkeley, CA: University of California Press, 2003).
6. Letter to the author, August 28, 2003.
7. Although not every Japan film includes a strip show, *A Girl Named Tamiko* (John Sturges, 1962) includes visits to Tokyo's seamier entertainments.
8. "Ozu on Ozu: The Talkies," 5.
9. Jan Dawson, *Wim Wenders* (New York: New York Zoetrope, 1976), 8.
10. Bill Thompson, "A Young German Filmmaker and His Road Movies," *1000 Eyes* (November 1976), 22.
11. Richie, *Ozu*, 25–26.
12. Kinowelt Home Entertainment, *"Paris, Texas"* (Wim Wenders interviewed by Roger Willemsen, Munich: 2001). This interview is included with the Criterion Collection's *Paris, Texas* DVD.
13. Shizuo Yamanouchi in Igarashi, *Ozu's Films from Behind the Scenes*.
14. Dawson, *Wenders*, 8.

15. Michel Boujut, *Wim Wenders* (Paris: Edilig, 1982), 8.
16. Wim Wenders, *The Road Trilogy* (Criterion, 2016) [booklet], 16.
17. Dawson *Wenders*, 9.
18. Bordwell, *Poetics*, 8.
19. In post-Occupation *Equinox Flower*, the family drinks not Coke but Bireley's Orange, a non-carbonated soft drink that originated in California but was unknown to most Americans living stateside. Like Harold Lloyd's personality, it was sweet and bland and became as ubiquitous in 1950s Japan as Lloyd had been in the 1920s. A poster for Bireley's is placed high on the wall of the pachinko parlor in *The Flavor of Green Tea Over Rice* and appears next to Chishu Ryu in close-ups of him early in the first pachinko parlor sequence.
20. Mark Betz, "Wenders Travels with Ozu," in Choi, *Reorienting Ozu*, 233–47.
21. In 1982, a time when Wenders was based in New York, its Japan Society held a complete retrospective of Ozu's films, and a group of silents from that retrospective subsequently toured the US.
22. Betz, "Wenders Travels with Ozu," 244–45.
23. Betz, "Wenders Travels with Ozu," 242–43.
24. Betz, "Wenders Travels with Ozu," 244.
25. Dawson, Wenders, 10.
26. Kogi Tanaka, *Talking with Ozu* [Ozu to kataru]. (Tokyo: Shochiku, 1993). This short film is available on Criterion's *Tokyo Story* DVD. Wenders repeats these sentiments in other filmed interviews.
27. Rintaro Mayuzumi, *Wim Wenders in Tokyo for Until the End of the World*, (Tokyo: NHK, 1990). Available on Criterion's *Until the End of the World* DVD.
28. Mayuzumi, *Wim Wenders in Tokyo*.
29. Carlos Clarens, "King of the Road," *Film Comment* (September–October 1977), 45.
30. See Geist, *The Cinema of Wim Wenders*, 141.
31. The film also includes, somewhat inexplicably, footage of the family's clapping game from *Tokyo Chorus*.
32. For more on this film, see Keiko McDonald, *Reading a Japanese Film: Cinema in Context* (Honolulu, HI: University of Hawai'i Press, 2006), 122–35.
33. Gina Marchetti, *The Chinese Diaspora on American Screens: Race Sex, and Cinema* (Philadelphia, PA: Temple University Press, 2012), 168.
34. https://www.rogerebert.com/reviews/dim-sum-a-little-bit-of-heart-1985.
35. David Bordwell, "Watch Again! Look Well! Look!" in Choi, *Reorienting Ozu*, 24–25.
36. Bordwell, "Watch Again! Look Well! Look!," 26.
37. Vincent Canby, *New York Times*, August 9, 1985.
38. For a more nuanced description of this situation, see Muriel Jolivet, *Japan: the Childless Society? The Crisis of Motherhood* (London: Routledge, 1997), 162ff.
39. This voice-over introduction exists only in those copies of the film distributed with English subtitles since the Japanese already knew this about themselves. Japanese copies of the film instead gave basic information about ballroom dancing. Linda C. Ehrlich, "*Shall We Dance?* (*Shall we dansu*, Japan, 1996. Directed by Suo Masayuki)," *Asian Cinema* (Spring 1998), 103.

40. For a detailed analysis of *An Abnormal Family* and more on Suo's Ozu-obsession, see Kirsten Cather, "Perverting Ozu: Suo Masayuki's *Abnormal Family*," *Journal of Japanese and Korean Cinema* 2, no. 2 (2010): 131–45.
41. Eccentric officemate Aoki's full name is Tomio Aoki, the real name of Ozu's enfant terrible Tokkankozo. Actor Naoto Takenaka, who plays Aoki, was given the same name in Suo's *Sumo Do, Sumo Don't*.
42. The version of the film distributed in Japan and Hong Kong contains eighteen minutes that were eliminated from the North American version. They are described in Ehrlich, "*Shall We Dance?*," 101–2. Ehrlich believes these give greater dimension to the women in the film, but neither scene appears to alter the film's depiction of the separation between the sexes.
43. Ehrlich, "*Shall We Dance?*," 96.

Afterword Part III: But is it modern?

The question of whether or not Ozu can be called a "modernist" has roiled cinema scholarship as much as the "meaning of the vase" in *Late Spring*.[1] As we have seen, traditional aesthetics in Japan are "modern" by Western standards; in fact they influenced Western modernism. Meanwhile, Japanese artists and consumers have at times embraced Western modernism, which their own culture had a hand in creating. In 1920s and 1930s Japan, "modernism" could mean anything Western. By this standard, Ozu was certainly "modern," as much for embracing Lloyd and Lubitsch as for looking to more avant-garde directors like von Sternberg, Lang, Pabst, and Ruttmann for inspiration.

Does Ozu's own idiosyncratic style make him modern or simply idiosyncratic? The best answer comes from Ozu himself, whose wistful comment to Takashi Kawamata, "I used to be one [avant-garde filmmaker] myself when the studio was in Kamata," suggests he saw himself as modern in the sense of avant-garde, at least in the Kamata days.[2]

Tadao Sato documents a youthful Ozu pestering established director Uzuhiko Ushiwara with the question, "What is the future of cinema?"[3] Merely an assistant cameraman at that time, he was nevertheless eager to push the envelope of what cinema could become.

Of the two posters hanging on the wall in Jiro's room in *Passing Fancy*, one is for the Tsukiji Little Theatre, a modern, leftwing, European-inspired theater, whose manifesto stated that it existed for drama, the future, and the people, and that it wanted a clean break from tradition.[4] Writing about the poster, Tadao Sato confirmed that "Ozu was the kind of director who paid very close attention to this kind of [décor]."[5] In other words, the poster wasn't there because it was handy but because Ozu wanted to promote the theater and proclaim himself sympathetic to its mission and/or to suggest that this film about the proletariat fit into its ethos.

Were Ozu's late films still modern or calcified, uninspired, and "old-fashioned" as some of his contemporary critics and certain film scholars have deemed them? Those close to Ozu when he made his late films have described him as being driven by an almost religious perfectionism.[6] Whether seen as parametric (Bordwell) or transcendental (Schrader), Ozu's films have been linked to those of Dreyer and Bresson,

Afterword Part III 251

modernists whose perfectionism explored religious subject matter.[7] In the last quarter of the twentieth century and the first quarter of the present one, Ozu's late films inspired avant-garde filmmakers around the world: Wenders and Handke, as we have seen, and numerous others, including Jim Jarmusch, Abbas Kiarostami, Claire Denis, and Hou Hsiao-hsien.

David Bordwell has judged *An Autumn Afternoon*, Ozu's last film, "in form and attitude a young man's work."[8] Such an assessment accords with the East Asian tradition which holds that fine artists improve with age, their late work having greater depth, subtlety, refinement, and value. In creating his late films, Ozu undoubtedly strove to fulfill the maxim repeated in *The Munekata Sisters*, "What is truly new never gets old." The history of art is, for the most part, the study of art that broke new ground, that was "modern" in its time and never got old. This is the work of Ozu.

Notes

1. See Mitsuhiro Yoshimoto, "The Difficulty of Being Radical: The Discipline of Film Studies and the Post-colonial World Order," in *Asian Cinemas: A Reader and Guide*, ed. Dimitris Eleftheriotis and Gary Needham (Honolulu, HI: University of Hawai'i Press, 2006), 27–40.
2. Igarashi, *Ozu's Films from Behind the Scenes*.
3. Sato, *Art of Yasujiro Ozu 6*, 92.
4. See Brian Powell, *Japan's Modern Theatre: A Century of Change and Continuity* (London: Japan Library, 2002), 58–65.
5. Sato, *Art of Yasujiro Ozu 5*, 95.
6. Inoue, *I Lived, But . . .*; Wenders, *Tokyo Ga*.
7. Bordwell, *Narration in the Fiction Film*, 275ff; Schrader, *Transcendental Style in Film*.
8. Bordwell, *Poetics*, 376.

Plot Synopses

For those readers who may not have seen all of Ozu's films, I include the following plot synopses for his extant films, along with the lead actors and information about existing digital versions. For complete, annotated filmographies in English for all of Ozu's films, readers should consult Donald Richie's *Ozu*, David Bordwell's *Ozu and the Poetics of Cinema*, or Kyoko Hirano's filmography in Kiju Yoshida's *Ozu's Anti-Cinema*.

Extant Silent Films, 1929–1935

Days of Youth (*Wakaki hi*, 1929)

Waseda student Watanabe (Ichiro Yuki) advertises his room for rent as a ploy to meet girls. When Chieko (Junko Matsui) shows up to take the room, Watanabe must move. Failing to find another place, he moves in with fellow student Yamamoto (Tatsuo Saito), who is also friends with Chieko. After some initial setbacks, both boys follow Chieko on a ski trip and, despite poor skiing skills, attempt to court her. However, they soon find out that she is there to become engaged to Hatamoto (Shinichi Himori), captain of the ski club. Despondent, the boys return to Tokyo. Undeterred by failure, Watanabe hangs another sign in the window, advertising their room for rent.

Ozu ensemble players Choko Iida, Takeshi Sakamoto, and Chishu Ryu also appear in this film in minor roles.

DVD available in a two-disc set, "The Student Comedies," issued by the British Film Institute, region 2 only.

I Graduated, But . . . (*Daigaku wa deta keredo*, 1929)

Nomoto (Minoru Takada), a recent graduate, turns down a job as a receptionist in a company because he feels it is beneath him. However, his mother (Utako Suzuki) has come to Tokyo with his fiancée, Machiko (Kinuyo Tanaka). Afraid to admit he does not have a job, Nomoto marries Machiko and only after his mother leaves confesses that he is unemployed. Without telling her husband, Machiko goes to work in a bar, where Nomoto sees her while on an outing with his friend Sugimura (Kenji Oyama). At home

254 Plot Synopses

he scolds Machiko for taking such a job but then admits it is he who has been irresponsible. He returns to the company he turned down, ready to become a receptionist, but they tell him the prior offer was just a test and offer him a good position instead.

Ozu ensemble player Takeshi Sakamoto has a small part.

Only ten minutes of this film survive and are included in the DVD set "The Student Comedies," issued by the British Film Institute, region 2 only.

A Straightforward Boy (Tokkan kozo, 1929)

Tatsuo Saito, Takeshi Sakamoto, and Tomio Aoki mug their way through this nonsense comedy, apparently based on O. Henry's "Ransom of Red Chief." Aoki would retain the name of this film as his stage name.

Thirteen minutes of this film survive and can be viewed on YouTube: https://www.youtube.com/watch?v=gshM6WBr1nU

Walk Cheerfully (Hogaraka ni ayume, 1930)

Kenji (Minoru Takada), a petty criminal and boxer, lives and works with Senko (Hisao Yoshitani). He falls in love with Yasue (Hiroko Kawasaki), a secretary, who works at the same company as Kenji's girlfriend, Chieko (Satoko Date). Yasue's boss (Takeshi Sakamoto) is trying to seduce her, so Chieko, aware that Kenji loves Yasue, helps the boss lure her to a love hotel. Kenji learns of the plan and rescues Yasue, but at the same time she realizes he is a criminal and rejects him. Vowing to go straight to win back Yasue, Kenji inspires Senko to do the same. Meanwhile, Yasue has been fired. All three find jobs at the same company, Kenji as a window washer and Senko as a driver. Kenji has not, however, been in contact with Yasue, who longs for him. Leaving work one day, she overhears Chieko and gangster Gunpei (Teruo Mori) trying to lure Kenji back to a life of crime. Kenji resists their overtures but is shot in the arm by Gunpei. Yasue and Senko come to his rescue, but the police show up soon after, having already arrested Chieko and Gunpei. Kenji and Senko willingly go to prison, eager to be cleansed of their criminal past. Upon their release, Yasue, her mother (Utako Suzuki), and her little sister (Nobuko Matsuzono) host a reunion for them.

Tomio Aoki (Tokkankozo) has a minor role.

DVD available in a three-disc set from Criterion's Eclipse Series 42: "Silent Ozu: Three Crime Dramas."

I Flunked, But . . . (Rakudai wa shita keredo, 1930)

Takahashi (Tatsuo Saito) lives with other Waseda students in a room above his aunt's house, where the boys can easily summon snacks from the bakery next door while they study. Takahashi and the bakery girl (Kinuyo Tanaka) are sweethearts. Takahashi has other friends as well, a network of students who work out elaborate, interdependent

Plot Synopses 255

cheating schemes, and, on the eve of their last, crucial exam, Takahashi is the designated lynchpin, assigned to write the answers on the back of his shirt. He does so, but early in the morning his landlady sees the marked-up shirt and sends it to the laundry. All of the boys in the cheating network flunk and must repeat their last year of college, while all of the roommates except Takahashi pass. Takahashi is despondent for a time, but when the roommates all fail to find jobs, he and his cronies are happy to be back in school, leading cheers for the school teams.

Chishu Ryu and Tomio Aoki (Tokkankozo) have minor roles.

DVD available in a two-disc set "The Student Comedies," issued by the British Film Institute, region 2 only.

That Night's Wife (*Sono yo no tsuma*, 1930)

Shuji Hashizume (Tokihiko Okada) robs an office to pay for his sick daughter's treatment. The police mount a massive search, but Hashizume eludes them and grabs a cab to get home. The cabbie turns out to be undercover detective Kagawa (Togo Yamamoto), but Hashizume's wife, Mayumi (Reiko Yagumo), uses her husband's pistol to keep him at bay while the couple watches over their child, whose illness has reached a crisis. When they nod off, Kagawa disarms them but agrees to delay arresting Hashizume so that he can stay with his daughter through the night. As day breaks, Kagawa feigns sleep, allowing Hashizume to escape, but he soon returns, preferring prison to a life on the run.

Tatsuo Saito plays the family's doctor and Chishu Ryu, a policeman.

DVD available in a three-disc set from Criterion's Eclipse Series 42: "Silent Ozu: Three Crime Dramas."

The Lady and the Beard (*Shukujo to hige*, 1931)

Absurdly old-fashioned to the point of wearing a beard and a samurai's padded underwear under his business suit, Kiichi Okajima (Tokihiko Okada) is a kendo champion and friend of young Baron Teruo Yukimoto (Ichiro Tsukida). On his way to the Baron's sister's birthday party, Okajima uses his kendo skills to foil an attempt by *moga* Satoko (Satoko Date) and her gang to rob Hiroko (Hiroko Kawasaki). At the party, the Baron's sister, Ikuko (Toshiko Iizuka), and her friends mock Okajima for his stubborn conservatism. Later he interviews for a job and again encounters Hiroko, who is the office receptionist. He fails to get the job, but Hiroko seeks him out to thank him for rescuing her earlier in the week and to suggest he might do better in interviews if he would shave his beard. He follows her advice and not only lands a job in a hotel-based travel agency, but, on a second trip to the Baron's home, excites the interest of sister Ikuko, who subsequently rejects a rich suitor. However, Okajima loves Hiroko. He visits her at home and later agrees to her mother's (Choko Iida) proposal that they marry. Satoko, however, appears at the hotel and tries to ensnare Okajima in a robbery. He foils her plot but meets her later and takes her to his room in an ostensible effort to reform her. She declares her love for him. He rejects her, but she remains in his room overnight. Ikuko and her family stop by in the morning. Shocked to find Satoko there, they retreat immediately, but Hiroko, who arrives shortly afterward, declares her faith in Okajima and remains. Touched by the couple's trust in one another, Satoko agrees to reform.

Mitsuko Yoshikawa plays the Baron's mother and Takeshi Sakamoto their butler.

DVD available in a two-disc set "The Student Comedies," issued by the British Film Institute, region 2 only.

Tokyo Chorus (*Tokyo no gassho*, 1931)

Insurance agent and father of three, Shinji Okajima (Tokihiko Okada) fights with his boss over the termination of an older employee, Yamada (Takeshi Sakamoto), and is fired. At home he fights with his son (Hideo Sugawara) to whom he has promised a bicycle. Eventually the boy gets his bicycle, but Okajima's daughter (Hideko Takamine) falls ill. To afford her medical treatment, Okajima sells his wife's kimonos. Unable to find another office job, he agrees to help his former teacher Omura (Tatsuo Saito) in his curry rice restaurant but soon discovers that his first duty will be to carry banners advertising the restaurant while Omura hands out leaflets. His wife Sugako's (Reiko Yagumo) dismay over her lost kimonos is nothing compared to her horror when, from a streetcar, her children spot their father carrying the banners. He explains that the job is only temporary until the teacher can find him something better, and she relents, offering to help out in the restaurant herself. In the last scene, Okajima's high school class gathers at the restaurant for a reunion with Omura, and Okajima is offered a job as an English teacher in a country town north of Tokyo.

Choko Iida appears as Mrs. Omura.

DVD available in a three-disc set from Criterion's Eclipse Series 10: "Silent Ozu: Three Family Comedies."

I Was Born, But... (*Umarete wa mita keredo*, 1932)

Salaryman Yoshii (Tatsuo Saito) moves with his two sons (Hideo Sugawara and Tokkankozo) and his wife (Mitsuko Yoshikawa) to a suburb of Tokyo, which is also close to his boss, Iwasaki (Takeshi Sakamoto). The sons struggle to establish their place in the local children's hierarchy, eventually enlisting the aid of the beer and sake delivery boy. The children's rituals include finding and eating sparrow eggs and "killing" and reviving one another through particular gestures. Iwasaki's son Taro (Seiichi Kato) is one of the gang, and one evening the Yoshii and Iwasaki families gather to watch Iwasaki's home movies. The sons are aghast by their father's undignified clowning in the films, an obvious effort to please the boss. Back home they throw a tantrum and, when Yoshii explains that he needs to please his boss so that they can eat and go to school, the

Plot Synopses

boys go on a hunger strike. The strike soon ends as real hunger sets in, and they begin to understand the compromises adult life entails.

Chishu Ryu appears in a minor role.

DVD available in a three-disc set from Criterion's Eclipse Series 10: "Silent Ozu: Three Family Comedies."

Where Now Are the Dreams of Youth? (*Seishun no yume ima izuko*, 1932)

As a student, Tetsuo Horino (Ureo Egawa) helps his buddies to cheat on exams, leads the cheerleading squad, and enjoys the attentions of the local bakery girl, Oshige (Kinuyo Tanaka). When his father dies unexpectedly, he must leave school and take over the family business. A year passes, and his buddies, having graduated, come to him seeking jobs. Still a student at heart, he helps them to cheat on the company's entrance exam while continuing to elude his uncle's (Ryotaro Mizushima) efforts to find him a wife. One day he meets Oshige, who is moving because the bakery has closed. He offers her employment and, his affection for her revived, asks his buddies if he should marry her. They agree reluctantly, neglecting to tell him that one of them, sad sack Saiki (Tatsuo Saito), is already engaged to her. When Oshige informs him of the true state of affairs, he upbraids his friends, Saiki in particular, for treating him as a boss and not as a friend. They explain that economic realities compel them to treat him with deference.

Choko Iida, Takeshi Sakamoto, and Satoko Date appear in minor roles.

DVD available in a two-disc set, "The Student Comedies," issued by the British Film Institute, region 2 only.

Woman of Tokyo (*Tokyo no onna*, 1933)

Chikako (Yoshiko Okada) works as a secretary and moonlights as a prostitute to pay for her younger brother Ryoichi's (Ureo Egawa) schooling. Ryoichi believes his sister stays out late to help a professor with translations and is devastated when his girlfriend, Harue (Kinuyo Tanaka), tells him that her policeman brother, Kinoshita (Shinyo Nara), knows the truth and is investigating. When Chikako returns late as usual, Ryoichi confronts her. She confesses, and Ryoichi leaves, walking the streets in despair. Worried, Chikako visits Harue in the morning, but Harue has not heard from him. Soon Kinoshita calls to inform her that Ryoichi has committed suicide. As the two women mourn over his body, callous newspapermen harass them, hoping to sensationalize the tragedy.

Chishu Ryu appears as one of the reporters; Hideo Sugawara appears as the boy who fetches Harue to the telephone.

Woman of Tokyo is titled after Chaplin's *Woman of Paris*, in which a young woman, separated from her fiancé, becomes a Parisian courtesan. When her fiancé finds her, she is torn between her love for him and her affluent lifestyle. Her ambivalence drives him to suicide.

258   Plot Synopses

DVD available in a two-disc set ,"Three Melodramas," issued by the British Film Institute, region 2 only.

Dragnet Girl (Hijosen no onna, 1933)

Gang leader and retired boxer Jyoji (Joji Oka) lives with his moll, Tokiko (Kinuyo Tanaka), a typist in a typing pool, whose boss, Okazaki (Yasuo Nanjo), is courting her. Student and aspiring boxer Hiroshi (Hideo Mitsui) asks to join the gang and, winning Tokiko's approval, is allowed in. Hiroshi's sister, Kazuko (Sumiko Mizukubo), disapproves, however, and asks Jyoji to dismiss her brother. Jyoji agrees, becoming infatuated with Kazuko, but Hiroshi continues to hang out with the gang. Jealous, Tokiko confronts Kazuko, but her gentle ways persuade Tokiko to go straight. Jyoji, however, is neither willing to go straight nor accept Tokiko as a "decent woman" like Kazuko. They fight, and she leaves him. Meeting boss Okazaki at a jazz club frequented by the gangs, she briefly considers becoming his mistress but returns to Jyoji instead. This time he agrees to go straight, but Hiroshi interrupts the reconciliation, fretfully announcing that he has stolen money from his sister's employer and has lost most of it gambling. Jyoji accepts responsibility for getting it back, and the couple decides to rob Tokiko's boss, Okazaki. Jyoji leaves the stolen money with the brother and sister but finds Tokiko unwilling to run from the police, who are hot on the couple's trail. He attempts to leave her behind, but she shoots him in the leg, and, in the midst of a final reconciliation and tearful embrace, they are arrested.

Chishu Ryu appears as a policeman.

DVD available in a three-disc set from Criterion's Eclipse Series 42: "Silent Ozu: Three Crime Dramas."

Passing Fancy (Dekigokoro, 1933)

Happy-go-lucky Kihachi (Takeshi Sakamoto) lives with his son, Tomio (Tokkankozo), next door to Jiro (Den Ohinata), a younger man with whom Kihachi works in a brewery. The two men meet young, beautiful, and homeless Harue (Nobuko Fushimi). Infatuated, Kihachi persuades restaurant owner Otome (Choko Iida) to take her in, and the older woman comes to regard Harue as a daughter. Kihachi hopes to marry the ingénue, but both she and Otome prefer Jiro, who denies his own infatuation with the girl. Tasked with persuading Jiro to marry Harue, Kihachi is nevertheless devastated and goes on a drinking binge. Teased by his schoolmates, the generally self-contained Tomio throws a major tantrum, and Kihachi confesses to being a neglectful parent. Father and son reconcile, and the good-hearted but irresponsible Kihachi gives Tomio money to spend on candy. The boy falls ill from overindulging and must be taken to the hospital. The impoverished Kihachi cannot pay the bill, so Jiro borrows money from the local barber (Reiko Tani) and, despite having finally proposed to Harue, decides to join a work gang headed to Hokkaido to pay back the debt. Kihachi insists on taking Jiro's

Plot Synopses 259

place, however, and is actually en route by boat to the northern island when, missing his son, he literally jumps ship and swims back toward Tokyo.

Chishu Ryu appears in a minor role.

DVD available in a three-disc set from Criterion's Eclipse Series 10: "Silent Ozu: Three Family Comedies"; also in single issue from Bo-ying.

A Mother Should Be Loved (*Haha wo kowazuya*, 1934)

At school two brothers (Seiichi Kato and Shusei Nomura) are told their father has died. Eight years pass, and the elder brother, Sadao (Den Ohinata), becomes distraught when he learns that his birth mother was his father's first wife and not the second wife (Mitsuko Yoshikawa), who raised him. His sensitivity is temporarily assuaged by his stepmother and uncle (Shinyo Nara), but he later reacts violently when he perceives that his stepmother treats him differently, more leniently in fact, than she does her own son, Kosaku (Hideo Mitsui). He leaves home to live with prostitutes in Yokohama and returns briefly only to provoke more arguments and recriminations. He returns to the brothel and rebuffs his stepmother when she follows him there. However, an elderly maid (Choko Iida) complains to Sadao about how badly her son treats her. Touched, he recognizes his own bad behavior and is ultimately reconciled to his stepmother and half-brother.

This film, today missing its first and last reels, was not one of Ozu's more successful efforts, and, to Westerners, its story seems to be much ado about nothing. It helps, however, to understand that in Japan children were adopted for a variety of formally sanctioned reasons. Fathers had an absolute right to their children, and upper-class families took babies away from prostitutes, mistresses, even abandoned wives, that the head of the house had fathered. Well-to-do families without sons sometimes adopted adult men, who then took the family name, as husband for a daughter and future head of the household. But these adoptees did not always receive the same love, respect, and acceptance that children born to both parents in a household did. Consequently, Sadao's sensitivity to the fact that the woman who raised him is not his birth mother would have elicited more understanding and compassion from Japanese in the 1930s than it does from Westerners.

Chishu Ryu appears as Hattori, a friend of Kosaku, who has amassed gambling debts.

What remains of this film can be viewed on YouTube. A Blu-ray version from the British Film Institute's "Ozu Collection" has been included on a DVD of *Late Autumn*, region 2 only.

A Story of Floating Weeds (*Ukigusa monogatari*, 1934)

Kihachi's (Takeshi Sakamoto) troupe of traveling players arrives in a small mountain village where Kihachi has fathered a child twenty years earlier. The players try to present their show, but the weather doesn't cooperate, and the country theater leaks badly. Kihachi, meanwhile, passes his time with Otsune (Choko Iida), his former mistress, and their son, Shinkichi (Hideo Mitsui). His current mistress, actress Otaka (Reiko Yagumo), discovers his secret and asks her young counterpart, Otoki (Yoshiko Tsubouchi) to seduce the boy, who does not know that Kihachi is his father. Otoki succeeds in her mission, but the youngsters fall in love, and Shinkichi refuses to give up Otoki. Enraged, Kihachi rejects Otaka, but the bad weather has so damaged the troupe's finances that they must disband. Kihachi briefly considers moving in with Otsune and Shinkichi but soon concludes that the boy, whose education he has supported through the years, would find him an embarrassment. Commending Otoki to Otsune, he leaves, determined to start afresh. At the station, he meets Otaka, and the two reconcile, agreeing to join forces to start a new troupe.

Reiko Tani and Tokkankozo appear as father-and-son members of the troupe.

DVD available in a two-disc set from Criterion, which includes the 1959 remake of the film, titled only *Floating Weeds*.

An Inn in Tokyo (*Tokyo no yado*, 1935)

In Ozu's last Kihachi film, Takeshi Sakamoto plays an itinerant worker with two sons (Tokkankozo and Takayuki Suematsu) and no wife. Turned away from factory after factory, the little family shelters in an inn for the lower classes. There they befriend Otaka (Yoshiko Okada) and her daughter, Kimiko (Kazuko Ojima). Otaka also needs work but has failed to find any. When the boys lose the family's only belongings, they no longer have enough money for the inn, but Kihachi discovers that his old friend Otsune (Choko Iida) runs a nearby restaurant. She not only puts them up but is able to arrange a job for Kihachi. He wants to marry Otaka, but she has disappeared. Eventually, he discovers her working in the local sake restaurant, and she confesses that she also works as a prostitute because Kimiko is sick and in the hospital. Without saying why, Kihachi tries to borrow money from Otsune to pay Kimiko's hospital bills, but she is jealous of his attentions to the younger woman and refuses the loan. In desperation, Kihachi steals the money, asks Otsune to look after his boys, and sends them to Otaka with the money. Then he heads to the police station to turn himself in.

This is Ozu's last extant silent film. His very last silent is the lost *College is a Nice Place* (1936).

Chishu Ryu appears as a policeman.

DVD available from Bo-ying.

Plot Synopses

Sound Films, 1936–1952

The Only Son (*Hitori musuko* 1936)

Widowed Otsune (Choko Iida) works in a silk factory in Shinshu, a mountain town near Nagano. Her young son, Ryosuke (Masao Hayama), is bright, and his teacher Okubo (Chishu Ryu) encourages him to go to high school. Otsune objects because she cannot afford to send him, but she later relents. Meanwhile, Okubo moves to Tokyo to seek his fortune. Twelve years later Otsune, having sent Ryosuke to high school and college in Tokyo, prepares to visit him there, but her visit is disillusioning. Ryosuke (Shinichi Himori) has married without ever consulting her; the couple has a baby, of which Otsune was never informed; and the only job Ryosuke has been able to find is as a poorly paid night school teacher. The young couple struggles to entertain Otsune graciously, but neither mother nor son can disguise the disappointment and bitterness each feels at Ryosuke's failure to do better for himself. They visit Okubo and discover that he has fallen out of the professional class entirely and instead operates a customer-poor cutlet (*tonkatsu*) shop. Ryosuke's wife, Sugiko (Yoshiko Tsubouchi), sells her good kimono so that the family can enjoy a day together in Tokyo, but just as they are about to set off, neighbor boy Tomio (Tokkankozo) is kicked by a horse, and Ryosuke insists that Tomio's mother (Mitsuko Yoshikawa) take the kimono money to defray her hospital bills. Otsune praises Ryosuke for his kindness and encourages him to try harder to succeed. She reveals that she has sold her house and land to pay for his education and now lives in the company dormitory. The film ends with her back in Shinshu, extolling her son's success but privately very glum.

DVD available from Bo-ying and Criterion.

What Did the Lady Forget? (*Shujo wa nani o wasuretaka*, 1937)

In Tokyo Dr. Komiya (Tatsuo Saito) and his wife, Tokiko (Sumiko Kurishima), entertain her niece Setsuko (Michiko Kuwano) from Osaka. Setsuko is a fashionable "modern girl," who smokes, plays golf, and drives. Being from Osaka, she is warm and outgoing but also outspoken and blunt. Komiya is bemused, but Tokiko is mortified by Setsuko's behavior. Meanwhile, Komiya's student Okada (Shuji Sano) is smitten by her. Tokiko expects Komiya to play golf on the weekend, but he plays hooky instead, sleeping at Okada's student apartment and visiting a bar, where Setsuko joins him, and then a geisha house. Tokiko discovers his deception when he has his friend and fellow golfer Sugiyama (Takeshi Sakamoto) send a postcard for him announcing fine weather only to have it rain. Meanwhile, Setsuko comes home drunk. When Tokiko finds out that Okada brought her home in this condition, she tells her friend Mitsuko (Mitsuko Yoshikawa), whose son Fujio (Masao Hayama) Okada had been tutoring, to fire him. When a confrontation between Komiya and Tokiko erupts, he slaps her, but later both he and Setsuko apologize to her. At the end, domestic peace restored, Setsuko goes home to Osaka after promising to marry Okada, and the Komiyas look forward to a night of marital pleasure.

Choko Iida appears as one of Tokiko's friends; Tokkankozo plays Fujio's friend.

DVD available from Shochiku Panorama Entertainment, "Ozu Yasujiro: 100th Anniversary Collection," region 3 only.

The Brothers and Sisters of the Toda Family (*Todake no kyodai*, 1941)

This film concerns a grown family consisting of two brothers and three sisters, who lose their father (Hideo Fujino) shortly after a family reunion. Three of the siblings, two sisters and the elder brother, are married and well-off, but the mother (Ayako Katsuragi) and the youngest, unmarried sister, Setsuko (Mieko Takamine), are thrown on their siblings' charity when the family discovers that the father had numerous debts and left no money to support his remaining dependents. Mother and daughter move in with the elder brother, Shinichiro (Tatsuo Saito), whose responsibility they are, according to Confucian precepts. His pretentious, self-centered wife (Kuniko Miyake) resents the intrusion, however, and mother and daughter move on to live with eldest sister Chizuru (Mitsuko Yoshikawa). She, too, finds them burdensome, so they take up residence in the family's dilapidated villa by the seashore. Meanwhile, the youngest son, Shojiro (Shin Saburi), introduced to us as an easy-going loafer but moved by his father's death to make something of his life, decides to immigrate to Tianjin in Japanese-occupied China to find work. Returning one year later, he castigates his siblings for not taking proper care of their mother. Joining her and Setsuko in the villa, he invites all of them, including their maid (Choko Iida), to accompany him back to China, and they agree. Meanwhile, Setsuko attempts to arrange a marriage between Shojiro and her friend Tokiko (Michiko Kuwano).

Yoshiko Tsubouchi appears as middle sister Ayako and Masao Hayama as Chizuru's son Ryokichi. Chishu Ryu and Takeshi Sakamoto have minor parts.

DVD available from Bo-ying.

There Was a Father (*Chichi ariki*, 1942)

Horikawa (Chishu Ryu) and his son, Ryohei (Haruhiko Tsugawa), live in Kanazawa, where Horikawa teaches junior high school. Horikawa leads his students on an excursion to eastern Japan, where one of the boys drowns in a boating accident. Although Horikawa had forbidden the boys to go boating, he feels responsible and resigns his post. Father and son return to the father's hometown, Ueda, where Ryohei goes to school. When the boy enters junior high school, however, Horikawa declares the commute too far and insists his son live in a dormitory. Later, Horikawa takes a job in Tokyo and is able to see his son only during school vacations.

After Ryohei (Shuji Sano) grows up, he takes a teaching job in distant Akita, still able to see his father only occasionally. Meanwhile, Horikawa has reconnected with

Plot Synopses   263

Hirata (Takeshi Sakamoto), a friend from his teaching days, and the two enjoy a reunion with their former students. Soon after the reunion, Horikawa has a heart attack and dies during one of Ryohei's rare visits. Ryohei marries Hirata's daughter, Fumiko (Mitsuko Mito), and together they take Horikawa's ashes back to Ueda.

Shin Saburi appears in a minor role.

DVD available from Bo-ying and Criterion. Criterion provides more and better English subtitles.

Record of a Tenement Gentleman (*Nagaya shinshiroku*, 1947)

Kohei (Hohi Aoki) loses his father in downtown Tokyo and follows Tashiro (Chishu Ryu) home. Tashiro's roommate, Tamekichi (Sokichi Kawamura), wants nothing to do with the boy, so the two men leave him with their neighbor Otane (Choko Iida). Otane resents his presence and does her best to get rid of him, particularly after he wets his futon one night, but Kohei won't leave her. She scolds him unjustly for eating her dried persimmons, but Tamekichi confesses to the crime, and the next day, having wet his futon once more, Kohei disappears. More attached to him than she has admitted, Otane searches for him, but it is Tashiro who finds him once again and brings him back. Otane decides to adopt him. They visit the zoo and a photography studio, and her friend Kikuko (Mitsuko Yoshikawa) buys him some new clothes. That night his father shows up to claim him, and Otane resolves to adopt one of the many war orphans that populate Tokyo.

DVD available from MediaDisc and Panorama Entertainment.

A Hen in the Wind (*Kaze no naka no mendori*, 1948)

Tokiko (Kinuyo Tanaka) is waiting for her husband, Shuichi (Shuji Sano), to come home from the war when her young son, Hiroshi, becomes ill. With no money and a hospital bill to pay, Tokiko accepts one assignation in a house of prostitution. Her friend Chieko (Akiko Ida) scolds her for making this desperate move. When Shuichi returns and discovers her infidelity, he is devastated and rapes her. The next day he visits the brothel and befriends a prostitute named Fusako (Chiyoko Ayatani), promising to find her an honest job. His boss, Satake (Chishu Ryu), agrees to hire Fusako and, additionally, advises Shuichi to forget the past and forgive Tokiko. Back home, Shuichi, still angry, knocks her down a flight of stairs. Shocked by his own actions, he finally agrees to forgive, forget, and move forward with their lives and marriage.

Takeshi Sakamoto appears as Tokiko's landlord, Sakai.

DVD available from Bo-ying.

Late Spring (Banshun, 1949)

Noriko Somiya (Setsuko Hara) is twenty-seven and still unmarried. Her Aunt Masa (Haruko Sugimura) worries that she will soon be too old to find a suitable husband, but Noriko is reluctant to leave her widowed father (Chishu Ryu) alone. She enjoys her single life as head of her father's home and her access to his friends. Aunt Masa, nevertheless, arranges for her to meet an eligible young man and, at the same time, proposes that her father marry Mrs. Miwa (Kuniko Miyake), a comely widow. Noriko is overcome with jealousy at the thought of someone taking her place in her father's house, but her friend Aya (Yumeji Tsukioka), a thoroughly Westernized divorcee, calls out Noriko's jealousy and urges her to pursue the marriage her aunt has arranged. Noriko acquiesces, and father and daughter make a final trip together to Kyoto, where Somiya's friend Onodera (Masao Mishima) lives. After the wedding, Somiya and Aya repair to a bar, where Somiya admits that he lied for Noriko's sake and never intended to remarry. Aya finds this admirable and promises to visit him.

DVD available from Criterion.

The Munekata Sisters (Munekata shimai, 1950)

The Munekata sisters, Setsuko (Kinuyo Tanaka) and Mariko (Hideko Takamine), live in Tokyo with Setsuko's unemployed husband, Mimura (So Yamamura), while their ailing father (Chishu Ryu) lives in Kyoto. Setsuko supports her family by running a bar, but it, too, is ailing. When her old flame, Hiroshi Tashiro (Ken Uehara), offers to lend money to keep the bar afloat, Mimura objects, and the bar closes. Meanwhile, Mariko befriends Hiroshi, who runs a furniture factory in Kobe, and tries to reunite him with Setsuko, urging her sister to divorce Mimura, who is self-absorbed and abusive. Setsuko finally agrees, but before she can act on her intentions, Mimura drops dead from a heart attack. Haunted by the thought that she has caused Mimura's death, Setsuko refuses to marry Hiroshi, opting instead to remain single.

Tatsuo Saito appears in a minor role.

DVD available from Bo-ying.

Early Summer (Bakushu, 1951)

Noriko Mamiya (Setsuko Hara), twenty-eight and single, lives with her extended family in Kamakura and works as a private secretary for Tokyo businessman Satake (Shuji Sano). Noriko enjoys a circle of women friends from her school days and is particularly close to Aya (Chikage Awajima), whose mother runs a traditional restaurant where businessmen, including Satake, entertain guests. Noriko is also close to her sister-in-law, Fumiko (Kuniko Miyake), but often at odds with her brother Koichi (Chishu Ryu), a doctor. Koichi's assistant, Kenkichi Yabe (Hiroshi Nihon'yanagi), widower and father of a toddler, lives next door and was a boyhood friend of Noriko's brother

Plot Synopses 265

Shoji, who never returned from the war. When Noriko's nephews (Zen Murase and Isao Shirosawa) run away after being disciplined by their father, Yabe helps her search for them.

When Satake proposes Manabe (who never appears onscreen) as a marriage prospect for Noriko, all of her family, including her parents (Chieko Higashiyama and Ichiro Sugai), are enthused, all except Noriko herself. Meanwhile, Koichi's medical establishment decides to send Yabe to a hospital in northerly Akita. Yabe's mother (Haruko Sugimura) is not enthusiastic about the move and confides to Noriko her wish that her son would remarry with someone like Noriko. Noriko immediately accepts this backhanded proposal—to her family's chagrin. In the end, however, they accept her decision. Off-screen she moves to Akita, and her parents move to the family seat in Yamato, where they join the father's older brother (Kokuten Kodo).

DVD available from Criterion.

The Flavor of Green Tea Over Rice (*Ochazuke no aji*, 1952)

Taeko (Michiyo Kogure) is dissatisfied with her marriage to Motoki Satake (Shin Saburi), whom she finds too pedestrian in his tastes. She thus sets a poor example for her niece Setsuko (Keiko Tsujima), whose mother (Kuniko Miyake) is trying to arrange a marriage interview (*omiai*) for her. Setsko runs away from the interview to join her uncle Motoki and his young protégé, Non-chan (Koji Tsuruta), to whom she takes a liking. When Taeko, who had accompanied her sister-in-law to the *omiai*, learns of Motoki's role in Setsuko's misdeed, the marriage reaches a breaking point. Without consulting her husband, Taeko makes an impromptu visit to her father in Osaka. Meanwhile, Motoki must leave sooner than expected on a business trip to Uruguay, and Taeko arrives home too late to see him off. Alone in their home, she misses him, and when he returns that night because his plane has had engine trouble, they are reconciled. The next day, Taeko details the reconciliation for her friends, and Setsuko meets Non-chan for a date.

Chishu Ryu appears as the owner of a pachinko parlor, and Chikage Awajima plays Taeko's friend Aya.

DVD available from Bo-ying.

Late Films, 1953–1962

Tokyo Story (*Tokyo monogatari*, 1953)

Shukichi Hirayama (Chishu Ryu) and his wife, Tomi (Chieko Higashiyama), set out from the Inland Sea town of Onomichi to visit their children in Tokyo and Osaka. Their son Koichi (So Yamamura) is a busy doctor in an outlying Tokyo neighborhood and has little time to spend with them. Their daughter Shige (Haruko Sugimura), a hairdresser with her own salon, is likewise busy, so the two children prevail upon Noriko

(Setsuko Hara), widow of their MIA brother, Shoji, to take the parents sightseeing. Subsequently, Shige and Koichi send their parents off to the spa town of Atami, but their inn's young customers keep the parents awake with their games and loud music, so they return to Tokyo sooner than expected. Shige indicates that they will be in the way of a hairdressers' meeting at her house that evening, so Tomi bunks in with Noriko while Shukichi meets with old friends from Onomichi and eventually returns to Shige's house drunk with one of the friends in tow. The parents, who have already visited with their youngest son, Keizo (Shiro Osaka), in Osaka on their outbound trip, find it necessary to stop there again because Tomi falls ill on the train. She recovers, and they make it back to Onomichi, but she falls critically ill soon after their return. The Tokyo children are summoned, and they arrive in time to watch her die. Keizo, who had been out of town, arrives several hours later. All three children leave soon after the funeral, but Noriko stays a few days longer to help Shukichi, and he urges her to forget his son Shoji and remarry. Younger daughter Kyoko (Kyoko Kagawa), who still lives at home, complains to Noriko about her siblings' rush to leave, and Noriko consoles her, explaining that children inevitably grow away from their parents as they establish careers of their own away from home. Noriko takes the train back to Tokyo, and Shukichi sits alone, looking out over the landscape.

DVD available from Criterion.

Early Spring (Soshun, 1956)

Bored with the monotony of his salaryman's life, Sugiyama (Ryo Ikebe) has an affair with a fellow-commuter nicknamed "Goldfish" (Keiko Kishi). Sugiyama also socializes with neighbors and war buddies, as well as Kawai (So Yamamura), who has quit Sugiyama's company to run his own bar. Sugiyama's wife, Masako (Chikage Awajima), spends time with her mother (Kumeko Urabe) and her widowed friend Sakae (Chieko Nakakita). When Masako learns of her husband's infidelity, she moves in with Sakae. Sugiyama is transferred to rural Mitsuishi. Prompted by family friend and mentor Onodera (Chishu Ryu), Masako joins her husband in Mitsuishi, and both agree to repair their marriage.

Haruko Sugimura and Kuniko Miyake appear in minor roles.

DVD available from Criterion, Eclipse Series, "Late Ozu," and the British Film Institute's Ozu Collection, "Three Melodramas," Region 2 only.

Tokyo Twilight (Tokyo boshoku, 1957)

During the war, Shukichi Sugiyama's (Chishu Ryu) wife left him for another man and moved to Manchuria, leaving him to raise their two daughters alone. When the film begins, his older married daughter, Takako (Setsuko Hara), has moved back home with her toddler to escape her disengaged, alcoholic husband (Kinzo Shin). Shukichi's uncommunicative younger daughter, Akiko (Ineko Arima), has fallen in with a dissolute crowd, and, unbeknownst to either Shukichi or Taeko, has become pregnant by her

Plot Synopses

self-centered boyfriend, Kenji (Masami Taura). Meanwhile, Shukichi's sister (Haruko Sugimura) announces that she has seen his estranged wife, Kisako (Isuzu Yamada), in Tokyo. As luck would have it, Kisako runs a mahjong parlor that Akiko frequents. Still embittered by her mother's desertion, Takako visits Kisako and insists that she not reveal her identity to the already troubled Akiko, who nevertheless guesses the truth. Emotionally distraught from an abortion and Kenji's disinterest, Akiko confronts her mother and shortly afterwards commits suicide. Without ever knowing about the abortion, Takako blames Kisako for Akiko's death and refuses to see her pining mother off when Kisako and her husband (Nobuo Nakamura) leave Tokyo for Hokkaido. She resolves, however, to return to her husband, believing that without two parents her young daughter might grow up feeling unloved as Akiko did.

So Yamamura makes a cameo appearance.

DVD available from Criterion, Eclipse Series, "Late Ozu," and the British Film Institute's Ozu Collection, "Three Melodramas," region 2 only.

Equinox Flower (*Higanbana*, 1958)

Business executive Hirayama (Shin Saburi) has found an appropriate match for his daughter Setsuko (Ineko Arima), but she wants to marry fellow worker Taniguchi (Keiji Sada), who is being transferred to Hiroshima. Angry that his daughter has not consulted him on what he considers a rash decision, Hirayama refuses to consent to the marriage until he is tricked by a family friend from Kyoto, Yukiko Sasaki (Fujiko Yamamoto), whose mother (Chieko Naniwa) is being treated in a Tokyo hospital. Hirayama's wife (Kinuyo Tanaka) and daughters (Miyuki Kuwano as younger daughter Hisako) are delighted, but Hirayama refuses to attend the wedding until, until at the very last moment, he changes his mind. Meanwhile, his former schoolmate Mikami (Chishu Ryu) asks Hirayama to check on his daughter Fumiko (Yoshiko Kuga), who works in a bar and lives with her musician boyfriend. Hirayama obliges, serving as a liaison between estranged father and daughter. Mikami and another former classmate (Nobuo Nakamura) invite Hirayama to a class reunion in the spa town of Gamagori, and there he and Mikami agree that in this day and age it is necessary to give in to daughters. Hirayama travels further south to Kyoto to visit the Sasakis, and they urge him to continue on to visit Setsuko in Hiroshima. He agrees reluctantly, but at the end looks forward to a complete reconciliation with his daughter.

Ureo Egawa appears as one of the reunion classmates. Miyuki Kuwano, who plays Hisako, is the daughter of Michiko Kuwano, who played the irrepressible niece in *What Did the Lady Forget?*

DVD available from Criterion, Eclipse Series, "Late Ozu," and from Shochiku Panorama Entertainment, "Ozu Yasujiro: 100th Anniversary Collection." English subtitles are better on the Criterion copy.

Ohayo (1959)

In addition to exhibiting their farting prowess, the Hayashi boys (Koji Shigaraki and Masahiko Shimazu) are consumed with a desire for their own television set. When their father (Chishu Ryu) scolds them for obnoxiously demanding one, they vow to stop talking, citing adults' indulgence in meaningless small talk, the *ohayo* (good morning) of the title, for example. The neighbors, already given to constant gossip, are sure the boys' mother (Kuniko Miyake) has a grudge again them, and many other misunderstandings follow. After the boys run away one evening, their father relents and buys a television, in part to help out his retired neighbor (Eijiro Tono), who is trying to make extra money as a salesman, and peace is restored in the home and in the neighborhood. The boys' aunt (Yoshiko Kuga) and their English tutor (Keiji Sada) are attracted to one another but can't seem to get beyond the small talk the boys had objected to.

Haruko Sugimura plays one of the neighbors.

DVD available from Criterion.

Floating Weeds (*Ukigusa*, 1959)

Made for Daiei instead of Shochiku and set on Shijima, an island off Honshu's Kii Peninsula, the film's plotline is identical to that of the 1934 *Story of Floating Weeds*. Ganjiro Nakamura stars as Komajuro, head of the acting troupe, Machiko Kyo as his disaffected mistress, Haruko Sugimura as the abandoned mistress and mother of his son (Hiroshi Kawaguchi). Ayako Wakao plays the young actress who seduces the son. Hideo Mitsui, who played the son in 1934, appears as the least scrupulous of the actors, and Masahiku Shimazu, from *Ohayo*, plays the little boy attached to the acting troupe, the part played by Tokkankozo in 1934. Chishu Ryu appears as the impresario.

DVD available in a two-disc set from Criterion, which includes the 1934 version, *A Story of Floating Weeds*.

Late Autumn (*Akibiyori*, 1960)

Mamiya (Shin Saburi), Taguchi (Nobuo Nakamura), and Hirayama (Ryuji Kita) conspire to marry off both Akiko (Setsuko Hara) and her daughter, Ayako (Yoko Tsukasa), wife and daughter of their deceased friend, Miwa. They designate widower Hirayama as Akiko's suitor and try to introduce Ayako to Goto (Keiji Sada). Mamiya and Taguchi have longed for Akiko since college (when she instead chose Miwa), and when she eventually declines Hirayama's advances, all three feel bereft. Meanwhile, Ayako resists Mamiya's efforts at matchmaking but accepts the offer of a friend her age to set her up with Goto. Another friend, Yuriko (Mariko Okada), scolds the three older gentlemen for interfering in the women's lives. At the end, Ayako marries Goto, Akiko is left alone, and the three male friends admit they had fun despite their missteps.

Plot Synopses 269

Kuniko Miyake, Chishu Ryu, Masahiko Shimazu, Koji Shigaraki, and Miyuki Kuwano appear in minor roles. Mariko Okada, who plays Yuriko, is the daughter of Tokihiko Okada, who starred in five of Ozu's silent films and died in 1934.

DVD available from Criterion, Eclipse Series, "Late Ozu."

The End of Summer (*Kohayagawake no aki*, 1961)

Manbei Kohayagawa (Ganjiro Nakamura), widower and jovial head of an Osaka-based brewery clan, has renewed his liaison with his former mistress, Tsune (Chieko Naniwa). While his married daughter, Fumiko (Michiyo Aratama), fumes about his affair, his younger daughter, Noriko (Yoko Tsukasa), and his widowed daughter-in-law, Akiko (Setsuko Hara), consider marriage proposals. After an initial heart attack from which he recovers, Manbei dies at Tsune's home in Kyoto. Son-in-law Hisao (Keiji Kobayashi) decides to sell the failing brewery to a large firm, Akiko elects to remain single, and Noriko looks forward to marrying Teramoto (Akira Takarada), the man she really loves, who has taken a job in distant Sapporo.

Daisuke Kato plays the uncle, Manbei's brother-in-law; Haruko Sugimura and Chishu Ryu appear in minor roles; and Masahiko Shimazu and Koji Shigaraki (the brothers in *Ohayo*) appear as cousins.

DVD available from Criterion, Eclipse Series, "Late Ozu."

An Autumn Afternoon (*Samma no aji*, 1962)

Kawai (Nobuo Nakamura) convinces widower Hirayama (Chishu Ryu) that it is time for his daughter Michiko (Shima Iwashita) to marry, insisting he has a good match in mind. Michiko is reluctant but indicates an interest in her brother Koichi's friend Miura (Teruo Yoshida). Koichi (Keiji Sada) discovers that Miura is already engaged, however, and a disappointed Michiko agrees to marry the young man Kawai has suggested. Meanwhile, Koichi and his wife, Akiko (Mariko Okada), sort through the ups and downs of modern married life, and Hirayama, Kawai, and Horie (Ryuji Kita) entertain their old teacher, "Gourd" (Eijiro Tono), whose own daughter (Haruko Sugimura) has grown too old to marry.

Kuniko Miyake and Daisuke Kato appear in minor roles.

DVD available from Criterion.

Selected Bibliography

Anderson, Joseph L. "Spoken Silents in the Japanese Cinema; or, Talking to Pictures: Essaying the Katsuben, Contextualizing the Texts." In *Reframing Japanese Cinema: Authorship, Genre, History*, edited by Arthur Nolletti, Jr. and David Desser, 259–311. Bloomington, IN: Indiana University Press, 1992.

Anderson, Joseph L. and Donald Richie. *The Japanese Film: Art and Industry*. Princeton, NJ: Princeton University Press, 1982.

Atkins, Jacqueline. "Wearing Novelty." In Jacqueline A. Atkins, John Dower, Anne Nishimura Morse, and Frederic A. Scharf, *The Brittle Decade: Visualizing Japan in the 1930s*, 94–143. Boston, MA: MFA Publications, 2012.

Atkins, Jacqueline A., John Dower, Anne Nishimura Morse, and Frederic A. Scharf. *The Brittle Decade: Visualizing Japan in the 1930s*. Boston, MA: MFA Publications, 2012.

Barrett, Gregory. *Archetypes in Japanese Film: The Sociopolitical and Religious Significance of the Principal Heroes and Heroines*. Selinsgrove, PA: Susquehanna University Press, 1989.

Barrett, Gregory. "Comic Targets and Comic Styles: An Introduction to Japanese Film Comedy." In *Reframing Japanese Cinema: Authorship, Genre, History*, edited by Arthur Nolletti, Jr. and David Desser, 210–26. Bloomington, IN: Indiana University Press, 1992.

Beardsley, Richard K., John W. Hall, and Robert E. Ward. *Village Japan*. Chicago, IL: University of Chicago Press, 1959.

Benedict, Ruth. *The Chrysanthemum and the Sword*. New York: Houghton Mifflin, 2005. Originally published 1946.

Betz, Mark. "Wenders Travels with Ozu." In *Reorienting Ozu: A Master and His Influence*, edited by Jinhee Choi, 233–47. New York: Oxford University Press, 2018.

Bordwell, David. "A Cinema of Flourishes: Japanese Decorative Classicism of the Prewar Era." In *Reframing Japanese Cinema: Authorship, Genre, History*, edited by Arthur Nolletti, Jr. and David Desser, 328–46. Bloomington, IN: Indiana University Press, 1992.

Bordwell, David. *Figures Traced in Light: On Cinematic Staging*. Berkeley, CA: University of California Press, 2005.

Bordwell, David. *Making Meaning: Inference and Rhetoric in the Interpretation of Cinema*. Cambridge, MA: Harvard University Press, 1989.

Bordwell, David. *Narration in the Fiction Film*. Madison, WI: University of Wisconsin Press, 1985.

Bordwell, David. *Ozu and the Poetics of Cinema*. Princeton, NJ: Princeton University Press, 1988.

Bordwell, David. "Visual Style in Japanese Cinema, 1925–1945." *Film History* 7 (1995): 5–31.

Bordwell, David. "Watch Again! Look Well! Look!" In *Reorienting Ozu: A Master and His Influence*, edited by Jinhee Choi, 21–32. New York: Oxford University Press, 2018.

Branigan, Edward. "The Space of *Equinox Flower*." *Screen* 17, no. 2 (Summer 1976): 74–105.

Brown, Kendall H. and Sharon A. Minichiello. *Taisho Chic: Japanese Modernity, Nostalgia, and Deco*. Honolulu, HI: Honolulu Academy of Arts, 2002.

Burch, Noël. *To the Distant Observer: Form and Meaning in the Japanese Cinema*. Berkeley, CA: University California Press, 1979.

Cather, Kirsten. "Perverting Ozu: Suo Masayuki's *Abnormal Family*." *Journal of Japanese and Korean Cinema* 2, no. 2 (2010): 131–45.

Cazdyn, Eric. *The Flash of Capital: Film and Geopolitics in Japan*. Chapel Hill, NC: Duke University Press, 2002.

Chion, Michel. *Audio-Vision: Sound on Screen*. Translated by Claudia Gorman. New York: Columbia University Press, 1994.

Chion, Michel. *Film, A Sound Art*. Translated by Claudia Gorman. New York: Columbia University Press, 2009.

Chion, Michel. *Le son au cinéma*. Paris: Cahiers du cinéma (Editions de l'Etoile), 1985.

Chion, Michel. *Words on Screen*. Translated by Claudia Gorman. New York: Columbia University Press, 2017.

Choi, Jinhee, ed. *Reorienting Ozu: A Master and His Influence*. New York: Oxford University Press, 2018.

Coates, Jennifer. *Repetition and the Female Image in Japanese Cinema, 1945–1964*. Hong Kong: Hong Kong University Press, 2016.

Conant, Ellen P., ed. *Nihonga, Transcending the Past: Japanese-Style Painting 1868–1968*. St. Louis, MO: Saint Louis Art Museum, 1995.

Cooper-Hewitt Museum. *MA: Space-Time in Japan*, exhibit catalog. New York, n.d.

Davis, D. William. "Back to Japan: Militarism and Monumentalism in Prewar Japanese Cinema." *Wide Angle* 11, no. 3 (1989): 16–25.

Davis, Darrell W. "Ozu, the Ineffable." In *Reorienting Ozu: A Master and His Influence*, edited by Jinhee Choi, 33–43. New York: Oxford University Press, 2018.

Davis, Darrell William. *Picturing Japaneseness: Monumental Style, National Identity, Japanese Film*. New York: Columbia University Press, 1996.

Dawson, Jan. *Wim Wenders*. New York: New York Zoetrope, 1976.

Desser, David, ed. *Ozu's Tokyo Story*. Cambridge: Cambridge University Press, 1997.

Desser, David. "Space and Narrative in *The Makioka Sisters*." In *Kon Ichikawa*, edited by James Quandt, 373–83. Toronto, ON: Cinematheque Ontario, 1998.

Dore, Ronald Philip. *City Life in Japan: A Study of a Tokyo Ward*. Berkeley, CA: University of California Press, 1958.

Dower, John W. *Embracing Defeat: Japan in the Wake of World War II*. New York: W.W. Norton & Co., 1999.

Dower, John W. "Modernity and Militarism." In Jacqueline A. Atkins, John Dower, Anne Nishimura Morse, and Frederic A. Scharf, *The Brittle Decade: Visualizing Japan in the 1930s*, 9–49. Boston, MA: MFA Publications, 2012.

Dower, John W. *War without Mercy: Race and Power in the Pacific War*. New York: Pantheon Books, 1986.

Selected Bibliography

273

Ehrlich, Linda. "*Shall We Dance?* (*Shall we dansu*, Japan, 1996. Directed by Suo Masayuki)." *Asian Cinema* (Spring 1998): 94–107.

Ehrlich, Linda and David Desser, eds. *Cinematic Landscapes: Observations on the Visual Arts and Cinema of China and Japan.* Austin, TX: University of Texas Press, 1994.

Fowler, Edward. "Piss and Run: Or How Ozu does a Number on SCAP." In *Word and Image in Japanese Cinema*, edited by Dennis Washburn and Carole Cavanaugh, 273–92. Cambridge: Cambridge University Press, 2001.

Gallicchio, Marc. *Unconditional: The Japanese Surrender in World War II.* New York: Oxford University Press, 2020.

Geist, Kathe. *The Cinema of Wim Wenders: From Paris, France to "Paris, Texas."* Ann Arbor, MI: UMI Research Press, 1988.

Geist, Kathe. "Yasujiro Ozu: Notes on a Retrospective." *Film Quarterly* 37, no. 1 (Fall 1983): 2–9.

Hasumi, Shigehiko, "Ozu's Angry Women," 2004. rouge.com.au/4/ozu_women.html.

Hendry, Joy. *Marriage in Changing Japan.* London: Croom Helm, 1981.

High, Peter B. "A Drama of Superimposed Maps: Ozu's *So Far from the Land of Our Parents*," *Gengobunkaronshū/Journal of Language Culture* 29, no. 2 (March 2008): 3–21.

High, Peter B. *The Imperial Screen: Japanese Film Culture in the Fifteen Years' War 1931–1945.* Madison, WI: University of Wisconsin Press, 2003.

Hirano, Kyoko. *Mr. Smith Goes to Tokyo: Japanese Cinema under the American Occupation.* Washington, DC: Smithsonian Institution, 1992.

Hotta, Eri. *Japan 1941: Countdown to Infamy.* New York: Alfred A. Knopf, 2013.

Igarashi, Makoto. *Ozu's Films from Behind the Scenes* [*Ozugumi no seisaku genba kara*]. Tokyo: Shochiku, 2003.

Inoue, Kazuo. *I Lived, But . . .* [*Ikite wa mita keredo*]. Tokyo: Shochiku, 1983.

Jansen, Marius B. *The Making of Modern Japan.* Cambridge, MA: Harvard University Press, 2000.

Joo, Woojeong. *The Cinema of Ozu Yasujiro: Histories of the Everyday.* Edinburgh: Edinburgh University Press, 2017.

Joo, Woojeong. "Rethinking Noriko's Marriage Narrative as Historical Allegory in Ozu Yasujiro's *The Moon Has Risen* and Other Occupation-Era Films." *Screen* 56, no. 3 (Autumn 2015): 335–56.

Kometani, Shinnosuke. *Chasing Ozu.* Translated by Kimiko Takeda. Tokyo: The Publishing Arts Institute, 2021.

McDonald, Keiko. *Cinema East: A Critical Study of Major Japanese Films.* East Brunswick, NJ: Associated University Presses, 1983.

McDonald, Keiko. *Reading a Japanese Film: Cinema in Context.* Honolulu, HI: University of Hawai'i Press, 2006.

Matsuura, Kanji and Akiko Miyamoto, eds. *Ozu Yasujiro Taizen.* Tokyo: Asahi Shinbun Publications, 2019.

Mayo, Marlene J., J. Thomas Rimer, and H. Eleanor Kerkham, eds. *War, Occupation, and Creativity: Japan and East Asia 1920–1960.* Honolulu, HI: University Hawai'i Press, 2001.

Mayuzumi, Rintaro. *Wim Wenders in Tokyo for Until the End of the World.* Tokyo: NHK: 1990.

Mellen, Joan. *The Waves at Genji's Door: Japan Through Its Cinema.* New York: Pantheon Books, 1976.

Mezies, Jackie, ed. *Modern Boy, Modern Girl: Modernity in Japanese Art 1910–1935.* Sydney: Art Gallery of New South Wales, 1998.

Miyao, Daisuke. "Ozu and the Aesthetics of Shadow: Lighting and Cinematography in *There Was a Father* (1942)." In *Reorienting Ozu: A Master and His Influence*, edited by Jinhee Choi, 119–31. New York: Oxford University Press, 2018.

Morioka, Michiyo and Paul Berry. *Modern Masters of Kyoto: The Transformation of Japanese Painting Traditions*. Seattle, WA: Seattle Art Museum, 1999.

Nitschke, Gunther. "MA: The Japanese Sense of Place." *Architectural Design* 36, no. 1 (March 1966): 117–56.

Nolletti, Arthur Jr. and David Desser, eds. *Reframing Japanese Cinema: Authorship, Genre, History*. Bloomington, IN: Indiana University Press, 1992.

Nornes, Abé Mark. *Japanese Documentary Film: The Meiji Era through Hiroshima*. Minneapolis, MN: University of Minnesota Press, 2003.

Nornes, Abé Mark. "The Riddle of the Vase: Ozu Yasujiro's *Late Spring* (1949)." In *Japanese Cinema: Texts and Contexts*, edited by Alastair Phillips and Julian Stringer, 78–89. London: Routledge, 2007.

Nygren, Scott. *Time Frames: Japanese Cinema and the Unfolding of History*. Minneapolis, MN: University of Minnesota Press, 2007.

Okada, Hidenori. "Ozu Yasujiro ni okeru kaiga to dezain" [Ozu Yasujro's painting and design]. In *Ozu Yasujiro Taizen*, edited by Kanji Matsuura and Akiko Miyamoto, 135–43. Tokyo: Asahi Shinbun Publications, 2019.

"Ozu on Ozu: The Silents." *Cinema* (USA) 7, no. 3 (Winter 1972–1973): 22–24.

"Ozu on Ozu: The Talkies." *Cinema* (USA) 6, no. 1 (1970): 3–5.

Phillips, Alastair. "Pictures of the Past in the Present: Modernity, Femininity and Stardom in the Postwar Films of Ozu Yasujiro." In *Screening World Cinema*, edited by Catherine Grant and Annette Kuhn, 86–100. New York: Routledge, 2006.

Phillips, Alastair. "The Salaryman's Panic Time: Ozu Yasujiro's *I Was Born, But . . .* (1932)." In *Japanese Cinema: Texts and Contexts*, edited by Alastair Phillips and Julian Stringer, 25–36. London: Routledge, 2007.

Pilgrim, Richard B. *Buddhism and the Arts of Japan*. Chambersburg, PA: Anima Books, 1981.

Prindle, Tamae K. *Women in Japanese Cinema: Alternate Perspectives*. Portland, ME: Merwin Asia, 2016.

Raine, Michael. "A New Form of Silent Cinema: Intertitles and Interlocution in Ozu Yasujiro's Late Silent Films." In *Reorienting Ozu: A Master and His Influence*, edited by Jinhee Choi, 101–17. New York: Oxford University Press, 2018.

Richie, Donald. *Ozu: His Life and Films*. Berkeley, CA: University California Press, 1974.

Rimer, Thomas. "Teiten and After, 1919–1935." In *Nihonga, Transcending the Past: Japanese-Style Painting 1868–1968*, edited by Ellen P. Conant, 44–56. St. Louis, MO: Saint Louis Art Museum, 1995.

Russell, Catherine. *The Cinema of Naruse Mikio: Women and Japanese Modernity*. Durham, NC: Duke University Press, 2008.

Russell, Catherine. "Insides and Outsides: Cross-cultural Criticism in Japanese Film Melodrama." In *Melodrama and Asian Cinema*, edited by Wimal Disanayake, 143–54. Cambridge: Cambridge University Press, 1993.

Sato, Barbara. *The New Japanese Woman: Modernity, Media, and Women in Interwar Japan*. Durham, NC: Duke University Press, 2003.

Sato, Tadao. *The Art of Yasujiro Ozu: Vols. 1–8*. Translated by Goro Iiri, 1974–1978.

Selected Bibliography 275

Sato, Tadao. *Currents in Japanese Cinema*. Translated by Gregory Barrett. Tokyo: Kodansha, 1982.

Sato, Tadao. "Japanese Cinema and the Traditional Arts: Imagery, Technique, and Cultural Context." In *Cinematic Landscapes: Observations on the Visual Arts and Cinema of China and Japan*, edited by Linda Ehrlich and David Desser, 165–86. Austin, TX: University of Texas Press, 1994.

Schrader, Paul. *Transcendental Style in Film: Ozu, Bresson, Dreyer*. Berkeley, CA: University of California Press, 1972.

Shillony, Ben-Ami. *Politics and Culture in Wartime Japan*. Oxford: Oxford University Press, 1981.

Sorensen, Lars-Martin. *Censorship of Japanese Films During the U.S. Occupation of Japan: The Cases of Yasujiro Ozu and Akira Kurosawa*. Lewiston, NY: Edwin Mellen Press, 2009.

Standish, Isolde. *A New History of Japanese Cinema: A Century of Narrative Film*. New York: Continuum International, 2005.

Stein, Wayne and Marc DiPaolo, eds. *Ozu International: Essays on the Global Influences of a Japanese Auteur*. New York: Bloomsbury Academic, 2015.

Takinami, Yuki. "Modernity, *Shoshimin* Films, and the Proletarian-Film Movement." In *Reorienting Ozu: A Master and His Influence*, edited by Jinhee Choi, 133–54. New York: Oxford University Press, 2018.

Tanaka, Kogi. *Talking with Ozu [Ozu to kataru]*. Tokyo: Shochiku, 1993.

Thompson, Kristin. *Breaking the Glass Armor*. Princeton, NJ: Princeton University Press, 1988.

Thompson, Kristin. "Notes on the Spatial System of Ozu's Early Films." *Wide Angle* 1, no. 4 (1977): 8–17.

Thompson, Kristin and David Bordwell. "Space and Narrative in the Films of Ozu." *Screen* 17, no. 2 (Summer 1976): 41–105.

Vasey, Ruth. "Ozu and the Nō." *Australian Journal of Screen Theory* 7, no. 80 (1988): 88–102.

Wada-Marciano, Mitsuyo. *Nippon Modern: Japanese Cinema of the 1920s and 1930s*. Honolulu, HI: University Hawai'i Press, 2008.

Wenders, Wim. *Tokyo Ga*. Berlin and New York: Wim Wenders Produktion, Chris Sievernich Filmproduktion, Gray City, Inc., 1985.

Wood, Robin. "The 'Noriko Trilogy': Three Films of Ozu with Setsuko Hara." *Cineaction* 26/27 (1992): 60–81.

Yoshida, Junji. "Laughing in the Shadows of Empire: Humor in Ozu's *Brothers and Sisters of the Toda Family* (1941)." In *Reorienting Ozu: A Master and His Influence*, edited by Jinhee Choi, 155–74. New York: Oxford University Press, 2018.

Yoshida, Kiju. *Ozu's Anti-Cinema*. Translated by Daisuke Miyao and Kyoko Hirano. Ann Arbor, MI: Center for Japanese Studies, 2003.

Yoshimoto, Mitsuhiro. *Kurosawa: Film Studies and Japanese Cinema*. Durham, NC: Duke University Press, 2000.

Yoshimoto, Mitsuhiro. "The Difficulty of Being Radical: The Discipline of Film Studies and the Post-colonial World Order." In *Asian Cinemas: A Reader and Guide*, edited by Dimitris Eleftheriotis and Gary Needham, 27–40. Honolulu, HI: University of Hawai'i Press, 2006.

Young, Louise. *Japan's Total Empire: Manchuria and the Culture of Wartime Imperialism*. Berkeley, CA: University of California Press, 1998.

Zeman, Marvin. "The Serene Poet of Japanese Cinema: The Zen Artistry of Yasujiro Ozu." *Film Journal* 1, nos. 3–4 (Fall–Winter 1972): 62–72.

Index

Note: Illustrations are indicated in bold.

An Abnormal Family (*Hentai kazoku: Aniki no yome-san*, 1984), 244, 249n40
Akasaka Palace, 149, 151, 157n88
Alice in the Cities (*Alice in den Städten*, 1974), 231–34
All Quiet on the Western Front (1930), 19, 37, 89
The American Friend (*Der amerikanische Freund*, 1977), 234
Anders, Allison, 232
Anderson, Joseph, 56, 63, 70
ankokugai eiga, 9
Anti-Comintern Pact, 94
Aoki, Hohi, 123, 263
Aoki, Tomio (Tokkankozo), 58, **205 fig. 10.1**, 249n41, 254–56, 258, 260–62, 268
Arima, Ineko, 192, 266–67
Asphalt (1929), 10, 23
Atsuta, Yuharu, 104, 120n57, 237
An Autumn Afternoon (*Samma no aji*, 1962), 43, 155n55, 158–59, 166–69, 171, 175, 177–78, 179n5, 179n16, 190, 199–201, 203, 207n23, 242, 251, 269, **colorplate 1A**
Awajima, Chikage, 264–66

bakudan sanyushi (Three Human Bomb Patriots), 99n5
Bancroft, George, 20, 36
Barrett, Gregory, 18, 81, 185
baseball, 26n8, 92, 96, 108, 135–38, 140–41, 155n55, 160n3, 167–68, 231, 242
Battle of Midway, 116, 119n47, 147

Beauty and the Beast (*La Belle et la Bête*, 1946), 150
Benedict, Ruth, 37, 82, 103
benshi (*katsuben*), 54–56, 63, 63n9
Berlin: Symphony of a City (*Sinfonie der Grosstadt*, 1922), 20, 22–24
Betz, Mark, 234–36, 248
Bordwell, David, 2, 4, 28, 31, 33, 35, 37, 39, 47, 49, 56, 63, 65–66, 70–73, 75, 81, 83–84n9, 92–93, 104, 109, 113, 115, 123, 127, 129, 134, 140, 142, 153, 154n30, 163, 166–67, 173, 179n5, 175n8, 183, 185–86, 193n31, 195, 200, 210, 212, 215, 218, 220, 228n44, 229, 234, 242–44, 250–51, 253
"both . . . and" mindset vs. "either . . . or" mindset, 102–3, 118n19, 121, 131, 137, 183
Branigan, Edward, 172
Bresson, Robert, 250
bridges, 164, 173, 177–78, 179n19, 190, 233, 246. *See also* passage
Broadway Daddies (1928), 34
Broadway Scandals (1929), 19, 34
The Brothers and Sisters of the Toda Family (*Todake no kyodai*, 1941), 101–9, 111, 127, 134, 137, 143, 151–53, 159, 163, 177, 179n10, 183, 188, 234, 262
Buddhism, 102, 105, 110–11, 119n55, 154n38, 180, 182–83, 185, 188–89; Buddha, 110–11, 141, 147, 184, 243; *butsudan*, 105, 111, 188–89, 240
Burch, Noël, 70, 163, 215

278 Index

Burma Campaign: Far Motherland (*Biruma sakusen: Haruka nari fubo no kuni*), 116

Cazdyn, Eric, 135
censorship, 20, 102–3, 122, 127, 133, 136, 146, 153n8, 208n32; censors, 89–90, 99, 99n5, 104, 117, 121–22, 125–27, 131, 134, 136–39, 147, 154n26. *See also* SCAP
The Champ, (1931), 36, 82
Chaplin, Charles, 75–76, 84n22, 93, 109, 257
Chichi to musume, 114, 132, 134, 155n45
Chigasaki, 126–28, 134
China: after 1949, 140, 228n42, 242; art, 147, 211; Japan's war and occupation 3, 87, 96, 98–99, 100n16, 101–2, 104, 106–9, 111, 116, 118n35, 119n36, 119n42, 119n47, 128, 143, 146, 148, 152, 156n77, 180, 228n42, 241, 262
Chion, Michel, 3, 52n6, 54–56
chivalry, 37, 195–96
Christianity, 16, 130–31, 146, 154n39, 180–83, 185, 188, 191–92, 192n6; Christian church, 16, 145, 148, 181; Japanese Christians, 139, 182
circle imagery, 164, 167, 179n8, 186–88. See also *samsara*; wheel
city symphony, 20, 23
Cold War orientalism, 230, 247n5
College is a Nice Place (*Daigaku yoitoko*, 1936), 86, 91, 260
communism, 17, 76–77, 84n27, 94, 102, 106, 140, 146, 182, 247n5; anti-communism, 122, 135, 153; Communist Party, 17, 76–77, 135, 146, 182
Confucianism, 84n20, 90, 102–4, 154n38, 180, 183, 191, 196–97, 262
continuity failures, 73–74, **73 fig. 4.3, 74 fig. 4.4,** 84n17
Crawford, Joan, 37, 94–95, 98, 127, 148

Daiei, 153n5, 231, 268
Daoism (Taoism), 211
daruma, 185
Date, Satoko, 11, **184 fig. 9.2,** 254–55, 257

Davis, William Darrell, 76, 104
Days of Youth (*Wakaki hi*, 1929), 32–33, 35, 40, 43, 46–47, 56–57, 58, 72, 185, 197, 220, 229, 233, 253
death (as theme), 29–33, 42–43, 51, 53n20, 91–93, 95, 105, 109, 111–16, 120n57, 120nn60–61, 125, 132, 140, 142, 161, 166–67, 175–78, 183, 188, 232–33, 242, 262, 264, 267; connection to Buddhism, 43, 92, 111–12 186, 188; funerals, 43, 82, 111–12, 148, 174, 177, 188–89, 192n4, 193n10, 193n23, 266; suicide, 15, 30–31, 42, 75–76, 90, 115, 122, 156n71, 157n83, 173, 196, 204, 257, 267
Depression, 35, 90–91, 93, 107, 115, 136
Desser, David, 4, 83n7
Dietrich, Marlene, **98 fig. 5.1,** 98–99, 148
Dim Sum: A Little Bit of Heart (1985), 241–44, 247n5
The Docks of New York (1928), 20, 36, 59
Don Quixote (1933), 37
doppelgänger, 37–39, 53n14, 129
Dore, Ronald Philip, 189–91
Dower, John, 89, 96, 105, 117n10, 123, 125, 132, 135–36, 154n23, 159n2
Dragnet Girl (*Hijosen no onna*, 1933), 9–16, **13 fig. 1.1, 16 fig. 1.2,** 19–20, 22–24, 26n13, 29, 32–33, **36 fig. 2.1,** 36–39, 56–62, **60 fig. 3.1,** 66, 69, 72–74, **73 fig. 4.3, 74 fig. 4.4,** 86, 89, 117n8, 128, 131, 180, 183, 197–99, 202, 204, 206, 208n32, 217, 229, 258
Dreams of Youth (*Wakodo no yume*, 1928), 86
Dreyer, Carl Theodor, 250

Early Spring (*Soshun*, 1956), 116, 156n70, 158–59, 159n1, 161, 169, 175–78, 186, 188, 201, 241, 244–46, 266
Early Summer (*Bakushu*, 1951), 140, 144–48, 151, 153, 156n81, 157n86, 158, 161, 163, 169, 175, 181, 187, 196, 198–99, 201, 203–4, 219, 230, 232, 234, 264
East of Eden (1955), 143

Index 279

editing, 83, 164, 190, 243; cart-before-the-horse, 55, 62–63, 70, 240, 243, 247; continuity, 66, 70, 84n17, 122, 210. *See also* continuity failures; 180° rule; 360° space

Egawa, Ureo, 86, 230, 257, 267, **colorplate 1B**

empty shots, 33, 42, 45, 70, 72, 94, 113, 130, 163, 165–67, 176–77, 179n10, 190–91, 214–15, 222–23, 239, 242–43, 246–47

The End of Summer (*Kohayagawawake no aki*, 1961), 1, 43, 154n39, 163–67, 169, 177–78, 179n8, 179n10, 188, 203, 208n31, 212–16, **213 fig. 11.1**, 222, 242, 269, **colorplates 2A–3B**

Enomoto, Chikatoshi, 222

Equinox Flower (*Higanbana*, 1958), 86, 119n53, 158–59, 171–78, **181 fig. 9.1**, 188, 181–83, 192, 203, 235–36, 239, 241, 245, 248n19, 267, **colorplate 1B**

Escapade in Japan (1957), 229–31

etiketto, 196, 246. *See also* chivalry

evanescence. *See* transience

Every Night Dreams (*Yogoto no yume*, 1933), 196, 203

feminism, 3, 13, 195–97, 202–4, 206; *feminisuto* tradition, 207n7. *See also* chivalry; *etiketto*; Japanese women

First Steps Ashore (*Joriku no dai-ippo*, 1932), 36, 59

The Flavor of Green Tea Over Rice (*Ochazuke no aji*, 1952), 148–52, **152 fig. 7.4**; original script, 102

Floating Weeds (*Ukigusa*, 1959), 132, 161, 169, 260, 268

Flower Drum Song (1961), 230, 244, 247n5

Flunky, Work Hard! (*Koshiben ganbare*, 1931), 29

Ford, John, 155n58, 236, 239

Forst, Willi, 94

Fowler, Edward, 127–28

Fuji, Mount, 109, 119n53

Fujiwara, Kamatari, 173

Garfield, John, 146

German Expressionist cinema, 2, 9–10, 20, 23, 37, 53n14, 95, 154n22

Germany, 2–3, 52n11, 53n14, 89–90, 93–95, 98, 103, 105–6, 115, 117n10, 118n28, 121–22, 127, 140–41, 233–34, 236; Teutonic, 105, 108, 138

The Goalie's Anxiety at the Penalty Kick (*Die Angst des Tormanns beim Elfmeter*, 1972), 232–33, 238

Goya, Francisco de, 108; *Red Boy*, 108, 127, 209

Greater East Asia Co-Prosperity Sphere, 158

Greater East Asia War, 102, 119n45, 151, 158, 182. See also Pacific War; World War II

The Green Years (1946), 129–30

Guadalcanal, 116

Gunkan March, 158–59

Hamada, Tatsuo, 84n17

Handke, Peter, 232, 238–39, 251

Hara, Setsuko, 144, 199–200, 232, 264, 266, 268, 269

Harunobu. *See* Suzuki

hashi. *See* bridges

Hashimoto, Meiji, 218

Hasumi, Shigehiko, 207n16, 244

Hattori Building, 138, 149

Hattori, Kintaro, 138

Heath, Stephen, 167

A Hen in the Wind (*Kaze no naka no mendori*, 1948), 52n7, 121, 123–26, 128–131, **129 fig. 7.1**, 134, 139, 153–54n21, 181, 186, 199, 202–3, 263

Hendry, Joy, 177

Hepburn, Katharine, 144, 148, 157n86, 199

He's Going to Nanking (*Kare shi nankin e iku*), 102

Higashiyama, Chieko, 265

Higashiyama, Kaii, 218

High, Peter B., 89–90, 116–17, 117n10, 139

Hino, Ashihei (Katsunori Tamai), 146, 148, 156nn77–78

Hirano, Kyoko, 4, 126, 153n5, 253

Hiratsuka Beach, 134

280 Index

Hiroshige. *See* Utagawa

Hiroshima, 103, 127, 173, 182, 236, 267

Hirotsu, Kazuo, 132, 134, 155n45

Hitler, Adolf, 52n11, 89, 94, 103–5, 115, 118n30

Hollywood, 1, 9, 17, 20, 28, 34, 37, 55, 77, 98, 108–9, 130, 145, 153, 206, 210, 218, 229–31, 247n5

Hot Water (1924), 64n17

Hotta, Eri, 103, 153n3

Hou, Hsiao-hsien, 251

humanism, 15–16, 18, 117, 131, 152, 206

I Flunked But . . . (*Rakudai wa shita keredo*, 1930), 29, 32, 35, 40, 56, 58, 60, 62, 66, **67 figs. 4.1, 4.2**, 74, 76, 91, 96, 220, 254–55

I Graduated, But . . . (*Daigaku wa deta keredo*, 1929), 32, 35, 48, **48 fig.2.3**, 91, 151, 204, 253

I Lived But . . . (*Ikite wa mita keredo . . .*, 1983), 207

I Was Born, But . . . (*Umarete wa mita keredo*, 1932), 27n21, 42, 45, 47, 56, 69, 81, 84n9, 85n32, 90, 108, 148, 161, 185, 190, 210, 230–32, 235, 240, 245, 256

iconography, 2–3, 9–10, 92, 180, 182, 190

ie, 114, 134

If I Had a Million (1932), 36, 94

Iida, Choko, 240, 247n3, 253, 255–63

Ikeda, Tadao, 9

Imamura, Shohei, 84n17

India, 19, 27n17; Indian independence, 19, 27n18, 117

An Inn in Tokyo (*Tokyo no yado*, 1935), 29, 34, 40, 43, 45, 51, 55–56, 58, 60–61, 69, 82, 91, 124, 126, 131, 157n89, 196, 203, 240, 260

internationalism, 16, 19, 37, 89–90, 98, 105, 114, 141, 152, 160n3; international displays (flags, maps, globes), 19, 50, **50 fig. 2.4**, 90, 98, 99n7, 114–15, 148, 159

intertitles. *See* title cards

Itami, Mansaku, 109, 119n50

Iwamoto, Mari, 139, 182

Iwasaki, Akira, 95, 121

Iwashita, Shima, 207n16, 269, **colorplate 1A**

Izumi, Kyoka, 122

Japan in Time of Crisis (*Hijoji Nippon*, 1933), 99n16

Japanese art, 210–12, 214–18; *nihonga*, 154, 209–10, 212, 218–26, 227n16, 227n30, 228n35, 228n39, 236; pre-Meiji, 209, 219, 221; pre-Edo, 212; *rinpa*, 215; *ukiyoe*, 209–10, **213 fig. 11.2**, 215–17, **217 fig. 11.3**, 219–20, 228n39; *yoga*, 209, 212, 218

Japanese theater: Kabuki, 7n1, 54, 90, 97, 147, 151; *naniwabushi*, 56, 58, 62, 223–24; Noh, 3, 137, 139, 190–92; *taishu engeki*, 56; Tsukiji Little Theatre. *See* Tsukiji. *See also shinpa*.

Japanese women: abortion, 72, 156n70, 267; abuse, 13, 125, 142, 195, 202, 206; apres-guerre, 128; good (decent) woman, 12, 14, 32, 53n17, 72, 195, 197, 199, 258; liberation, 122, 135, 137, 144, 148, 195–97, 199, 206; prostitution, 9, 30–31, 37–38, 51–52, 76–77, 84n27, 91, 123–25, 129–30, 157n89, 186, 196, 203–4, 239, 257, 259–60, 263; rape, 25, 38, 52, 125, 130, 202–3, 263; sexual harassment, 14, 26, 202–3, 206, 208n29, 254; Shochiku representation of, 197, 203; suffering, 142, 196–97, 207n7, 264, 266–67. See also Confucianism; chivalry; *etiketto*; marriage; *moga*

Jodoji, 188–89, 193n23

Joo, Woojeong, 4, 53n17, 75, 84n27, 109–10, 116, 118n19, 133, 142, 148, 152, 157n85, 163, 179n20, 195, 207n5

Jurong Prison Camp, 139

Kagamijishi (1935), 7n1

Kagawa, Toyohiko, 182

Kamata district, 7, 16, 83n9, 86, 250

Kano, Sanraku, 215

Kawamata, Takashi, 86, 155n55, 250

Kawasaki, Hiroko, 254–55

Kido, Shiro, 16, 55, 84n9, 121, 197, 203, 229

Kinema Junpo, 59, 89, 108

Kings of the Road (*Im Lauf der Zeit*, 1976), 231–34

Kinoshita, Keisuke, 84n17

Kiss and Tell (1945), 129–30

koan, 191

Kobayakawa, Kiyoshi, 224–25

Kogure, Michiyo, 150, 157n89, 265

Kometani, Shinnosuke, 155n55, 207n22

Komparu, Zenchiku, 192

Korea, 105, 130, 140, 158; Korean War, 140, 146, 230, 241

Kurishima, Sumiko, 261

Kurosawa, Akira, 96, 117

Kusunoki, Masatsura and Masahige, 173, 179n20

Kuwano, Kayoko, **98 fig. 5.1, 221 fig. 11.4**, 261–62, 267

Kuwano, Miyuki, 267, 269

The Lady and the Beard (*Shukujo to hige*, 1931), 11, 35, 66, 76, 95, 106, 183–85, **184 fig. 9.2**, 198–99, 255

Lady Windermere's Fan (1925), 17–18, 26n15

Lang, Fritz, 11, 17, 19, 23, 37, 39, 94, 250

Late Autumn (*Akibiyori*, 1960), 157n88, 168, 171, 177–78, 183, 188, 192n4, 199–201, 203, 208n31, 234, 241, 259, 268

Late Spring (*Banshun*, 1949), 66, 114, 132–41, **133 fig. 7.3**, 144–45, 147–48, 153, 155n45, 155n55, 161, 163, 166, 168–69, 172, 175–76, 178, 188, 190, 199–200, 202, 206, 210, 234–39, 241, 244, 250, 264, 241

The Left-Handed Woman (*Die linkshändige Frau*, 1977), 238–39

Leise fliehen meine Lieder (*The Unfinished Symphony*, 1933), 94–95

Lightning Over Water (1980), 233

Lloyd, Harold, 35, 64n17, 109, 248, 250

Love Letters (1945), 129

Lubin, Arthur, 229–31

Lubitsch, Ernst, 17–18, 36, 52n13, 94, 250

ma space, 164, 190–91, 211, 216, 221, 232–34, 243, 247. See also *susabi*

McDonald, Keiko, 193n23

The Makioka Sisters (*Sasameyuki*), 106, 134; film (1983), 45

male protagonist types: chaste warrior, 185; democratic fathers, 81; *nimaime*, 15–16; *tateyuku*, 15–16

Man with a Movie Camera (*Chelovek s kino-apparatom*, 1929), 27n21

Manchukuo. See Manchuria

Manchuria, 90, 99, 106–8, 118–19nn36–37, 119n39, 119n41, 119n47, 143, 156n71, 158, 160n3, 205, 266; Manchurian Incident, 89, 90, 107

Marais, Jean, 150

Marco Polo Bridge Incident, 99

marriage, 33, 82, 135–36, 140, 142–45, 148, 153, 161, 168, 170–71, 174, 176–78, 181–82, 195, 199–202, 204, 206, 208nn25–26 241, 245, 247, 263, 265–67; arranged (miai) marriage, 35, 132, 134, 145, 149–50, 155n45, 164–65, 199–201, 208n25, 262, 264–65, 269; love marriage, 134, 149, 176, 201, 208n25; remarriage, 114, 166, 169–70, 175, 191, 199–200, 202–3, 241, 264–66; *shudan miai*, 132

Marx, 76; Marxists, 107. See also communism

May, Joe, 10

Meguro Gajoen, 219, 227n29

Meiji period, 93, 135, 139, 141, 182, 212; Civil Code, 196; Meiji Revolution (Reformation), 102, 130, 195

Mellen, Joan, 104, 107–8

Miki, Suizan, 219–20, 222, 228n31, 228n34

military: American, 133–34, 138, 140, 182–83, 236–37; Japanese, 26, 34, 90, 96, 103, 109–11, 115, 116–17, 120n61, 123, 134, 160n3, 182; militarism, 90, 94, 122, 130, 136, 160n3, 204–5, 227n30, 237

mirrors. See doppelgänger

Mitsui, Hideo, 258–60, 268
Mitsukoshi, 225, 228n40
Miyake, Katsumi, 218
Miyake, Kuniko, 230–31, 237, **237 fig. 12.1**, 262, 264–66, 268–69
Miyao, Daisuke, 119n55, 120n57
mobo (modern boy), 24
Modern Times (1936), 93
modernism, 2, 4, 9, 19, 49, 70, 76, 90, 92, 118n19, 119n41, 140–42, 144, 196, 212, 218, 234, 250–51; anti-modernist, 93, 103, 110, 130; modern love, 10, 149; modernization, 93, 102, 138–39, 148, 151, 160n3, 269. *See also* Westernization
moga (modern girl), 11, 96, 99n16, 128, 135, 137, 195, 197–98, 224–25, 228n39, 255, 261
A Mother Should Be Loved (*Haha wo kowazuka*, 1934), 26, 32, 37, 43, 61, 90, 95, 104, 144, 259
mu, 180, 190, 214
Muddy River (*Doro no kawa*, 1981), 239–41
muga, 191
mukokuseki (stateless) aesthetic, 9, 26
The Munekata Sisters (*Munekata shimai*, 1950), 140–45, 147–49, 154n21, 156n70, 158, 191, 200, 202, 210, 220, 251, 264

Nakamura, Ganjiro, 268–69, **colorplate 3B**
Namiko (*The Tragedy of Hototogisu*), 153n10
Nanjing (Nanking), 102, 160n3
Naritayama, 183
narrative: 1–3, 7, 9, 16–17, 21–22, 24, 56, 59, 63n2, 65–85, 91–92, 97, 161, 163–79, 183, 211–12, 215, 218, 233, 241; ambiguous (open-ended), 3, 70–73, 77, 142–43, 153n21, 243–44; coherence, 54, 71–72, 163–74, 178. *See also* parallelism; substitution
Naruse, Mikio, 29, 52n13, 53n21, 84n9, 109, 138, 196, 203, 229, 240
National Policy (*kokusaku*), 102–4, 106–7, 109–10

Nazi, 52nn10–11, 89, 94–95, 98, 102–3, 106, 117n10, 122, 234, 236
New Wave: French, 232–34; Japanese, 86, 146, 206
New Yorker Films, 1, 159n1, 231
Die Niebelungen (1924), 19
Nikolai Cathedral, 145, 148
Nipper (RCA dog), 26, 58, 86, 217–18
No Blood Relation (*Nasanu naka*, 1932), 229
Noda, Kogo, 132, 143, 148, 200, 208n31, 231
Nosferatu (1922), 23
nostalgia, 4, 39, 41, 44, 47, 57, 97, 107, 128, 143, 150, 159, 161, 241
Nygren, Scott, 103

Occupation of Japan 3, 87, 96, 119n45, 121–22, 127–28, 130–32, **133 fig. 7.3**, 133–40, 143–46, 148, 151, 153, 154n23, 158, 161, 179n20, 196, 201, 206, 230, 234, 237. *See also* SCAP
Ofuna district, 86, 156n81
Ogata, Korin, 216
Oguri, Kohei, 239–41
Ohayo (*Good Morning*, 1959), 1–2, 46, 148, 161, 169, 175, 183, 188, 199, 231–33, 240, 268–69
Ohinata, Den, 258–59
Oka, Joji, **13 fig. 1.1**, 16, 36, **36 fig. 2.1**, 59, 229, 258
Okada, Mariko, 268–69
Okada, Tokihiko, **79 fig. 4.6**, 100n17, **184 fig. 9.2**, 255–56, 269
Okada, Yoshiko, 100n17, 157n89, 257, 260
okesa, 57
Okinawa (Ryukyu Islands), 1, 151, 230; Battle of Okinawa, 147, 157n83
Olympia (1938), 105
Olympics, 105, 118n28, 160n3
omiai/miai. See marriage
omoshirogara, 159–60n3
180-degree rule (cuts or line), 44, 66, 68, 70, 79, 136, 191, 242, 245, 247
The Only Son (*Hitori musuko*, 1936), 66, 82, 86, 91–96, 98, 105–6, 115, 126–27, 138, 175, 187, 261

Index 283

Onna keizu, 122
Onomichi, 175–76, 188–90, 193n23, 238, 265–66
Osaragi, Jiro, 123, 143
Our Dancing Daughters (1928), 34, 52n7, 95
Ozu, Yasujiro: personal life, 7, 9, 49, 82, 85n32, 86, 100n18, 101–2, 116–17, 119n42, 120n60, 121, 139–40, 152, 156n77, 180, 193n10, 208n39, 209–10, 218, 227n28, 250; personality, 1, 46, 82, 109, 117, 191, 208n31, 232, 237–38, 247n3

Pabst, G.W., 27n22, 37, 94, 250. See also *Pandora's Box*
pachinko, 150–51, 231, 248n19, 265
Pacific War, 87, 108–9, 116, 119n45, 140, 153, 159n2. *See also* World War II; Greater East Asia War
Pan Am, 151, **152 fig. 7.4**
Pandora's Box (*Die Büchse der Pandora*, 1929), 23
parallelism, 13, 80, 113, 127, 153n10, 168, 175. *See also* substitution; twinning; visual puns
parametric style, 2, 65, 83n9, 127, 244, 250
Paris, Texas (1984), 232–36
passages, 46–47, 164–66, 168–69, 172, 176, 178, 190, 232–33, 245–46. *See also* bridges; death; marriage
Passing Fancy (*Dekigokoro*, 1933), 26, 32–34, 36, 46, 51, 56, 58, 62, 64n17, 66, 81–82, 90, 108, 185, 204–6, **205 fig. 10.1**, 210, 223, 240, 250, 258
patriarchy, 76, 104–5, 195–96, 206
Pearl Harbor, 103, 108–9, 119n45, 119n47, 128, 160n3
perspective systems: climbing, 219; multi-point, 211; one-point, 211–12, 214, 217, 219
Phillips, Alastair, 135
photography, still, 210, 219, 227n28, 233–34, 263
Poil de carotte (1932), 37, 52n10

police, 10, 12, 14–15, 17–18, 20, 24–25, **25 fig. 1.3**, 30–31, 33, 38, 56, 61, 65–66, 76–77, 83, 117n10, 124, 136, 190, 196, 198, 230–31, 254–55, 257–58, 260; police state, 17–18, 26
The Pride of the Yankees (1942), 135, 138
Prohibition, 10
puns. *See* visual puns

Rain (1932), 37
Raine, Michael, 10, 55, 63n9
Rayns, Tony, 75
Record of a Tenement Gentleman (*Nagaya shinshiroku*, 1947), 46, 121–28, 130–31, **131 fig. 7.2**, 134, 136–37, 140, 144, 150, 181–82, 234, 240, 263
Renaissance, 210–11, 218
Richie, Donald, 2, 4, 46, 57, 83n9, 109, 157n86, 168, 172, 230–31, 238, 253
The Rogue Song (1930), 35, **184 fig. 9.2**
romantic love, 13, 16, 149, 199–201. *See also* marriage: love marriage; modernism: modern love
Russell, Catherine, 28, 207n7
Ruttmann, Walther, 20, 23–24, 94, 250
Ryoanji, 140, 190, 238
Ryu, Chishu, 116, 150, 158, 191, **237 fig. 12.1**, 237–38, 242, 248n19, 253, 255, 257–69

Saburi, Shin, 174, 262–63, 265, 267–68
Sada, Keiji, 267–69
Saeki, Shunko, 219–20, 222, 225, 227n30, **colorplate 4**
Saigo, Takamori, 123, 130, **131 fig. 7.2**, 137, 140
St. Luke's Hospital, Tsukiji, **181 fig. 9.1**, 181–83, 192n6
Saito, Tatsuo, **50 fig. 2.4, 67 fig. 4.2, 221 fig. 11.4**, 230, 253–57, 261–62, 264
Sakamoto, Takeshi, 116, **187 fig. 9.3**, 253–54, 256–63
same-sex bonding, 195, 204
samsara, 186, 188, 192. *See also* circle imagery; wheel

284 Index

Sano, Shuji, 100n17, **112 fig. 6.1**, 116, 261–64

Sato, Barbara, 195, 208n25

Sato, Tadao, 15, 20, 83n4, 124, 133, 186, 207n7, 209, 250

Satomi, Ton, 208n31

saundoban, 55–56, 63

Sayonara (1957), 230

SCAP (Supreme Commander for the Allied Powers), 121–22, 125–26, 130, 136, 138, 146, 149, 153n8

Schrader, Paul, 180, 250

Sesshu. *See* Toyo

Seventh Heaven (1927), 35

Shall We Dance? (*Shall we dansu*, 1996), 161, 244–47, 249n42

Shigaraki, Koji, 268–69

Shillony, Ben-Ami, 103, 108

Shimazu, Masahiko, 268–69

Shimazu, Yasujiro, 59, 83–84n9

Shimomura, Kazan, 223

Shinoda, Masahiro, 136

shinpa, 31, 75–76, 122, 197

Shinto, 37, 102, 122, 183, 185, 223

Shintoho, 143

Shochiku, 7, 16, 55, 59, 84n9, 86, 109, 116, 119n53, 121, 144, 156n81, 229, 230–31, 268

Shoda, Kakuyu, 222, 225, 228n34

Siegfried, 19, 104–5, 118n30

silent "sound," 3, 54–63; "sound bridges," 62–63

sojikei staging, 153n21, 220, 242. *See also* twinning

Sorensen, Lars Martin, 96, 123, 127, 129–30, 136–39

Sotatsu. *See* Tarawaya

space, rendering of, 211–25, 232–34, **color-plates 2A–3B**; space-time continuum, 97, 164, 190, 211. See also *ma* space, *mu*, 180° rule, 360° shooting space

Speedy (1928), 35

Spione (1928), 11, 17, 39

Stagecoach (1939), 155n58

Standish, Isolde, 76, 84n22, 119n39, 207n4

Sternberg, Josef von, 17, 20, 23, 36, 59, 94, 250

still life shot. *See* empty shots

A Story of Floating Weeds (*Ukigusa monogatari*, 1934), 32–33, 38, 40–41, 45–49, 56–57, 61, 68–69, 75, 82, 90, 97, 108, 113, 132, 161, 169, **187 fig. 9.3**, 185–88, 220, 233, 259–60, 268

A Straightforward Boy (*Tokkan kozo*, 1929), 254

Stratocruiser, Boeing, 151, **152 fig. 7.4**

Street Without End (*Kagirinaki hodo*, 1934), 52n13, 109, 138

stupa, 111, 113, 119n55, 166, 188–89, **colorplate 1B**

substitution, 3, 74, 77, 172

Sugimura, Haruko, 264–69

Sumo Do, Sumo Don't (*Shiko funjatta*, 1992), 244–45, 249n41

Suo, Masayuki, 161, 244–47

susabi, 191

Suzuki, Harunobu, 215

symbolism, 2–3, 7, 9, 11, 14, 17, 23–24, 28–53, 72–75, 77, 80, 92, 97, 114, 124–25, 164, 166, 175–78, 180, 186, 189, 202–4, 210, 233, 240

synecdoche, 3, 24, 25, 63

tagasode-byobu, 45, **45 fig. 2.2**

Taisho period, 152, 209

Takamura, Kotaro, 218–19

Takarazuka Revue (Girls's Opera), 150, 231

Takata, Biichi, 212, 219–20

Takenaka, Naoto, 249n41

Takashimaya, 219, 225

Talbot, Dan, 1–2, 231

Tamai, Katsunori. See Hino, Ashihei

Tanaka, Kinuyo, 11, **16 fig. 1.2, 60 fig. 3.1**, 86, **129 fig. 7.1**, 193n10, 253–54, 257–58, 263–64, 267

Tanaka, Masasumi, 148

Tanizaki, Jun'ichiro, 27n17, 53n14, 106, 134

Tateishi, Harumi, 219–20, 222, 228n31

Tawaraya, Sotatsu, 215–16

Taylor-Jones, Kate, 153–54n21

Teusler, Rudolf, 181, 192n6

That Night's Wife (*Sono yo no tsuma*, 1930), 9–10, 17–20, 23–25, 27n17, 29, 32, 34, 37, 45–46, 65–66, 76, 90, 98, 114, 136, 183, 209, 235, 255

There Was a Father (*Chichi ariki* 1942), 103, 108–17, **112 fig. 6.1**, 119n55, 120n60, 122, 124, 134, 144, 159, 166, 169, 177, 186, 188, 191, 210, 220, 234, 262–63

Thompson, Kristin, 2, 28, 31, 66, 70, 83n4, 134, 136, 167, 170, 218

360° cutting style (shooting space), 44, 66, 136

The Three Penny Opera (*Die Dreigroschenoper*), 23, 27n22

title cards, 44, 54–55, 57, 61, 62–63, 63n2, 66, 68, 78

Die Tochter des Regiments (1933), 37, 52n11

Tojo, Hideki, 103–5, 121

Tokkankozo. *See* Aoki, Tomio

Tokutomi, Kenjiro (Roka), 153n10

Tokyo Chorus (*Tokyo no gassho*, 1931), 29, 34, 44, 46, 49–51, **50 fig. 2.4**, 56–58, 66, 68–71, 75–76, 78–81, **79 fig. 4.6**, 83, 90, 97–98, 100n17, 125, 127, 223–24, 235, 248n31, 256

Tokyo Story (*Tokyo monogatari*, 1953), 65, 148, 155n58, 156n70, 158, 161, 166, 174–77, 188, 190–91, 199, 202, 204, 206, 230, 232, 238, 240, 242–43, 265–66

Tokyo Twilight (*Tokyo boshoku* 1957), 143, 154n21, 156n70, 158, 161, 202, 206, 266–67

Tokyo-Ga (1985), 237

tonari-gumi, 126

Torii, Kiyonaga, 216

Torii, Kiyonobu, 217, **217 fig. 11.3**

Toyo, Sesshu, 214

Tracy, Spencer, 206

transience, 39–44, 46–47, 49, 51, 71, 113, 166, 178, 180, 240

Tripartite Pact, 105

Trümmerfilme, 121

Tsukiji, 181–83; Tsukiji Hoganji, 182–83, 193n10; Tsukiji Little Theatre, 250

twinning, 220–21, **221 fig. 11.4**. See also *sojikei* staging

Uemura, Shoen, 223, 228n35

Underworld (1927), 17, 20, 23

Until the Day We Meet Again (*Mata au hi made*, 1932), 16, 19, 55, 157n89, 204, 207n5

Until the End of the World (*Bis ans Ende der Welt*, 1991), 237, **237 fig. 12.1**

Ushiwara, Uzuhiko, 250

Utagawa, Hiroshige, 210, 212, **213 fig. 11.2**, 214–15

Vertov, Dziga, 27n21

visual puns, 33–34, 51, 94, 138

visual "sound." *See* silent "sound"

Wada-Marciano, Mitsuyo, 9, 75–77, 83n9, 84n27

Wako Building. See Hattori Building

Walk Cheerfully (*Hogaraka ni ayume*, 1930), 9–11, 13–15, 20–25, **25 fig. 1.3**, 26n13, 31–32, 34, 38–40, 43, 45–48, 65–66, 68, 70, 72–73, 86, 90, 96, 98, 106, 110, 114, 125, 183–84, 198, 202–3, 212, 233, 254

Wang, Wayne, 241–44

war orphans, 121, 123, 130, 137, 182, 263

Watanabe, Kazan, 115

Watteau, Jean-Antoine: *The Dance*, 150, 209

Watts, Alan, 191

Weimar cinema. *See* German Expressionist cinema

Wenders, Wim, 141, 180, 231–39, **237 fig. 12.1**, 241, 243, 246–47, 248n21, 248n26, 251

Western aesthetics, 210–11; *horror vacui*, 211, 225

Westernization (modernization), 9, 93–94, 96, 103, 122, 128, 130, 138, 160n3, 195. *See also* modernism

What Did the Lady Forget? (*Shujo wa nani o wasureta ka*, 1937), 1, 95–99, **98 fig. 5.1**, 102, 106, 132, 135, 137, 142, 148–49, 198, 206, 220–22, **221 fig. 11.4**, 225, 261, 267

Wheat and Soldiers (*Mugi to heitai*), 146, 148, 156nn77–78

wheel, 47, 91–92, 186–88, **187 fig. 9.3**, 192. *See also* circle imagery

Where Now Are the Dreams of Youth? (*Seishun no yume ima izuko*, 1932), 32, 49, 51, 58, 86, 90–91, 96, 104, 106, 128, 169, 199–200, 204, 220, 230, 257

White, Pearl, 200, 206, 207n19

Wings of Desire (*Der Himmel über Berlin*, 1987), 236, 238

A Woman of Paris (1923), 75, 84n22, 257

Woman of Tokyo (*Tokyo no onna*, 1933), 30–32, 36, 38, 42–44, 46, 53n17, 61–62, 73, 75–78, **78 fig. 4.5**, 84n22, 93–94, 100n17, 106, 113, 157n89, 203–4, 257

Wood, Robin, 195, 199–200, 202–4, 206, 208n27

World War I, 37, 93–94

World War II, 52n10, 103, 121, 145, 173, 182. *See also* Greater East Asia War; Pacific War

Wrong Move (*Falsche Bewegung*, 1975), 238

Yagumo, Reiko, 255–56, 260

Yamaguchi, Hoshun, 218, 227n27

Yamakawa, Shuho, 225

Yamamoto, Isoroku, 109, 116, 119n47

Yamamoto, Kikuo, 26n4

Yamamoto, Shunkyo, 219

Yamamura, So, 156n70, 264–67

Yamanaka, Sadao, 101, 117n8

Yamanouchi, Shizuo, 144, 247n13

Yamato, 147–48; aircraft carrier, 147, 157n83, 158; region, 147, 265; *yamato-e*, 147, 219

Yokohama, 16, 259

Yoshida, Junji, 99n16, 104

Yoshida, Kiju, 4, 253

Yoshikawa, Mitsuko, 256, 259, 261–63

Young, Louise, 118n36, 119n41, 160n3

Yuki, Ichiro, 229, 253

Zen, 140, 180, 185, 189, 190–92, 223; Renzai, 180, 192n4

Zentsuji, 146–48; prison camp, 146, 156n81, 203